JUNG'S FOUR
AND SOME
PHILOSOPHERS

T0350027

Jung's Four
and
Some Philosophers

A Paradigm for Philosophy

THOMAS M. KING, S.J.

University of Notre Dame Press
Notre Dame, Indiana

Library of Congress Cataloging-in-Publication Data

King, Thomas Mulvihill, 1929–
    Jung's four and some philosophers : a paradigm for philosophy /
Thomas M. King.
        p.   cm.
    Includes bibliographical references and index.
    ISBN 0-268-03252-1 (alk. paper). — ISBN 0-268-03251-3
(pbk. : alk. paper)
    1. Philosophers—Psychology. 2. Typology (Psychology) 3. Jun-
gian psychology.   I. Title.
B104.K56   1999
190—dc21   98-53803
                                                            CIP

The paper used in this publication meets the minimum requirements
of the American National Standard for Information Sciences—Permanence
of Paper for Printed Library Materials, ANSI Z39.48-1984.

Contents

Part III
Three with a Perceiving Faculty as Dominant

Introduction

The argument of the present book can be stated in two sentences: First, the four personality types of Jung offer a significant way of understanding the differences among philosophers. Second, Jung's account of "individuation" provides a pattern to understand the development of a philosopher's ideas. I have come to the first claim only after recognizing that philosophers of genius disagree. They have understood one another's arguments and even worked together for years (e.g.: Plato and Aristotle, Whitehead and Russell), yet continue to be at odds. This suggests that many philosophic differences have a basis apart from philosophy. So I propose elements from the psychology of Jung to gain a perspective on the philosophers, their message, and their development.

The writings of C. G. Jung (1875–1961) are collected in twenty volumes, but the elements relevant to the present study can be stated briefly: There are four personality types, identified as Thinking, Feeling, Intuition, and Sensation. These occur in pairs: Thinking and Feeling are the two faculties of Judging, while Intuition and Sensation are the two faculties of Perception. Jung would see everyone having all four "Functions," but usually one of the four dominates while its opposite is repressed, for example, Thinking is favored and Feeling is repressed. In the alternate pair (Intuition and

Sensation), one of the two is favored over its opposite and is called the Auxiliary; but here the contrast between the two is less extreme. For example: a person can have a dominant Thinking and repress one's Feeling, that is, relegate it to the Unconscious, or one might do the reverse and favor Feeling. The same person would have either Intuition or Sensation as auxiliary. The integrated personality would have all four Functions in balance. This might be symbolized in dreams or images by four units balanced to form a cross, a square, a swastika, etc.—often included in a circle.

When a young person sets out in the world, generally one identifies with the strongest Function; that is, the Ego associates with the Dominant Function. But the time comes—frequently in the mid-thirties—when the individual feels life is empty; something is missing. The original sense of purpose is gone and one is dispirited and confused. At this point the individual feels called upon to make a difficult search for the rejected Function—only to find this Function underdeveloped, childish and primitive. This Function can appear suddenly, and the Ego finds its appearance both fascinating and threatening. The repressed Function seems to dwell in a land of wonder and mystery (the Unconscious).

Under the attraction of this entrancing and threatening Function, the Ego becomes confused and uncertain about its approach to life. For a while it might alternate back and forth between the Dominant and the Repressed—Jung calls this Enantiodromia (after Heraclitus). During this troubled time some people fluctuate between Thinking and Feeling, while others fluctuate between Intuition and Sensation, depending on which Function originally was Dominant. The resolution of confusion might restore the Dominant to control and the repression is more or less continued. Or the Ego might do the opposite: identify with the repressed Function and neglect the Dominant. But the resolution Jung preferred (Individuation) involved a synthesis of the opposing Functions. Jung generally called this synthesis the Self (also the Transcendent Function, the Image of God, the Symbol, Wholeness); it is a wondrous reconciliation of the opposites that ends the confusion. The Self contains all four Functions in balance, but frequently the balance is seen to involve only two, the Dominant and Repressed. Since Individuation takes one into a world beyond the familiar, the process is often a religious awakening. Jung claimed that to be truly healed a person must develop a religious outlook on life.

This is the basic pattern that the present study will show in twelve philosophers. But first, an ordinary example might clarify the pattern. Take the person said to identify with Thinking, while Intuition was the auxiliary and Feeling was repressed. This works for a while, but maybe in the early thirties the person is overcome by a great outpouring of emotion. The person is amazed and afterwards might protest: "I was not myself"—human feelings have appeared. After several such occasions the person might question the rationalism (Thinking) by which one has lived; one loses the certainty one had known and is disoriented. The Feelings have appeared unexpectedly, and they act at random apart from control of the Ego; they are primitive, childish, and lack nuance. At this point the person can further repress the Feelings, or, instead, identify with the Feelings and renounce the rationalism (Thinking) that had been dominant. But instead of either alternative, one can undertake the painful task of working through the confusion to unite Thinking and Feeling in a "higher" synthesis, a synthesis that seems to come as a gift. This is Individuation, and it is what Jung tried to achieve in his patients. This process will be shown in the writings of philosophers.

Individuation is symbolized in a person's dreams and spontaneous imagery. The repressed Function is often seen as being under the sea (Jung regarded the sea as the primary symbol of the unconscious), or buried in the ground, or lost in a dark forest. The Ego, identifying with the dominant Function, sets out on a difficult and unfamiliar journey (a sea voyage, a night venture into the forest) to locate the missing Function. Perhaps on the way one meets a dark figure, the Shadow (elements of one's character one does not want to recognize), or the Anima/Animus (an entrancing figure of the opposite sex)—figures of central importance to Jung, but only of minimal importance in the present text. The individual might become bewildered or overpowered, but, *if* all goes well, there will be a reconciliation of the Functions. This integration is often symbolized as a circle (Mandala) or a circle containing a Quaternity (the four Functions in balance). This expresses wholeness, the goal to be attained. An abundance of circles and squares is found in the drawings and doodles of people under tension; they frequently occur in the drawings and dreams of children; they are found in religious symbols. But often only three conscious Functions appear, perhaps with a place left for the Fourth (the Repressed Function that is missing or separate); healing would involve the Three becoming Four. Three with a missing Fourth, or Three becoming Four, or a hesitation between Three and Four, etc., are basic Jungian symbols; Three-to-Fours are often found in dreams—and in the writings of philosophers.

The four Functions in balance can be seen in many crosses, emblems, corporate logos, the compass rose, etc. There are also many examples of four centered elements with one of them different.

Some familiar examples of Quaternity (the Four), Mandala, and Three-becoming-Four can be seen in the Bible: Genesis speaks of the four rivers of Paradise (Gen. 2:10); Ezekiel sees a bright cloud and "from the midst of it came the likeness of four living creatures. . . . each had four faces"; later Ezekiel sees "four wheels beside the cherubim. . . . the four had the same likeness, as if a wheel were in a wheel. . . . they went in any of their four directions. . . . and every one had four faces" (Ezek. 1:5, 6; 10:9–11). The book of Revelation picks up on Ezekiel to tell of the divine throne, and "on each side of the throne, are four living creatures, full of eyes in front and behind"; then the four creatures break four seals to bring on four horsemen. Revelation ends with the account of a "foursquare" city that comes down from heaven (Rev. 4:6; 21:15). All of these examples are from the more visionary books of the Bible.

Three-becomes-Four when the Lord speaks through Amos: "For three transgressions of Damascus, and for four, I will not revoke the punishment" (Am. 1:3); then the phrasing of three-becoming-four is repeated for seven additional cities ("For three transgressions of Gaza, and for four," "For three transgressions of Tyre, and for four," "For three transgressions of Edom, and for four," etc.). In the book of Daniel, Nebuchadnezzar stands at the door of the fiery furnace and asks, "Did we not cast three men bound into the fire? . . . But I see four men loose, walking in the midst of the fire, and they are not hurt; and the appearance of the fourth is like a son of the gods" (Dan. 3:24, 25). Later Daniel saw "the four winds of heaven" stirring up the sea, and "four great beasts came out of the sea." He tells of each, but "the fourth beast . . . was different from all the rest" (Dan. 7:2, 3, 19). In the book of Job, three familiar friends appear in chapter 2 to accuse Job of wrongdoing; this continues until chapter 32, when Elihu, a young stranger (youth and strangeness are often signs of the Fourth), joins "Job's three friends" in accusation. In Revelation the four living creatures around the throne are three beasts and a man.[1]

It is to be noted that in these passages abundant mention is made of Four, or of Three with a separated Fourth. But there is no reason in the biblical text to associate the Three or the Fourth with specific psychic Functions, such as Thinking or Feeling, as Jung would do. But even Jung himself could speak at great length of the Four, the Quaternity, Three becoming Four, without identifying these with the Four Functions of Thinking, Feeling, Intuition, and Sensation.[2] He is considering them as they occur in the alchemists and visionaries, where they frequently appear without being identifiable as Thinking and the rest. He and others have seen this symbolism in literature. Here I show the symbolism in philosophers, and in working with *philosophers*—as opposed to visionaries, poets, and others—it is more evident that the Quaternities, Three/Fours, and Unions of Opposites are related to the specific Functions of Jung.

Consider the Three and the search for the missing Fourth as found in a philosopher. In Plato's *Republic*, Socrates has identified three of the four virtues, but he has trouble defining justice, the fourth. He tells of a search into a land of mystery that suggests the Unconscious. Socrates advises Glaucon to "light a candle and search." He explains the situation,

> If there were four things, and we were searching for one of them, wherever it might be, the one sought for might be known to us from the first, and there would be no further trouble; or we might know the other three first, and then the fourth would clearly be the one left. . . . Is not a similar method to be pursued about the virtues, which are also four in number? (I, 690–91)

The method concerns Three with a separated Fourth, and to find the missing element a search is made into the dark woods:

> Socrates: . . . we may consider three out of the four virtues to have been discovered in our State. The last of those qualities which make a state virtuous must be justice, if we only knew what that was.
>
> Glaucon: The inference is obvious.

Socrates: The time has arrived, Glaucon, when like huntsmen, we should surround the cover, and look sharp that justice does not steal away, and pass out of sight and escape us; for beyond a doubt she is somewhere in this country: watch therefore and strive to catch a sight of her, and if you see her first, let me know. . . . Offer up a prayer with me and follow.

Glaucon: I will, but you must show me the way.

Socrates: Here is no path . . . and the wood is dark and perplexing; still we must push on.

Glaucon: Let us push on.

Socrates: Here I saw something: Halloo! . . . I begin to perceive a track, and I believe that the quarry will not escape. . . . we are stupid fellows.

Glaucon: Why so?

Socrates: Why, my good sir, at the beginning of our enquiry, ages ago, there was justice tumbling out at our feet, and we never saw her; nothing could be more ridiculous. Like people who go about looking for what they have in their hands. . . . (I, 695–97)

This dramatic account of a search for the missing Fourth where "the wood is dark and perplexing" is perhaps the most vivid philosophic account of a search for the missing Function (here Sensation, found in their "Hands") in the Unconscious. The missing Fourth involves religion: "Offer up a prayer with me." Whenever a philosopher introduces a perplexing search, or a land of mystery, or a troubled ocean voyage, the present study will interpret the passage as a search for the missing Function in the Unconscious.

Beyond the four Types indicated above, Jung also speaks of the difference between the Introvert and the Extrovert—all four Types can be one or the other. But the present text makes little of this distinction; most of the philosophers considered are Introverts (Extroverts are less inclined to develop an elaborate philosophic system).

Also, Jung has made a distinction between the faculties of Judgment (Thinking and Feeling) and the faculties of Perception (Intuition and Sensation). The Judger is a person who likes closure, while the Perceiver likes to keep options open for new experience. This difference is important in the present study and serves to outline the sections. That is, in Part One three Perceivers are presented, then in Part Two six Judgers, and finally in Part Three three additional Perceivers.

A popular form of these personality types has been worked out by Isabel Briggs Myers and her husband. They developed a test by which a person can identify one's type, and their work has led to an abundance of empirical studies relating type to levels of academic achievement, family relationships, job suitability, and so on.[3] Currently in the U.S. there are many programs that help people understand themselves by knowing their Jungian or Myers-Briggs type. Those interested have formed the Association for Psychological Type and publish their own journal—*Journal of Psychological Type*—at Mississippi State University. The Myers-Briggs classification gives each individual a set of four identifying initials: an I or an E (Introvert or Extrovert); an N or an S (Intuition or Sensation); a T or an F (Thinking or Feeling); a P or a J (Perception or Judgment). Thus, if the person considered earlier in this Introduction took the test, he or she might be given the initials INTP, Introvert, Intuitive, Thinker, and Perceiver. The present study will suggest Myers-Briggs initials for each philosopher.[4] For purposes of clarity, this study will generally capitalize words from the special vocabulary of Jung: the Self, the Functions, Feeling, and the like. This is to indicate they are Jungian terms and not terms of the author being treated. Also the four Functions will often be abbreviated by a single letter: T, Thinking; F, Feeling; N, Intuition; and S, Sensation. Jung abbreviates the ambiguity of Three and Four in several ways: 3+1 or 3:4 (see *A*, 224, 225, 251); these abbreviations will be used. (An extended treatment of the types is found in Jung's *Psychological Types*, 330–407; a good account of Individuation is found in the same book, 57ff., and *ACU*, 275ff.)

Several quotations from Jung could assist in getting a better hold on Jungian themes important to the present study. Jung tells of one coming to a psychic standstill:

> Whenever a damming up of libido occurs, the opposites, previously united in the steady flow of life, fall apart and henceforth confront one another like antagonists eager for battle. They then exhaust themselves in a prolonged conflict the duration and upshot of which cannot be foreseen, and from the energy which is lost to them is built that third thing [Self] which is the beginning of the new way. (*PT*, 89)

In terms of the Three and the Repressed Fourth Jung writes of the opposition between the functions of consciousness, three of which are fairly well differentiated, while the fourth, undifferentiated, "inferior" function is undomesticated, unadapted, uncontrolled, and primitive. Because of its contamination with the collective unconscious, it possesses archaic and mystical qualities, and is the complete opposite of the most differentiated function. (*PR*, 121)

The inferior function is the one of which least conscious use is made. This is the reason for its undifferentiated quality, but also for its freshness and vitality. It is not at the disposal of the conscious mind, and even after long use it never loses its autonomy and spontaneity, or only to a very limited degree. Its role is therefore mostly that of a *deus ex machina*. It depends not on the ego but the *self.* Hence it hits consciousness unexpectedly, like lightning and occasionally with devastating consequences. It thrusts the ego aside and makes room for a supraordinate factor, the totality of the person, which consists of consciousness and unconsciousness and consequently extends far beyond the ego. This self was always present but sleeping, like Nietzsche's "image in the stone." (*ACU*, 304)

In encountering the repressed Function the individual feels distress and confusion; there are Three, but where is the Fourth?

The incomplete state of existence is, remarkably enough, expressed by a triadic system, and the complete (spiritual) state by the "tetradic" system. The relation between the incomplete and the complete state, therefore, corresponds to the "sesquitertian proportion" of 3:4. This relation is known in Western alchemical tradition as the axiom of Maria. It also plays a not inconsiderable part in dream symbolism. (*ACU*, 360)

In meeting the missing Fourth, one begins the Enantiodromia, a battle of opposites (Dominant and Repressed) that can lead to healing:

The confrontation of the two positions generates a tension charged with energy and creates a living, third thing—not a logical stillbirth in accordance with the principle *tertium non datur* but a movement out of the suspension between opposites, a living birth that leads to a new level of being, a new situation. The transcendent function manifests itself as a quality of conjoined opposites. (*SDP*, 90)

In the study that follows I have taken the Jungian elements and expanded them to give a diagram of Quaternity that associates philosophical elements with each of the Functions (see fig. 1). I have arbitrarily put T at the top of the figure; for purposes of consistency

I will continue this arrangement (T on top) throughout the text. Putting terms from many philosophers together in a single figure has its limitations, for in different philosophers the same term can have very different meanings. For example, the word "feeling" is highly ambiguous; it can be placed under three of the Functions—as an S: "There is no feeling in my right arm"; as an F: "You have hurt my feelings"; as an N: "I have a feeling we cannot trust him." (Jung comments on this ambiguity, *SDP,* 141–42.) There are many others: "Good" can be one's aim and thus tell of the N (Aristotle: the good is that at which all things aim) or it can be F (Kant: nothing is good without qualification except a good will). The word "thinking" is often used without implying the T: "I am thinking I like this." Though there are many such ambiguities, I venture a common model in figure I.1. In the figure the unity of elements associated with each of the Functions is not immediately evident. The text that follows the figure will give a better understanding of the unity, yet other elements of unity will be seen only as the study advances. The figure is offered here largely for future reference.

The individual types could be considered as pairs. First the Judging types: Thinking and Feeling. The Thinker (often symbolized as

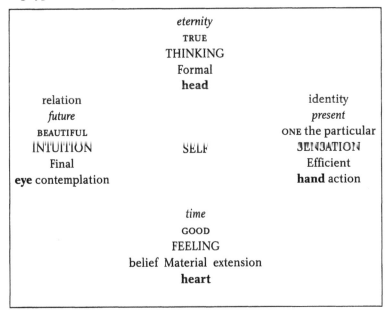

Figure I.1

the Head) gives primacy to logical consistency. Truth is seen as an abstract and timeless quality in which the Thinker is at home. The Thinker looks for the eternal essence of things with little concern for present needs or human feelings. The Thinker is reserved, detached, curious, and quite adaptable—until one of the Thinker's principles is violated. In contrast, the Feeler (often symbolized by the Heart) gives primacy to human values, emotions, and the nuances of personal relations. The Feeler believes that time (duration) with others and their presence makes all the difference. Familiar things (things had for a long duration) take on a sentimental value. The Feeler knows how things and people are placed and what is "fitting." The Thinker and Feeler could be set in contrast: While the Thinker overlooks the "personal" dimensions, the Feeler does not understand why logic is so important. The Thinker's world is abstract, coherent, and principled; the Feeler's world is one of human concerns, loyalties, and ethical sensitivity. But both of these are Judging types, and they seek a reconciliation of Head and Heart, of intellect and feeling, of truth and love.

The Intuitive and Sensate are Perceivers: The Intuitive (often symbolized as the Eye) is always looking beyond the present data to discover new interrelationships and broader, more ultimate meanings. The Intuitive looks to the future, new possibilities, and ever more comprehensive understandings, while the Sensate (symbolized as the Hand) is down to earth, aware of the small details, the tangible, the concrete singular, the present. The Sensate prefers facts and hard data to airy speculation. While the Intuitive does not see the trees for the forest, the Sensate does not see the forest for the trees. The world of the Intuitive is always "beyond," "behind," "apart from," the evident world; it is made of "escapes" (passings beyond) and interrelationships; that is, present things point beyond themselves; they are "other"; they are doorways leading to new horizons. In contrast, the Sensate knows the present, individual object; each thing is simply itself; it is what it is and refers to nothing ("One" in the above chart refers to what is *indivisum in se et divisum ab omni alio*"). But both N and S are Perceiving types, and they seek a reconciliation of Eye and Hand, of vision and fact, of forest and trees.

Thus, Perceiving philosophers vs. Judging philosophers offers one basis on which to compare different philosophers: the Perceiving-philosopher tries to reconcile elements that suggest S and N, while the Judging-philosopher tries to reconcile elements that suggest T and F.

One Quaternity familiar to most philosophers is the four virtues of Plato considered above, and another is the four causes of Aristotle: formal and material, final and efficient. They could be considered in pairs and taken as T and F, N and S. Accordingly one could contrast the "worlds" of the different types:

> The T: the world is a precise system wherein everything can be deduced; it functions like a great equation.

> The F: the world is human beings set in space and time, and all people and things have their proper place.

> The N: the world is the supreme synthesis, and objects have little or no identity in themselves but exist only in relation to the whole.

> The S: the world is only the totality of independent units (building blocks); each unit is simply itself.

The present study considers four Intuitives (Plato, Sartre, Whitehead, and Teilhard) and four Thinkers (Descartes, Spinoza, Kant, and Kierkegaard). It treats two Sensates (Locke and Hume) and two Feelers (Augustine and Rousseau). The emphasis on the Intuitives and Thinkers may say something about my own preferences; but I also believe most philosophers are in one of these two types.

Here a psychological perspective is used to understand why philosophers differ. But beyond that I claim that a philosopher's type and the subsequent move to Integration enter into the substance of a philosopher's ideas. This is justified by a series of essays on individual philosophers. As each essay begins, the Dominant Function of the philosopher is identified and a brief set of quotes is offered to justify the claim; this is followed by suggested Myers-Briggs letters. Some of the essays will be more convincing than others, but hopefully the accumulated evidence will establish my claims. It is obvious that studies of the philosophers who show little development will be weaker cases.

The elements from Jung significant to the present study could be summarized as:

1. The pervasive presence of the Dominant.
2. The pervasive absence of the Repressed.
3. The Repressed must be sought in a place of mystery.
4. The Enantiodromia of Dominant and Repressed leading to a synthesis, the Self.
5. Images of 3:4 and Quaternity, of circles and squares.

This study gives Jung's psychology, terminology and symbols an importance that is probably excessive. To diminish the excessive psychological tilt, I offer a final reflection to return to a more philosophic context. Still, it is good to recall that philosophy developed out of the advice given to Socrates—"Know thyself"—this made philosophy a personal quest. Socrates is said to have considered philosophy "the soul's search for salvation" (Barrett, 5), "a lifelong quest for salvation" (Morgan, in Kraut, 242). Today philosophy is not understood that way. But many noted philosophers have claimed that philosophy brings deliverance to the soul (Plotinus, Boethius, Descartes, Spinoza, and others). The present study would hope to restore to philosophy the "quest for salvation."

Many years ago I had intended to write a novel, but it never got started; it involved four characters and one of them was missing. I later became aware of Jung's Four and saw how closely they described the four characters of my novel. I am INTP and early in my novel one of the four had disappeared; eventually the remaining three (a T, N, and S) found themselves at odds with one another and went in search of the missing F. Later I learned of Jung and got the basic insight for the present work while reading Gilson's *Being and Some Philosophers*—so I pattern my title after his. In 1962, I began writing. But an excessive involvement with Jung left me feeling confined within my own head. In 1964, I chanced upon an essay by Sartre that told of the intentionality of consciousness and I felt liberated (from my own psyche). So I set the project aside for twenty-six years. During that time I did my dissertation on Sartre's phenomenology of religion, taught theology, and wrote books on Sartre, Teilhard, and Merton—and a book of my own thoughts on religion and the deliverance of the soul (*Enchantments: Religion and the Power of the Word*). But the ideas of Jung have stayed with me many years after my original insight, and now I bring the matter to completion.

Though greatly influenced by Jung, I still have many reservations. Some touch on the present work (I see Jung's description of the types excessively oriented to troubled individuals and find the Myers-Briggs understanding more balanced). But the present work is not an evaluation of Jung's considerable achievement. Rather, it assumes the Jungian schema and uses it to bring a fresh perspective on philosophers and their ideas.

There is an immense secondary literature on Jung; some of it is positive and some is highly critical. Much of the criticism involves elements beyond the scope of the present study, though some does not. Some critics have found Jung's fascination with the number four to be excessive and find his association of the mystic 4 and 3:4 with his four personality types to be arbitrary (see Kaufmann, III, 308). On these points I believe the present work offers considerable support to the claims of Jung. Beyond that, Kaufmann claims that even Jungians are now ignoring his four psychological types and adds, "Jung's typology has had little influence in America." In considering the immense popularity of the Myers-Briggs type indicators developed out of Jung, it is difficult to understand this claim. A recent book on Jung claims that apart from his work on the interpretation of dreams, "Jung's most enduring contribution to the field of psychology [is] his theory of psychological types" (Hopcke, 49).

June Singer and Mary Loomis, two Jungian therapists, have argued that the Dominant and Repressed Faculties are not always opposed in bi-polar confrontation (Singer, 348—49). That is, for example, one could have a dominant T with a strong F. They would see the possibility of both Faculties working together and giving a period of great creativity. Jung knew some of his disciples raised this objection, yet he insisted the Faculties were bi-polar (SL, 16—17, 260). I would agree with Singer and Loomis in finding that opposing Faculties can work well together; this is most evident in the presentation of Teilhard that follows.

There was considerable development in the thought of Jung that I have not found necessary to consider; I have worked with his mature ideas. The best presentation of his development would seem to be Raymond Hostie's *Religion and the Psychology of Jung*, pp. 111—154. Some mention should be made of Jung's familiarity with philosophy. He tells of reading Plato, Kant, and Schopenhauer and often refers to them in a general sort of way. He appeals to Kant in claiming that we can know only the phenomena. He also makes a number of disparaging references to Kierkegaard and Heidegger but does not show any real familiarity with them. He would protest, "I am an empiricist, not a philosopher," and I would take him at his word.

For their assistance in developing the present manuscript I would like to thank Avery Dulles, S.J., John K. Kearney, John Haught, Julia Lamm, Nicole Schmitz-Moormann, and Wilfried VerEecke.

Notes

1. Similar examples could be found in Eastern texts: the Mandukya Upanishad tells of the "four conditions" of the self; the fourth is Atman, in the pure state "neither consciousness nor unconsciousness." The four conditions form the sacred word AUM (OM): the *a* the *u* and the *m* are the first three, while "the word OM as one sound is the fourth state of supreme consciousness" (*Upanishads*, 83, 84).The *Bhagavad Gita* tells of three heavenly kingdoms and one of earth (*BG*, 46); it tells of "four orders of men," and "four kinds of men who are good," and the four resemble the four types of Jung (*BG*, 62, 75). Buddhists have made extensive use of circles with inscribed squares as an aid to meditation. See Jung's contrast of East and West in *PR*, 55ff.

2. See *PR*, 34–105. These pages are an extended treatment of the Three and the Four, of Circles and Squares, etc. in dreams, art, literature, alchemy, and gnosticism. But in this treatment Jung never tries to identify the Four with specific Functions; he simply shows the extent of the Symbol. Frequently in these passages the Three-Four appears without evidence that would tie the elements to particular Functions. But an advantage of the present study of *philosophers* is that the Three and Four are often clearly identified with philosophical elements that are associated with the Functions. Perhaps that is because philosophers are better able to identify the elements than the poets, gnostics, alchemists, and others studied by Jung.

3. The account that best relates Myers-Briggs types to achievements, job suitability, etc. is *Gifts Differing*, by Isabel Briggs Myers with Peter B. Myers (Palo Alto: Consulting Psychologists Press, 1980). The same address offers tests for determining type and other materials; a type test is also available on the Internet. *Gifts Differing* offers a good statement of the types and brings out well several small but significant differences between the authors and Jung. The most important of these concern the role of the Auxiliary Function (see pp. 17ff). I would side with Myers-Briggs on this point. They claim that an extreme version of any Dominant has a weak or missing Auxiliary. Accordingly in this text I would see Kierkegaard's lack of a significant Auxiliary explaining some of the jarring quality in the synthesis he called Faith. This work of Isabel and Peter Myers tells of extensive testing for types with many charts and statistics. Several small and more popular accounts of the types are available at

weekend workshops on types and their interplay. The best of these accounts would seem to be *Facing Your Type* and *Facing Other Types*, by George J. Schemel (Typrofile Press, Church Road, Box 223, Wernersville, Pa. 19565).

4. The Dominant would refer to one of the two interior letters, thus, NT in INTP. To determine which of the two is the Dominant: If one is a P *Introvert* (as in INTP), the Dominant is either T or F depending on which letter is in one's type (so the INTP would have T, not N, as Dominant); if one is a P *Extrovert* (as in ENTP) the Dominant is N or S. If one is a J Introvert, the Dominant is N or S; if one is a J Extrovert, the Dominant is T or F. I am fairly confident I have identified the Dominants of the authors considered herein, but my identification of the other letters of their type was sometimes tentative.

Bibliography

As the work deals intensively with one author per chapter, I offer a bibliography of the works of that author at the end of the appropriate chapter. As Jung was considered at length in the introduction, the Bibliography on Jung is presented here.

Most of the references to Jung are to the volumes of his complete works in the Bollingen Series; they are translated by R. F. C. Hull and published by Princeton University Press. An extended account of the Types is to be found throughout *PT*, but especially on pp. 330–407.

A	*Aion*
ACU	*Archetypes and the Collective Unconscious*
PA	*Psychology and Alchemy*
PR	*Psychology and Religion*
PT	*Psychological Types*
SDP	*The Structure and Dynamics of the Psyche*
SL	*The Symbolic Life*
TE	*Two Essays in Analytical Psychology*
MDR	Some of the quotes from Jung are in *Memories, Dreams, Reflections*. Edited by Aneila Jaffe, translated by R. and C. Winston. New York: Pantheon, 1963.

Other Works

Anonymous. *Bhagavad Gita*, translated by Juan Mascaro. New York: Penguin Classics, 1962.

Anonymous. *Upanishads,* translated by Juan Mascaro. New York: Penguin Classics, 1962.

Barrett, William. *Irrational Man.* New York: Doubleday Anchor Books, 1958.

Hopcke, Robert H. *A Guided Tour to the Collected Works of C. G. Jung.* Boston: Shambhala, 1989.

Hostie, Raymond. *Religion and the Psychology of Jung.* New York: Sheed & Ward, 1957.

Kaufmann, Walter. *Discovering the Mind. 3vols.* New York: McGraw-Hill, 1980.

Morgan, Michael L. *The Cambridge Companion to Plato,* edited by Richard Kraut. Cambridge: Cambridge University Press, 1992.

Myers, Isabel Briggs and Peter Myers. *Gifts Differing.* Palo Alto: Consulting Psychologists Press Inc., 1980.

Singer, June. *Boundaries of the Soul,* New York: Doubleday, rev. ed., 1994.

Part I
Three with a Perceiving Faculty as Dominant

1 Plato: Socrates Welcomes a Stranger
The Dominant Gives Way to the Self

Plato/Socrates as a Dominant N: The identification is most evident in texts that tell of dialectic: dialectic involves an ascending power in argument (*dialegein*) or thought (*dianoein*). One passes *through* (*dia*) elements as one ascends to ever wider comprehensions. Education is a "journey upwards" involving "the ascent of the soul into the intellectual world" (*Dialogues*, I, 776). A true education starts with a principle, and one is required to explain it by a higher principle, and that principle by a higher, and so forth until one finds a resting place in the best of the higher (I, 485). Beauty also involves an ascending process: beginning with the beauties of earth, one ascends to a more inclusive beauty, and then to the beauty of all fair forms, and from fair forms to fair practices, and from fair practices to fair notions, until one arrives at the notion of absolute beauty (I, 335). In all of these, objects are not seen for themselves (S) but for their ability to point "beyond" themselves, for their "otherness." As the Intuitive is concerned with the eyes (sight, insight) so with Plato: "The soul is like the eye," "Raise the eye of the soul to the universal light," "From vision we possess philosophy" (I, 768, 770, 799, 739). Philosophers (N) are set in contrast with the "practical class" (S), those "fond of fine tones and colors" (I, 739).

(Note, however, that both N and S are "Perceivers"—not "Judgers," as T and F are.) Plato's Myers-Briggs type would be INTJ.

The terms of each philosopher that are relevant to a Jungian interpretation will be presented in a Quaternity format. Arbitrarily, here and throughout, T will be on the top and N on the left. The present Quaternity has terms from Plato identified with Jungian Functions (see Figure 1.1). The first term under each letter tells of the Four virtues; the second tells of the Four divisions of the line; the third of studies (*Republic*); the fourth of rejected definitions of knowledge (*Theaetetus*); the fifth of the balance achieved in the *Sophist* (BEING is listed at the center reconciling Same and Other); the sixth the cosmic elements (*Timaeus*).

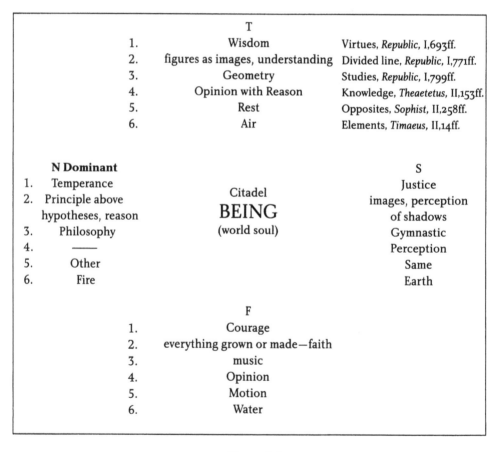

	T	
1.	Wisdom	Virtues, *Republic*, I,693ff.
2.	figures as images, understanding	Divided line, *Republic*, I,771ff.
3.	Geometry	Studies, *Republic*, I,799ff.
4.	Opinion with Reason	Knowledge, *Theaetetus*, II,153ff.
5.	Rest	Opposites, *Sophist*, II,258ff.
6.	Air	Elements, *Timaeus*, II,14ff.

N Dominant		S
1. Temperance		Justice
2. Principle above	Citadel	images, perception
hypotheses, reason	**BEING**	of shadows
3. Philosophy	(world soul)	Gymnastic
4. ——		Perception
5. Other		Same
6. Fire		Earth

	F
1.	Courage
2.	everything grown or made—faith
3.	music
4.	Opinion
5.	Motion
6.	Water

Figure 1.1

I. The Republic: Quaternity in State and Soul

Most of the writings of Plato are in the form of dialogues, and the earlier dialogues are dominated by Socrates. It is difficult to determine how much of Plato's material goes back to the historical Socrates and how much originates with Plato. But here the question is of only minor importance, for Socrates will be considered the voice of Plato's N. When Socrates steps aside in the late dialogues, this will be seen as the N stepping aside so that the opposing Functions can be reconciled and the Self might appear. But even in the many dialogues wherein Socrates takes the lead, the N can be seen as making increased allowance for the Repressed S.

The early writings of Plato involve much dialectic, yet they often reach no conclusion. In these writings philosophy seems to be the dialectical process itself: by argument one continually sees "beyond" what is immediately evident to the senses. These early dialogues often consider a virtue such as courage or temperance. Frequently Socrates' partner in dialogue would define these by particular examples; but Socrates moves away from particulars (S) and pushes for a more general understanding (I, 66). This move to the more general is the N. In these dialogues Socrates speaks eloquently of a rejection of sense knowledge and the body. We are told that the true philosopher "would like, as far as he can, to get away from the body and to turn to the soul"; for "in attempting to consider anything in company with the body she [the soul] is obviously deceived" (I, 448). The soul does best apart from sensation, with "neither sounds, nor sights, nor even any pleasure." Such are the values in the early texts of Plato.

Some years after he had told of the philosopher escaping the body,[1] Plato wrote the *Republic*. As the *Republic* begins, Socrates would treat the soul, but, since the soul is difficult to study, Socrates decides to explain the soul by an extended analogy with the state (I, 631). The result is that Socrates speaks of both the state and soul and the one will illuminate the other. This tells much of the present study, for it too will understand many philosophic texts as telling of the "soul" of the philosophers. So, when Socrates tells us that in speaking of his Republic he is also speaking of the soul, this gives some justification for the present study.

In the *Republic* Socrates tells of the Four virtues of the state and

5

the same Four virtues of the soul. The Four will be seen to conform with the Four Functions of Jung, but what a Jungian would find more striking is the many references to Three with a missing Fourth; the Fourth must be found in the dark. Socrates identifies the Four virtues: the state should be "wise and valiant and temperate and just" (I, 690–91). This Quaternity would give first place to temperance, which will be seen as N—Plato's Dominant; accordingly it is that by which a man is "master of himself." Wisdom will be seen to correspond to T (Plato's Auxiliary); valiance (courage) will be seen to correspond to F, and finally justice will correspond to S. Wisdom is identified as a kind of knowledge; while valiance (courage) concerns a "true opinion . . . about real and false dangers" (I, 693). Temperance "has more of the nature of harmony and symphony" (I, 694). Thus, temperance is identified with the N as it concerns the interrelationships, the "harmony," uniting all the parts. It is found in the man who is "master of himself"; in Jungian terms it is for the one in whom Consciousness is in control of the other Faculties. [2]

Socrates easily identified three of the virtues, but he finds it difficult to define justice. There are Three, but where is the Fourth? What is justice? As he seeks to define the missing Fourth, Socrates uses imagery suggesting a search in the Unconscious: prayer is necessary, and they must travel to obscure regions. Socrates instructs, "Light a candle and search, and get your brother and Polemarchus and the rest of our friends to help discover justice" (I, 690). The tone of the passage has changed as the Fourth is sought. To discover means to define, to bring before consciousness, and Socrates explains why this is necessary: "not to help justice in her need would be an impiety" (I, 690). The Jungian 3:4 is evident as Socrates explains,

> If there were four things, and we were searching for one of them, wherever it might be, the one sought for might be known to us from the first, and there would be no further trouble; or we might know the other three first, and then the fourth would clearly be the one left. . . . And is not a similar method to be pursued about the virtues, which are also four in number? (I, 690–91)

The Jungian symbolism is again evident as Socrates says, "If the three were discovered by us, justice would be the fourth or remaining one" (I, 696).

Socrates seems to insist that the Fourth is difficult to find. He reports:

> we may consider three out of the four virtues to have been discovered in our State. The last of those qualities which make a state virtuous must be justice, if we only knew what that was.

Glaucon, with whom Socrates is talking, responds: The inference is obvious.

Socrates: The time has arrived, Glaucon, when like huntsmen, we should surround the cover, and look sharp that justice does not steal away, and pass out of sight and escape us; for beyond a doubt she is somewhere in this country: watch therefore and strive to catch a sight of her, and if you see her first, let me know. . . . Offer up a prayer with me and follow.

Glaucon: I will, but you must show me the way.

Socrates: Here is no path, I said, and the wood is dark and perplexing; still we must push on.

Glaucon: Let us push on.

Socrates: Here I saw something: Halloo! I said, I begin to perceive a track, and I believe that the quarry will not escape. . . . we are stupid fellows.

Glaucon: Why so?

Socrates: Why, my good sir, at the beginning of our enquiry, ages ago, there was justice tumbling out at our feet, and we never saw her; nothing could be more ridiculous. Like people who go about looking for what they have in their hands—that was the way with us—we looked not at what we were seeking, but what was far off in the distance; and therefore, I suppose, we missed her.

Glaucon: What do you mean?

Socrates: I mean to say that in reality for a long time past we have been talking of justice, and have failed to recognize her. (I, 695–97)

This illustrates well what Jung would see as a search into the Unconscious for the missing Fourth. When justice finally is found, it turns out to be *in their hands*, that is, it is S. "In their hands" also suggests that the missing Function has been a missing part of themselves.

Justice can now be defined. Its many definitions show how closely it corresponds to the "in itself" quality characteristic of the S. Justice is "doing one's own business and not being a busybody," "one man should practice one thing only, the thing to which his nature was best adapted." Justice is "the power of each individual in the state to do his own work" (I, 697). Justice is "the having and doing what is a man's own, and belongs to him" (I, 697). Such is justice for the state, and so for the individual: "The just man does not permit the several elements within him to interfere with one another, or any of them to do the work of the others" (I, 707). In these passages justice involves each unit confined to itself and acting *in itself* without "meddlesomeness and interference" with others. It is radically nonrelational. Justice is the inner quality of each element, apart from an overall integration or harmony (N) with the rest. To pick up an image from the Introduction: Justice is each single tree being itself, while Temperance is the harmony, the overall forest. As Socrates ascended in ever broader generalities (N), he had overlooked the concrete singular, the S, an object being simply itself. This was what had to be found in the dark forest.

But the passage could also illustrate another image from the Introduction where the missing Function was spoken of as "the stone that was rejected"—only to become the cornerstone. The S (justice) was rejected; now it is the cornerstone of the whole system. Justice is "the ultimate cause and condition of the existence of all of them [temperance and courage and wisdom], and while remaining in them is also their preservative; and we were saying that if the three were discovered by us, justice would be the fourth or remaining one" (I, 696).

Later in the *Republic* Socrates speaks of education. He proposes that the early years of education should involve gymnastics, music and geometry (without pressing the point, these could be seen as S, F, and T). But until one has spent time on these three studies, one does not consider the "coping stone" of education: philosophy. One begins dialectic/philosophy (N) only when one is thirty years old.[3] And in studying philosophy one is to give up gymnastics (I, 799). The renunciation of gymnastics could suggest that the S function is to be ignored so that one might concentrate on the N—the Dominant is developed at the expense of the Repressed.

When the *Republic* treats human knowing, the eye of the body is set in contrast with the eye of the mind, and the eye of the mind is favored. This is explained in terms of a line that is divided into four parts: two parts for the eye of the body and two parts for the eye of the mind.[4] (The reader of Plato's text can lose track of which part of the line he is considering, so I have numbered the parts and added numbers in brackets to facilitate reading.)

> Now take a line which has been cut into two unequal parts [part 1–2 has been cut from part 3–4] and divide each of them again in the same proportion [giving parts 1, 2, 3, and 4], and suppose the two main divisions to answer, one to the visible [1 and 2] and the other to the intelligible [3 and 4], and then compare the subdivisions in respect of their clearness and want of clearness, and you will find that the first section [1] in the sphere of the visible consists of images. And by images I mean, in the first place, shadows, and in the second place, reflections in water and in solid, smooth and polished bodies and the like. (I, 771)

The next section [2] of the line is said to include "everything that grows or is made." Then the third and fourth divisions are distinguished from one another, and the third division is better than the first two, but it too has its limitations. In considering the parts that conform to the eye of the mind,

> There are two subdivisions, in the lower [3] of which the soul uses the figures given by the former division [1 and 2] as images; the enquiry can only be hypothetical, and instead of going upwards to a principle descends to the other end. . . .

But the final section [4] of the line is different:

> in the higher [4] of the two [3 and 4], the soul passes out of hypotheses, and goes up to a principle which is above hypotheses, making no use of images as in the former case, but proceeding only in and through the ideas themselves.

Images [1] and things [2] would seem to be S and F (the F identification is not evident), but the two higher parts of the division correspond well to Jungian Functions: part 3 to T and 4 to N. In explaining 3 Plato tells of geometry: geometricians assume the reality of the "absolute square and the absolute diameter and so on." Since geometry is based on assumptions that are not proven (the axioms of geometry are simply accepted), geometry itself turns out to be fundamentally unproven. But the final form of knowledge [4] is that "which reason herself attains by the power of dialectic." Now all assumptions are left behind; they serve simply as points of departure from which the mind can ascend. Thus, dialectic [4] "is the coping stone of the sciences, and is set over them; no other science can be placed higher—the nature of knowledge can no further go" (I, 794).[5]

Socrates explains:

> and now, corresponding to these four divisions, let there be four faculties in the soul—reason [4] answering to the highest, understanding [3] to the second, faith (or conviction) [2] to the third, and perception of shadows [1] to the last. (I, 773)

In this text all four Faculties are recognized and accepted, and, here in speaking of 2 as faith, its association with the F Function is more evident than it was above. The body is also present and does more than mislead (as Socrates had earlier affirmed); it now makes a contribution, however small. But the four are not centered about a midpoint to form a balanced Quaternity; they are spread out to form a line and the four are given radically different values.[6]

Later in the *Republic* Plato returns to consider the four faculties, and again they are found in pairs:

> At any rate, we are satisfied, as before, to have four divisions; two for intellect and two for opinion, and to call the first division science, the second understanding, the third belief, and the fourth perception of shadows, opinion being concerned with becoming, and intellect with being. (I, 793)

Immediately after telling of the division of the line, Socrates tells a parable concerning prisoners in a cave: the prisoners have spent their lives chained to the floor of the cave watching shadows projected before them on a wall. When one prisoner is forced to turn around, he sees the images making the shadows. Then this prisoner is dragged out of the cave so that he can see objects themselves; finally he can look to the sun and see it as it is (I, 775). The whole parable is said to tell of "the ascent of the soul into the intellectual world" (I, 776). Here, as in the division of the line that preceded, the sense world (the shadows) is not simply dismissed as error; it is given some measure of truth. That is, the S is not entirely rejected.

As the *Republic* continues, Socrates proposes that the state should educate certain qualified individuals in dialectic/philosophy and thus lead them to higher states of contemplation and virtue. But he would not leave them in the bliss of a higher state, contemplation (N). They would be forced to descend again to the sense world (go back into the cave) and rule over those who live there. Upon their return, they should serve as rulers of the state, as they have seen the higher truth. Having seen the light, they will better understand the shadows and images of the cave. But they do not need to learn anything from the shadows and images (S); they are simply to rule the cave dwellers according to the higher truth (N) they have contemplated through philosophy. In Jungian terms the conscious mind (the world of light) should assume complete control over the unconscious (the shadows of the cave). In the *Republic* such is the well-ruled state and the well-ruled individual. The philosopher is made king; the luminous and royal figure of reason is in control, and the dark shadows of the unconscious are to obey.

II. The Conscious Mind and the Passions

Socrates knew that most states and most individuals are not ruled by reason. The military or the merchant class might seize control—an individual's soul might be dominated by a craze for power. But Socrates would consider it worse still if the state should become a democracy. Democracy brings about a chaos in which everyone does what comes into their head at the moment. In a democratic state, eating, dieting, exercising, and philosophizing are all valued equally. Likewise, in an individual soul there might be a democracy of the appetites: every impulse is as good as the next. One lives by appetite and is no longer virtuous.

But tyranny is even worse than democracy. An individual knows tyranny when a drive alien to reason assumes total control of one's life; one is said to have gone mad. One is driven by an uncontrollable urge that dominates the reason and all other appetites.

Plato claims we all have strains of such madness within us, and for evidence he, like modern psychology, points to our dreams. "Even in good men, there is a lawless wild-beast nature, which peers out in sleep" (I, 830, 848). One can partially give way to this inner beast, and then there is a moderate indulgence; but it is difficult to stop with moderation and one passes easily into total indulgence. Now a single passion acts as tyrant, and seemingly the chaos of conflicting appetites is ended. Perhaps this passion is eros and one becomes shameless. "Love is the lord of the house within him, and orders all the concerns of his soul" (I, 831). Such a one is goaded into a frenzy to satisfy the horrid pangs of love and loses all control. Earlier, these passions

> were only let loose in the dreams of sleep. But now that he is under the dominion of Love, he becomes always and in waking reality what he was then very rarely and in a dream only; he will commit the foulest murder, or eat forbidden food, or be guilty of any other horrid act. Love is his tyrant, and lives lordly in him and lawlessly, and being himself a king, leads him on, as a tyrant leads a State, to the performance of any reckless deed by which he can maintain himself and the rabble of his associates. (I, 833)

The tyrant in the state is now "the waking reality of what we dreamed." And the longer the tyrant lives, the more tyrannical he becomes. Though others might envy him his prosperity and success, his appetite has become insatiable; he is beset with fear and is the most miserable of men. The difference between being ruled by a passion and being ruled by reason can be seen in the larger context of the state: "Tyranny is the wretchedest form of government" and it is set in contrast with a monarchy: "the rule of a king [is] the happiest" (I, 835; see I, 838)—that is, consciousness guided by reason. "Then if the man is like the state, ... must not the same rule prevail?" (I, 835).

Because Plato wanted to keep the passions under control, his ideal State would put strictures on the poets: they were not allowed to speak ill of heroes and gods and could use only approved musical forms. The ideal State would expel those poets unwilling to limit themselves to social betterment. Why? When sentimental poets tell of the pangs of love, the listeners lose their self-control and break down in tears. Before hearing the poet these people had disciplined their emotions, but in listening to poetry their passions stir to life and overpower their reason. Poetry has released the "wild beast," and the tyranny of the passions can begin.

In the *Republic* a line had been divided into four parts, two of which symbolized the mind and two the physical; accordingly there were two faculties of intellect and two of opinion. *Two* faculties of mind suggest that Plato has T as a strong Auxiliary. The image of two higher and two lower is presented visually at the conclusion of the *Republic*. There Socrates tells of Er, who died in battle and descended to the nether world, but twelve days later returned to life. Er told of traveling with a great company of the dead "to a mysterious place at which there were two openings in the earth; they were near together, and over against them there were two other openings in the heaven above. In the intermediate space there were judges seated." (I, 872) The two openings on earth and two in heaven form a Quaternity with judges in the middle. The two heavenly and two earthly pick up the fourfold division of the line found earlier in the *Republic*, where two parts were spiritual and two were physical (a similar two-and-two division can be found in the *Gorgias*, where there are four arts and four shams and each of these is divided into a two and two). But in this final image of the *Republic* the Four are not stretched out to form a line. Rather they form a Quaternity, with judges in the all-important middle, the place where the Self should appear.

The *Republic* has offered a sober and rational ideal of sanity with consciousness/reason in full control. But in a later dialogue (*Phaedrus*) the absolute control has been relaxed to allow for Eros; this could be seen as allowing for the F, one of the two less-developed Functions. Eros again (as in the *Republic*) is identified as a type of madness, yet the *Phaedrus* speaks in praise of the madness of love, Eros, the very drive the *Republic* had criticized as "a mad and furious master" (I, 593). Now the *Phaedrus* is claiming that "the madness of love is the greatest of heaven's blessings" (I, 250)! Madness was seen to be opposed to reason, but it is no longer simply dismissed; several forms of madness, and especially love, are said to take one to a realm higher than the sane man can know. That is, there is a region above sanity! Reason is no longer ultimate. Now the lover can reach spiritual heights equivalent to those of the philosopher (provided the lover is not devoid of philosophy) (I,253). Eros is closely akin to philosophy, one scholar of Plato speaks of his eros and philosophy as "two aspects of one and the same impulse" (Raven, 108).

In the *Phaedrus* the sight of a beautiful body awakens one to a recollection of heavenly Beauty. Beauty shines "in clearness through the clearest aperture of sense," that is, through the eyes, the *physical* eyes, not the eyes of the soul (I, 255). Gazing at the beautiful, one becomes a lover. But here there is a special need for philosophy, for without it the lover will rush forth to seize the beautiful one and give eros a physical expression. The philosopher, in the presence of earthly beauty, exercises restraint, and in doing so his spirit rises. His spirit passes beyond the individual object of physical beauty and then beyond the whole physical world, till he finally beholds heavenly Beauty. This is eros acting "under the direction of the better elements of the mind," but in being allowed to act at all it attains an expression not allowed in the *Republic*. The *Phaedrus* tells of a spiritual ascent, as did the *Republic*, but now eros facilitates the long and arduous work of philosophy/dialectic that was proposed by the *Republic*. Thus eros could have become a tyrant; but, if moderated by philosophy, it could also assist one in rising to divine contemplations. In the *Phaedrus* the lover moved by the madness of eros is given a place beside the sober philosopher of the *Republic*.[7]

III. Enantiodromia and a New Definition of Being

The *Parmenides* is generally considered a late dialogue of Plato's, even though it presents Socrates as a young man. It is written in a playful style, but scholars have found its complex arguments "of an unprecedented obscurity" (Raven, 208). In this dialogue, the aged and revered Parmenides is talking with the young Socrates, and Parmenides claims that only Being exists. This would make Becoming (any movement) unreal, as it is apart from Being. Our senses tell of a changing world, yet Parmenides offers highly rational arguments that would deny all reality to the sense world (see Taylor, 350–52). There is only Being itself, which is timeless and unchanging. Thus, Parmenides is more radically dominated by his N than Socrates was in the *Republic*, for there Socrates had allowed sense objects some measure of reality (as above in the fourfold division of the line). But Parmenides denies all reality to sense. The *Parmenides* often takes a turn that is playful and elusive, but in the end the great Parmenides gets the better of the argument.

A scholarly consensus would see Plato's *Parmenides* followed by the *Theaetetus*. In this late dialogue Socrates seems more estranged from the sense world than in the *Republic*: "We ought to fly away from earth to heaven as quickly as we can; and to fly away is to become like God, as far as this is possible" (II, 178). With such a claim it seems the original Socrates is again speaking, and, as in the early dialogues, there is much dialectic and no conclusion. The subject of the *Theaetetus* is the definition of knowledge (*episteme*). The dialogue contains an abundance of Jungian symbols: Socrates talks of "square figures" and says he is a midwife, not one who delivers babies, but one who delivers souls. The image of birth suggests to a Jungian the coming birth of the Self. Socrates will illustrate his method by assisting Theaetetus in defining knowledge. With Socrates acting as midwife, Theaetetus offers three definitions of knowledge. The three will be shown to correspond with the S, F, and T, and Socrates will show that all three are inadequate. In reaching this conclusion, Socrates has delivered Theaetetus of three "wind-eggs," that is, three claims that will not hold up to criticism.

Consider the three definitions: Theaetetus's first attempt would take the definition of Protagoras: "Knowledge is perception" (II, 153); according to this definition the wind would be cold if one finds it cold and hot if one finds it hot. Evidently, "perception" means sense perception (S). Each individual speaks of one's own sensation, and, since sensation/perception is knowledge, each individual is right: "What seems to a man is to him." Each individual is sufficient to one's self and there is said to be no common wisdom. There are only separate trees and no forest; the self-sufficiency of the individual again suggests the in-itself, the S. Again, those who claim that knowledge is perception are the ones who "believe in nothing but what they can grasp in their hands" (II, 157). They are the Sensates. But Socrates rejects their claim, for all that perception gives us is an ongoing flux of sensation. If the Sensates were correct, Reality would be a matter of change/becoming rather than Being.[8]

In this dialogue the position of the "divine" Parmenides, N, ("only Being is") is set in opposition to that of the "earthy" Protagoras, S (only becoming is). The arguments of Parmenides would draw Socrates into pure Being wholly apart from the sense world, while those of Protagoras would drag him into the flux of sense phenomena wholly apart from Being. In telling of the two opposing claims, Socrates tells of feeling like he is caught in the middle of the playing field at the palaestra; he is pulled in both directions by the opposing players (II, 183). This is what Jung would call the Enantiodromia, the battle of the opposites, N vs. S, or Parmenides vs. Protagoras. Parmenides is the rational N, while Protagoras is the flux of sensation who now is associated with "the river-gods," further telling of the S in the Unconscious.

Socrates is asked to deal with the arguments of Parmenides, and to everyone's surprise he refuses. The refusal could be explained by the *Parmenides*, wherein it seems that Socrates was beaten at his own game. The present study suggests the refusal was based on the similarity between the dialectic of Parmenides and that of Socrates. Parmenides had won the debate (with the young Socrates and another youth), but as a pure N he allowed no reality for Sensation. Socrates was unwilling to go that far, and also unwilling to say why. So rather than consider Parmenides anew, he turned back to consider Protagoras; here Socrates by his dialectic can show well Protagoras' inadequacy. Having rejected Protagoras, Theaetetus proposes a second definition of knowledge: "Knowledge is true opinion." The Greek (*ten alethe dozan*) could be translated as "true judgment" or "true belief" (see Taylor, 339). This could be seen as associated with the F (Jung speaks of the F holding opinions without being able to defend them). This is the second definition of knowledge. In being associated with F, a judgment is involved (the T and F are Judging Faculties while the N and S are Faculties of Perception).

When Socrates shows the second definition of knowledge to be inadequate, a third definition is proposed: knowledge is "true opinion combined with reason [*meta logou*]" (II, 206).[9] This means that, beyond holding an opinion, one is able to defend it and show it is self-consistent. This is the T. Socrates see this as an improvement, for now the opinion cannot be refuted by logic; but still it is inadequate, as it is based only on assumption. This too is rejected. Thus, Socrates has shown three things: "Knowledge is neither sensation, nor true opinion, nor yet definition and explanation accompanying and added to true opinion" (II, 216). Having identified only three things that knowledge is not, Socrates decides that Theaetetus has given birth to nothing but wind-eggs.

As the early dialogues of Plato could reach no conclusion, so the *Theaetetus*. But as the *Theaetetus* ends, Socrates leaves to defend himself in court, in the trial that will condemn him to death. Thus, having rejected S, F, and T, and refusing to deal with Parmenides (N), Socrates himself (N) goes to his death. The death of Socrates had been treated at length in the earlier dialogues of Plato. It seems a little unusual to refer again to his coming trial, but with this reference Socrates no longer dominates the writings of Plato. From now on (with one possible exception) Socrates seems never again to lead a Platonic dialogue.[10]

Socrates as N has brought Plato to the fullness of Being by an upward ascent into the Light, the fullness of consciousness, but in doing so he gave little recognition to the physical world, to becoming, to things in themselves. Parmenides did the same with his disciples, but he was more extreme than Socrates. But for both Parmenides and Socrates something is still missing: Sensation, the individual, the particular; the S is largely in the Unconscious. Socrates was the noble voice of Plato's N, but now Plato sends him to his demise and looks for another who can bring about the Integration he is seeking. He needs someone who can hold a middle position in the dispute between the radically transcendent (other) claim of Parmenides and the radically immanent (present sensation) claim of Protagoras.

Someone new appears! He is identified only as a Stranger from Elea, the hometown of Parmenides, yet he appears on the scene from nowhere and he has no name. Socrates asks, "Is he not rather a god . . . who comes to us in the disguise of a stranger?" (II, 221). He is the mysterious and unnamed one, "divine he certainly is," who will reconcile the Opposites. He first appears in a dialogue said to take place on the day after the *Theaetetus*. Socrates welcomes the Stranger and asks him to conduct the discussion—then Socrates quietly steps aside. Though the Stranger is identified as a disciple of Parmenides, he will break with Parmenides, and in the process Plato will break with Socrates. The Stranger will end the radical domination of Plato's N and work out a compromise that will resolve the Enantiodromia. The dialogue is called the *Sophist*, a dialogue in which the Stranger sets out to define the elusive Sophist (Protagoras, who had identified knowledge with perception [S], was the prime Sophist). The Stranger will try to bring the Sophist before consciousness (II, 223). But the wily Sophist has his verbal tricks: he is said to run into the darkness (the Unconscious?) and that makes it difficult to see who he is. Again (as in looking for Justice in the *Republic*) a difficult search must be made in darkness to discover the missing S.

The Sophist is said to deal in falsehood, but even to allow that falsehood exists would oppose the basic claim of Parmenides. For Parmenides there is no falsehood. For falsehood is a kind of non-being and not-being is not; only being is: "Never will you show that non-being is." For Parmenides, Being is one and unchangeable, while the opposites of these, division and change, are forms of nonbeing. As such, they are not. If the Stranger (or Plato) is to allow any reality to change, to falsehood, or sense experience, he must first show that nonbeing can *be*. To do so, the Stranger fears he must renounce his father (teacher), that is, Parmenides, for the Stranger will be forced to maintain, "In a certain sense notbeing is and that being, on the other hand, is not" (II, 248). The claim appears to be nonsense and a double contradiction; it is the kind of speech Parmenides and Socrates would not allow. Even those listening to the Stranger find their heads are spinning.

The Stranger, too, has problems with the claim. He is troubled as he sets out to argue that not-being is; he tells of having "no heart for this argument." For to make his defense he must go beyond what sane people say, so he warns, "I tremble at the thought of what I have said, and expect that you will deem me mad." The madness is that he will have to *set reason aside* and go beyond being into the darkness of nonbeing. One cannot descend into the Unconscious without taking some risk, so the Stranger speaks of his defense as a "perilous enterprise" (II, 249). But out of concern for others, he will venture beyond Consciousness (beyond where things can be rationally and clearly stated). The clarity of the Conscious mind allows no double-talk, yet the Stranger is forced to defend double-talk (not-being is, and being is not). A claim that seems akin to madness.

The Stranger tells of a long-standing war between the Giants and the Gods; they are fighting over the nature of Being. The groups are not further identified, but the Giants clearly represent the materialists and Protagoras was such.[11] The Sensate imagery is evident:

> Some of them [the Giants] are dragging down all things from heaven and from the unseen to earth, and they literally grasp in their hands rocks and oaks; of these they lay hold, and obstinately maintain, that the things only which can be touched or handled have being or essence, because they define being and body as one, and if any one else says that what is not a body exists they altogether despise him, and will hear of nothing but body. (II, 253)

These Giants are said to be wild and primitive figures (such are the figures from the Unconscious). The worst of them are "terrible fellows," "real aboriginals, children of the dragon's teeth." They would "drag everything down into matter" and shamelessly assert "that nothing is which they are not able to squeeze in their hands" (II, 255). They are Plato's undeveloped S, they are the wild and primal powers of the tangible world that Plato has long repressed. They could not show themselves as long as Socrates (N) dominated the mind of Plato. But when Socrates retires, the Giants/Protagoras/Sophists, that is, the repressed S, can come into its own. The Stranger undertakes the "perilous" confrontation of opposites.

In contrast with the Giants there are the Gods. They too are not identified, but Parmenides had been called a god, and in the *Theaetetus* Socrates wanted to fly away and "become like God." The "Gods" are said to "cautiously defend themselves from above, out of an unseen world, mightily contending that true essence [Being] consists of certain intelligible and incorporeal ideas" (II, 254). They are Plato's N; they resemble Socrates/Parmenides and they too have been unyielding. So between the Gods and the Giants "there is always an endless conflict raging concerning these matters." The endless conflict suggests the passage in the *Theaetetus* wherein Socrates told of feeling pulled in opposite directions, like one on the central line of a playing field. Then as now it was the Enantiodromia of the N (Parmenides) pulling him in one direction and the S (Protagoras) pulling him in the other. But now the Stranger will end the conflict by boldly confronting both Giants and Gods, seeking to establish a common Center. He would set up a "citadel"—a stable position between the conscious and the unconscious where N and S can agree. This is the process of Integration.

Jung speaks of ending the domination of the conscious Function by having the ego initiate a dialogue with the repressed Function. Jung says that in some cases,

> the "other" voice [the Repressed] is more or less distinctly heard. For such people it is technically very simple to note down the "other" voice in writing and to answer its statements from the standpoint of the ego. It is exactly as if a dialogue were taking place between two human beings with equal rights, each of whom gives the other credit for a valid argument and considers it worthwhile to modify the conflicting standpoints by means of thorough comparison and discussion. . . . in most cases a long conflict will have to be born, demanding sacrifices from both sides. (*SDP*, 88–89)

Jung will describe this as a "bringing together of the opposites for the production of the third: the transcendent function" (*SDP*, 87). So in the *Sophist*, the Stranger will be "demanding sacrifices from both sides"; he will press both to give a little on their respective claims. This will lead to the production of the transcendent Function.

To effect the reconciliation the unruly Giants (S) must be drawn into a dialogue. They had been claiming that only sensible objects are real ("things only which can be touched or handled"), but some of the Giants are led to concede that the virtues are real even though they are intangible. In making this concession and allowing for the intangible, they have softened their position—they no longer simply identify with the S. Then the Stranger must get the Gods, "the friends of ideas," to likewise modify their position. The Stranger argues that if reality is fixed and immovable being, Being would be "devoid of life and mind, and [exist] in awful unmeaningness an eternal fixture" (II, 257).[12] The Gods are unwilling to go this far and likewise are willing to modify their claim. Then the Stranger proposes a definition of Being to which both the Giants and Gods are led to agree; "Being is simply power" (II, 255). It is "an active or passive energy, arising out of a certain power which proceeds from elements meeting with one another. . . . Any power of doing or suffering in a degree however slight was held by us to be a sufficient definition of being" (II, 256). Note: the power arises out of "elements meeting with one another." The deadlock has been broken and the N and the S are meeting. An energy is released as the opposites meet (for Jung, the reconciliation of opposites involves a release of psychic energy; see *PT*, 251–53; *PR*, 81). By defining Being as power, the Stranger has broken the deadlock of the Enantiodromia.[13]

The Stranger then sets up "five classes." This involves Being and two sets of opposites: there is Rest and Motion, and Same and Other; these Four could be presented as a Quaternity surrounding

	Rest	
Other	BEING	Same
	Motion	

Figure 1.2

Being (see fig. 1.2). The claim that a Quaternity is formed with Being at the Center would be more evident if Plato spoke of the elements as "Four." He does not, but still in telling of two sets of opposites with all Four sharing in Being, the Quaternity arrangement is readily suggested; while BEING is the quintessence (see Jung's *PR*, 100, where the unifying Fifth is so identified). Since all four share in Being,[14] Being would be what Jung considered the Self (both Other and Same *are*, and so with Rest and Motion).

Having established this middle position as a "citadel," the Stranger would like to get the Gods and Giants to agree to his conclusion. But he finds both the Philosophers (Parmenides, the Gods— N) and the Sophists (Protagoras, the Giants—S) are difficult to locate. But difficult for opposite reasons. "Because the Sophist runs away into the darkness of not-being, in which he has learned by habit to feel [*tribe*, "rub," a sense word] about, and cannot be discovered because of the darkness of the place" (II, 262). The Philosopher presents an opposite problem: "And the philosopher, always holding converse through reason with the idea of being, is also dark from excess of light; for the souls of the many have no eye which can endure the vision of the divine" (II, 262).

The difficulty is that the Philosopher is in pure light (Consciousness) and the Sophist in pure darkness (Unconsciousness).[15] So the Stranger finds them both difficult to locate. The image of being unable to see because of too much light (ideas) and too much darkness (sensation) was already presented in the *Republic* (I, 777). But in the *Republic* no attempt was made to find a middle point. Now the Stranger is setting up a point between light and darkness. For Jung, the self appears at "a point midway between the conscious and unconscious" (*TE*, 221).

In this passage, Plato, speaking through the Stranger, has criticized the divine Philosophers, the "friends of ideas." Yet all the while, Socrates, the philosopher who told abundantly of heavenly ideas, the one who until now was the hero of all the dialogues of Plato, sits by in silent approval.[16]

The Stranger is asked to define the Philosopher, but the Stranger postpones the task, for he is determined to go after the Sophist and have a good look at him. And again (as in the *Republic* when Socrates sought to define Justice) there is the image of hunting in the dark; in each case, it is the S that is being sought. But the Sophist is "not easily caught, for he seems to have abundance of defences which he throws up, and which must every one of them be stormed before we can reach the man himself" (II, 271). This is the tricky realm (the Unconscious) into which the Stranger would lead his auditors. But he tells them they can take heart, for "the citadel is ours, and what remains is easier" (II, 271). The "citadel" refers to the new definition of Being established above. The citadel allows for both the being of nonbeing and the nonbeing of being. With this established, it is considered only a cleanup operation to catch the Sophist himself. They seek him and find him in "the union of sense and opinion" (II, 274; this would be in the union of S [sense] and F [opinion], the *two* repressed Functions; recall that Plato had a strong T as Auxiliary and this gave him the two spiritual and two physical as in the divided line in the *Republic*). Having found the Sophist, they would "exhibit him in his true nature." The Sophist finally is defined and the dialogue can end.[17]

Having established a new definition of Being (or "a mark to distinguish real things") as a Citadel, the dialogues of Plato take a different tone. After the *Sophist*, the *Statesman* seems to be the next Platonic dialogue, and again the Stranger takes the lead, while again Socrates sits by in silence. Here the Stranger praises the mean, the middle ground, and that is new and fundamentally different. Now the "mean" is the mark that distinguishes between good men and bad. This is not the teaching of the *Republic*. Now the mean and balance are the ideal. So the beauty of every work of art is centered on measure and balance, and the task of the Statesman is to balance all extremes (II, 311)! The Stranger has established a middle ground (a citadel between Consciousness and Unconsciousness). To explain the value of mean and middle ground, the Stranger refers back to the *Sophist* and its claim that nonbeing is real. Once this is accepted, moderation and the mean will characterize the thought of the Stranger. So he tells of skills, crafts, and practical politics—elements that were ignored in the *Republic*. But even theory will be different: "We shall some day require this notion of a mean with a view to the demonstration of absolute truth" (II, 312). The absolute truth is no longer pure N. Eternal nature will be found "in measure and the mean" (II, 402).

In a late dialogue (the *Laws*), Plato introduces a second Stranger to tell of the state he envisions, a state very different from the republic. Telling of both monarchy and democracy, the Stranger adds, "You must have both these forms of government in a measure; the argument emphatically declares that no city can be well governed which is not made up of both" (II, 468). The *Republic* had praised monarchy and rejected democracy, but the state proposed in the *Laws* will set up "a mean between monarchy and democracy" (II, 519). Beyond the discipline of the *Republic* the Stranger calls for a freedom (II, 468). In the *Republic* Plato was speaking of both the state and the soul. Is he doing the same in the *Laws*? In that case, the monarchy of consciousness is ended; the appetites are allowed some limited recognition, some democracy, some freedom, for a citadel has been established on the "middle ground." Heavenly principles will no longer be invoked without regard for the present fact, for "a perfectly simple principle can never be applied to a state of things which is the reverse of simple" (II, 322). Now principle is not all-powerful. Plato has made some concession to the dark of the cave. The dark unconscious voices have been given some freedom.

Plato has moved from his N to establish a middle ground that in its balance resembles the Self of Jung; it balances Other and Same, the N and the S. This gives a different tone to the writings that followed the *Sophist*. This can best be seen by comparing the government proposed in the *Laws* with that proposed in the *Republic*. The government proposed in the *Laws* is ruled by a "Nocturnal Council." The term is not explained, but it is said to meet daily after the first light of dawn and before the sun rises (II, 686); that is, in the middle time *between* the night and the daylight (between Unconsciousness and Consciousness?). While in Plato's republic the leaders of the state had gazed at the pure light of the sun; this gave them all they needed to make their decisions. That is, the darkness had no part to play. Now that a mean has been established, they meet at dawn, between the darkness of night and the full light of day. In Jungian terms, the Self has appeared; it is the middle ground between the Unconscious and Consciousness.

The *Laws* tell of balance, yet Plato ends the work with a final Quaternity showing consciousness clearly in control. He again introduces the four fundamental virtues (with minor differences). "We said that virtue was of four kinds. . . . and that mind was the leader of the four, and that to her the other virtues and all other things ought to have regard" (II, 697). The conscious mind is still in control, but in saying that the other virtues "ought to have regard" for mind, he has used a gentle phrase suggesting the mind's control is no longer absolute.

IV. With S Acknowledged, Plato Develops an Interest in Physical Science

In his later years Plato's interest turned increasingly to cosmology and astronomy. This interest is evident in a late dialogue, the *Timaeus*. Timaeus dominates the dialogue by a long monologue on the creation of the universe. In announcing that he will be dealing with the physical world, he says he will present only opinion and belief. Socrates is asked "to accept the tale which is probable and enquire no further" even though it might contain inconsistencies (II, 13). Socrates assents. That is, Timaeus is allowed to violate the canons of Socratic discourse: there will be only probability, there will be a lengthy speech and no dialogue, and inconsistencies are to be overlooked! Yet Socrates meekly agrees: "We will do precisely as you bid us." This renunciation of dialectic and a concern with the physical world, with opinion, and a lengthy account of the probable illustrates the change in Plato. The godlike philosophers have accepted that the "Giants" have something to tell them—though it is only probable.[18]

The *Timaeus* tells of the world being created out of four elements in two sets of pairs: fire and earth, air and water. They were the four elements commonly recognized in Greek thought of the time. The dialogue is filled with Four and 3:4 symbols. Even the opening line has Socrates ask, "One, two, three; but where, my dear Timaeus, is the fourth of those who were yesterday my guests?" Three are there and one is missing! Because this line illustrates so well 3 and the missing 4th, Jung quotes it on many occasions (e.g.: see Jung, *ACU*, 234, 235, 243, 378, 389).[19]

Timaeus is said to have "made the nature of the universe his special study," so he will give an account of its origin. To do so he introduces the four conventional elements set in pairs: there is fire and earth, there is air and water. How two of these four elements would conform to the Jungian Quaternity is evident in the following passage that associates fire with the visible (N) and earth with the tangible (S):

> Now that which is created is of necessity corporeal, and also visible and tangible. And nothing is visible where there is no fire, or tangible

which has no solidity, and nothing is solid without earth. Wherefore also God in the beginning of creation made the body of the universe to consist of fire and earth. (II, 14–15)

Timaeus says that originally there was only fire (the visible) and earth (the tangible—the two are the N and S) and these two were in radical opposition. In order to unite two such diverse elements, Timaeus claims two mediums are necessary: air and water. When these are added, the world is comprised of "elements which are in number four," and thus they form "a perfect whole." Air and water could be seen as the auxiliary Functions (T & F). Then, in Jungian terms, by the addition of the auxiliary Functions, the Dominant and the Recessed are able to unite; the completed Four brings about what Jung calls Wholeness and Plato "a perfect whole."

The *Timaeus* calls the four elements "the four most beautiful bodies" or the "four forms of bodies which excel in beauty" (II, 34). Then it goes on to claim that each of these is constructed out of right triangles, and the right triangles are divided into two classes: right triangles with two equal sides (isosceles triangles) and right triangles with no equal sides. Timaeus then claims that each of the four elements is composed of tiny building blocks (atoms of a sort), and the atoms themselves are formed out of the right triangles. The atoms are of two types: "there are generated from the triangles which we have selected four kinds—three from the one which has the sides unequal; the fourth alone is framed out of the isosceles triangle. Hence they cannot all be resolved into one another. . . . But three of them can be thus resolved and compounded . . ." (II, 34). The fourth element that is "framed out of the isosceles triangle" is identified as the earth; it is the tangible and is set apart from the other three to give Three plus One, and the one is the tangible earth, the separated S. The earth alone is formed of isosceles triangles (four isosceles triangles can be joined at their right angles to form a square and six squares can be put together to form a cube).

The cube has more stability than the other forms, so "earth is the most immovable of the four and the most plastic of all bodies" (II, 35). The other three (fire, air, and water) are more ethereal and as such they can be resolved into one another, but earth cannot be so resolved. The tangible earth is the separated Fourth.

Timaeus' somewhat imaginative account speaks of the entire

universe as a single animal and the animal is said to have a single soul; the single animal contains all lesser animals within it (an image common among the pre-Socratics). This large animal is in the form of a perfect sphere "having its extremes in every direction equidistant from the centre." It is composed of the same basic opposites that were considered in the *Sophist* (Same and Other), and again, as in the *Sophist*, they would be united in Being: in making this Being, the Creator "compounded a third and intermediate kind of essence [Being], partaking of the nature of the same and the other." This is the Being, the citadel, proposed in the *Sophist*. Again it is the union of S and N in a central "intermediate kind" of Being. Its formation is explained:

> He [the Creator] took the three elements of the same, the other, and the essence [Being], and mingled them into one form, compressing by force the reluctant and unsociable nature of the other into the same. When he had mingled them with the essence [Being] and out of the three made one, he again divided this whole into as many portions as was fitting, each portion being a compound of the same, the other and the essence. (II, 17; Jowett regularly speaks of *ousia* as "essence" where others translate it as "being.")

Plato's image becomes increasingly complex as the resulting mix of Same, Other, and Being is marked with an ascending series of numbers and divided into two long strips. The strips are joined together at their centers to form a letter X. Then the ends of each strip of the X are bent around until they form a three-dimensional sort of sphere. When this is done, each strip begins to rotate: Same on the outside and Other on the inside. The circles form Mandalas of sorts and one is said to have a rectangular figure inscribed within it. It rotates to the right, while the motion of the Other is to the left. The fixed stars are placed in the outer circle of Sameness, while the sun, moon, and five planets are set in the inner circle of Otherness, and the two strips rotate independently. The fixed stars are constant (same) while the other seven (planets, sun, and moon) move freely and are the other. Thus, Same and Other have a cosmic meaning and they can be *seen* in the physical world.

When the time comes to populate the universe with animals,

they are to be created according to the heavenly ideal in both nature and number, and "there are four such." The first heavenly ideal
of animal is the gods whom the Creator formed largely from fire; so
using the identification of fire (as presented above), the gods would
correspond to the N (as did the Gods in the *Sophist*):

> There are four such [ideals]; one of them is the heavenly race of the
> gods; another, the race of birds whose way is in the air; the third, the
> watery species; and the fourth, the pedestrian and land creatures. Of
> the heavenly and divine, he (the Creator) created the greater part out
> of fire, that they might be the brightest of all things and fairest to be-
> hold, and he fashioned them after the likeness of the universe in the
> figure of a circle. (II, 21)

These fiery gods are the stars moving around in a perfect circle.

When human beings are set into the universe, a primary importance is given to their physical sight, which is considered as a divine
gift. Through this gift humans can observe the stars and determine
the mathematics involved; this draws them to philosophy. So *physical
sight* is the greatest gift given to humanity. The Creator gives sight
so that on seeing the circular and regular movement of the heavens
we may properly employ the revolution of our minds, that is, the di-
anoetic part. This restores us to our heavenly identity. The motions
of the heavens are "naturally akin to the divine principle within us,"
and by physically seeing the harmony and revolution of the heavens
we can have our divine nature renewed. We may thus attain "that
perfect life which the gods have set before mankind, both for the
present and the future" (II, 66).

In the *Timaeus*, physical science has replaced dialectic! Physical
science is again given primacy at the end of the *Laws*. There the nation will be ruled by members of the "nocturnal assembly," and the
training required to be an assembly member differs from that of the
guardians in the *Republic*. Anyone

> who has not contemplated the mind of nature which is said to exist in
> the stars, and gone through the previous training, and seen the con-
> nection of music with these things and harmonized them all with laws
> and institutions, is not able to give a reason of such things as have a
> reason. And he who is unable to acquire this in addition to the ordinary
> virtues of a citizen, can hardly be a good ruler of a whole state. (II, 702)

Here one is to contemplate "the mind of nature which is said to exist in the stars." The object of contemplation is not the "Good" seen with the "eye of the mind" as in the *Republic*. Now one contemplates the physical world with the eye of the body, and this is the contemplation necessary for one to become a leader. The soul of the cosmos is seen in its movements. Now the ruler-to-be does not contemplate the Form of forms with the eye of the mind, he studies the night sky with the eye of the body. He thus comes to know a "world-soul" of sorts that is found in the sense world. A Plato scholar would see this world-soul "as the link that he [Plato] had long been seeking between the world of Ideas and the world of sense" (Raven, 238). The link that unites the opposites has become visible; the world soul is the middle element.

The importance of both astronomy and this visible Soul is further developed in the *Epinomis*, a dialogue that follows closely on the *Laws* and is often regarded as appendix to the *Laws*. (Though some scholars have questioned its authenticity as a work of Plato—including Jowett, whose translation I have been following—others accept it, notably A. E. Taylor, whose translation I now use.) The *Epinomis*, like the *Timaeus* and the final pages of *The Laws*, considers astronomy. Here the visible heavens (called Uranus) is identified as the source of all good things and the one who has given us number; in the *Republic* the Good (seen by the eye of the mind) was the source of all good on earth. Now Uranus, the physical heavens seen as a god, is the object of contemplation. We are to "accept his gift of number and let [one's] mind expatiate over the whole heavenly circuit" (P&E, 227). The virtue proposed in the *Epinomis* is piety, and one is to grow in piety by studying the planetary orbits. This is the altered contemplation offered in the final writings of Plato. In his earlier writings astronomy was largely dismissed, as it concerned only the passing world (I, 789). But in the latter writings astronomy has usurped the place of dialectic; it is "the goal," while dialectic is reduced to being a "touchstone" (see A. C. Lloyd in Taylor, 206). Ryle speaks of the change as an "intellectual revolution" (Ryle, 14). The revolution concerns the acceptance of the S. The movement of the stars manifests the perfect circle; the physical and the ideal have been united. The earthy S has been integrated into the divine N. Now the philosopher contemplates the World Soul visible in the cosmos; it, like the citadel in the *Sophist,* is the median element uniting the divine Ideas (N) and the particulars of Sense.

The writings of Plato show many Quaternities and Threes-becoming-Fours; the early dialogues show an N moving free of the body. Then there is a limited acceptance of sense knowledge in the *Republic,* and later *(Sophist)* a full acceptance of sense knowledge and a unity of opposites in Being. Socrates once had told of being caught on a playing field between proponents of Being and Becoming. Then he stepped aside to allow a Stranger to resolve the Enantiodromia, much as the Dominant must step aside to allow for the appearance of the Self. The reconciliation of opposites in Plato offers a vivid example of Jungian Integration. In other authors the Jungian patterns will not be as evident as they are in Plato. But to see the significance of a Jungian approach to the philosophers, one would have to consider how the world appears to one who is the reverse of Plato: Sensation as Dominant and N as Repressed. Such a one would seek an Integration of similar elements, but from an opposite starting point. John Locke was such a philosopher. Unlike Plato, who set out to develop a philosophy "making no use of images," Locke tried to develop a philosophy based wholly on images of sense. Locke was an S and Plato was an N, and both of them moved to Integration late in life.

Notes

1. Many believe Plato (428/7–348/7 B.C.) started writing in his early thirties, shortly after Socrates, his teacher, was put to death by the Athenians (399 B.C.). Some, appealing to a text of Diogenes Laertius, have claimed he began writing before Socrates died, a position not widely accepted (Kraut, 33); others have seen him not really writing until the 370s (Ryle, 216). In any case, he wrote over many years. There is considerable agreement on the *general* order of composition; here I will assume a version of this agreement.

2. See the importance of Temperance in Plato's adventures in Sicily (*PE,* 117, 125); there Temperance is again associated with control and harmony.

3. Ryle has a unique understanding of Plato and a complex theory of why dialectic is postponed: Plato did not teach it to the young because this had produced political trouble in Athens (Ryle, 154).

4. This Quaternity and the one that follows picks up on a Quaternity that was common in Greek thought of the time: Simonides speaks of the good man as "four-cornered"; Protagoras speaks of the "quadrilateral," the four great virtues. A similar Quaternity also telling of the well-balanced person is

found in the "Four H Clubs" (head, heart, hand, and hearth) once common in the U.S.

5. For a careful account of the difference between *noesis*, 3, and *dianoia*, 4, see Ian Mueller in Kraut, 184.

6. Similar Quaternities, with two of the four associated with the body and two with the soul, are found in the *Gorgias*: "Now, seeing that there are these four arts, two attending on the body and two on the soul for their highest good." It turns out that in imitation of the true arts flattery "has distributed herself into four shams or simulations of them, she puts on the likeness of some one or other of them, and pretends to be what she simulates" (I, 523). The "four arts" to which he refers are gymnastics and medicine for the body; legislation and justice for the soul; the "four shams" that correspond are attire and cooking for the body, and sophistry and rhetoric for the soul.

7. A similar spiritual ascent through the power of Eros is found in the *Symposium*, where the ascent is narrated at a drinking party where many participants become more or less drunk (not wholly conscious), a situation far removed from the sobriety of the *Republic*. The *Laws*, a later work of Plato's, will also speak positively of drinking until one is not entirely sober. These mixes of philosophy and alcohol would have no place in the *Republic* or earlier dialogues. Becoming open to "spirits" suggests Plato has become more open to the Unconscious.

8. In this dialogue Socrates responds well to the claims of Protagoras (S), but when he is asked to respond to the claims of Parmenides (N), he refuses. Socrates was known for his willingness to debate any point with anyone, but he refuses to debate the claim of Parmenides because of "the unbidden guests (arguments) that will come swarming in on our feast of discourse" (II, 186). This refusal could mean that Parmenides had shown Socrates the weakness in his own position, though Socrates would not simply deny sense knowledge. Socrates could not accept the pure N of Parmenides and yet could not explain why not.

9. In additional contexts Plato has set Belief (opinion) and Belief-with-Reason in contrast, as when telling of the rhapsodes "who recite in order to be believed and not with any view to criticism or instruction" (see I, 281, 99, 116, etc.).

10. As mentioned above, there is some uncertainty about the order in which Plato wrote the dialogues. Many commentators argue that the *Philebus* (wherein Socrates leads the discussion) is later than the *Theaetetus*. It may be. The *Philebus* is not considered in this study, but it too contains an example of 3 becoming 4. Having divided existing things "into three classes," Socrates adds, "I say that a fourth class is still wanted. . . . add this as a fourth class to the three others" (II, 355). One could compare Plato's break with Socrates with Jung's break with Freud. In each case a senior mentor had shown the way until the disciple could no longer accept the teaching of the master. Jung tells of his break: "When I parted from Freud, I knew that I was plunging into the unknown. Beyond Freud, after all, I knew nothing; but I had taken the step into darkness" (MDR, 199). In setting Socrates aside, Plato seems to take a similar step.

11. There is no agreement as to whom Plato is referring: it could well be

the conflict between the Italian Idealists and the Ionian Atomists. Cornford sees no need to look for one set of persons who held the materialist position to the exclusion of others (Cornford, 232).

12. Earlier Socrates spoke of philosophy as a way of dying; the true philosopher "is always pursuing death" (I, 447). This was the way to be with the gods in timeless being, in eternal fixity. Now the gods are said to have life, that is, now even they share in Becoming.

13. Cornford has written forcefully against Jowett's translation of "I hold the definition of Being is simply power." He renders it: "I am proposing as a mark to distinguish real things that they are nothing but power." Cornford's objection is that the Greek word used is *horos* and not *logos*, thus he does not see Plato committing himself to a definition of Being (Cornford, 234).

14. The best way to see N as Other is to see N as the ascending power found in dialectic; one is always passing beyond, always seeking an unnamed Other not immediately present; likewise, physical beauty awakens yearnings for the heavenly Beauty that is always other and elsewhere. The "otherness" is evident in the dialogues that reached no conclusion; they were dialectic for dialectic's sake, the process of going beyond and beyond. The *Theaetetus* again has Socrates wanting to flee the body, and again the dialogue has much dialectic and no conclusion: knowledge has shown itself as "other" than the three definitions considered.

15. In the *Republic*, the philosopher was to rise from the dark of the cave to the light of the sun. In the higher world the eyes of the philosopher were blinded by the light, but gradually his eyes adjusted. When he later returned to the cave, he would again be blinded. So Plato warns that whenever one sees someone stumbling about, one should not leap to conclusions. One "will first ask whether the soul of that man has come out of the brighter life, and is unable to see because unaccustomed to the dark, or having turned from darkness to day is dazzled by excess of light" (I, 777). This is similar to the dilemma in the *Sophist* where the extremes of both light and darkness make it difficult to see.

16. In the *Republic* the philosopher was able to contemplate the sun, but in a later work, the *Laws*, Plato argues that looking directly at the sun blinds one, leading to a sense of darkness at noonday (II, 639). As in the *Republic*, the philosopher is blinded by an excess of light; but in the *Republic* the blindness was excused. In the *Sophist* and the *Laws*, blindness from an excess of light seems no different from the blindness of being in the dark.

17. The Sophist illustrates what Jung calls the Shadow, a sort of bête noire one cannot escape. Such is the Sophist throughout the dialogues of Plato, a negative counterpart of Socrates who bears a resemblance to Socrates that is too close for comfort. Jung's "Shadow" is not developed in the present study.

18. In the *Republic* Socrates had said opinion is to be found "in the interval between pure being and absolute not-being" (I, 742). There and in the *Theaetetus* opinion was not considered true knowledge. In the early dialogues there was much dialectic (N) and no conclusion, no final teaching. Now there is much final teaching and little dialectic. Plato's "citadel" has been duly established "in the interval between pure being and absolute not-being." Starting

with the *Sophist* and the retirement of Socrates, there is little dialectic, unless one believes (as many do) that the *Philebus* comes after the *Sophist*. But here and in the later dialogues probable opinions are proclaimed freely and without argument or defense.

19. Jung has written an extended consideration of the *Timaeus* (P&R, 122–27). But other than this dialogue and several citations of a single line from the *Symposium* ("Eros is a mighty daemon"), Jung seems to have had only minimal familiarity with Plato—and with most other philosophers. In treating the *Timaeus*, Jung tells of Plato's presentation of the four elements (fire and earth, air and water) and suggests that fire and earth are present and "either air or water is missing" (P&R, 122). It is difficult to see why Jung would read the passage this way; his reading suggests that *two* elements are present and two (or one) are missing! By doing so he would have the missing element as the unity of the opposing two. With such a reading the opening line telling of three with a missing four would not seem to apply, or it would read, "Two are here, where is the third?" Later in the dialogue (as will be seen) Fire, Air, and Water are seen to be made out of similar triangles, whereas Earth is made of isosceles triangles. Thus, Earth is clearly the separated Fourth. Taking the passage this way makes a better reading of both the 3+1 and the Quaternity; it also picks up on Plato's long-standing difficulty in accepting the tangible (Sensation). For additional times that Jung has cited the opening of the *Timaeus*, see P&R, 70, 164; SDP, 314, 513; ACU, 388. In one of his early writings Jung seemed to identify Socrates as a T with N suppressed: "the strongly rationalistic attitude of Socrates repressed the Intuitive Function as far as possible, so that it had to make itself felt in the form of concrete hallucinations since it had no direct access to consciousness. But this is not the case with the Intuitive type" (PT, 145–46). I can ascribe this claim only to his lack of familiarity with the texts of Plato and with the fact that he had not fully developed his own understanding of the types.

Bibliography

Works of Plato

I and II

The Dialogues of Plato, in two volumes, translated by B. Jowett. New York: Random House, 1892. To enable readers to know which dialogue is quoted, the page numbers on which the dialogues begin are indicated:

Vol. I: *Charmides*, 3; *Lysis*, 31; *Laches*, 55; *Protagoras*, 81; *Euthydemus*, 133; *Cratylus*, 173; *Phaedrus*, 233; *Ion*, 285; *Symposium*, 301; *Meno*,

349; *Euthyphro*, 383; *Apology*, 401; *Crito*, 427; *Phaedo*, 441; *Gorgias*, 505; *The Republic*, 591.

Vol. II: *Timaeus*, 3; *Critias*, 71; *Parmenides*, 87; *Theaetetus*, 143; *Sophist*, 221; *Statesman*, 283; *Philebus*, 343; *Laws*, 407.

P&E *Philebus and Epinomis*, translated with commentary by A. E. Taylor. New York: Nelson, 1956.

PE *The Platonic Epistles*, translation, introduction, and notes by J. Harwood. Cambridge: The University Press, 1932.

Other Works

Cornford, Francis M. *Plato's Theory of Knowledge*. Indianapolis: Bobbs Merrill, 1957.

Kraut, Richard, editor. *The Cambridge Companion to Plato*. Cambridge: Cambridge University Press, 1992.

Raven, J. E. *Plato's Thought in the Making*. Cambridge: Cambridge University Press, 1965.

Ryle, Gilbert. *Plato's Progress*. Cambridge: Cambridge University Press, 1966.

Taylor, A. E. *Plato: The Man and His Work*. New York: Meridian Books, World, 1961.

2 John Locke: A Late Encounter with the "Bottom"
The Dominant Finally Looks to the Unconscious

Locke as an S: "All knowledge is founded on, and ultimately derives itself from, sense" (*Drafts*, 1). "Sense-perception is the true and only source from which the knowledge of natural law [morality] is derived" (*ELN*, 97). Our senses perceive only individual units, so "particular matters of fact are the undoubted foundations on which our civil and natural knowledge is built" (*CU*, 36). At the basis of "all our reasoning and knowledge is nothing but particulars"; "Whatever is, whether in God or out of God, is singular" (*E*, II, 404, 304n). Locke proposed a "corpuscular" theory wherein the world is composed of minute, autonomous corpuscles. He told of our tendency "to consider the substances we meet with, each of them, as an entire thing by itself, having all its qualities in itself, and independent of other things" (*E*, II, 260). He proclaimed action to be "the great business of mankind" (*E*, I, 387), and claimed his own philosophy could be proven by "experience and observation" (*E*, I, 211). He is often called the philosopher of "common sense" (*E*, I, 10n).

Locke does not have the many Quaternities of Plato, but the

elements of his Enantiodromia are abundant (see fig. 2.1). Locke's Myers-Briggs type would be ESTP.

	T	
	Inscription	
N		**S Dominant**
Divine Revelation		Sense Experience
Vision		Hand—action
Relations		Corpuscles
Theory		Particulars
	F	
	Tradition	

Figure 2.1

I. Locke's Theory of Knowledge

John Locke was born near Bristol in England in 1632 and began studies at Oxford as a young man of twenty. The experimental sciences had recently come into prominence and he was drawn to them, especially to medicine; he soon fell in with the group that gathered around the chemist Robert Boyle. His editor observes: "He thus early showed his love for facts rather than abstractions" (*E*, I, xix). Facts were in vogue at the university, yet he was troubled while he was there. A schoolmate recalled him as "a man of turbulent spirit, clamorous and discontented"; he was an extrovert who "preferred intercourse with persons to intercourse with books" (see *E*, I, xix). When he was about thirty, he wrote a series of essays on how we come to natural-law morality. In one of these he considered different kinds of knowledge:

> However, there are three kinds of knowledge which, without an over-careful choice of terms, I may call inscription, tradition, and sense-experience. To these may be added a fourth kind, namely, supernatural and divine revelation, but this is no part of our present argument. For we do not investigate here what a man can experience who is divinely inspired, or what a man can behold who is illuminated by a light from heaven, but what a man who is endowed with understanding, reason, and sense-perception, can by the help of nature and his own sagacity search out and examine. (*ELN*, 123–25)

The Jungian symbol of Three with a separated Fourth is evident, and the Fourth has the quality of the wonderful and miraculous that Jung associates with the Unconscious. By "inscription" (the first kind of knowledge), Locke is referring to innate knowledge, what is "inborn in us," "stamped upon [our] minds in their very first being." He denies that we have any such innate knowledge. Reason itself contains nothing to work with; in Jungian terms, the T acting alone is insufficient to know anything. Locke then considers "tradition"; he allows that most people pick up their values from those around them and make no attempt to ground their "belief," but it is this grounding he wishes to consider. In telling of a "tradition" that people "believe," this would be associated with the F. That brings Locke to the conclusion that "sense perception" is "the basis of our knowledge of the law of nature [morality]" (ELN, 131).

Thus, in his early thirties, Locke was claiming that moral laws can be discovered experimentally just as the laws of science are. "The foundation of all knowledge of it [the natural moral law] is derived from those things which we perceive through our senses" (ELN, 133).

In saying that morality is "derived" from sense knowledge, he is not saying that it is "visible" or immediately contained in sensation. Rather it takes argumentation and reasoning, and these move us apart from what is directly perceptible. It takes a great labor of the reason ("the discursive faculty of the mind" [ELN, 149]) to bring what is found in sensation into the light of understanding. Thus, Locke is giving primacy to the S, but not the S alone. The S must work together with the T.

> For only these two faculties [reason and sense perception working together] appear to teach and educate the minds of men and to provide what is characteristic of the light of nature. . . . As long as these two faculties serve one another, sensation furnishing reason with the ideas of particular sense objects and supplying the subject matter of discourse, reason on the other hand guiding the faculty of sense, and arranging together the images of things derived from sense perception, thence forming others and composing new ones, there is nothing so obscure, so concealed, so remote from any meaning that the mind, capable of everything, could not apprehend. (ELN, 147)

Throughout the writings of Locke, these same two faculties will be found working in tandem, while the F and the N are ignored. Thus

Locke, a dominant S, will be seen as taking a starting point radically different than Plato's with his dominant N; yet both had T as Auxiliary.

These early *Essays* served as a quarry from which Locke later would extract his arguments. When it came to writing his masterpiece, *An Essay Concerning Human Understanding*, the same pattern is found. Revelation is set aside as the other three contenders are considered. Innate ideas and tradition are seen to be inadequate, so knowledge is found to be based on sensation, but only if the senses act in coordination with reason. Thus the Three and separated Fourth is implicit in his major text. Again Sensation and its Auxiliary, Thinking, will constitute the scope of human understanding.

In 1664 (when Locke was thirty-two) he delivered an official lecture; the text has a playful quality that suggests all of it cannot be taken at face value. Still it tells abundantly of a troubled state of mind as he compares philosophy to "the encompassing sea" that allows one no repose. He seems to speak from experience:

> Many things are found there [in philosophy], delightful in variety, stupendous in depth, with which you may divert the mind, but whenever you betake yourself so as to rest there with certainty, you will find nothing stable, nothing firmly fixed, and the endless waves, abounding on all sides and overwhelming, toss the uneasy and anxious mind without being able to appease its thirst and its longing for happiness. (*ELN*, 223–25)

Such was Locke in his early thirties.

Locke was highly skeptical of what he was taught, and his early writings show him plagued by doubt and uncertainty. As he continued through his thirties, he often gathered with friends for philosophic discussion. In the spring of 1671, when he was thirty-nine, he told of gathering with five or six others for discussion. As they considered the "principles of morality and revealed religion," they reached a standstill (*E*,I, xvii). Locke traced their impasse to the fact that they did not know the kinds of objects their minds were fit to consider. Locke proposed making this difficulty the subject of their next meeting and prepared a page of his own thoughts. Eventually the page became his lengthy work (998 pages), *An Essay Concerning Human Understanding*. Several months later he tells of it being completed, but it seems he continued to rewrite and add to it until it was published in 1690, nineteen years after it was begun. The work soon became popular, but he continued making changes in later editions. He tells of it being "written by incoherent parcels, and after long intervals of neglect, resumed again"; some parts were reworked many times.

Three early drafts of the *Essay* have recently become available; the first of these was completed soon after the initial discussion. The opening passage of this draft tells of the work he intended; it stresses both sensation and the particular; that is, his own identity as an S:

> I imagine that all knowledge is founded on, and ultimately derives itself from, sense, or something analogous to it, and may be called sensation, which is done by our senses conversant about particular objects, which gives us the simple ideas or images of things, and thus we come to have ideas of heat and light, hard and soft, which are nothing but the reviving again in our minds of those imaginations, which those objects, when they effected our senses, caused in us. . . . therefore, I think that those things which we call sensible qualities are the simple ideas we have, and the first object of our understandings. (*D*, 1; spelling and punctuation modernized)

The completed *Essay* insists that human knowledge has limits that must be recognized. He spoke of his text as a clearing of the ground and a removing of the rubbish that lies in the way of knowledge. The first rubbish to remove is the claim that the mind is furnished with innate ideas (for example: an innate grasp of the principle of contradiction). In contrast to such claims, he would propose "the historical, plain method" (*E*, I, 27). That is, he would consider empirical knowledge and not speculations about eternal truths. By calling it a "plain method" he seems to allude to the "common sense" that characterizes the *Essay*. Over and over again the work insists on the limits of our knowledge, and in this way it differs from his earlier essays telling of the mind "capable of everything." As a Sensate he was a practical man. He tells of writing the work for his own use, but he hoped it might be of use to others (*E*, I, 12). He would have us set aside our speculations and employ our minds "about what may be of use to us; for of that they [our minds] are very capable" (*E*, I, 29).

Locke tells abundantly of the limits of our knowledge, yet he claimed this speculative limit does not matter. We were made for action, not speculation, and "the Candle that is set up in us shines bright enough for all our purposes" (*E*, I, 30; see also *RC*, 55). The image of a candle with its limited light suggests the limitation of a Dominant S when it comes to speculation. But though we are "sensible of our short-sightedness," we can rest assured that our minds are "very capable" of grasping what may be of use to us (*E*, I, 29). The present human state, "not being that of *vision*," leaves us groping in the dark. While the angels and souls of the just in heaven have a more complete knowledge (*E*, II, 361, 407). For they are endowed with "more *comprehensive* faculties" and are capable of collecting together the "almost boundless *relations*" of things (*CU*, 7). Their "comprehensive" minds see the "relations" (*N*), what the Sensate lacks. So in our present life we must "content ourselves by what is attainable."

Again Locke would use the image of exploring the sea to tell of the human condition: "It is of great use to the sailor to know the length of his line, though he cannot with it fathom all the depths of the ocean. It is well he knows that it is long enough to reach the bottom, at such places as are necessary to direct his voyage, and caution him against running upon shoals that may ruin him" (*E*, I, 30–31). As to the broader questions: "we need not be troubled that some other things escape our knowledge" (*E*, I, 31).

In all these passages Locke is seeing human knowledge as limited. But he is aware of unexplored "depths of the ocean" that are beyond our earthly human comprehension; he looks forward to understanding the rest in the time of "vision" when the just souls stand in the presence of God. In the meantime, Locke intended to establish "the bounds between the enlightened and dark parts of things; between what is and what is not comprehensible by us" (*E*, I, 31–32). In Jungian terms, he will set the limits of human Consciousness and will not try to explore what concerns the Unconscious. Consider what Locke finds missing: we lack "*vision*," we do not see the "*relations*" that are perceived by angels with their "more *comprehensive* faculties." All of these terms are associated with the N; they are found in a realm beyond the human—what Jung would term the Unconscious. But, as for us, our mind "stirs not one jot beyond those ideas which *sense* or *reflection* have offered for its contemplation" (*E*, I, 142). Therefore, we do not know general truths, yet we should not complain; rather let us "be content to glean what we can from *particular* experiments" (*E*, II, 352). Locke will center his attention on the particular, that which Socrates rejected.

The image of the sea was used to tell of our limitation: we should not "let loose our thoughts into the vast ocean of Being; as if all that boundless extent were the natural and undoubted possession of our understandings" (E, I, 31). For those who let their "thoughts wander into those depths where they can find no sure footing" become taken up with idle disputes and skepticism (E, I, 31). He claims that by not venturing into questions we cannot answer, we will be safe from claiming knowledge we do not have.

The *Essay Concerning Human Understanding* would limit human knowledge to what can be known by the S and T working together. Locke would have no sympathy with "symbolic" ways of knowing or probings into mystery. There is a clear line between light and dark and the line should be observed. Calling for "order and clearness" in thinking, he went on to say that the "figurative application of words" is nothing more than attempts "to insinuate wrong ideas, move the passions, and thereby mislead the judgement" (E, II, 146). He advised parents to have their son's love of poetry "stiffled and suppressed as much as may be"; while music is mostly a waste of time (EW, 284, 311). In the meantime, some things are seen in broad daylight, while the greater part of our concerns are given "only the twilight, as I may say, of probability" to guide us in our present limited state (E, II, 360). The "dark side," "our ignorance," is "infinitely larger than our knowledge" (E, II, 212). He had let his line of exploration descend down into the ocean and found his line was limited. Our knowledge is "narrow," so we should consider our ignorance and "launch not out into that abyss of darkness (where we have not eyes to see nor faculties to perceive anything)" (E, II, 212). On this earth we are in a "fleeting state of action and blindness." Not being in the state of "vision" we must "in many things content ourselves with faith and probability" (E, II, 195).

In the *Essay Concerning Human Understanding*, Locke speaks of two types of sensation: external and internal. By the internal sense we can observe the workings of our own mind, and "though it be not sense, as having nothing to do with external objects, yet it is very like it, and might properly enough be called *internal sense*" (E, I, 123; *Drafts*, 7). So he would conclude, "External and internal sensation are the only passages I can find of knowledge to the understanding" (E, I, 211). So the phrase "sensation and reflection" recur constantly in this text, and by the two we come to know only particulars as they appear to us.

By our external senses we receive "ideas" from objects.[1] All the objects of sense are singular, and thus "the immediate object of all our reasoning and knowledge is nothing but particulars" (*E*, II, 404). (Recall the Sensate is concerned with the concrete singular.) These particulars imprint their image (idea) in our minds. Then the understanding considers the different images and sees which images are the same and which are different; it affirms the first and negates the second. Thus the two faculties (S and T) work together. And "the perception of the agreement or disagreement of our particular ideas is the whole and the utmost of all our knowledge" (*E*, II, 404). Apart from this we may have thoughts that take us to the clouds, but however elevated these thoughts seem, they do not rise "one jot beyond those ideas which sense or reflection have offered for its contemplation" (*E*, I, 142).

Shortly before Locke's *Essay* appeared, Newton published his famous *Principia;* this proposed a vast mathematical account of the universe that offered a consistent explanation of many physical events. Locke inserted a passage into his *Essay* commending Isaac Newton for his ability "to retain such a train of particulars [which] may be well thought beyond the range of human faculties" (*E*, II, 175). By this he would see Newton's principles as only a manifestation of Newton's remarkable ability to hold so many particulars together in his mind. For knowledge concerns only particulars; we cannot really know the general—the N is missing.

II. *The Physical World of the Sensate*

Locke adopted the "corpuscular" theory that had been proposed by Robert Boyle and other experimentalists. That is, all things are made of minute corpuscles; some gatherings of corpuscles send forth tiny invisible particles that strike our eyes and ears to give sensation. The basic corpuscles are said to have "extension, figure, rest and motion" (*E*, I, 158).[2] These qualities are actually in the things we perceive and are called primary qualities, while color, sound, smell, etc. are secondary qualities that arise only within our faculties. Color and taste are no more to be found in an orange than pain is to be found in the blade of a knife. Locke distinguishes the primary qualities from the secondary in that the four primary ones are perceived by two faculties, that is, "both by seeing and feeling [touching]," they make impressions "both on the eyes and touch"

(*E*, I, 158). And one can be certain of the things "he sees and feels" (*E*, II, 327, 331). They are thus validated by the eye and the hand, the two faculties suggested by the N and the S. The world of Locke is composed of swarms of particular particles, and one wonders what he makes of their relationships (the missing N). Locke claims "relations" or "relationships" are created by the mind as it compares two objects, and, apart from the mental act of comparison, they have no independent reality: "The nature therefore of relation consists in the referring or comparing two things one to another," and accordingly a relation is "not contained in the real existence of things, but something extraneous and superinduced." A relation arises "by way of considering or comparing two things together, and so [is] also an idea of my own making" (*E*, I, 428, 430; II, 145).[3] The texts that deny the objective reality of all relations are clear enough, yet it is difficult to reconcile these texts with others that speak of all finite things as dependent on God (dependency is a relationship).[4]

The minute particles are said to strike against one another and by impulse communicate their motion. "Bodies operate one upon another, and that is manifestly by impulse and nothing else."[5] He tells us it would be "impossible to conceive" any other type of interaction. Thus, the only world of which we can conceive is made of minute independent units bumping into one another and this bumping constitutes their minimal relationship. He then finds himself wondering how familiar objects (a rock, a cat, etc.—objects made of bumping corpuscles) can ever hold together. Experience makes it clear that such things do hold together, but lacking an N he cannot understand what unifies: "they unite, they consolidate; these little atoms cohere, and are not, without great force, separable. He that could find the bonds that tie these heaps of loose little bodies together so firmly; he that could make known the cement that makes them stick so fast one to another, would discover a great and yet unknown secret" (*E*, I, 412). He spends five pages showing why the cohesion of particles is "incomprehensible." One of his commentators observes, "Cohesion seems to have held the secret of nature for Locke" (Yolton, *Locke and the Compass of Human Understanding*, 85). It was the secret he could not discover, for his philosophy was centered on the S where things are entirely loose and separate.[6]

The "heaps of loose little bodies" of which he speaks is the world of the Sensate. That is, there are heaps of loose trees, and no forest;

there is nothing that would make the trees "cohere." There are only unrelated bodies bumping into one another, and cohesion is incomprehensible—the N is lacking. In a similar way, Locke is often considered a Nominalist, for he was unwilling to allow true general ideas, that is, universals. Rather, he would see us inventing "universals" only for convenience in action and communication. To allow real universals would allow more than the "particulars," for universals serve to comprehend particular objects—but the N of comprehensive Vision is lacking.

After he has presented a world of bumping particles, Locke goes on to talk of an interacting world. But this is a world he would postulate, as it cannot be known by our senses. Locke again tells of our limitation: "we are so far from being admitted into the secrets of nature, that we scarce so much as ever approach the first entrance towards them. For we are wont to consider the substances we meet with, each of them, as an entire thing by itself, having all its qualities in itself, and independent of other things" (E, II, 260).

Such is the S. But these radically independent substances, that seem to comprise the Sensate world, are not the final story. In truth, all things turn out to be interconnected! Locke explains that if you put a piece of gold anywhere by itself, separate from the reach of all other bodies, it will immediately lose all its color and weight, and perhaps malleability too. Water by itself would cease to be fluid. Likewise plants, animals, and ourselves would be radically changed if we were in isolation. All have a "dependence . . . wholly on extrinsical causes and qualities of other bodies that make no part of them." This radical dependence on what is outside or "other" suggests the N; but the dependence is the secret of nature that we cannot know. He would see us as quite wrong "when we think that things contain *within themselves* the qualities that appear to us in them" (E, II, 260–61). Sensible qualities arise only by their relationship with us. Again, things and qualities seem to be radically relational, yet Locke would deny the objectivity of relationships: "things, however absolute and entire they seem in themselves, are but retainers to other parts of nature. . . . Their observable qualities, actions, and powers are owing to something without them; and there is not so complete and perfect a part that we know of nature, which does not owe the being it has, and the excellences of it, to its neighbors." (E, II, 262). It is difficult to see how such a world, where things "are but retainers to other parts of nature" that owe their very "being" to their neighbors, does not involve real relationships.

These passages go on to speak of "invisible fluids," or "particles," or "streams" that keep the machinery of the universe going. But the particles and fluids are invisible and unknowable. Observant people might make guesses about them, but we cannot really know. Apart from such guesses, the true nature of things will not be known "without revelation" (*E*, II, 264). Thus, Locke would postulate an interacting world, a world where the identity of everything seems to consist in it being only a "retainer" of influences upon it. These interrelations would seem to be the "dark parts of things" he warned we cannot know, while the world we deal with is composed of independent particulars which must be studied as such (see *E*, I, 32).

One way of reading Locke would have us experience only individual objects seemingly unrelated, while beyond what we can know is a radically interrelated universe. This the angels know and we will know after death, but now it either wholly escapes our apprehension or, having a faint glimpse of it, we grope after it in the dark (*E*, II, 407). The present study would attribute this arrangement and some of its confusion to Locke being an S, with his N, the Faculty that interrelates, largely unrecognized in the dark of the Unconscious.[7] Accordingly, any general theory is considered by Locke as "a sort of waking dream" (from a letter quoted in Yolton, *Locke and the Compass of Human Understanding*, 59).

It has been argued that Locke's understanding of science changed over his lifetime: as a young man he saw science as natural history, but after he became aware of the theory of Newton he came to see science as involving the "mathematico-deductive method" (Axtell in Yolton, *John Locke*, 165 82). Newton's *Principia* came out shortly before the first edition of Locke's *Essay*, and Locke was among the first to appreciate the *Principia*. He became a friend of Newton and after reading the *Principia* began seriously studying mathematics, something he had not done previously; he also began to take principles more seriously than his sensate theory of understanding would allow. He made small changes in his *Essay* but was either unwilling or unable to adjust the entire theory to include the new understanding he came upon in his final years (Yolton, *Locke and the Compass of Human Understanding*, 89).

In 1697 at age sixty-five, Locke wrote a short work (*Conduct of the*

Understanding) that makes further concession to the *Principia* and also seems to allow for the N in ways that his *Essay* had not. This is most evident in his insistence that we "bottom" our knowledge in a principle or general truth (*CU*, 17, 23, 46, 56, 94–96). In this "bottoming" of truth the particular details are said to "have their consistency" (*CU*, 94). That is, the details hold together. The "consistency" would unite the lesser truths into a unifying principle, though Locke believed most scientists will not find this possible. Locke compares such general truths to "the lights of heaven." He even compares Newton's universal gravitation to the teaching of Jesus (*CU*, 95); in both cases it is their generality that seems to require a sort of revelation. At one time Locke had defined revelation as "what a man can behold who is illuminated by a light from heaven" (*ELN*, 123). At that time revelation was the mysterious Fourth he set aside to consider human knowing. In his final work the heavenly light is included in human knowing; it is what gives "consistency" to particulars. This late essay even suggests the unity of opposites: "General knowledge drawn from particulars are the jewels of knowledge" (*CU*, 60). Generalities and particulars come together to form jewels! A similar suggestion of the unity of opposites is found where he speaks of us having a "touchstone" of truth.

III. The Man of Action

Locke was far from being a scholarly recluse. He was involved in the events of his time: he was secretary of the Board of Trade and consulted widely on commerce, the colonies, medicine, gardening, linenmanufacture, and the system of coinage. He has been described as a "consummate political animal," "a tough-minded and worldly person, extremely shrewd and prudent in all his financial and political dealings," he was "interested in practical things almost to the point of obsession" (Wood, 27). So when Locke published his *Essay Concerning Human Understanding*, he considered it largely a practical work for "the improvement of useful knowledge." Since our understandings were made for practical purposes, he judged our inability to see the minute particles (considered above) to be the will of God. For God designed our sense faculties for "the business we have to do here," our faculties are for "our business in this world" (*E*, I, 402) and we are better off without seeing the minute corpuscles. If someone were given "microscopial eyes," "such an acute sight would not serve to conduct him to the market and exchange" (*E*, I, 403). It is for such practical purposes that we are well designed, for "action [is] the great business of mankind" (*E*, I, 387).

The opening passages of the *Essay* make several striking references to the hands, often suggestive of S, of action. It begins: "Reader, I have put into thy hands what has been the diversion of some of my idle and heavy hours." He tells of being reluctant "to let it go out of my hands" (*E*, I, 10n). He would tell of the limits of knowledge but urge his readers to "busy their heads and employ their hands" without throwing "away the blessings their hands are filled with, because they [their hands] are not big enough to grasp everything" (*E*, I, 29).

A similar preoccupation with hands in found in his *Second Treatise on Government*, probably written in the summer of 1681. The 126 pages of this work have 56 references to hands: "every man's hands," "hands to administer justice," "hands of nature," "business at hand," "hands of a few," "hands of distinct persons," "power in their hands," "hands of justice," "lay violent hands upon," etc. His late essay on education tells of the young being "formed by the hands" of the teacher who shows a strict "hand" and "a gentler hand" and "skillful hands to guide" to prepare the pupil for "assaults on all Hands." His *Conduct of the Understanding* ends with the assurance that a profitable remedy "is always at hand."

During the lifetime of Locke, England was divided by a series of political and religious troubles. In that context he wrote and developed his political philosophy. As an Extrovert with a dominant S he was a practical man, and many of the changes in his theory can be understood in terms of contemporary events. Hearing of a political theory, he explained his concern: "whether it be now practical." He wanted to see a study of politics based on "the testimony of daily experience" (*PW*, 138). Experience would show how individuals of different faiths might share "the same civil interest, and hand in hand march to the same end of peace and mutual society" (*PW*, 138). His understanding of religious toleration changed over the years, and the changes seem less theoretical than efforts to find the amount of individual freedom that could be tolerated practically at a particular time in English history.

In 1661, he wrote, "No one can have a greater respect and veneration for authority than I" (*PW*, 148). At this time he allowed the ruler to employ his power "upon the multitude that are as impatient of restraint as the sea, and whose tempests and overflows cannot be too well provided against" (PW, 142). The rulers are to exercise a strong hand. He tells of an earlier time when the people of the nation had let their "passions free reign," but now we can look back upon our miseries "as men do when, having recently been tossed about on a stormy sea, they stand safe on the shore and look with pleasure at the futilely threatening waves" (PW, 153).[8] So in 1661 he called for a leader with "absolute and arbitrary power over all the indifferent actions of his people."

But times changed. Twenty years later, he saw great danger in the arbitrary power of rulers and put his trust in democracy and the unruly mob he had criticized. But, for Locke, whether power should be with the authorities or with the people was largely a practical question (Wootton, in PW, 35). He was still the observant scientist following the "plain historical method," and asking which political system would work *now*. Locke was always a religious man, but still, practical man that he was, he would speak of using religion for a social good (regulating "our Religion, Politics and Morality" by what is good for human life [EW, 226; see PW, 390]).

Locke has been seen as the first political thinker to make labor the cornerstone of his ideas (Wood, 34). Work with one's hands gives one property rights. For Locke, God made humans to labor and the need to labor is a mark of the goodness of God (PW, 440). Locke speculated about the condition of primal human beings in a state of nature where all things were common property. Yet each primal man had something distinctly his own: "the labour of his body, and the work of his hands." This meant the acorns or apples under the trees belonged equally to all, but they became private property by the worker's act of picking them up. "His labour hath taken it out of the hands of nature, where it was common, and belonged equally to all her children" (PW, 275). Accordingly, one gains title to a piece of land by cultivating it (PW, 278). For God has given the earth "to the use of the industrious and rational (and labour was to be his title to it)" (PW, 277). Yet there are practical limits: "As much as anyone can make use of to any advantage of life before it spoils, so much he may by his labour fix a property in. Whatever is beyond this, is more than his share, and belongs to others" (PW, 276). Some have objected that this limit on property might work well with the small independent farmers Locke had known, but would be difficult to apply to the industrial capitalism that was then taking shape. Yet Locke himself was clear, "Every man should have as much as he can make use of" (PW, 279), and anything further would result in idleness.

Labor gives rise to property, and then property gives rise to the social body: "The reason why men enter into a society is the preservation of their property" (PW, 373, 262). Apart from property-defense, humans could live as separate individuals. In his political theory as well as in his theory of the natural world, reality is constituted by separate individuals. Each one is "absolute lord of his own person and possessions, equal to the greatest, and subject to nobody" (PW, 324). These separate individuals have no intrinsic relationships,[9] no social nature that would bring them together; relations arise only when free individuals consent to become a society. (The forest arises only by consent of the trees!) "That which makes the community, and brings men out of the loose state of nature into one politic society, is the agreement which everyone has with the rest to incorporate and act as one body, and so be one distinct commonwealth" (PW, 369). It has been observed that nowhere in his many writings does Locke make "sociability" a basis for law (von Leyden, in ELN, 53). He was committed to what has been termed a "systematic individualism" (Wootton, in PW, 86–87).

An earlier section showed that when Locke presented his corpuscular theory of matter, he had difficulty seeing how the individual corpuscles might cohere. Now he has the same difficulty in considering human beings. They too are presented as prone to bump into each other, so to protect themselves they would gather with others to form a body politic. The bond between them is only their free consent, a consent that can be revoked. When Locke considered either particles or people, the individual unit was primary. The body politic is formed only to enable individuals to pursue their private ends (Wootton, in PW, 38); they form societies for "the preservation of their property," their "lives, liberties and estates." And even then each individual would retain the right to judge when to oppose the government as being tyrannical (Wootton, in PW, 52; Dunn, 33). In a similar way, Locke did not see the Christian Church as a community founded by Christ, but rather "a voluntary society of men, joining themselves together of their own accord" for common worship. There is no such thing as "a Christian commonwealth" (PW, 396), there is only the

Christian individual acting as "every private man's search and study discovers it unto himself," for "each has the supreme and absolute authority of judging for himself" (*PW*, 407, 422). His understanding of religion was "profoundly individualistic" (Wootton, in *PW*, 67). Thus with particles, peoples, and believers, Locke can allow nothing but separate individuals. It is the world of the S, where all that is real is singular. Yet it was the singular, the particular, that Socrates wanted to ignore.

Locke undertook writing his *Essay Concerning Human Understanding* in 1671 in order to show how our human understanding can know "the principles of morality and revealed religion." The text had concluded that our human faculties can know God, moral truths, and all we need to know for practical purposes. But when friends pressed him to show how the principles of morality could be demonstrated, he made several attempts and was not satisfied with any of them. This quest for the natural moral law was behind his writing the *Essay*, but he finally came to the conclusion that only revelation—especially Christian revelation—could give one the principles of true morality. One of his critics observes, "This is not an inspiring conclusion to a philosophical quest that had covered three and a half decades" (Dunn, 85).

As an older man, Locke turned increasingly to revelation—the mysterious Fourth, the "light from heaven" he had set aside three decades earlier when he wrote his *Essays on the Laws of Nature*. In his later years he would be claiming that it is Christian revelation that gives us morality, and this revelation is authenticated by miracles. So in the final decade of his life Locke wrote a lengthy tract arguing that miracles authenticate a teaching; he wrote another tract on seeing all things in God. Then he wrote hundreds of pages of an essay, *The Reasonableness of Christianity*, yet the point of the essay seems to be that Christian faith is above human reason. Then he filled hundreds of additional pages with a study of the Epistles of St. Paul. These religious works contain much argumentation; in these detailed studies of Christian revelation Locke seems to be seeking the moral principles he could not find in his rational philosophy of particulars.

But apart from his difficulty in showing how we can know moral principles, there is another reason Locke would try to extend his understanding beyond what he had allowed in his monumental *Essay*. As indicated above, it was in 1687, shortly before the first edition of the *Essay* appeared, that Newton published the *Principia*.

Locke and many of the educated people of Europe were amazed at the vast and coherent mathematical understanding of the universe it contained. In its sweeping generalities and unified vision, it seemed to be the kind of science that Locke's *Essay* had considered impossible. Yet Locke was one of the first to recognize the importance of the *Principia* and made small changes in the text as he prepared later editions of his *Essay*. But in 1697 he wrote a book with a different spirit than his *Essay,* the small work titled *Conduct of the Understanding*. While his earlier *Essay* told of our limitations and our "invincible ignorance" (*E*, II, 216), now he announces we are "born with faculties and powers capable of almost anything" (*CU*, 13)! Earlier he had told of dropping his line into the ocean and discovering his limits. Now he criticizes those who confine their exploration to "where the light shines" and do not "venture out into the great ocean of knowledge"; they "do not dig and search for it (truth) as for gold and hid treasure" (*CU*, 8, 9). The very images, leaving the light, venturing into the great ocean, and digging for hidden treasure, show that Locke is willing to probe beyond the familiar; and the images he uses (leaving the light, venturing into the ocean, digging for treasure, etc.) are the ones Jung associates with exploring the Unconscious. At one time Locke confined human knowledge to the practical. Now he complains of those who think knowledge beyond what "serves their ordinary business is above their capacities" (*CU*, 83). Now he would have us learn by analogy, an ambiguous type of knowledge not considered in the *Essay*.

In the *Conduct of the Understanding*, Locke tells of temples containing sacred images that influence people's lives, but Locke, venturing into psychology, tells of contemporary people having inner images that do the same: they have "invisible powers that constantly govern them" (*CU*, 3). He goes on to tell of needing courage in "the struggles of the mind" and of occasions "when the mind frights itself (as it often does)." The mind beholds things "wrapped up in impenetrable obscurity." But he advises that if we proceed in orderly fashion, things in the "mist that appeared hideous giants not to be grappled with, will be found to be of ordinary size and shape" (*CU*, 83–84). For one familiar with Jung, all these images suggest that the sixty-five-year-old Locke has been exploring his Unconscious. Accordingly, this late work will allow for the missing N.

This late work speaks of the comprehensive truths whereon "the mind is brought to the source on which it bottoms" (*CU*, 23). Bottom and bottoming are mentioned often in this brief work (*CU*, 23, 46, 56, 94, 95). It is the process of looking for wider truths wherein separate facts might gain their "consistency." He saw Isaac Newton providing a bottoming-truth in his theory of universal gravitation: for he showed how "all bodies gravitate to one another." This general truth resembled what is found in "the lights of heaven." And Locke compared it to the general truth found in Revelation: "Our Savior's great rule, that we should love our neighbour as ourselves" (*CU*, 95). Note the two examples that he gives of bottom-truths: one concerns gravitation and other concerns mutual love. One binds particles together and the other binds people. Both concern the missing coherence! When Locke wrote the *Essay Concerning Human Understanding* he saw the coherence of separate particles creating an unanswerable problem. Now the unanswerable problem is answered—by a light from heaven.

Whether it is gravity binding all atoms together or love binding all humans together, a heavenly light has intervened through Newton to give coherence to the atoms and the facts of science, and through Jesus to give coherence to human individuals. The heavenly light is the N; it is the repressed Function giving consistence to the trees and making them a forest.

Both Locke and Plato proposed philosophies of government, but there are radical differences in their starting points. Locke's politics is based on free and separate individuals forming a state, while Plato's philosophy is based on the common good with little recognition of the individual. In other words, Locke saw political society as the development of separate trees, while Plato saw the trees only in terms of their function in the forest. A similar contrast is found in their theories of knowledge: Locke is centered on the particulars known by the senses with little room for the general, while Plato generalizes so readily that sensation and particulars seem not to count. Locke has a world of bumping particles in which the whole is problematic, and Plato has a unified world where the particles are problematic.

The present study would understand these differences in terms of the personality types of Jung: Locke was a Dominant S while Plato was a Dominant N. But the differences can also be understood in terms of their development: Locke's *Conduct* moves away from the consideration of the details of experience (natural history) to tell of bottoming our knowledge in a principle, and he even started a study of mathematics. In contrast, Plato was an N and a mathematician who in his later years moved away from the highly speculative philosophy and mathematics he once advocated to take an interest in experimental evidence (natural history). The changes in each could be ascribed to scientific developments of the times, but they could also be seen as each philosopher late in life giving recognition to what Jung would call the repressed Function. Both Plato and Locke came to appreciate the missing element, but only after each came to a fearful confrontation of the Opposite. Both saw the opposite as threatening "giants" (*Plato*, II, 273; Locke, *CU*, 83), but giants that could be modified.

Plato tells clearly of an Enantiodromia (most evident in the battle of Gods and Giants in the *Sophist*), and he went on to bring the opposites together in a "citadel" of sorts that resembled the Self of Jung. The conflict of opposites in Locke is not as evident as it was in Plato, and Locke's development seems less complete than the development of Plato. Still, the late work of Locke, *Conduct of the Understanding*, gives hints of opposites reconciled when it tells of bottoming particular truths to give them consistence. There is some suggestion of the appearance of the Self in Locke when he speaks of having a "touchstone" to distinguish the true from the false, and a similar suggestion when he speaks of general truths drawn from particulars as "the jewels of knowledge" (*CU*, 60).

Locke's *Essay Concerning Human Understanding* would strictly limit what we know to the working of the S and the T, while his N (and F) remained largely unrecognized. He was a highly disciplined man who developed a system of education to produce well-disciplined individuals, favoring discipline in both the individual and the state (Consciousness in control). He grew up in turbulent times, and as a troubled man he wrote his *Essay Concerning Human Understanding*. There he had tried to establish the S (assisted by the T) in firm control. He advised us to know the limits of our faculties and avoid the ocean of deep questions we cannot answer. This remained the message of the *Essay*, but the *Conduct* shows a different spirit, one that is willing to struggle with mystery, with the "hideous giants" that seem to dwell in the mists.

I will extend the basic Jungian paradigm to other philosophers in order to bring a new perspective on their work. The next philosopher to be considered is Jean-Paul Sartre. Like Plato, he will be seen as an N with T as Auxiliary. Like Plato, he will be seen as a highly theoretical N who struggled unsuccessfully for many years to become the practical activist; that is, he sought to involve his S. Like Plato's guardians, Sartre had been brought up to dwell in a higher world among "the airy simulacra of things" (he would call himself a Platonist). From the heights he could see the wider goals of society. But, like Plato in Syracuse, Sartre had trouble in descending to practical problems on the streets of Paris. Unlike Locke, the consummate politician, both Plato and Sartre had difficulties with practical politics.[10]

In the chapter that follows, Sartre will be seen to have a distressing encounter with his Repressed (S) in *Nausea*, an early novel. A lengthy Enantiodromia will be seen to run through the rest of his writings, and gradually a unity of opposites is approached.

Notes

1. Locke has a distinctive understanding of two words that are relevant to the present study: ideas and thinking. His editor would find the term "Ideas" to be "of most comprehensive generality," adding that "it would be difficult to find an adequate synonym, but perhaps *phenomenon* would be the nearest," though it also includes ideas that have been abstracted from the phenomena (*E*, I, 32n). Thus, "red" would be considered an idea. He sometimes used idea and image interchangeably. He would compare our ideas to images in a mirror and claim "the immediate object of perception is an idea" (*E*, I, 174; *E*, II, 8). He even suggested that we should have a dictionary composed entirely of pictures.

Locke will often speak of intuition and even compare it to the eye. But he does not mean intuition in the sense of Jung. His editor explains it is simply "the self-evident perception of agreement or disagreement between the ideas which it interprets" (*E*, II, 177n). It would be the mind seeing and affirming two images to be either the same or different. Likewise, Locke uses the word "thinking" in a wider sense than is generally common (see *E*, I, 183); it often seems equivalent to any activity of the mind.

2. The four properties could be seen as conforming to the Jungian Quaternity of Figure, Motion, Rest, and Extension, but sometimes Locke will make small variations in identifying them. One commentator has claimed that the minute particles of Locke "have only the non-relational qualities" (Yolton, *L&C*, 36). This could be seen to say that reality does not include relations—the N; see below.

3. Because of such passages, a commentator observes that "Locke is usually

read as denying the reality of relations, as his own words frequently suggest." But then the commentator excuses Locke on the ground that in such passages he is speaking only of our *ideas* of relations (Yolton, 104). This surely gives Locke considerable benefit of the doubt in a text he had worked over with great care. But apart from this solution, the difficulty remains of reconciling the texts denying relations with his abundant talk of relations (especially cause and effect). Fraser (editor of Locke's *Essay Concerning Human Understanding*) tells of several commentators finding the work "a mass of incoherent and mutually contradictory propositions" (*E*, I, 118n). This could be seen in the way he will occasionally give voice to his N, even in his *Essay.*

4. Copleston observes, "When speaking of relations in general, he seems to say that they are all mental; but this does not prevent him from speaking about some particular relations as though they were not" (108). In a similar way, Hume and Whitehead would wonder how Locke could insist on the concrete singular, and then speak of systems of interrelationships.

5. The passage is found in the first three editions of the *Essay*, but Locke removed it from the fourth edition, seemingly because he was impressed by his reading of Newton's *Principia* (see Yolton, *L&C*, 24n).

6. He allowed these passages to remain in his later editions of the text even though he was aware of Newton's presentation of gravity as a cohesive power.

7. *An Essay Concerning Human Understanding* comprises Four Books, and the Fourth Book divides many things into Fours: there are "four sorts" of knowledge, "four sorts" of judgments, "four degrees" of reason, "four sorts of arguments," "four" causes of error, and four "wrong measures of probability" (*E*, II, 168, 198, 388, 410, 442, 448).

8. Much as Plato's *Republic* had used the image of the state to tell of the soul, Locke might be doing the same: he might be seeing in the state the turmoil and the discipline that he needed to control his personal life. His philosophy of education stressed a training in self-discipline.

9. Locke, however, does make some allowance for the family as a natural unit of society.

10. Plato speaks of his involvement in the politics of Syracuse as "my misguided journeying"; he tells of going to Syracuse lest he appear "wholly a man of mere words who would never lay his hand wholly to anything" (*PF*, 146, 120). Sartre will be shown also as a man of words who would try to "lay his hand" to politics.

Bibliography

Works of Locke

CU *Locke's Conduct of the Understanding,* with introduction and notes by Thomas A. Fowler. New York: Burt Franklin, 1971 reprint.

Drafts   *Drafts for the Essay Concerning Human Understanding and Other Philosophical Writings*, edited by Peter H. Nidditch and G. A. J. Rogers. Oxford: The Clarendon Press, 1990.

E, I; E, II   *An Essay Concerning Human Understanding*, in two volumes, collated and annotated by Alexander Campbell Fraser. New York: Dover, 1959 reprint of 1894 original.

ELN   *Essays on the Law of Nature*, edited by W. von Leyden. Oxford: The Clarendon Press, 1954.

EW   *The Educational Writings of John Locke*, introduction and notes by James L. Axtell. Cambridge: Cambridge University Press, 1968.

PW   *Political Writings of John Locke*, edited and with an introduction by David Wootton. New York: Mentor, 1993.

RC   *The Reasonableness of Christianity*, edited, abridged, and introduced by I. T. Ramsey. Stanford: Stanford University Press, 1958.

Other Works

Copleston, Frederick, S. J. *A History of Philosophy*, vol. 5, part I. New York: Doubleday Image, 1964.

Dunn, John. *Locke*. Oxford: Oxford University Press, 1984.

Wood, Neal. *John Locke and Agrarian Capitalism*. Berkeley: University of California Press, 1984.

Yolton, J. W. *Locke and the Compass of Human Understanding*. Cambridge: Cambridge University Press, 1970.

Yolton, J. W., ed. *John Locke: Problems and Perspectives*. Cambridge: Cambridge University Press, 1969.

3 Sartre: *Jean sans Terre* Tries to Descend
The Repressed Takes Over; Then a Move to Integration

Sartre as N: Sartre tells of having lived in "Platonist fashion," for as a child he fled his "unjustifiable body" and regarded words as "the quintessence of things" (*W,* 32, 57, 59). He claimed, "I think with my eyes"; "the word intuition . . . delighted me beyond all measure. . . . Perception . . . became a holy act"; "I'm only a desire for beauty, and outside that: void, nothing" (*WD,* 15, 83, 282). "Everything starts with sight [*vue*] and ends with sight (*intuition*)" (*T&E,* 13). He claimed his philosophy's "essential way of proceeding is by intuition" and not by logical conditions as in Kant (*TE,* 35). "There is only intuitive knowledge. Deductive and discursive argument . . . are only instruments which lead to intuition" (*BN,* 210). Human reality is consciousness, and the nature of consciousness is to be "other," to "project itself into the future"; "it transcends itself"; in its inmost nature it is a only a relation with nothing substantial about it; it is a "flight" (*LPE,* 92; *PI,* 100; *BN,* 72, 442, lxvii, 705). "All existence as soon as it is posited is surpassed by itself" (*PI,* 272). The status of both his Repressed and Dominant are evident when a journal entry considers a man reaching into a hole, "The hands meet monsters which the eyes cannot see. His eyes are still in the kingdom of light" (*WD*, 150).

Figure 3.1 has columns between the N and S to show Sartre's incomplete Integration. These columns tell of an N that is partially S and an S that is partially N, but there is no complete Integration. Sartre's Myers-Briggs type would be INTJ.

		T		
N Dominant				S
For-itself	Practico-	Theoretico-		In-itself
Pure subject	theoretical	practical		Pure object
Divine gaze	Dialectical	Analytical		Stone
Eye	reason	reason		Hand
Nothingness	Praxis	Practico-		Being
Absolute evil		inert		Absolute good
Beauty				Nausea
		F		

Figure 3.1

I. An Idealist Discovers Existence

In 1963 Sartre finished writing a somewhat playful account of his childhood. For a long time he had planned to call it *Jean sans terre*, but finally it was published as *The Words*. By the earlier title Sartre saw himself as a "Platonist" living in abstraction above the world. So he told of his natural place being "a sixth floor in Paris with a view overlooking the roofs" (*W*, 38). This is the N, above it all, seeing the "whole picture," living "in the aether among the airy simulacra of things." He tells of making efforts to descend to the real world, but to do so "I had to wear leaden soles." In the meantime, "I live in the air out of habit, and I poke about down below without much hope" (*W*, 38). While working on this autobiography he had a dream: "I had to give a four-part lecture in a foreign country. I left after the third part, wondering whether they had understood that I had not finished" (dream of Dec. 7, 1960; Cohen-Solal, 443). For the third lecture to finish as four, Jean must descend to the earth and act (S); the attempted descent became a theme of his philosophy, biographies, and fiction (see Charme, 1–54).

Sartre claimed his "Platonism," his "idealism," his "blindness," took him thirty years to shake (*W*, 32, 157). At thirty he was writing *Nausea*, a semiautobiographical novel telling of Antoine Roquentin shaking free of his abstract world. Sartre explained: "I was Roquentin; I used him to show, without complacency, the texture of my life" (*W*, 158; for additional parallels between Sartre and Roquentin see Cohen-Sohal, 18, 80, 89).

Antoine is said to live in Bouville, and even the geography of the city suggests to a Jungian the ominous transformation that Antoine undergoes there: "Bouville. The vegetation has only surrounded three sides of it. On the fourth side there is a great hole full of black water which moves all by itself" (*N*, 156). He has lived in Bouville for three years, and during his fourth year Antoine senses a metamorphosis overtaking him like an illness: "I am quietly slipping into the water's depths, towards fear" (*N*, 8). He is entering the Fourth, the black water.

The metamorphosis is Sensation presenting itself to the Intuitive; so Antoine first notices the change as "something new" about his hands, "a sort of nausea in the hands" (*N*, 4, 11, 123). And observations on the hands run through this novel and the writings of Sartre. The nausea began when he was holding a stone and was overcome by a strange distaste, for he sensed the stone existed; the nausea came again while holding a doorknob: "From time to time objects start existing in your hand" (*N*, 123; Jung associates existence with S). He is drawn to pick up soiled papers from the street and crumple them in his hand; some papers are "covered with blisters and swellings like a burned hand." When finished, he wipes his "muddy hands on a wall or tree trunk." He is disturbed, for his life is changing beyond his control: "I'm afraid of what will be born and take possession of me — and drag me—where?" (*N*, 5–6).

Jungian symbols abound as Antoine sees four pages before him, the sun spreading four false reflections on his table, and four small sausages hanging in a window; there are four-storey houses, and four street lamps in the central square where there are "four cafés, the 'Railwaymen's Rendezvous' and three others" (*N*, 14, 81, 46, 24). It is in the Railwaymen's Rendezvous (the separated Fourth) that he watches the hands of four players at a card table; one player is hidden in shadow: "There are four of them. . . . I cannot make out the fourth player" (*N*, 20). He soon will make out the Fourth. He returns to his room and lies dazed on his bed staring at the ceiling where he sees "first rings of light, then crosses" (*N*, 31).[1]

Antoine goes to the art museum, where he looks at the paintings: "I saw hands and eyes." The Enantiodromia continues as he describes the hands and eyes in each portrait. Leaving the art museum he goes to the Bouville library to continue writing a historical study. There, between *three and four* in the afternoon "an immense sickness flooded over" him as he realizes that only the present moment and its sensations are real: "The true nature of the present revealed itself; it was what exists, and all that was not present did not exist. The past did not exist. Not at all. Not in things, not even in my thoughts. . . . things are entirely what they appear to be—and behind them . . . there is nothing" (*N*, 95–96). All that is real is sense data and the present (S). He feels possessed by an immense sickness. "I am the Thing. Existence, liberated, detached, floods over me. I exist" (*N*, 98). His attention focuses on his hand resting on the library table:

> It is lying on its back. It shows me its fat belly. It looks like an animal turned upside down. The fingers are the paws. . . . I feel my hand. I am these two beasts struggling at the end of my arms. . . . I feel its weight on the table which is not me. It's long, long, this impression of weight, it doesn't pass. . . . [I let my hand] hang against the back of the chair. Now I feel a weight at the end of my arm. It pulls a little, softly, insinuatingly it exists. I don't insist: no matter where I put it it will go on existing; I can't suppress it, nor can I suppress the rest of my body . . . nor all the sensations going on inside. . . . (*N*, 98–99)

The Introvert Intuitive is discovering Sensation; his hands are alien to him and his body unfamiliar. He is disturbed by sensations and the present; as an Intuitive he had been living for the future when he would publish his historical study. Now, in finding only the present (S) to be real, he cannot continue his research into the past. His attention turns to his knife lying on the table:

> I open it. Why not? It would be a change in any case. I put my left hand on the [writing] pad and stab the knife into the palm. . . . It bleeds. . . . I watch with satisfaction, on the white paper, across the lines I wrote a little while ago, this tiny pool of blood which has at last stopped being me. Four lines on a white paper, a spot of blood, that makes a beautiful memory. (*N*, 100)[2]

He leaves the library to tend to his hand and hurries along the street, but "the houses close around me, as the water closes over me" (N, 100). He is drowning in existence. He sees himself as an object, and is afraid of going mad.

Antoine hurries to a bar where a gramophone is playing, and the music brings him relief. As he hears the recorded voice, "the world vanishes, the world of existence." He becomes lost in the song. The singer had once existed, but now there is only the recorded sound. "The turning record exists, the air, struck by the voice which vibrates, exists," but the song itself does not exist. The song is only an abstract sequence of notes. One can destroy the record and stop the sound, but the song is not destroyed; for it is above existence—a timeless essence. Beyond all existence the song remains in its rigor (N, 103). So the song relieves his nausea, for while the song unfolds existence vanishes and he enters an ideal and necessary world of order. But when the music is over, he returns to realize: "I exist, that's all. And that trouble is so vague, so metaphysical that I am ashamed of it" (N, 105).

The following day he has arranged to have the noon meal with the Self-Taught Man, a timid scholar who has been spending much time in the library. The Self-Taught Man lives in an abstract world of books (much as Sartre claimed he too had lived the first thirty years of his life). At the restaurant table the Self-Taught Man tells of a prison artist who made a large woodcarving; "he did the delicate parts with the file: the hands and eyes" (N, 108). The Self-Taught Man tells of being a Humanist and loving all Humanity. But Antoine presses him on his abstract love; he finds that, though the Self-Taught Man praises the young people in the café, he is unable to say anything about them as individuals. He does not see them. He sees only the abstraction "young lovers" and not the real people sitting before him. When Antoine points this out, the Self-Taught man labels him "a misanthrope." This too is an abstraction; "misanthropy also has its place in the concert: it is only a dissonance necessary to the harmony of the whole" (N, 118). So Antoine refuses to be called a misanthrope: "I *am not* a humanist, that's all there is to it."

As the Self-Taught Man rambles on with abstractions, Antoine's stomach begins to turn over: "I want to vomit—and suddenly, there it is: the Nausea" (N, 122). For a moment he is about to stab the cheese knife into the eye of the Self-Taught Man. (Yesterday he had stabbed his hand [S]; now he wants to stab the eye [N] of the man who thinks as a Platonist; this is the Enantiodromia, the N and S at war.) He gets up from table as everything seems to be spinning around him. Leaving the café he hastens along the street till he reaches a balustrade that overlooks the sea.

> I turn back, lean both hands on the balustrade. The *true* sea is cold and black, full of animals; it crawls under this thin green film made to deceive human beings. The sylphs all round me have let themselves be taken in: they only see the thin film that proves the existence of God. I see beneath it! (N, 124)

Staggering along in a daze he boards a passing tram.

> I lean my hand on the seat but pull it back hurriedly. . . . I murmur: "It's a seat," a little like an exorcism. But the word stays on my lips: it refuses to go and put itself on the thing. . . . Things are divorced from their names. They are there, grotesque, headstrong, gigantic and it seems ridiculous to call them seats or say anything at all about them: I am in the midst of things, nameless things. . . . They demand nothing, they don't impose themselves: they are there. (N, 125)

Soon he is sitting in a park looking at a chestnut tree, "black, knotty hands reaching towards the sky." But he is speechless, "Words had vanished and with them the significance of things, their methods of use, and the feeble points of reference which men have traced on their surface" (N, 127). He tries to see relationships between things in the world around him, but it does not work.

> each of them escaped the relationship in which I tried to enclose it, isolated itself, and overflowed. Of these relations (which I insisted on maintaining in order to delay the crumbling of the human world, measures, quantities, and directions)—I felt myself to be the arbitrator; they no longer had their teeth into things. (N, 128)

These passages show the N and the S separating completely. The N is the world of relationships and words (words would situate all things in a great concert where all things are related). But to develop an overall harmony one must become blind to things *in themselves*. Relationships and harmonies are found to be only feeble human tracings over the surface, while each thing exists simply in itself. "To exist is simply *to be there*; those who exist let themselves be encountered, but you can never deduce anything from them" (N, 131). The branches ("empty hands") of the tree move, but the movement itself is simply an additional Thing. The world of existence has presented itself: it is a mass of unrelated Things; each unit is itself (S) without rapport or meaning beyond. The N is empty talk and the S is the reality of things (there are only trees and no forest). Antoine has slipped into the dark waters. But yet there is a touch of hope: he has understood. "The Nausea has not left me, and I don't believe it will leave me so soon; but I no longer have to bear it, it is no longer an illness or a passing fit: it is I" (*N*, 126). When Antoine stabbed his hand and staggered confused from the library, he repeated to himself a jumbled rendition of the Cartesian *cogito*: "I am, I exist, I think, therefore I am; I am because I think, why do I think? I don't want to think any more" (*N*, 100). But as the nausea took hold of him, the substantial "I" that Descartes found in the *cogito* vanished:

> Now when I say "I," it seems hollow to me. . . . A pale reflection of myself wavers in my consciousness. Antoine Roquentin . . . and suddenly the "I" pales, pales, and fades out. Lucid forlorn consciousness. . . . Nobody lives there anymore. A little while ago someone said "me," said my consciousness. Who? (*N*, 170)

A Jungian might say that he has made a dangerous descent into the Unconscious ("on the fourth side is a great hole of black water"), and in the process his ego has disintegrated. (While working on *Nausea* Sartre had a distressing experience with mescaline; afterwards he had flashbacks and feared losing his sanity [Cohen-Solal, 102].) But Sartre had also been writing articles in which he worked out a careful study of the *cogito*.

II. Two Separate Regions of Being

Sartre spent the academic year of 1933–34 in Berlin where he studied phenomenology under Edmund Husserl. Husserl (1859–1938) considered the *cogito* the starting point of philosophy, and Sartre would agree (*BN*, 103). So upon returning to France, Sartre wrote an essay to introduce Husserl's understanding of "intentionality" to a French audience; it was also his own understanding: every consciousness is a consciousness *of* something, but consciousness does not absorb its object into itself. Rather, it is other; to know is to explode towards. This is intentionality. Through it consciousness is purified, it is bright as a great wind, there is nothing in it except a movement to flee itself, a sliding beyond itself; if by the impossible you would enter "in" a consciousness, you would be siezed by a whirlwind and cast out, next to the tree, in the dust; for consciousness has no "within," it is nothing but the outside of itself and it is this absolute flight, this refusal to be substance which constitutes it as consciousness (*SI*, 32–33).

Consciousness is human reality; it has no "within," it is other than itself, and Sartre associated it with the "Other" found in Plato's *Sophist* (*BN*, 756). The Other in Plato's *Sophist* was considered above, and there and here it is associated with the N of Jung. As pure otherness, it would have "no 'within.'" Sartre (using terminology from Hegel) would call consciousness the For-itself and the object known the In-itself: these would form the N and the S, the elements of Sartre's Enantiodromia.

But Sartre would also differ with Husserl, for, unlike his teacher, Sartre would not locate the Ego in consciousness; for him consciousness must be "all lightness, all translucence" (*TE*, 42). Thus Sartre locates the ego outside of consciousness; it is "before" consciousness as one more sort of object of consciousness—it is an artificial construct. When Antoine said of consciousness, "Nobody lives there anymore," Sartre was presenting a well-thought-out position: human reality has no identity; it is endlessly other than itself. It has constructed the ego only to give itself a permanence, an identity. But, for Sartre, it does not work: consciousness cannot identify with itself; it is endlessly other and never the same—never the S. This is the basic theme of Sartre's psychological studies: we cannot *be* ourself no matter how hard we try.

In *Nausea* Antoine was relieved of nausea when he entered a café and heard a gramophone playing a recorded song. The song was said to be "above" existence; only the record and the sound existed (Jung associates existence with Sensation). While taken up by the song, Antoine was delivered from the nausea of existence. Sartre would develop this idea at length in *The Psychology of the Imagination* (1940). And again the work tells of the radical separation of the N and the S.[3]

Sartre considers a man awaiting the performance of Beethoven's Seventh Symphony. He hopes it will be played well; that is, he hopes the temporal analogue (the performance) will achieve the ideal. The hope implies that the symphony itself (as apart from the performance) transcends time. Should the concert be interrupted, Beethoven's symphony is not interrupted—only its performance. One cannot act upon the symphony. Nothing can change it. The symphony is an eternal essence of sorts. Many at the concert close their eyes so they may lose themselves in the ideal. While sound waves strike their ears, they enter the induced dream of "esthetic contemplation" (*PI*, 281). They have entered the unreality of the symphony. For Sartre they have not entered an alternate world, a sort of Platonic world that is also real (*PI*, 280). Rather, they only have let go of reality, let go of existence.

When the performance ends, the dreamer awakes "and comes suddenly in contact with existence. Nothing more is needed to arouse the nauseating disgust that characterizes the consciousness of reality" (*PI*, 281). Thus, Sartre concludes that the real is always nauseous and beauty is always imaginary. When one contemplates Beauty, one is not seeing reality at all. Beauty (N) is the timeless set of relationships in which I render myself unreal (other); while existence is the sickening individuality of things (S). This philosophy was implicit in *Nausea* where Beauty and Nausea alternated; they are Sartre's Enantiodromia.

In September 1939 Sartre was drafted into the French army, taken prisoner in June of 1940, and released in March of 1941. He returned to Paris, and Sartre the contemplative surprised his literary friends by calling on them to take direct action against the Nazi occupation. He organized a literary resistance, but his efforts went nowhere and the group soon folded. He returned to writing the book he had been working on for ten years. One critic observes, "Sartre learned from this experience that however much he praised direct action and despised contemplation, he was himself made for the latter" (Desan, 10). He was still the Platonist, *Jean sans terre*, though like Plato he tried unsuccessfully to ground himself in politics.

In 1943, Sartre published a highly contemplative work that he had started in 1930, *Being and Nothingness*. And the book tells of two realities: being and nothingness. Sometimes Sartre will call these two by the terms of Hegel: the in-itself and for-itself, and sometimes by the terms of Plato: Same and Other. The present study, working with Jung, would identify Being/In-itself/Same with S, and

identify Nothingness/For-itself/Other with N. The in-itself is immanence and the for-itself is transcendence.

Being, what Sartre often calls the in-itself, is said to be simply itself. "It is an immanence . . . it is glued to itself"; it "is what it is—in
the absolute plenitude of its identity" (*BN*, lxxvii, 120). It is solid
(*massif*); it is full positivity and knows no otherness (*BN*, lxxviii,
lxxix). While, in contrast, Nothingness (consciousness, the for-
itself) is "the Platonic Other" (*BN*, 756). "The for-itself is the foundation of all negativity and all relation. *The for-itself is relation*"; it
negates the in-itself; it is "flight," flight from self: it has no being
apart from being other; it has only a borrowed existence (*BN*, 442,
19, 756). As other it is even other than itself; it "must be what it is
not and not be what it is" (*BN*, 82).

To explain what he means by identifying consciousness (human
reality) with nothingness, Sartre considers *fascination*. Here the
knower is only a pure negation. The only qualification that the
knower

> can support is that he *is not* precisely this particular fascinating ob-
> ject. In fascination there is nothing more than a gigantic object in a
> desert world. Yet the fascinated intuition is in no way a *fusion* with the
> object. In fact the condition necessary for the existence of fascination
> is that the object be raised in absolute relief on a background of
> emptiness. (*BN*, 216)

The emptiness is the act of seeing, of knowing. Knowledge and the
knower "are nothing except the fact 'that there is' being" (*BN*, 218).

Sartre insists that consciousness itself is wholly without substance
(*BN*, 215); it is nothing. And that gives rise to the basic human problem. Consciousness would like to attain being; it would like to be its
own self; it would like to coincide with itself in self-identity. But consciousness is endlessly other, so it cannot be itself (consciousness is N
and cannot also be S). Consciousness is empty; it is a negation of itself, so it sees emptiness in the world. To give an example, Sartre offers
a Jungian image, a circle with a missing fourth: "For example, if I say
that the moon is not full and that one quarter is lacking, I base this
judgement on full intuition of the crescent moon" (*BN*, 105; an image
involving 3:4). For Sartre, the "absence" is not in the object known,
but only read into things by consciousness.

Consciousness is said to be haunted by its absent being. It wants to be being-in-itself, but not the opaque in-itself, the object that it has renounced. It wants to be the synthesis of for-itself and in-itself; that is, it wants both "the necessary translucency of consciousness along with the coincidence with itself of being-in-itself" (*BN*, 110). It wants to be both other than solid being and also solidly its *self*; it is that which "can exist only as a perpetually evanescent relation, but it would be [desires to be] this self as substantial being" (*BN*, 110). It wants to be God, "an absolute being which would be itself as other and other as itself" (*BN*, 446). In Jungian terms, it wants to be S as N and N as S, the synthesis of opposites.

This desired *self*, this union of opposites, relation and substance, nothingness and being, N and S, is sometimes seen as beyond the world, and then it is called God. So Sartre, like Jung, would term the union of opposites both the "*self*" and God. But Sartre argues such a union is impossible, as the terms contradict. Yet, for Sartre, though God is impossible, God remains the fundamental human value; in other words, "man is the being whose project is to be God," "man fundamentally is the desire to be God" (*BN*, 694). Thus, God is the human ideal. But Sartre argues that God is impossible, for "God" involves contradictory properties (e.g.: Being and Nothingness).

So humans are left striving in vain to attain "consciousness and being," a synthesis that is "always indicated and always impossible" (*BN*, 762). The apparent synthesis gives rise to the "magical," that is, the degradation of the for-itself into an in-itself (*BN*, 206). The magical is "an irrational synthesis of spontaneity [for-itself] and passivity [in-itself]. It is an inert activity, a consciousness rendered passive" (*E*, 84). The reign of magic "is blinded ideas, plugged by matter, matter possessed by mind and in revolt against mind" (*LPE*, 161). When one beholds "magic," one's consciousness is under a spell and refuses to see its situation with lucidity. The spell is the apparent reconciliation of the N and the S. Lucidity would bring one to Sartre's despairing conclusion: "Man is a useless passion" (*BN*, 754), the dramatic claim by which Sartre gained considerable popular fame. Here both his atheism and his human frustration come down to the irreconcilability of the N and the S.

Sartre identifies his massive volume *Being and Nothingness* as a study in "existential psychoanalysis." By this process one comes to see the absurdity of any human project; so Sartre explains that all human activities are equivalent, and "all are on principle doomed to failure. It amounts to the same thing whether one gets drunk alone or is a leader of nations" (*BN*, 767). For all human acts are nothing but vain attempts to achieve the impossible union of in-itself and for-itself (*BN*, 767). Sartre suggests that others have practiced a similar self-psychoanalysis (Antoine did so in *Nausea*) and come to the same conclusion. They would see no point in doing anything, as did Antoine: "I know very well that I don't want to do anything" (*N*, 173). *Being and Nothingness* sees no value in action, though it was published after Sartre called for direct action. *Being and Nothingness* is a contemplative work, for much of it was written earlier; its author was *Jean sans terre*.

Having said that human action in the world is futile, Sartre goes further to imply that it is impossible. He asks, how could consciousness and things interact? He replies: "Indeed it is impossible for a determined process to act upon a spontaneity [consciousness], exactly as it is impossible for objects to act upon consciousness. Thus any synthesis of two types of existence is impossible; they are not homogeneous; they will remain each one in its incommunicable solitude" (*BN*, 540). The N and S are in solitude and human action is impossible—or is it?

III. The Dramatic Leap from Contemplation to Action

In June of 1943 as Sartre published *Being and Nothingness*, he also produced a play, *The Flies*, his version of the Greek story of Orestes. As the play begins, Orestes has long practiced an existential psychoanalysis similar to Antoine's. By his travels he has *seen* everything, but he has *done* nothing. He is "free as the strands torn by the wind from spiders' webs that one sees floating ten feet above the ground." He claims, "My mind's my own, gloriously aloof" (*NE*, 59); he is Orestes *sans terre*. So Orestes feels unsatisfied: "I'm a mere shadow of a man; of all the ghosts haunting this town today, none is ghostlier than I" (*NE*, 88). These passages tell well of one who knows only his conscious Function; he is strangely unreal. The Intuitive has seen everything, but something is missing.

Orestes announces that to come down among others he must assume a burden of guilt. He decides to kill his mother and her lover and thereby avenge the murder of his father many years before; but the killing seems more like personal therapy for Orestes than any desire to avenge his father's murder. He announces to his sister that he will go "down to the city," "down into the depths, among you." He will bloody his *hands* with an irrevocable deed, and afterwards be able to boast, "I have done *my* deed." He will end his lofty Platonism. After he does so his sister congratulates him: "Give me that hand, your strong right hand. Your fingers are short and square, made to grasp and hold. Dear hand!" (*NE*, 105). The idealist finds the rejected hand is now esteemed (as cornerstone?). By the double killing Orestes claims he has been delivered from the lightness of pure speculation.

The next hero of Sartre's fiction is Mathieu, a philosophy professor idolized by his students (in *The Age of Reason*, published in 1945, but much of it written in 1939; the professor and students in the novel are patterned after Sartre and his devoted disciples). Mathieu has reflected himself out of the world and he too finds himself unable to do anything. Yet his "sole care had been to hold himself in readiness. For an act. A free, considered act that should pledge his whole life" (*AR*, 54). But he can do nothing decisive. A friend (patterned on Sartre's friend Paul Nizan) tells Mathieu that he did well in freeing himself, but he adds, "Now it's done, you are free. . . . You have spent thirty-five years cleaning yourself up, and the result is nil. . . . You live in a void. . . . you're adrift, you're an abstraction, a man who is not there" (*AR*, 131). Mathieu agrees and adds, "I've finally lost all sense of reality: nothing now seems to be altogether true." That is, Mathieu is *sans terre*, while his friend is a man of action. Mathieu tells his friend, "Everything you touch looks real"; while Mathieu is living "above" the real and cannot descend to act.

Later, Mathieu was sitting in a night club with a lady friend and observed his left hand lying flat on the table. To impress his friend "he jabbed the knife into his palm and felt almost nothing. When he took his hand away, the knife remained embedded in his flesh, straight up with its haft in the air" (*AR*, 220). Blood spills on the table cloth and over the floor. The hand-stabbing repeats the account in *Nausea*. And again (as in *Nausea*) the text is filled with allusions to the hand (the first 80 pages mention the hand(s) 36 times). Mathieu has bloodied his hand, but it is only a pointless gesture. He remains unable to act.

Later Sartre continued the story of Mathieu in *Troubled Sleep*, published in 1949. Mathieu has been drafted into the French army in 1940, and there he hopes to become part of the action. He and his comrades are ordered to delay the German advance; seeing a single German crawling down the road, he realizes this is his moment of action. He shoots and kills the man; then he begins laughing, for he has finally done something:

> For years he had tried in vain to act; one after another he had been robbed of action as fast as he had determined to act; he had been about as firm as a pat of butter. He had pressed a trigger, and, for once, something had happened, something definite. . . . *His* dead man, *his* handiwork, something to mark *his* passage on the earth. (*TS*, 193)

Both his eyes and hands are involved: "He was blinded by blood; his hands were red to the wrists. He rubbed his eyes, mingling the blood on his hands with that on his face" (*TS*, 198). Again, the killing is more a matter of Mathieu's personal therapy than an act of national defense.

In the meantime, Sartre had presented another fictional character who has been living *sans terre*: Hugo, in the play *Dirty Hands*, produced in 1948. Hugo is said to be an intellectual, "a fellow who doesn't work with his hands" (*NE*, 167). He is writing for a Communist paper somewhere in Eastern Europe in the final days of World War II. Yet he fears he can only write and not act. He is told: "It seems you want to *act*. . . . Only you can't do anything with your hands." "He won't work with his hands." Hugo acknowledges his limitation and would do violence to his hand, if it would help: "I would cut off my hand to grow up all at once" (*NE*, 186).

A party leader gives Hugo the assignment of killing Hoederer. Hugo has been longing for some "direct action" and this is the opportunity he has sought. Hoederer is also a Communist, but purists in the party think he is compromising party ideals by working out a pragmatic arrangement with the U.S. Pentagon. Since Hoederer is the man of action, Hugo can observe, "Everything he touches (S) seems real" (*NE*, 182). Hoederer can act in the real world because he is willing to compromise his principles; he will even lie to others in the party so that the party can gain power. Hugo begins to admire Hoederer, and this will make the assassination difficult. He is impressed by Hoederer's effectiveness, still he objects to Hoederer lying to the other party members. Hoederer responds:

> How you cling to your purity, young man! How afraid you are to soil your hands! All right, stay pure! What good will it do? Why did you

join us? Purity is an ideal for a yogi or a monk. You intellectuals and bourgeois anarchists use it as a pretext for doing nothing. To do nothing, to remain motionless, arms at your sides, wearing kid gloves. Well, I have dirty hands. Right up to the elbows. I've plunged them in filth and blood. (*NE*, 218)

In coming to admire Hoederer, Hugo wonders if he can carry out the assassination he has planned. Suddenly, in a moment of confusion and surprise, he turns on Hoederer: "Hoederer, I am looking you straight in the eyes and I'm aiming and my hand's not shaking." He shoots three times and Hoederer falls dead. It seems that Hugo has finally dirtied his hands with action, but it is not that simple. He is not sure if *he* has killed a man or if he was overtaken by the excitement of the moment; perhaps emotional drives beyond his control acted through him. If so, there would be no human deed, only a mindless accident. But several years after the event, Hugo is able to claim his deed was intended; he had killed out of principle. And this unity of intention (N) and deed (S) brings Hugo down to earth; it is his salvation, for he, after the event, has assumed the deed as his free act.

In 1951 Sartre produced the play, *The Devil and the Good Lord;* it tells of Goetz, a philosopher of sorts who is also *sans terre*. Goetz has been striving to be purely Evil, an "unalloyed monster," but he finds he is ineffective, "nothing but a useless uproar"; he is without weight (*DGL*, 55, 123). Like other characters in Sartre's fiction he regards his hands as alien objects: "Look at these hands. There's workmanship! We should all praise the Lord for giving us hands" (*DGL*, 61). But Goetz suddenly renounces his commitment to Evil; he decides to be totally Good: "I was a criminal—I will reform. I turn my coat and wager. I can be a saint" (*DGL*, 64).

The newborn saint prays to receive the stigmata. When it does not come, the stage directions say, "*He draws a dagger from his belt, stabs the palm of his left hand, then the palm of his right hand*" (*DGL*, 102). Now there is "blood on his hands," and soon another character pretends to have the stigmata too (*DGL*, 119).

Three characters in Sartre's fiction, Antoine, Mathieu and Goetz, could all be described as *sans terre*, and each has stabbed his own hand. The repeated image tells of Sartre's N fascinated by his S (his hand), but at the same time trying to reject and deny it. Mathieu, Orestes, Hugo, and Goetz, all come down to earth when they dirty their hands in the definitive act of killing another. Their bloody hands bring them deliverance.

Goetz tried to live pure Evil, and then pure Good, but neither worked. The problem was the purity. As Sartre was writing of the fictional Goetz, he also was writing a more theoretical treatment of Good and Evil (*Saint Genet*). And there the terms Good and Evil bear a striking resemblance to what he had earlier (in *Being and Nothingness*) presented as the in-itself and for-itself![4] But there is one radical difference: in 1943, the in-itself and for-itself were presented as regions of being irreconcilably separate, but now the two (Good and Evil) are so much alike that Goetz can hardly distinguish between them: "Is it good? Is it evil? The understanding is confused" (*DGL*, 56); "The loneliness of Good—how am I to distinguish it from the loneliness of Evil?" (*DGL*, 124); "a man needs good eyesight to distinguish the good Lord from the Devil" (*DGL*, 132). Goetz then realizes, "Monster or saint . . . I wanted to be inhuman" (*DGL*, 139). Both Good and Evil (Lord and Devil, saint and monster—in-itself and for-itself) are escapes from the human. They are both absolutes; as such they are inhuman poses by which people seek to avoid living and acting in the real world. By Evil one might identify with the lofty gaze (the for-itself, pure nonbeing), and by Good one might identify with that which is simply given (the in-itself, pure being). But, in identifying with absolute Evil or absolute Good, one is not able to act in the human world, where all events are relative. By aligning one's self with either absolute, one is unable to be human. So when Goetz pretends he is a saint he claims, "I shall have eyes for nothing but the earth and the stones. . . . I shall destroy the man [destroy his own humanity]" (*DGL*, 126, 131). The eyes gazing at the stone are the for-itself gazing at the in-itself (here and elsewhere in Sartre the eye and stone combination symbolizes the for-itself and in-itself).

The fascinating gaze is also Sartre on the sixth floor overlooking the stones of Paris. He is pure gaze, for the lofty place that gives him freedom and perspective also leaves him unable to act; action requires that he come down and make a real difference among his fellows. In renouncing pure Evil, Goetz had attempted to be pure Good. He descended from his lofty perspective and tried to identify totally with the objects gazed at, the helpless poor of earth (a move clearly undertaken in bad faith [*DGL*, 66]). But by identifying or pretending to identify with the poor, he still can do nothing, for to be among the masses he must pretend to be the helpless object. He has simply assumed the inertia of the Good (the in-itself, the S), and again he is unable to act. Eventually he realizes that identifying with either pure Evil or pure Good leaves him in a dream world, a phantasy wherein one makes dramatic gestures that accomplish nothing: "So then, all was nothing but lies and make-believe? I have effected nothing; I merely went through the motions" (*DGL*, 138). He decides to renounce both the purity of Evil and the purity of Good and enter the messy human scene where good and evil are part of every act. He will "be a man among men" (*DGL*, 145). To do so, like Hoederer, he accepts killing and lying even to his associates, for only thus can one be effective in the present world.[5]

In 1952 Sartre published his lengthy study (625 pages; parts had been published earlier) of a writer whom he knew and befriended, Jean Genet. Genet, like Goetz, once gave himself totally to Good and then totally to Evil. Sartre's study traces Genet through the *aporias* and contradictions of the process. To be pure Evil Genet tried to transform himself into an illusion, and this left him in a strange dream world unwilling to do actions that were real. Eventually he developed the practical skills of the professional thief. Since the skilled thief must perform practical *acts* (jimmying open a window, etc.), Genet has become a *working man* and this ends his dream world. For the man of action things no longer appear as wondrous symbols that accomplish nothing, they are practical tools (*SG*, 403).

Sartre developed the fictional character of Goetz at the same time as he worked on the philosophical/psychological study of his friend Genet. Both are presented as trying at one time to live as pure subject (for itself/Evil) and at another time as pure object (in itself/Good). But fascinated by the extremes, Goetz and Genet were unable to act. They renounced both absolutes to engage in the relativity of human life. But, in writing of Genet, Sartre says:

> Being, Nonbeing, Nonbeing of Being and Being of Nonbeing, Sovereign Good, Sovereign Evil: he [Genet] will now see these only as reflections which the two pieces shoot back and forth to each other. He has only to reweld these pieces for freedom to be established in its prime dignity. Then, perhaps, he will be tempted by real morality. (*SG*, 186)

A footnote to the passage says, "Good without Evil is Parmenidean Being, that is, Death, and Evil without Good is pure Nonbeing" (*SG*, 186). So Sartre calls for a synthesis of the two, "a Hegelian '*Aufhebung*'," for the "abstract separation of these two concepts expresses simply the alienation of man" (*SG*, 186). But it was Sartre himself who had insisted on their separation, a theme that dominated *Being and Nothingness*, a work that told abundantly of alienation. Now in the name of action Genet will begin to "reweld these pieces" and overcome his alienation. In *Being and Nothingness*, the separation of the in-itself and for-itself was the basis of Sartre's atheism (there could be no union as they were contradictory). Now he calls for "a Hegelian '*Aufhebung*'"—that will be achieved in the future! This *Aufhebung* would be the union of opposites that Jung called the Self and Sartre called God, the N (for-itself) reconciled with the S (in-itself). See my treatment in Matczak, 351ff.

Though Sartre told of the synthesis, he continued to have the same difficulty with action. In 1960, he presented his final work of fiction: a play, *The Condemned of Altona*. The central character, Franz, had been trained by his father, a German industrialist when the Nazis were in power, to take over the family ship-building plant. Franz served in the Nazi army and is haunted by memories of his wartime service. The play opens after the war, and Franz has been living for thirteen years as a recluse in the family mansion. Like other Sartrean heroes, he is "pure," a "puritan" (*CA*, 34, 69, 168); he is pure gaze and his hands are alien to him: when his hands shake beyond control, he addresses them: "Come on, boys, come on! There! There!" (*CA*, 34, 69, 168, 89). Franz has the same difficulty as other Sartrean heroes: "Do you know why I reproach myself? I've done nothing. Nothing. Nothing. Never" (*CA*, 137, 171). Franz has already killed some people, and it was killing that delivered Orestes, Mathieu, Hugo, and Goetz from contemplation. Franz has a similar understanding of what action means, "To act means to kill" (*CA*, 145); but Franz claims that throughout his life he was only performing dutifully as the "formidable machine" his father had made him. He has not freely acted and his deeds were not really his own. His father was also a machine, serving the "firm" he thought he controlled (*CA*, 172). Neither has committed a free human act, until the end of the play when they finally commit suicide together and achieve some sort of deliverance!

Thus, Sartre's fiction has six contemplatives making a dramatic leap to action (one is Bariona in a play of the same name and written in 1940, a play not considered here). The contemplatives could be seen as Sartre himself trying to appropriate his S. But even in 1960, *The Condemned of Altona* shows he is still the distant gaze, the N, trying to descend to the street, a descent that succeeds only in the act of a double suicide (Franz and his father). Does the suicide suggest a sacrifice of Ego/Consciousness so that action might follow (the N being sacrificed for a synthesis, much as Socrates [Plato's N] goes to his death in the *Theaetetus* so that the Stranger might tell of a synthesis)?

IV. The Opposites Will be Reconciled by Action

In *Being and Nothingness* Sartre had told of the for-itself as fleeing the in-itself, but in fleeing the in-itself it is also seeking to become the in-itself. But the in-itself it seeks to become is not the in-itself it rejected; it is the in-itself-for-itself (God). This was the impossible and contradictory synthesis.

> The for-itself arises as the nihilation of the in-itself and this nihilation is defined as the project toward the in-itself. Between the nihilated in-itself and the projected in-itself the for-itself is nothingness. . . . the for-itself, being the negation of the in-itself, could not desire the pure and simple return to the in-itself. . . . what the for-itself demands of the in-itself is precisely the totality detotalized [the in-itself-for-itself]. (*BN*, 693)

Thus, the for-itself (N) does not want to return to being an in-itself (S); it wants to be S while remaining N. A variation of the above text seems to occur in 1960 as Sartre speaks of the human "project, as a mediation between two moments of objectivity" (*SM*, 99; that is, the for-itself as mediation between two moments of in-itself). He reflects on his days as a student in philosophy: "The total concrete was what we [students] wanted to leave behind us; the absolute concrete was what we wanted to achieve" (*SM*, 19). In Jungian terms: the S was what they wanted to leave behind; the N-S was what they wanted to achieve—and the whole sense of the passage is that this synthesis is possible or will be possible someday.

Achieving the absolute concrete through action is the subject of the massive philosophical work of Sartre's later years, *Critique of Dialectical Reason;* only one of its two volumes appeared in his lifetime. He would see it as a total refutation of his earlier philosophical stances (Cohen-Solal, 412); "my outlook changed so fundamentally after the Second World War" (*BE&M,* 33). He would dismiss his earlier ethics as "idealism." The changes could be seen as a renunciation of the absolute opposition of for-itself and in-itself and a call for their reconciliation.

Sartre's "theology" can be confusing. In *Being and Nothingness* (1943), God was the impossible synthesis of in-itself and for-itself. But with his change after the war, Sartre started calling for what seems to be that very synthesis. Yet in doing so he would identify God differently: not as the impossible synthesis, but as either of the terms (in-itself, for-itself) in radical isolation from the other! (This I have argued elsewhere; see Matczak, 851–64.) The change meant that he would call for the *reconciliation oppositorum;* that is, for a Jungian, he will allow the appearance of the Self. Accordingly, he would pull back from his earlier claim that "Man is a useless passion." He would reject the idealism of the Left (N) and the idealism of the Right (S)—idealism of evil (N) and idealism of good (S)—the elements he had separated so totally in *Being and Nothingness* (*SM,* 29). Now he wants "to give man both his autonomy and his reality among real objects, avoiding idealism [N] without lapsing into a mechanistic materialism [S]" (*BE&M,* 37). That is, he comes down from his lofty vision without simply identifying with the stones of the street.

As indicated above, Sartre had returned from his time in the army calling for a common action against the occupying Germans. He led in forming a group of writers, *Socialisme et Liberté,* that fell apart after a year. Shortly after the war he was claiming Existentialism is not a contemplative philosophy, for "existentialism defines man by his action." But Sartre himself remained a writer, who, like the characters in his fiction, talked of "direct action" but lived apart. In February of 1948 he formed a political action group called *Rassemblement Democratique Revolutionnaire,* which he supported financially. But, after a difficult year and a half spent working with others, he resigned and the group fell apart. These two groups were his only attempts at political action in union with others, a theme fundamental to his writings (Cohen-Solal, 311). Then in the early fifties he had a sometimes friendly and sometimes stormy relationship with the Communist party, but he never joined. He remained a solitary contemplative overlooking Paris, the party, and the world. "However much he praised direct action and despised contemplation, he was himself made for the latter" (Desan, 10).

As a young philosopher Sartre told of lacking a sense of his own historicity (*WD*, 69)—he was above the historical process. But that changed slightly when he was in the army. In 1945 his associate, Merleau-Ponty, wrote for the two of them: "We have learned history, and we maintain that we can never forget it." But Sartre reflected on the claim of Merleau-Ponty and called the "we" a polite form of speech; for he still was the contemplative: "In order to learn what he [Merleau-Ponty] already knew, I still needed five years" (*St*, 235). In the intervening years, Sartre felt he was "lost in the political labyrinth." In 1948 one can see the change as he writes, "The idea is never purely practical nor purely theoretical; it is practico-theoretical or theoretico-practical" (*T&E*, 15). The terms are approaching each other; he is working at a reconciliation. In 1950 he claimed he "finally discovered the reality of the event. In a word, it was Merleau-Ponty who converted me. . . . He enlightened me" (*St*, 255). The content of the enlightenment is that he was acting and making some kind of history, whether he recognized it or not. The stages of this enlightenment can be seen in Sartre's fictional heroes: Antoine was apart from history and entirely passive, while each character that followed tried to renounce contemplation and to act, that is, commit an irrevocable deed with a free intent, though the free intent may come only after the deed. His literary characters did this with only questionable success.

The enlightenment of which Sartre speaks can best be understood in terms of the different starting points of Sartre's two major philosophical works: *Being and Nothingness* (1943) and *Critique of Dialectical Reason, I* (1960). The first is a contemplative work based on the self-validating *cogito* of Descartes as developed by Husserl; there, with lofty remoteness, Sartre told of the vanity of all human activity (*BN*, 767). "For a thoughtful person every enterprise is absurd" (*B*, 31).

But the later work, *Critique of Dialectical Reason*, has no self-validating starting point; it could be said to start with the "enlightenment" he received from Merleau-Ponty: the human being is maker of history. That is, he has renounced the pure N and by an enlightenment assumed that the N and S can unite in real human action. Again and again he had his fictional heroes renounce the self-evident starting point of his earlier work and try to live an enlightenment that is not self-evident at all. Sartre's associate, Francis Jeanson, saw the change involving *une sorte de grace divine* (Jeanson, 253). Sartre explains the difference in terms of his break with the more contemplative Husserl: "Husserl could speak of apodictic certainty without much difficulty, but this was because he remained on the level of pure, formal consciousness apprehending itself in its formality; but, for us, it is necessary to find our apodictic experience in the concrete world of history" (*CDR*, 35). The starting point has shifted; now history offers an "apodictic experience" on which philosophy can be based! But this remains only a nonvalidated enlightenment that lacks the certainty claimed by Descartes and Husserl for the *cogito*. Sartre has shifted from the *cogito* to tell of the N and S working together to form history.

With the change Sartre came to speak of human reality as praxis, an active (not a contemplative) term taken from Marx and Engels. Praxis refers to the free human action by which the events of history come about; it is said to involve both necessity and freedom (*CDR*, 79). By his understanding of praxis Sartre is objecting to the Marxists who claim that the "forces" of history override human freedom. In voluminous prose (*Critique of Dialectical Reason* has 1,430 pages of small type) he will attempt to show how free human acts can mix with the necessity of events to give rise to history.

In this *Critique* Sartre is claiming that the human individual acts only in a world already humanized. For example: one might deal with an economic crisis; but an economic crisis does not exist apart from the human world. It has no meaning "for the block of stone in the mountain, nor for God." (One might paraphrase: not "for the in-itself [mountain], nor for the for-itself [God].") An economic crisis has meaning only in a human world, a world Sartre would term the practico-inert. In Sartre's later philosophy the duality, praxis and practico-inert, more or less replaces the earlier duality, for-itself and in-itself. Instead of consciousness he will refer to lived experience, the *vécu*, and instead of the the in-itself he will tell of *la force des choses*. The opposition of the earlier terms has been softened. In *Being and Nothingness*, the terms for-itself and in-itself were developed as part of a contemplative understanding, best illustrated by the passage from *Being and Nothingness* quoted earlier concerning fascination, where consciousness becomes pure gaze (nothingness) looking at the object (being), yet each remained in "incommunicable solitude" (*BN*, 540). But, in recognizing that humans make history, Sartre softened the duality to speak of praxis and the practico-inert.[6]

The for-itself had been identified with the disinterested gaze of God and the in-itself with the stone that is wholly inert. But both of these allow no room for the human world. So while Goetz (above) was seeking absolutes he claimed, "I shall look no more at a human face. I shall have eyes for nothing but the earth and the stones." By taking this remote stance, he would destroy the human world, that is, the world in which one acts (praxis) in a world already humanized (practico-inert). Goetz would asssume the position of a divine eye that would contemplate from afar an objective world in which he was not involved. Thus he would be absolute Evil.

But soon Goetz will renounce both absolute Good and absolute Evil in order to act among humans, so he claims he must have an empty sky (that is, no God, no remote and pure for-itself). For the later Sartre, the absolutes of which he had made so much eliminate the relative world of humans; now in choosing the relative world of humans Sartre would eliminate the absolutes (God and the rock, for-self and in-self). Sartre (Goetz) cannot allow both God as absolute and man as relative. By identifying one's self as absolute for-itself, one can take a godly view and contemplate the fascinating stone (the world not humanized) as absolute object. Thus, the god-and-stone dyad is often found in Sartre's later writings and is rejected; it is a reference to the for-itself/in-itself duality. Consider several phrases: to encounter pure matter one "would have to be either a god or a stone"; "Matter could not be matter except for God, and for pure matter." In each of these Sartre is rejecting the contemplative view that involves extremes, a pure subject (God) viewing a pure object (stone). Instead of the for-itself (all but unmentioned in the *Critique*) Sartre speaks of dialectical reason. Dialectical reason (like the for-itself) always involves a withdrawal from what is to what is not; so it is the source of novelty and change. But dialectical reason itself can become analytical reason, "a particular practical moment of dialectical Reason." This is thought making "itself into a directed inertia in order to act on inertia"; "thought must become a thing" to act on things (*CDR*, 58–59). Thought, consciousness, here renders itself inert to understand and act on the inert! That identifies Sartre's change. That thought would become inert was once considered "magical" (see above, where the for-itself maintained its "purity") and was rejected. But now, thought's ability to assume "inertia" and thought's making itself a "thing" are what enable thought to act in the world! But if thought can be a thing, there can no longer be the clarity of pure consciousness, consciousness as an absolute. Once Sartre had written: "A pitiless clarity ruled over my mind; it was an operating room, hygienic, without shadows, without nooks or crannies or microbes" (*WD*, 271). This purity of consciousness was what he must lose to accept an enlightenment concerning the making of history.

Sartre once spoke of perception (contemplation) as a "communication between two absolute substances, the thing and my soul" (*WD*, 83). This was the radical opposition presented in *Being and Nothingness*, the opposition between the for-itself and the in-itself as absolutes (likewise *Nausea* was an attempt to present things "absolutely, without men" [*WD*, 145], that is, things as pure in-itself).[7] This is the world in which one is unable to act, for both the object and the subject are absolutes which could not unite.[8] But Sartre's later philosophy renounced the purity of the absolutes (as did Sartre's dramatic heroes, Bariona, Orestes, Hugo, Mathieu, Goetz, and Franz). Each of these renounced the purity of consciousness, the for-itself, to dirty his hands with the relative world where history is made. Thus, praxis and the practico-inert can be seen as relative versions of what had been absolutes (the for-itself and in-itself). Now the subject is partially object (thought as thing) and the object is partially subject (thing as thought).

Sartre tells of two alternatives by which people have understood history: "Either we reduce everything to identity (which amounts to substituting a mechanistic materialism for dialectical materialism)— or we make of dialectic a celestial law which imposes itself on the universe" (*SM*, 99; parenthesis in source). The celestial law was himself speculating above the world. The choice is between identity/ mechanistic-materialism (S) or celestial/dialectic (N). But Sartre rejects both; instead, he would restore to the individual the power to advance "beyond his situation by means of work and action" (*SM*, 99). Action itself will serve as "the negating transcendence of contradiction" (*CDR*, 80). To understand history he recommends the "progressive-regressive method." The progressive movement would consider the free human intent (projects), N, while the regressive movement would consider the concrete particular facts, S, that are simply given. It is only by the reciprocal movement of progression and regression, synthesis and analysis, that one can comprehend history, a history that Sartre believes will eventually have a single meaning (*SM*, 20).

One familiar with Jung could see both *Nausea* and *Being and Nothingness* as Sartre's radical attempts to differentiate (separate) the N and the S. They told of *deux regions d'être absolument tranchées* (*BN*, lxxvi); so, in terms of Jung, by allowing no synthesis there could be no Self/God-image/Transcendent Function. At that time Sartre's philosophy was based on the self-validating *cogito*, an apodictic starting point within consciousness. But then an "enlightenment" took him beyond the reflective lucidity of consciousness into the turmoil of history. The clarity and purity of the *cogito* were renounced as he tried to enter the disturbing and ambiguous tide of events that largely escaped his control. The *Critique of Dialectical Reason* that tells of the change can be seen as an extended shuttling back and forth between N and S trying to move towards a synthesis, the Self, that is, the God-image he had thoroughly rejected in his earlier texts. In the *Critique* Sartre rejected Husserl's "apodictic certainty" characteristic of "pure, formal consciousness" (see quote above), so that he might act in the world; a similar rejection of apodictic certainty was found when Plato rejected the certainty of Socrates to have Timaeus speak only of the probable. In each case one is trying to move from the purity of a contemplative stance into the ambiguity of actual events. In Jung's terms, it is a move from the pure clarity of Consciousness to a Reconciliation (Self) located on the border between Consciousness and the Unconscious (*TE*, 221). The process involves a renunciation of the clarity of Consciousness to gain a sense that one is a little more real and so is the world. So as a contemplative Orestes had felt unreal, like a spiderweb floating ten feet above the ground, until he acted; Hugo felt things in his world were unreal, until they were handled by Hoederer, the man of action. Action takes one into the ambiguity of events. And the move to action was made by an abundance of Sartrean heroes as they renounced their "purity." A similar move from a purity and clarity of

Consciousness to a murky reconciliation of opposites will be found in many additional authors in the present study; it is the process Jung called Integration.

Plato seems to have abandoned the purity and clarity of his political ideas in attempts to shape directly the politics of Syracuse (he did the same in offering a physical cosmology that was only probable); Sartre made similar attempts to shape directly the politics of his time. Both of these philosophers have had considerable impact on the history of ideas, but when they tried to dirty their hands with action they had little effect. On several occasions, Sartre tried to join with others and shape world politics, but he seems to have remained a contemplative to the end. His biographer would have it that after each failure he consoled himself by writing another contemplative tome (Cohen-Solal, 375).

Here (and elsewhere) I have claimed that Sartre began calling for the in-itself-for-itself synthesis (*Aufhebung*) he earlier had rejected; his writings even came to urge an ideal state where *freedom and necessity* would be united (*CRD*, 377). For one familiar with the early writings of Sartre it is hard to imagine two terms more difficult to reconcile. This future synthesis/state suggests the Jungian Self. But in these writings from the 1950s (Sartre's involvement with Marxism), it seemed to be a synthesis that humanity could achieve entirely on its own. In his *Critique* he went out of his way to present this synthesis as wholly within the human with no appeal to God. It involved no divine intervention, none of the quality of mystery or of gift-received that suggests religion. But with time Sartre went on to denounce the Communist party and disown Marxism itself. In 1980, shortly before he died, he talked at length with a young Jewish friend, Benny Levy. Through Levy he became interested in Jewish messianism. He saw this to mean that ultimately there will be a united humanity, an end that "is at bottom social *as well as religious*" (*HN*, 106; emphasis added). Human laws will be transcended "from above, not from below" (*HN*, 107). Something above the human! Sartre develops the point:

> this world will end and, at the same moment, another world will appear—another world that will be made of this one but in which things will be differently arranged. There is also another theme I like: the Jewish dead—and others too for that matter—will come back to life. (*HN*, 105)[9]

This and other messianic references are brief and puzzling. But they suggest the wondrous (*deus ex machina*) solution that often characterizes the appearance of the Self. In this conversation shortly before his death Sartre suggests a deliverance apart from the human system; it will *not* be attained through the development of certain facts today (*HN*, 106, 107). Such a wondrous deliverance characterizes the appearance of the Self.

Sartre, as an N, seems to have had a disturbing encounter with his Repressed S when he was about thirty; this was recounted in *Nausea*, a novel with many 3:4s and indications of Enantiodromia. There, and in *Being and Nothingness*, he told of a radical separation of the N and the S. Then he engaged himself in the slow effort to integrate the two. There are indications that he moved in this direction and even that some reconciliation took place late in his life.

In treating Plato, Locke, and Sartre, I have considered three Perceivers reconciling their N and S. It soon will be argued that Judgers are seeking to reconcile their F and T. That means they would have a different Enantiodromia and a different reconciliation. Saint Augustine had a Dominant F, and he will be considered next. He also had a confrontation with his Repressed when he was about the same age as Sartre. As with Sartre (Antoine) this seems to have involved Augustine in a distressful loss of ego. As a Feeler Augustine had different elements to reconcile and proceeded to effect a clearer reconciliation than Sartre's.

Notes

1. He receives a letter "folded in four" in an envelope whose lining is "three-quarters the envelope's weight." A set of books has "three or four" pictures per volume; his train will leave in "three quarters of an hour," and his finances will last "three or four years" (*N*, 60, 90, 146, 173).

2. Earlier in the novel a minor character had held out her arms "as if awaiting the stigmata," and soon after Antoine stabs himself another character stretched out his palms "as if he were about to receive the stigmata" (*N*, 27, 116).

3. This work also has an emphasis on the hand: in six pages (99–104) the hand[s] is mentioned 26 times. See also 106, 178, 180, "our hands and eyeballs," "our hands, our eyes," etc.

4. Perhaps the association Evil and Good with for-itself and in-itself is surprising. But consider the meanings Sartre has given to the terms: In *Being*

and Nothingness the in-itself was Being, wholly positive and Parmenidean Being (*BN*, 752). But nine years later Sartre would give the Good these same attributes: the Good is Being, absolute plenitude, it exists by itself in absolute positivity, it is Parmenidean Being (*SG*, 155, 158, 186). There is also a close parallel between what *Being and Nothingness* presented as the for-itself in 1943 and what is called Evil in 1952: the for-itself is nonbeing, it is other than self and other than being; it assumed its own marginal existence only if one fixed one's gaze on Being (*BN*, 726, 756; *SI*, 32; *TE*, 82). But in 1952, it is Evil that has these properties: Evil is pure nonbeing, it is other than itself, other than being, and always elusive; it can be seen only out of the corner of one's eye (*SG*, 186, 163, 30, 163). Earlier the for-itself was an explosion and cause of itself (*SI*, 32; *TE*, 82); now it is Evil that is an explosion and cause of itself (*SG*, 28, 19). Earlier the contents of the in-itself and the for-itself had left them as two regions of being that cannot unite; this left the human as a useless passion. But in Sartre's writing about Genet a radical change has taken place; the two are no longer two separate regions of being, leaving man a useless passion; rather, they are two artificial constructs that divide a true unity! This is the change in the latter Sartre. It is the *reconciliation oppositorum;* Integration is affirmed! See my treatments of this resolution in *Sartre and the Sacred*, pp. 120–22, 185–86, and in Matczak, pp. 851–64.

5. The fiction of Sartre always considered the problems he was working with in his personal life. Goetz gave his wealth to the poor to identify with them; but it did not work, as he was the lordly one who had the money to give. While writing this, Sartre gave generously to a political group he had founded, but he discovered that giving set him apart from those who received. A more significant issue concerns Goetz's and Sartre's willingness to kill and lie for an ultimate good. Sartre had been considering himself a Marxist. At the same time the extent of Soviet slave-labor camps had gained wide attention in Europe. He, and the journal he founded, *Les Temps Modernes*, justified the camps as a necessary part of the present world with its mixture of good and evil. In this mixed world he would have us work to bring about the final Marxist state. Sartre had visited the Soviet Union in 1954, and when he returned he praised all that he saw; later, when he had turned against the Soviets, he explained his earlier statements: "I lied" (Cohen-Solal, 351). This would seem to be the kind of lie that Hoederer and Goetz had advocated.

6. The present chapter begins with a Quaternity chart. By having the praxis/practico-inert terms closer to the center, the chart tries to illustrate the softening of the radical opposition found in *Being and Nothingness*.

7. Seeing things purely as themselves was nausea. Simone de Beauvoir said that Sartre hated greenery, was disgusted by raw meat, and detested the countryside (Cohan-Solal, 272). Each such object told of a world unworked by the human; each can be seen as a pure in-itself apart from the practico-inert, apart from matter humans have worked on.

8. God had been the impossible synthesis, for-itself-in-itself. But with Sartre's change God has become identified only with the for-itself: Goetz

said, "You see this emptiness over our heads? That is God. You see this gap in the door? It is God. You see that hole in the ground? That is God again. Silence is god. Absence is God." And he prayed, "Tell me: art Thou, indeed, the night? Night, the tormenting absence of everything! For Thou art the One who is present in the universal absence" (*DGL*, 141, 124). Sartre envisions someone telling Flaubert that God is "this infinite emptiness, everywhere, this cold, our eternal despair, what do you think it is if not Him" (*IF*, 532). This is God as the nothingness of *Being and Nothingness*, the wholly negative absolute Sartre rejects in his later writing; it can be identified simply with the for-itself and not the for-itself-in-itself (God) of *Being and Nothingness*.

9. Many of Sartre's old associates felt that Levy had excessive influence on Sartre at a time when his health was declining. Beauvoir tells of herself and Sartre's friends being "horrified by the nature of the statements extorted from Sartre" (*HN*, 6). In any case, Sartre approved the transcript of these interviews.

Bibliography

Works of Sartre

AR   *The Age of Reason*, translated by Eric Sutton. New York: Bantam, Modern Classics, 1968.

B   *Baudelaire*, translated by Martin Turnell. New York: New Directions, 1967.

BE&M   *Between Existentialism and Marxism*, translated by John Mathews. New York: Random House, 1974.

BN   *Being and Nothingness*, translated by Hazel Barnes. New York: Washington Square Press, 1966.

CA   *The Condemned of Altona*, translated by Sylvia and George Leeson. New York: Random House, Vintage Books, 1961.

CRD   *Critique de la Raison Dialectique*, I, Paris: Gallimard, 1960

DGL   *The Devil and the Good Lord*, and two other plays (*Nekrassov, Kean*). The first was translated by Kitty Black; the latter two by Sylvia and George Leeson. New York: The Philosophical Library, 1957.

E   *The Emotions: Outline of a Theory*, translated by Bernard Frechtman. New York: Philosophical Library, 1948.

HN   *Hope Now*, Jean-Paul Sartre and Benny Levy, translated by Adrian van den Hoven, with an introduction by Ronald Aronson. Chicago: University of Chicago Press, 1996.

IF   *La Idiot de la famille*, 3 volumes. Paris: Gallimard, 1971, 1975; my translations.

LPE   *Literary and Philosophical Essays*, translated by Annette Michelson, New York: Random House, Vintage Books, 1949.

N   *Nausea*, translated by Lloyd Alexander. New York: New Directions, 1964.

NE   *No Exit* and three other plays (*The Flies, Dirty Hands, The Respectful Prostitute*). The first two were translated by Stuart Gilbert and the latter two by Lionel Abel. New York: Random House, Vintage Books, 1949.

PI   *The Psychology of the Imagination*, translator not identified. New York: Citadel Press, 3d edition, 1965.

SG   *Saint Genet: Actor and Martyr*, translated by Bernard Frechtman. New York: New American Library, 1971.

SI   *Situations*, I. Paris: Gallimard, 1947; my translations.

St   *Situations*, translated by Benita Eisler. New York: George Braziller, 1965

SM   *Search for a Method*, translated by Hazel Barnes. New York: Random House, Vintage Books, 1963.

TE   *The Transcendence of the Ego*, translated by Forrest Williams and Robert Kirkpatrick. New York: Farrar, Straus and Giroux, 1957.

T&E   *Truth and Existence*, translated by Adrian van den Hoven. Chicago: University of Chicago Press, 1992.

TS   *Troubled Sleep*, translated by Gerard Hopkins. New York: Bantam, 1968.

W   *The Words*, translated by Bernard Frechtman. New York: Fawcett, 1966.

WD   *The War Diaries of Jean-Paul Sartre; November* 1939—*March* 1940, translated by Quintin Hoare. New York: Pantheon Books, 1985.

Other Works

Anderson, Thomas C. *Sartre's Two Ethics*. Chicago: Open Court, 1993.

Charmé, Stuart. *Meaning and Myth in the Study of Lives*. Philadelphia: University of Pennsylvania Press, 1984.

Cohen-Solal, Annie. *Sartre: A Life,* translated by Annie Cancogni. New York: Pantheon, 1987.

Desan, Wilfrid. *The Marxism of Jean-Paul Sartre.* New York: Doubleday Anchor, 1966.

Jeanson, Francis. *Le Problème moral et la pensée de Sartre.* Paris: Editions du Seuil, 1965.

King, Thomas M. *Sartre and the Sacred.* Chicago: University of Chicago Press, 1974.

Matczak, S. A. *God and Modern Philosophy.* A collection with an article by Thomas M. King, "The Atheism of Jean-Paul Sartre," 851–64. New York: Learned Books, 1976.

Part II
Six with a Judging Faculty as Dominant

4 St. Augustine: A Long and Troubled Conversion
The Search for the Repressed and Integration

Augustine as F: Augustine explains the title of his *Confessions:* to confess is simply "to lay open our feelings [*affectum*]" to God (*C*, 257). So the *Confessions* tell abundantly of Augustine's feelings: "This, my God, is what I feel when I hear your Scripture" (*C*, 293); one's "feelings vary" (*C*, 284). As a child, "I desired to express my inner feelings," "to give birth to what I was feeling" (*C*, 25, 32); as a youth, "I lived and I felt [*sentiebam*]," and a book "altered my way of feeling [*affectum*]" (*C*, 38, 56). Jung tells of the F getting into "the feeling of feeling itself." So Augustine tells of his youth: "I was not yet in love, but I loved the idea of love. . . . Being in love with love I looked for something to love"; "I . . . loved to feel sad and went looking for something to feel sad about" (*C*, 52, 54). His life story revolves around friendships: "Human friendship, knotted in affection, is a sweet thing" (*C*, 46); "Expressions of feeling, which proceed from the hearts of those who love and are loved in return . . . were like a kindling fire to melt our souls together," and all one wants from a friend is "demonstrations of good feeling" (*C*, 78). Speaking "out of the natural feelings" (F) of his soul, he felt "too weak to discover truth [T] by pure reason" (*C*, 190). His *Confessions* contains abundant accounts of weeping: *C*, 30, 31, 75, 78, 91, 132, 194, 206, 207, 210, 242, 249; he tells of weeping even while discussing philosophy (*HL*, 259, 268, 383). Life itself is concerned "with the affections of the heart" (*CI*, 39). For Augustine's Quaternity, see figure 4.1. Augustine's Myers-Briggs type would be ESFJ.

T
Truth/Number/Measure
Eternity/Timeless
Reason

N	Trinity/Word	S
Fitting	Wisdom/Truth	Beautiful
	Happy-Life	

F Dominant
Good/Feelings
Extension/Time/Space
Memory/Authority

Figure 4.1

I. Augustine's Conversion and the Finding of Truth

St. Augustine was born in Tagaste in North Africa in 354. As a boy he was greatly taken by literature, history, and fiction, but he hated arithmetic, a subject often associated with the T: "'One and one make two; two and two make four' was a horrible kind of singsong to me" (*C*, 32). Though he was much involved with his feelings, at the age of nineteen he read a text of Cicero's and was suddenly surprised by an interest in philosophy/Wisdom/Truth; this could be seen as an appearance of his T. He explained, Cicero "urged on and inflamed me with a passionate zeal to love and seek and obtain and embrace and hold fast wisdom itself, whatever it might be" (*C*, 57). His passionate zeal was awakened, but he was not ready for wisdom and soon became involved with other concerns; he felt estranged from wisdom. "A mist was cutting me off, my God, from the pure brightness of your truth" (*C*, 45); the mist suggests the T is in his

Unconscious. Augustine took a mistress, followed his ambition, and life went on much as before.

As a young man Augustine spent nine years with the dualistic religion of the Manichees. He was fascinated by the way they called out to him, "Truth, Truth," and promised to explain all things by reason. They spoke in veiled language and Augustine "thought they were concealing in their veils some important secret which they would later divulge" (*HL*, 47). Augustine reflected back on his time with them: "O Truth, Truth, how I panted for you even then deep down in the marrow of my soul" (*C*, 58). At this time Truth was veiled and the hunger for it was buried deep in the marrow of his soul.

At age twenty-six or twenty-seven Augustine wrote several books on "The Beautiful and the Fitting." The books no longer exist, but Augustine tells of their content:

> I saw that in bodies themselves there was one sort of beauty which comes from a thing constituting a whole, and another sort of grace which comes from the right and apt relationship of one thing to another, such as one part of the body to the whole body. . . . I defined and distinguished the beautiful as being that which is beautiful in itself and the fitting as being that which derives its grace from its appropriateness to something else. (*C*, 83, 85)

The passage could be seen as Augustine dealing with an object *in itself* (S, Beauty) and an object *in relationship* (N, Fitting). That could mean that he was passing beyond his Dominant and was differentiating his Auxiliaries, the S and the N. Jung sees this Differentiation of the Auxiliaries as the beginning of a move to differentiate the missing Fourth. Augustine claimed the ideas for these books sprang spontaneously from the depths of his heart: "Sweet truth, I was straining these ears to try to hear your inner melody" (*C*, 87).

Augustine was distressed by the lack of discipline among his pupils in the African schools, so he went to Rome. Soon he would take a teaching appointment in Milan and his mother would follow him there. But, when she arrived, she found him "despairing of ever discovering the *truth*." For he had discovered "how abject and helpless the soul is before it learns to cling to the solidity of truth." Such a soul is adrift and "carried this way and that, changing its course now here, now there; its light is clouded over and it cannot see the truth" (*C*, 84). The image of being adrift while truth is clouded over again suggests the troubled journey into the Unconscious: "I searched through shadows and on slippery ways. . . . I had come to the depths of the sea, and I had no confidence or hope of discovering the truth" (C, lll). He would vary the image, but still it is truth he is seeking:

> Thus there grew up before me a forest yielding no way of escape and into which I was loath to force my way; amid these circumstances my mind was unceasingly disturbed with the desire of finding truth. . . . In such perils there remained no other alternative than to implore the help of Divine Providence with tears and piteous supplications, and this I did unremittingly. (IS, 416)

Socrates offered a prayer as he set out searching for justice in a forest; St. Augustine also offered a prayer as he set out searching for truth in a forest. In each case the assistance must come from a heavenly source (see the final passages on Sartre above).

At age thirty, Augustine reflected on his busy life and considered making a change: "I must give up all this vanity and emptiness and devote myself entirely to the search for truth" (C, 128). Accordingly, he gathered regularly with a group of like-minded friends to converse about philosophy, yet he continued his teaching duties.

For many years Augustine believed that Christian writings had nothing to say to him, for he thought they spoke of God as a physical object with a body. He tells of always knowing better than that. But through listening to the sermons of St. Ambrose, bishop of Milan, he learned of the spiritual sense of scripture. Hearing that the Christian Church did not teach that God was physical, he took his first interest in Christianity. But though he wanted to know of a God that was not physical, he could not understand how anything not physical could be real. In other words, he believed God to be immaterial but could not conceive of a reality apart from space and time:

> I was still forced to think of you as a corporeal substance occupying space, whether infused into this world or diffused through the infinite space outside the world. . . . And the reason was that if I tried to imagine something as not being in space it seemed to me to be nothing, and by "nothing" I mean absolutely nothing, not even a void. For if a body is taken out of its place and the place remains empty of any kind of body, whether of earth, water, air, or sky, it will still be an empty

place, a "nothing" that is nevertheless in a spatial context. . . . So, Life of my life, I thought of you as an immensity through infinite space, interfused everywhere throughout the whole mass of the universe and extending beyond it in every direction for distances without end, so that the earth should have you, the sky should have you, all things should have you, and they should be bounded in you, but you would be boundless. (C, 136)

This passage is quoted at length, as extension (place/quantity, space/time) is associated with F. Augustine is not able to conceive of anything existing apart from "place," from spatial or temporal extensions, for his "mind was intent on the things which were in space" (C, 146). At this time he thought of the mind itself as "a rarified form of body in space" (C, 106). So his mind "made for itself a God to fill the infinite distances of all space" (C, 152).

Augustine came upon the writings of the Platonists (largely the works of Plotinus) and there found the advice given Socrates: Know thyself. Feeling the support of divine assistance, he was able to enter within and find an incorporeal Light blazing upon him and before which he "trembled in love and dread." Though trembling, he could ask the Light a fundamental question concerning his dilemma: "Is *Truth* therefore nothing because it is not extended through any kind of space, whether finite or infinite?" (C, 150). And from afar he seemed to hear the divine response: "I am that I am."

The event continued the somewhat philosophical conversion that began when he read Cicero many years before. Augustine asked whether truth was extended, and his question brought up two elements associated with the T: truth and nonextension. In this moment of illumination Augustine realized that Truth is real, even though it is not extended; it cannot be "located." He realizes God is the same. Hearing the voice in his heart, he could no longer doubt: "I had discovered that above my changing mind was the unchangeable and true eternity of truth" (C, 154). Both "Eternity" and "Truth" are apart from the world of the F, the world of feelings, extension, and time. At this time Augustine fell into a deep sleep and woke to find God "infinite in a different way," that is, "not in the sense of being diffused through space." He looked around him at other things only to see them "bounded in you [God], not in a spatial sense, but because your being contains everything in the hand of your truth" (C, 152).[1]

Augustine summed up what he learned from the Platonists: "They taught me to seek for a truth which was incorporeal" (C, 156). His awakening enabled him to see a whole new world, but he could not enter it as his "slavery to lust" had become a habit he could not break, so he could not devote himself to philosophy. He had a divided will: "So my two wills, one old, one new, one carnal, one spiritual, were in conflict, and they wasted my soul by their discord." But he could no longer claim he did not see the truth, for he had seen it with great clarity (C, 165), yet he seemed unable to change his way of life. "I was detained by woman's charm and the lure of honors" (HL, 48).

The final event in the conversion of Augustine occurred in August of 386 when he was thirty-one. A friend, Pontitianus, dropped by and saw the epistles of St. Paul on Augustine's reading table. Surprised at his interest in Christianity, the friend began telling of St. Anthony of Egypt and the desert monks. He then told what he recently heard while traveling in Germany: two members of the emperor's court were walking in the woods when they came upon a small hermit's hut that contained a copy of Athanasius's *Life of St. Anthony*. They had long struggled to achieve standing at court, but upon reading the life of Anthony they renounced this struggle, for they could be friends of God that very moment. They decided to become monks. Hearing of their liberation produced turmoil in the heart of Augustine:

> you, Lord, while he was speaking, were turning me around so that I could see myself; you took me from behind my own back, which was where I had put myself during the time I did not want to be observed by myself, and you set me in front of my own face, so that I could see how foul a sight I was. . . . If I tried to look away from myself, Pontitianus still went on with his story, and again you were setting me in front of myself, forcing me to look into my own face. (C, 173)

It was more than twelve years since Cicero had inspired him to search for wisdom, yet he could not devote himself to the task as he could not renounce his lust. Yet now he was hearing of two young men—less educated than he—who responded without delay, and they "were given wings to fly."

When his friend left, Augustine felt he no longer had an excuse.

Unlearned men had achieved victory, and he, with all his learning, kept delaying because he could not control his passions. He began "boiling with indignation" at himself and hurried out to a garden behind his house. He tells of an Enantiodromia with his will "turning and twisting this way and that . . . a will half maimed, struggling, with one part rising and another part falling"; his commitment to the Truth was in conflict with his passions. He only needed to will to go to God and he would already arrive, but he found the will "is not entire in itself when it gives the order, and therefore its order is not obeyed." He was divided against himself with two wills "because one of them is not entire, and one has what the other lacks" (C, 177).

From day to day, Augustine had postponed accepting the chastity he judged integral to Christian life. But finally, while weeping in the garden behind his house, he was able to say, "Now, now, let it be now!" With this the voices of lust were softened, yet he still hesitated to take the final step. He seemed to see before him the chaste dignity of Continence as a feminine presence:

> she was calm and serene, cheerful without wantonness, and it was in truth and honor that she was enticing me to come to her without hesitation, stretching out to receive and to embrace me with those holy hands of hers, full of such multitudes of good examples. . . . in them all was Continence herself, not barren, but a fruitful mother of children. . . . She smiled at me and there was encouragement in her smile. (C, 181)

Within Augustine a tempest was raging and without a downpour of tears. "Now, now, let it be now!" He flung himself on the ground under a fig tree and let the tears freely fall. "Why not now? Why not finish this very hour with my uncleanness?"

Then Augustine heard—or thought he heard—a child's voice saying, "Take it and read. Take it and read." The words seemed like a divine command telling him to read the text of St. Paul. So he hurried back inside his house and picked up the text. Selecting a passage at random he read: "Not in rioting and drunkenness, not in chambering and wantonness, not in strife and envying: but put ye on the Lord Jesus Christ, and make not provision for the flesh in concupiscence." With this, all his hesitations were swept away. He quickly went to tell his mother and her joy was great. Then with amazement he considered what had happened and wondered where his own freedom had been all the years he was bound by lust and ambition and unable to live the chaste and philosophic life he had wanted to live.

The appearance of Continence as an entrancing lady within him is an example of what Jung would call the Anima. The Anima is a fascinating lady who often has contradictory qualities; so Augustine's lady is Continence, yet a fruitful mother; she is serene, yet cheerful; she was alluring him to chastity.

II. The Struggle of Conversion Continues

The account of Augustine's conversion presented above is found in his *Confessions*, a text written more than a decade after the event. In reading only this account, one would think his conversion was complete with his decision to observe chastity in August 386. But Augustine has left a series of writings from the months that followed his conversion, and these show that his philosophic struggles continued. He needed time to appropriate what had happened and he developed breathing difficulties, so a month after his decision he quit teaching and took his mother and philosophic friends to a mountain retreat at Cassiciacum, an unidentified location not far from Milan. There they would devote their attention to philosophy, and, at the insistence of Augustine, careful accounts were written of all that was said. Augustine led the group in prayer, yet he insisted he wanted to work with reason alone. It seems that at Cassiciacum he was trying to get a hold on the fascinating Truth (T) he had found, a truth he would identify with number and measure (HL, 82). A Jungian could see him as spending the time differentiating his T and thus integrating it into his conscious mind.

Augustine explained his going to the mountains as an attempt to set aside his needless desires, recover his senses, and return to himself (BV, 137). A passage from Jung might clarify this return to self: "[One] has to reckon very seriously with an acceptance of the inferior, because undifferentiated, functions. No attempt at mediation will be successful if it does not understand how to release the energies of the inferior functions and lead them towards differentiation" (PT, 86). The seeking of a philosophic truth at Cassiciacum could be seen as an attempt to differentiate the T and "release the energies" it contained so that he would no longer live a divided life.

As the Cassiciacum conversations begin, Augustine compares those present to seafarers making their way to the port of *philosophy*. He tells of some philosophers like himself "wandering in the midst of fog." He encountered a tempest and did not yet feel "free of the mists which could confuse my course" (*HL*, 47). Now the mists refer to a basic philosophic problem that continually recurs during his talks at Cassiciacum: Can we know truth at all? The Platonists had played an important part in Augustine's conversion, but many within the Platonic tradition (the Academics) had maintained that we cannot know truth, so they suspended all assent: "the Academics for a long while steered my course amid the waves while my helm had to meet every wind" (*HL*, 47). At one time, their skepticism had hindered Augustine from looking for truth. But now he would answer the Academics; he claimed they continued to regard some statements as "truth-like," so he asked how they could identify something as "truth-like," if they did not know truth?

At Cassiciacum Augustine saw his search for truth as "a necessary and important occupation," yet progress was slow and he spent his time "cleansing" himself from vain and pernicious opinions (*HL*, 142; recall that the F has many opinions). The Truth for Augustine was highly personal, for he claimed one could discover Truth only if one entered philosophy with one's entire being (*HL*, 142). He saw himself so driven by the love of finding truth he often lay awake through much of the night (*HL*, 244). At times Augustine's conversations with his friends show they have truth firmly established, but these are followed by other times when truth is compared to Proteus and slips from their grasp (*HL*, 180, 182, 319). He would reach impressive conclusions, only to say he held them "with more misgiving than assurance" (*L*, 5). The soul finds it difficult to approach the mysterious presence of truth: "It [the soul] trembles, pants, and burns with love, and, driven back from the light of truth, returns, not from choice but from exhaustion, to its familiar darkness" (*WL*, 11).

At this time Augustine believed Christ to be the truth he was seeking, but it was a matter of belief and not knowledge. So he seemed unable to see what he was after (*HL*, 260–61). He speaks at length in praise of reason, calling it "a mental operation capable of distinguishing and connecting the things that are learned" (*HL*, 308). This "distinguishing and connecting" is the work of a logician; in praising reason, Augustine was adjusting to his T.

Augustine told of rejecting arithmetic as a child and hating the singsong of number. But now he was seeking number and claiming that it is present in all branches of study: poetry, music, and astrology; "all things are seen as presented to reason as *numerically proportioned.*" Reason "came to feel that it possessed great power, and that it owed all its power to numerical proportions. Something wondrous urged it on. And it [reason] began to suspect that it itself was perhaps the very number by which all things are numbered" (*HL,* 319). Thus, number, "that most hidden something by which we enumerate," would be "the discloser of universal truth." Numbers "have a real existence of their own" (*C,* 222), and it is by our ability to grasp the nature of numbers that the human is greater than the animals (*HL,* 326).

After hating arithmetic, Augustine is now discovering the wonder of "sempiternal number" and "the divine numbers of wisdom" (*IS,* 333). Numbers are said to dwell in a "shrine" or a "sanctuary" of their own (*T,* 140, 151–52); this could be seen as the rejected T dwelling in a sacred place—the Unconscious. Jung used a biblical image to tell of the missing function being brought back to consciousness: the stone that was rejected has become the cornerstone. For Augustine, the Reason/number/truth he had rejected as a child is becoming the cornerstone of his mind.

At Cassiciacum and throughout the rest of his life Augustine was fascinated by number, but he does not speak of numbers in a familiar way as would a T. For Augustine, numbers are wondrous symbols filled with hidden meanings.[2] He alludes to major philosophic issues concerning eternity and the soul, and then adds, "Whoever has grasped the meaning of simple and intelligible numbers will readily understand these matters" (*HL,* 321). A contemporary critic speaks of Augustine's "curious ideas about numbers," for numbers were seen as strange and magical symbols, not practical tools (see also *CG,* 375). As Augustine had disliked arithmetic as a child only to exalt number in his later years, so as a child he had disliked grammar. Later, in regaining his missing T, he would speak of "the almost heavenly power and nature of grammar" (*C,* 30; *HL,* 322). Grammar is the structure or form (T) of language; it once was rejected, but now, filled with "almost heavenly power," it is being restored.

Shortly after returning from Cassiciacum, Augustine writes of two restless nights when he encountered his reason as a partner in dialogue:

> While I was turning over in my mind many and divers matters . . . all at once a voice spoke to me—whether it was myself or another inside or outside of me I do not know, for that is the very thing that I am endeavoring to find out. Reason thereupon spoke to me as follows. (*HL*, 343)

Here he meets his own reason as a somewhat alien voice, an inner identity with whom he is summoned to speak. Jung sees such a dialogue as an important step towards healing and even developed techniques for encouraging the dialogue. When the opposing functions ignore each other, the person is divided, but when they are brought into dialogue a reconciliation is approaching. In *The Soliloquies*, Augustine (F) is able to dialogue with his reason (T), and this turns out to be a difficult and painful process. As it begins, reason advises him to pray. Following Augustine's lengthy and impassioned prayer, reason asks him what he wants to know. He answers, "I desire to know God and the soul." Reason asks, "Nothing more?" "Absolutely nothing" (*HL*, 350; for passages telling of a similar desire see also 351, 370, 381, 392, 412). Reason is further identified as the sight of his soul (*HL*, 360; *IS*, 86).

Augustine's quest for God and soul has brought him into a painful, personal struggle. Yet Augustine insisted on the philosophical nature of his quest: "I am searching for what I am to *know*, not what I am to believe" (*HL*, 352). He is searching for the T, not the F (belief, opinion). He wants to embrace Wisdom; he tells of wanting to see Truth "with no veil between." To do this he is willing to surrender everything to Reason, "Lead me, drive me, where you will, through what means you will, how you will. Demand from me whatever difficult and arduous tasks you choose" (*HL*, 374). In Jungian terms, the Hero (Consciousness) is willing to sacrifice everything to find his missing lady, the Anima (in Augustine's Latin, reason [*ratio*] is a feminine noun). Reason responds by reminding him of his weaknesses and the hero is brought down to size. He cries out, "Why do you torment me; why do you probe so deeply, why do you go down so low?" But reason rebukes his emotional excess, "Restrain your tears and control your feelings" (*HL*, 376). Finally reason leads him through a series of tedious deductions. The passages seem to tell of the T differentiating itself: "If this world will endure forever, it is true that the world will endure forever," and "If it will not endure, is it not likewise true that it will not endure?" "If it is a tree, I think you will not deny that it is a true tree," etc. Such passages abound in this essay, and they seem to be first attempts at strict rational thinking; they show Augustine discovering logic and the a priori judgment, that which the T has always known. Since he has lived by his feelings, it seems he must discover the elements of logical thinking, and reason even suggests that "the science of argumentation is *truth itself*" (*HL*, 419). Augustine is going through a painful time of self discovery; Jung would speak of the process as "a turning away from life and a descent to the *deus absconditus*, who possesses qualities very different from those of the God who shines by day" (*PT*, 253).

This is Augustine, many months after his conversion, still seeking the hidden God and telling of never experiencing such obscurity. He fears that reason will question him further and asks how reason could exist in the soul with so few people knowing it is there. This is the question of the F who is beginning to locate the buried T (a T beginning to locate his Feelings would ask how we can have feelings that we do not feel). Reason tells Augustine of Truth being buried, but adds that those interested in finding it "cannot contain themselves until they behold in all its breadth and fullness the whole countenance of Truth, whose splendor already glows" (*HL*, 423). Again, Truth has a wondrous quality; the phrases also suggest that Truth dwells in the Unconscious.

Augustine objects that reason has wandered about, luring him on while laying snares for him. Having made several unsuccessful tries at obtaining Truth, he still feels helpless: "For we were seeking to discover what truth is, and I see that we have, even at the present time, not been able to search it out in this forest of things, after having explored almost all the bypaths. What are we to do?" (*HL*, 410–11) Augustine and reason reach a minimal understanding concerning the immortality of the soul and end their dialogue. The dialogue has used the imagery Jung associates with the unconscious (a search for truth in the forest of things, etc.). When Jung tells of coming to grips with the Anima, he claims "one finds behind her cruel sport a superior knowledge" (*ACU*, 31). In the *Soliloquies* Augustine has been searching for that knowledge, only to find himself a victim of the "cruel sport." This essay, written eight months after his garden experience, seems to be the last written text telling of his current struggles. The dialogue can easily be read as an account of Augustine searching for his missing Function.

Both the *Confessions* and the Cassiciacum discussions say much concerning the "happy life" *(beata vita)*. Augustine tells of three false approaches to happiness, but adds, "As I see it, however, a fourth alternative remains in which the happy life may be found" (*WL*, 6).[3] This separate Fourth tells of the happy life found in God who is both wisdom and truth (*WL*, 20); then the passage speaks of the happy life as the perfect love of God. At the time of Augustine, as at the time of Plato before him, there was a common agreement that there were four virtues, but in writing as an F Augustine presents them as four forms of love:

> For in speaking of virtue as fourfold, one refers, as I understand it, to the various dispositions of love itself. Therefore, these four virtues . . . I would not hesitate to define as follows: temperance is love giving itself wholeheartedly to that which is loved, fortitude is love enduring all things willingly for the sake of that which is loved, justice is love serving alone that which is loved and thus ruling rightly, and prudence is love choosing wisely between that which helps it and that which hinders it. (*WL*, 22)[4]

But to come to these blessed virtues one must use "all the powers of the soul." By doing so one can attain "to the heights of wisdom and truth, the enjoyment of which is nothing other than the happy life". (*WL*, 28–29)

III. The Union of Opposites

Throughout the essays that were written in the months following Augustine's conversion, there are abundant appeals to circles and squares. These could be seen as the mandalas (circles) that Jung would find in the troubled dreams of his patients; Jung calls them "the traditional antidote of chaotic states of mind" (*ACU*, 273, 18). They appear to those "confronted with the problem of opposites in human nature and are consequently disoriented; or again in schizophrenics whose view of the world has become confused owing to the invasion of incomprehensible contents from the unconscious" (*ACU*, 387–88). Jung understands their appearance as an attempt at self-healing; they are attempts to hold together the disordered elements that are dividing the personality. So Augustine would speak of "gathering myself together from the scattered fragments into which I was broken and dissipated" (*C*, 40).

At his mountain retreat at Cassiciacum, Augustine was trying to heal his inner division and, like the patients of Jung, he speaks frequently of circles and squares, figures mentioned many times in the dialogue Augustine had with his reason (considered above; see *HL*, 355, 356, 357, 420, 424); the last of these passages tells of lines being drawn from the circumference of a circle to its center—this could be seen as the move toward a reconciliation of opposites at a central point. (Jung tells of the power of the circle as it suggests a balance: "through the construction of a central point to which everything is related" [*ACU*, 388]). In one of the dialogues of this period the account of circles and squares runs for ten pages: there a square is said to be better than a triangle (as 4 is better than 3), but a circle surpasses all other plane figures and the center point of the circle is even likened to the soul (*IS*, 71–80, 85, 88, 89).[5] He speaks of a circle and of "drawing lines from it to the center" (*HL*, 424). (For Jung the Center is where the Transcendent Function will appear.) For Augustine the center of a circle is that "by which the other parts are mutually measured; it rules over all, as it were, by a kind of law of equality." He then compares the circle to the soul and urges that the soul return to its self, to its own center (*IS*, 242). The Wisdom is within, but to get to it people must know the way, "the way to descend from themselves to Him, and by Him to ascend to Him" (*C*, 93; see Jung, *ACU*, 19 for descent and ascending; a theme that will also be seen to occur in Teilhard).

Before his conversion Augustine spoke abstractly of a unity that would contain "the nature of truth and the supreme good" (*C*, 85). But this unity first appears as an inner reality in *De Libero Arbitrio*, a work probably written in 387–88, a year or so after the time of his dramatic conversion. Here he tells of the Wisdom to which he aspired and defines it as "the truth in which the highest good is seen and possessed"; he repeats, "the truth wherein the highest good is seen and possessed"; and the true and the good are again united as Wisdom when he explains: no one is happy "except by the highest good which is found in the contemplation and possession of that truth which we call wisdom" (*T*, 134). Here Wisdom can be seen as the synthesis wherein the true and the good (the T and the F) are reconciled. Truth is said to water one from within; the treacherous sea has been crossed and the opposing Function makes its power available to the conscious mind. Wisdom is now his possession (and the possession of every wise man). Wisdom "shows all things good that are true." Wisdom is not simply number or argumentation alone, it is the reconciliation of truth and value (T and F, the True and the Good). Wisdom is no longer the elusive Proteus, the Truth hidden in a forest, in a mist, behind a veil, or in the depths of the sea. Now Truth is perceived and held (*cernitur et teneretur*). "Wisdom will shine forth to you from its seat within [*ipsa interiora sede*]." In terms that suggest the F and the T Augustine defines the Happy Life: "To *love* Him and to *know* Him, that is the happy life" (*T*, 60).

In the *Confessions* Augustine would address God as "the one true and good landlord and farmer of this field of yours, my heart" (*C*, 43). And he would exclaim in prayer: "O eternal truth and true love and beloved eternity" (*C*, 149). That is, Truth and Love (T and F) are joined in a beloved (F) eternity (T). But much later, when he was writing of the Trinity, he would see the Trinity embodying this synthesis of T and F:

> Or does this Wisdom, which is called God, not understand itself and not love itself? . . . Or are we to think that the Wisdom which God is, knows other things and does not know itself, or loves other things and does not love itself? And if it is absurd and impious to say or to believe such things, then, behold, there is a trinity, namely, wisdom, the knowledge of itself, and the love of itself. For so do we find a trinity in man, that is, the mind, and the knowledge by which it knows itself, and the love by which it loves itself. (*Tr*, 464)

The passage again tells of a reconciliation, for it shows wisdom containing both knowledge and love. This same study of the Trinity would also see opposites united in certain words:

> The word, therefore, which we now wish to discern and study is knowledge with love. Hence, when the mind knows and loves itself, its word is joined to it by love. And because the mind loves its knowledge and knows its love, then the word is in the love and love in the word, and both are in him who loves and who speaks. (*Tr*, 285)

Augustine's *City of God* would also pick up on the Trinitarian image within. There he would see his mind as incapable of error when it knows his being, his knowing, and his loving: "I am assured both that I am, and that I know this; and these two I love" (*CG*, 371–72).

It can be noted that Augustine is a Judger (J), so the opposites that are united in him to form the Jungian Self are the opposites located on the J axis, F and T (not those of the P axis, N and S, as was the case in earlier presentations of Plato, Locke, and Sartre). Accordingly, Augustine has Knowledge and Love joined in Being to tell of the Trinity; while Plato had Other and Same joined in Being to form a trinity of sorts ("out of the three made one" [II, 17]).[6]

Augustine came to see that Truth was abiding within him and teaching him. Many times he would use Truth or Wisdom or Teacher as a name for Christ or God; he would address the Father saying, "Your Son, the Truth, has said. . . ." Augustine would claim that in hearing someone speak his inner sense for truth would tell him whether what he heard was true—almost like the inner voice of Socrates that would advise him at critical moments. (Like Socrates, he tells of divine ideas within us.) Augustine has a Teacher within him telling him whether he is hearing the truth. Should someone interpret the Scriptures for him he asks, "But how should I know whether what he said was true? And if I did know it, would it be from him that I knew it? No it would not; it would be from inside me, from that inner house of my thought, that Truth . . . would say: 'He is speaking the truth,' and at once I would be sure" (C, 260).

So Augustine would call upon this inner voice: "Let Truth, the light of my heart, speak to me." "Speak to me! Teach and instruct me!" (C, 290). We ordinarily think of learning as coming from a teacher in school, but any external teacher can only bring one to ask the right questions so that the student might better "hear that Teacher who teaches within" (T, 55). We are to consult "the Truth that presides over the mind itself from within," and by listening to the inner Truth the student becomes "an inward disciple of the truth" (T, 56). Augustine explains that "the nature of the soul [is] to live in union with the Divine Ideas." In making a true judgment, one "does so in the light of those Ideas with which it is united" (T, 177–78). Such is the truth buried within that Augustine has finally discovered, with many Platonic overtones, though Augustine abundantly criticized Plato.

Augustine would return to Africa and there become bishop of Hippo; he became well known as a writer and preacher. A number of his sermons have come down to us, and there is a fascinating detail from his Christmas preaching that would suggest Truth has risen from the Unconscious. Augustine left us fifteen Christmas sermons. Unlike the Christmas sermons of today that tell of the shepherds coming to Mary and Joseph in the stable, and so forth, the sermons of Augustine hardly consider these Gospel events. Rather, nine of Augustine's talks develop the scriptural text, "Truth is sprung out of the earth" (a phrase taken from the Latin translation of Psalm 85:11).[7] Augustine's fascination with the phrase would suggest that, for him, Truth has come forth from the Unconscious, the unlikely place from where Christ the Teacher has emerged.

Throughout his life Augustine had an ongoing concern with extension (place/quantity/time/space), a concern of the F. Cicero had awakened him briefly to an interest in Wisdom (a timeless reality), but later he could not imagine how anything apart from time and space could still be real. He told of his situation: "The very force of truth itself was staring me in the face, but I turned my panting mind away from what was incorporeal and concentrated on line and color and swelling magnitudes" (C, 85). He concentrated on extended objects and tried to conceive of God in physical terms: God was like an ocean, or like a mass of bodies, or like a fine vapor. All the terms tell of extension, "swelling magnitudes." Hardly had he developed such notions than he realized it was only his mind creating "a god to fill the infinite distances of all space" (C, 152). But this situation changed with his reading of the Platonists, for following their advice he was able to discover Truth within himself, and Truth was a reality without extension. Amazed to find a Reality that cannot be situated, he came to know a God apart from place: "Place there is none, we go backwards and forwards, and there is no place" (C, 234). God is apart from all space: "How absurd it is to believe that God is contained within the boundaries of any place although it be infinite" (WL, 16).

Augustine will likewise play with the idea of God apart from time, yet "all times are in you. . . . all things of tomorrow and after tomorrow, all things of yesterday and before yesterday, you will accomplish today and you have accomplished today" (C, 23). "Your today is eternity. . . . You made all times and before all times you are; nor was there ever a time in which there was no time" (C, 267). By his discovery of God he had found a reality that was timeless, unextended in time or space (C, 150). He had found something of which by itself the F cannot conceive: timeless numbers and timeless truth.

One of the essays written immediately following his conversion is titled "On the Quantity of the Soul." The essay tries to show that the soul (like God) is a reality that cannot be quantified; the soul is not "long or wide or anything like that" (*IS*, 128). By this claim Augustine is trying to argue that the soul is beyond extension (F); his soul is eternal while his ego is in time. At Cassiciacum he often told of seeking to know "God and the soul." And the soul turns out to be like God. For just as God is without "parts extended in length and breadth, with size and bulk and separated parts," so is the soul. The soul is made in the image and likeness of God (*C*, 60).

But though Augustine will often present God, the soul, and number as apart from time, he is also concerned with the unity between eternal number (T) and time (F). This is evident in the set of philosophical essays written immediately after his conversion. They were concerned with the "big questions" of philosophy: our ability to know truth, what is happiness, how can there be evil if God is good, and so forth. But the longest of these essays concerns music. The work was not completed, but the entire text concerns only rhythm. Augustine had only a limited interest in music (*C*, 242), so how explain his extended concern (210 pages!) with rhythm during a troubled time? Consider his surprising definition of music: it is the science of measuring well (*IS*, 175). The definition tells only of rhythm, and rhythm is the joining of eternal Number to Time. And that is Augustine's project during his crisis: unite the T and the F. In his own words, he is concerned with "number-traces belonging to time-intervals" (*IS*, 324).

"On Music" is presented as a dialogue with a master speaking to his disciple. And again, this essay at the time of Integration has much concern with three and four:

> Master: . . . those three numbers whose harmony you were wondering at could only have been brought together in the same relation by the number four. . . . So that now, not one, two, three only, but one, two, three, four is the most connected progression of numbers. . . . Tell me now, one and three make what?
>
> Disciple: Four.
>
> Master: Well, two, the lone middle number, can't be joined with anything but itself, can it? And so tell me now what twice two makes?
>
> Disciple: Four.
>
> Master: So then, the mean agrees with the extremes and the extremes with the mean. And, therefore, just as there is a certain virtue in three

in that it is placed in order after one and two, while consisting of one and two, so there is a certain virtue in four in that it falls in counting after one, two, and three, while consisting of one and three, or twice two. . . .

Master: Try and see whether the property we attributed to the number four can be found in other numbers or not? [It cannot so] . . . you certainly see that from one to four is the most complete progression, either from the point of view of odd and even numbers, since three is the first whole odd number and four the first whole even (this subject was treated a little while ago). Or because one and two are the beginnings and seeds, as it were, of numbers, three is made from; and this accounts for three numbers. And when they are brought together by proportion, the number four appears and comes to be, and is joined to them by rule, to become the final number of the measured progression we seek. (IS, 200–202; additional praise of Four occurs later in this dialogue [e.g.: "there could be no other progression than from one to four either in feet or times." [IS, 212–13])

This lengthy passage telling of the wonders of Four is found in the treatise on music, a treatise that was to show that rhythm consists in numbers found in time.

For Augustine poetry is musical speech, and he would see it leading us to things divine by an orderly path and steps of ascent. Rhythm is the fourth and final step of this ascent: "Reason understood, therefore, that in this fourth step of ascent—whether in particular rhythm or in modulation in general—numeric proportions held sway and produced the finished product" (HL, 317–18).

At this period (shortly after his conversion in the garden), Augustine also intended to write treatises on other liberal arts. He seems to have begun some, but if he did write them they are lost. But what he would say is evident from a treatise written together with his study of music, "Free Choice of the Will." He speaks of pantomime, dance:

Ask what there is in pantomime [dance] to cause delight, and number will answer that it is present there. Now examine the beauty of a graceful body, and number will be found to be at work in space. Examine beauty in bodily movement, and you will see how number plays a role in the proper timing. (T, 150)

In a similar way Augustine would interpret other forms of art:

> Even men who create beauty in working with bodily materials make use of numbers in their art and fashion their products in accordance with them. While producing their work, they manipulate their hands and tools until what is being formed externally is made as perfectly as possible to conform with the inward light of number. (*T*, 151–52)

This play between number/measure/form (T) and extension (F) is considered at length in the *Confessions*. In considering the creation of the world Augustine wonders how "the Word which is eternally spoken" could be spoken in time (*C*, 262). How could the world have a beginning in time, while eternal Reason who created it has no beginning or end (*C*, 263). He is perplexed about measuring time, for what he measures no longer exists (only the present exists) (*C*, 273–78). In the first nine books of the *Confessions*, Augustine gives a highly personal account of his own life. Then one is surprised to find the final four books taken up with issues relating time to eternity (measure, number). It is not evident how these books belong in a personal account. But if one sees measure as a bringing together of time and eternity, or as a bringing together of extension and number, then one can see these latter chapters telling of bringing together Augustine's F and T, and that too has a place in his confessions. The final Chapters of the *Confessions* concern the creation of the world, and many have seen them as an unsuitable ending for what had been a story of his inner life. But when seen in the context of a Jungian reading, they too would be part of Augustine's personal story.

The present consideration of Augustine tells mostly of his extended conversion, with only occasional references to works written in his later years. The later works are less philosophical and concern mostly his preaching and teaching as priest and bishop. In their impersonal instruction of others, they do not readily lend themselves to a Jungian analysis. But all the writings of Augustine, with their mixture of an impersonal Platonism (N) and his own personal deliverance shaped the culture of the West for a thousand years.

Many years after Augustine a radical change was introduced into Western philosophy through the writings of René Descartes. Like Augustine, he too was a Judger who also knew the separation between reason and extension (T and F), but, as a Dominant T, he would come to the problem of Integration very differently than Augustine.

Notes

1. Here mention is made of the "hand" of God's truth, a striking phrase; it and similar phrases in Augustine have given me some second thoughts about the close association of S and the Hand. Yet I believe it is generally the case. Consider other mentions of the hand of God in the *Confessions:* 33, 66, 84, 90, 117, 118, 146, 152, 158, 181, 130, 251, 253, 261! In partial defense, one could note in addition the many times Augustine speaks of divine speech and of listening to the divine word: "I want to hear" how God made the world; "I should lay the ears of my body open to the sounds . . . ", we "hear him and rejoice greatly at the Bridegroom's voice," etc.; "I heard your voice behind me, calling me back" (*C*, 260, 263, 290). In each case the ears are listening to statements of divine Truth. As statements they are J, that is, Judgments. Augustine claims that we begin by the words of divine authority (F, opinions of a sort), and move from there to the use of our reason (T): "There is no sounder principle in the Catholic Church than that authority would precede reason" (*WL*, 39; see other similar claims in the same work, pp. 11, 33). The same idea is put well when Augustine writes, "With regard to the acquiring of knowledge, we are of necessity led in a twofold manner: by authority and by reason. In point of time, authority is first; in the order of reality, reason is prior" (*HL*, 303). The sequence from authority to reason (F to T) is found throughout Augustine; a sequence that tells of an F on the J axis. In a consideration of the senses he considers the ears before the eyes, and hearing is primarily the hearing of speech (*HL*, 316). If he speaks of the hand of truth (*C*, 152), he can also speak of "the hand of my mouth"! (*C*, 265).

Also, Augustine has often told of rejecting sense and thereby seeing or contemplating God. This, and his frequent references to the hand, could argue that Augustine is an N not an F; it could also argue against the general thesis of this study. But these passages could be partially explained in terms of Augustine having N as a strong Auxiliary; they could also be seen as the Platonist influence on Augustine, especially at the time of his conversion. The Platonists (N) had readily available for him a highly developed vocabulary concerning things of the spirit, a vocabulary centered around the contemplative approach of the N (for a balanced account of Neo Platonism and Plotinus in Augustine, see O'Connell, pp. 18, 75–80). Augustine could be seen as adopting much of their vocabulary in trying to articulate his own experience, and the Platonists speak often of rejecting "sensation." In passing to the T Augustine tells of rejecting extended objects (F). This is so his T might appear. This is clear in a letter concerned with contemplating God. He insists: God is not "visible in any locality or space relation," he is not "distributed through portions of space," he is "without space relations," not "a corporeal God with separate parts occupying different places" (*L*, 133–64, 224–26). His character as a J is further evidenced as the visible world is seen as if it is speaking judgments to him: natural objects proclaim, "He made us," "We exist because we were created," etc. (*C*, 215, 260).

2. A text from soon after Augustine's conversion illustrates his mystical treatment of numbers; it also shows his fascination with the number four. He quotes a passage of St. Paul: "All things are yours, and you are Christ's, and Christ is God's." Since the passage of St. Paul has four elements (things, you, Christ, God), Augustine uses the occasion to develop the meaning of the number four: "If one counts from the beginning of the series, one gets 1, 2, 3 and 4. . . . Furthermore the sum of $1 + 2 + 3 + 4$ is 10. Accordingly the number 10 rightly signifies the teaching which presents God as the maker and the creature as the made. . . . Now just as the sum of $1 + 2 + 3 + 4$ is 10, so $(1 + 2 + 3 + 4)$ multiplied by 4 is 40. But suppose that the body is correctly signified by the number 4 because the body consists of the celebrated four elements (the dry and the moist, the cold and the hot), and because the three-dimensional character of the body is produced by a progression, which also is contained in the number 4." That the body is "signified by the number 4" is a theme of Jung's; in contrast Jung would have the heavenly identity signified by three. This use of four and three is found elsewhere in Augustine: "For a trinity is present in the Creator, while the number 7 signifies the creature, by reason of his life and body. In the case of his life, there are three Commandments: to love God with our whole heart, our whole soul, and our whole mind; with the body there are four very discernible elements of which it is composed" (*CI*, 84). For further accounts of the body composed of four elements in Augustine, see *IS*, 36, 60, 61.

To understand the use of numbers to Augustine consider the lengthy quote above concerning four, a passage that continues for several pages. It juggles numbers around to finally come up with why John's Gospel speaks of a fishing net containing 153 fish (*ETDQ*, 99). Elsewhere he offers another interpretation of the 153 fish (see *CI*, 84–85). There are other similar passages in Augustine telling of the mystical power of number, often with a stress on the number four. *IS*, 202 again has $1 + 2 + 3 + 4 = 10$. In a dialogue Augustine writes, "Those three numbers whose harmony you were wondering at could only be brought together in the same relation by the number four. . . . So that now not one, two, three only, but one, two, three, four is the most closely connected progression of numbers" (*IS*, 200). "The course of the day and year are accomplished through the number four; the days are carried through in intervals of hours: morning, noon, evening, and night; the years, by the spring, summer, autumn, and winter months" (*CI*, 84). In a text written long after his conversion he continued to have a fascination with numbers, but there he tells of the wondrous perfection of the numbers six and seven (*CG*, 374–76).

3. Another three becoming four is found in "The Teacher": "We have done our best to find out three things. . . . But there is a fourth point I would like to find out from you" (*T*, 44). Here seems no point in trying to associate the three or four things with individual Functions.

4. Later he returns to consider the four virtues as the four rivers of Paradise and to see the four rivers of Paradise as the four Gospels nourishing the Church.

5. These passages contain many references to geometrical figures, and all references are to triangles, squares, radii, and circles (none to rectangles, ellipses, etc.). See also *HL*, 241; *L*, 35; *IS*, 16, 25.

6. Jung saw the Trinity as the three Conscious Functions. I have proposed a different way of understanding the Trinity in a Jungian context (the Dominant and Recessed united in the Transcendent Function; such an understanding is well illustrated here by Augustine). See further considerations of the Trinity in the Epilogue to this study.

7. Here is an example of how Augustine uses this text: "If Mary is earth, let us realize what we are saying when we sing, Truth is sprung out of the earth" (*SCE*, 97); the fifteen sermons use the phrase twenty-one times. The RSV translation of the Psalm reads, "Faithfulness will spring up from the ground." Jung mentions Augustine's use of this phrase (*PT*, 234).

Bibliography

Works of St. Augustine

C   *The Confessions of St. Augustine*, translated by Rex Warner. New York: Mentor, New American Library, 1963.

CG   *The City of God*, translated by Marcus Dods, George Wilson, and J. J. Smith. New York: The Modern Library, Random House, 1950.

CI   *Christian Instruction*, including: "Admonition and Grace," "Christian Combat," "Enchiridion of Faith," "Hope and Charity," translated respectively by John J. Gavigan, John Courtney Murray, Robert P. Russell, and Bernard M. Peebles. Fathers of the Church (a series), New York: Cima, 1947.

ETDQ   *Eighty-Three Different Questions*, translated by David Masker. Fathers of the Church (a series), Washington, D.C.: Catholic University of America Press, 1977.

HL   *The Happy Life*, including: "Answer to Sceptics," "Divine Providence and the Problem of Evil" (De Ordine), "Soliloquies," translated by Ludwig Schopp, Denis J. Kavanagh, Robert P. Russell, and Thomas F. Gilligan. Fathers of the Church (a series), New York: Cima, 1948.

IS   *The Immortality of the Soul*, including: "The Magnitude of the Soul," "On Music," "The Advantage of Believing," "On Faith in Things Unseen," translated respectively by Ludwig Schopp, John J. McMahon, Robert Catesby Taliaferro, Luanne Meagher, Joseph Deferrari and Mary Francis McDonald. Fathers of the Church (a series), New York: Cima, 1947.

L   131–64 *Letters 131–164*, translated by Wilfrid Parsons. Fathers of the Church (a series), New York: Cima, 1948.

SCE   *Sermons for Christmas and Epiphany*, translated and annotated by Thomas Comerford Lawler. Ancient Christian Writers (a series), Westminster, Md.: Newman Press, 1952.

T   *The Teacher*, including: "Free Choice of the Will," "Grace and Free Will," translated by Robert A. Russell. Fathers of the Church (a series), Washington, D. C.: Catholic University of America Press, 1967.

Tr   *The Trinity*, translated by Stephen McKenna. Washington, D.C.: The Catholic University of America Press, 1962.

W   *The Catholic and Manichaean Ways of Life*, translated by Donald A. Gallagher and Idella J. Gallagher. Washington, D.C.: The Catholic University of America Press, 1965.

Other Works

O'Connell, Robert J. *St. Augustine's Confessions: The Odyssey of Soul.* New York: Fordham University Press, 1989 (earlier edition, Cambridge: Harvard University Press, 1969).

5 Descartes: Thought and Extension Divided
Philosophical Troubles Pass and the Dominant Rules

Descartes as a T: "I thought I could do no better than . . . devote my whole life to cultivating my reason and advancing as far as I could in the knowledge of the truth (*PWD*, I, 124). "I am, then, in the strict sense only a thing that thinks; that is, I am a mind, or intelligence, or intellect, or reason—words whose meaning I have been ignorant of until now. But for all that I am a thing which is real and which truly exists. But what kind of a thing? As I have just said—a thinking thing" (*PW*, II, 18).[1] "I was a substance whose whole essence or nature is simply to think" (*PW*, I, 127). "I could take it as a general rule that the things we conceive very clearly and very distinctly are all true" (*PW*, I, 127). "We ought never to let ourselves be convinced except by the evidence of our reason" (*PW*, I, 131). Descartes is known for the claim that he doubted all things, but one commentator observes that he never doubted his reason (Frankfort, 16, 28). For Descartes's Quarternity, see figure 5.1. Descartes's Myers-Briggs type would be INTP.

	T Dominant	
	Thinking	
	reason—intellect	
	True	
N		S
Imagination		Sensation
(Mechanics)	F	(Medicine)
	Memory	
	Opinion	
	Ethics	
	Good	
	Extension, place	

Figure 5.1

I. Descartes as Both Rationalist and Dreamer

Descartes does not entirely fit the Jungian model as it was presented. For, though in his philosophy the T is clearly dominant, in his mature personal life he never seems to have lost contact with the unconscious elements of his personality. This left him with a somewhat double character: he claimed to work only with clear and distinct ideas, while he maintained a Catholic faith and morality that he set apart from all doubt! He had other traits not consistent with his rationalist image: he liked rhetoric and praised poets for their enthusiasm and imagination; he had several dreams that he considered divinely inspired, and in one dream the Spirit of Truth confirmed him in his mission; he always treasured the early hours of the morning when he could meditate in a semiconscious state: "I awake to mingle the reveries of the night with those of the day" (Vrooman, 194, 76). In short, Descartes was more than the detached intellect his philosophy would imply. One commentator sees him taking some dreams so seriously that he rested his philosophy on the "infirm foundation of irrational dreams," while acting "as if he were that phantasm of his thought 'a thinking thing'" (Cole, 130, 131). But most puzzling is that, while insisting on the certainty of mathematical knowledge, he could claim that God could make the radii of a circle unequal! He even claimed God could make two contradictory judgments both true (Frankfurt, 7). Strange claims for a rationalist! He could be understood as a young man who anguished greatly over the problems of philosophy, but then, through a deep acceptance of his Catholic faith, he passed beyond the philosophical anguish of his youth to spend his time defending and clarifying his earlier insights. Thus it would seem that personally he knew some Integration, though this does not show in his philosophy. This would leave his philosophic writings with a static quality; he seems to be defending a great insight of his youth.

In 1619 Descartes was a troubled twenty-three-year-old plagued by fundamental doubts and serving in an army far from home. On November 10 (a date with much personal significance for Descartes because of pressures from his father; see Cole), he meditated alone in an overheated room and believed he came upon "the foundations of a marvelous science," the key that would unify all knowledge. The following night he was disturbed by three troubling dreams that seemed to confirm his mission.[2] He asked for divine assistance and vowed to go on pilgrimage to the shrine of the Virgin Mary at Loreto. He also resolved to tell the world what he had discovered, but by 1628 he had not finished his first essay, *Rules for the Direction of the Mind in the Search for Truth*, a work published only after his death. This early text spoke of only two sure ways of being safe from error: intuition and deduction. He explains the meaning of each term:

> By "intuition" I do not mean the fluctuating testimony of the senses or the deceptive judgment of the imagination as it botches things together, but the attention of a clear and attentive mind, which is so easy and distinct that there can be no room for doubt about what we are understanding. . . . intuition is the indubitable conception of a clear and attentive mind which proceeds solely from the light of reason. . . . Thus everyone can mentally intuit that he exists, that he is thinking, that a triangle is bounded by just three lines. (*PW*, I, 14)[3]

Intuition is the first and principal way by which the mind can proceed safe from error. Yet it is important to note what Descartes means by intuition. It is the faculty by which one intuits "simple natures" or "simple propositions." The propositions so perceived would be judgments that are innate to the intellect and identical with its workings. As examples Descartes suggests the principle of contradiction, and the fact that if two quantities are equal to a third quantity they are equal to each other. Thus, Descartes speaks of intuiting "propositions." What he means by intuition refers to the Jungian T, not the N.

Having explained "intuition," Descartes adds a second way of knowing also free from error: "deduction, by which we mean the inference of something as following necessarily from some other propositions which are known with certainty" (*PW*, I, 15). The other propositions known with certainty are the primary ones intrinsic to the intellect. Descartes would have us develop our deductive ability so that we would come to see the principles deduced with the same intuitive clarity by which we had intuited the original claims. That is, he would effectively reduce deduction to intuition, and he recommended mathematical exercises to assist us in extending what we see by "intuition."

Though Descartes claimed that all knowledge depends on the intellect (*PW*, I, 30), he added that we have two instruments of knowledge beyond the intellect: "there are *only two* of these, namely imagination and sense perception." Thus we have three modes of knowing. If the imagination is identified as the faculty which "botches things together" (a phrase from the above quote), then intellect, imagination, and sense could be seen as the three faculties T, N, and S.[4] That means one of the Functions is missing—but not for long! On the following page he again tells of the intellect alone being capable of knowledge, yet now we are told "it can be helped or hindered by *three* other faculties, *viz.* imagination, sense-perception, and memory" (emphasis added). Here—and without explanation—the three has become four and the Fourth is the memory, a faculty easily associated with the F (consider all that Augustine wrote on the wonders of memory).

Now Descartes claims,

> there are only four faculties . . . , *viz.* intellect, imagination, sense-perception and memory. It is of course only the intellect that is capable of perceiving the truth, but it has to be assisted by imagination, sense-perception and memory if we are not to omit anything which lies within our power. (*PW*, I, 39)

Thus to be complete "four faculties"—not three—are needed.

Descartes goes on to say that when the intellect is concerned with matters in which there is nothing corporeal or similar to the corporeal, the intellect cannot receive any help from the other three faculties. But when it would consider something that refers to the body, "the idea of the thing must be formed as distinctly as possible in the imagination" (*PW*, I, 43). To reach the physical the imagination must work with the senses and memory. Thus the imagination (as N) can be seen as the Auxiliary Function; it assists the intellect in reaching the two lesser Faculties, and, since it can visualize the physical, it assists in understanding the extended world.[5] But the intellect itself is in no way physical.

In 1629 Descartes published his *Discourse on Method*, a work that would make him famous. There he tells again of his anguish and uncertainty as he sat in a stove-heated room ten years earlier and made a wonderful discovery. His engaging narrative notes how prone we are to accept the opinions of others. So we need to rid ourselves of all opinions, and he had many opinions of which to rid himself (*PW*, I, 117, 118, 122). But it soon became evident that some of his knowledge was more than opinion. He recalled how mathematics pleased him in his student days, for mathematicians and only mathematicians offered certainty and self-evident reasonings. So he dedicated his life to cultivating his reason. He presents his famous, *Cogito, ergo sum*, and sees this as a truth he cannot doubt; it becomes "the first principle" of his philosophy. "I knew I was a substance whose whole essence or nature is simply to think, and which does not require any place, or depend on any material thing, in order to exist" (*PW*, I, 127).

Descartes has presented thinking as apart from "any place" or "any material thing," and this would give rise to a basic mind/body dualism that runs through his writings and the Cartesian tradition: mind is radically apart from place or extended things. In many passages Descartes tells of the two:

> But I recognize only two ultimate classes of things: first, intellectual or thinking things, i.e. those which pertain to mind or thinking substance; and secondly, material things, i.e. those which pertain to extended substance or body. (*PW*, I, 208)

> I conceive of myself as a thing that thinks and is not extended, whereas I conceive of the stone as a thing that is extended and does not think, so that the two conceptions differ enormously; but they seem to agree with respect to the classification "substance." (*PW*, II, 30)

> ... there is a great difference between the mind and the body, inasmuch as the body is by its very nature always divisible, while the mind is utterly indivisible. (*PW*, II, 59)

Thus, there are two radically different kinds of substance, and each possesses a principal attribute: with mind it is thought, with body it is extension (*PW*, I, 210). All other attributes are merely "modes" of thought or extension—the modes would be the particular thoughts one had or the particular shape of the extended object. He would speak of the two in a variety of terms: "thought and extension," or "thinking substance itself" and "extended substance itself," and so forth. One was the soul and the other was the body. He would speak of his "I" as "entirely distinct from the body," for the nature of the soul is thought, while the nature of the body is extension. In considering extension he would allow no real difference between space, quantity, and corporeal substance (that is, he would allow no vacuum). He would claim that to take even the smallest fraction of extension from a body is taking away that much of its substance, for extension is what a body is (*PW*, I, 226).

In telling of thought and extension as two independent substances, he can be seen as stating the opposition between the T and F Functions. Since the two substances are fundamentally separate, he would be left with the problem of bringing body and soul together in the human being (for Descartes the problem does not apply to animals, as animals have no mind; they are like wind-up toys, machines that can be explained by their moving parts). But with the human there is the problem of bringing body and soul together, that is, in reconciling the Opposites.

Descartes claimed that matter is fundamentally extension, so to take away from an object's extension is to take away from its substance. Thus, the matter of Descartes (a T, on the J axis) difffers from the matter of Plato and Sartre (who were Ns, on the P axis). The Intuitives were seen to regard matter as S, that is, as self-enclosed units one can touch with the hand, atoms of a sort. For Plato and Sartre a partial loss of extension would not involve a substantial change. But Descartes and Augustine are both on the J axis, so they would see matter as extension located somewhere, matter is situated (and mind is not). Both Descartes and Augustine would try to reconcile number and extension (T and F), but they would come at the problem from opposite sides. Descartes was at home with number and extension was in a world apart, while Augustine was at home with extension (time and space) and numbers were in a world apart. Yet both Descartes and Augustine were concerned with rhythm, that which associates number (T) with duration (F).[6]

II. Problems of a Dualist

Having set up a radical distinction between thought and extension, between mind and body, Descartes could not show how they would interact. Yet the difficulty was more evident to his disciples and critics than it was to Descartes. He had a long, close friendship with princess Elizabeth of Bohemia who wrote to him asking how the soul can be governed by the passions (the body) when soul and body have nothing in common. Descartes wrote to the princess that the body causes the soul to have feelings and passions, and the soul causes the body to move; this happens through an inexplicable union between the soul and body. This "inexplicable" union did not satisfy the princess: nor was she satisfied that, instead of explaining the matter, he responded with vague moralizing and practical advice.

So Descartes set about writing a little "treatise on the passions" which he gave the princess in 1646. He had already suggested the pineal gland (*conarion*) as the place where the body might act on the mind (*PW*, I, 100). He also considered this gland the place of the *sensus communis* which he identified or associated with the imagination (*PW*, II, 22, 59). But his descriptions of how body and mind interact are not very satisfying. He tells the princess that passions are caused by material spirits that rise and move "the little gland in the middle of the brain" so that material spirits become "coarser and more agitated" (*PW*, I, 349, 364). He tells at length of inner vapors moving through brain cavities and of the blood producing "a certain very fine wind," but vapors and fine wind are no closer to "thought" than any other physical object. Nowhere does Descartes explain how *physical objects* becomes *thoughts of physical objects*—not a small problem. He allows that sensation and imagination are involved, but still the transition from body to mind, from extended-substance-without-thought to the thinking-substance-without-extension, is not considered. One reads his *Treatise on the Passions* and other works that touch on the difficulty and one wonders why Descartes did not see the problem of the princess. The difference can be seen as the opposition of the T and F Faculties. Above it was suggested that Descartes was not the rationalist he claimed to be. Perhaps his more-than-rationalist identity kept him from seeing the problem, the mind-body problem that continues to bedevil philosophers.

In one of his early writings Descartes gave an image to explain his overall work that suggests a Quaternity. He compared philosophy to a tree: the roots of the tree are metaphysics: metaphysics reveals the principles of knowledge "including the explanation of the principal attributes of God, the non-material nature of our souls and all the clear and distinct notions which are in us" (*PW*, I, 186). The roots are clearly the T as it considers the innate ideas of the intellect. Then the trunk of the tree is said to be physics and the three principal branches are identified as medicine, mechanics, and morals. Physics includes the world of experience, so it proceeds beyond the pure intelligence to involve the imagination and senses. Descartes added that it is from the branches, not the roots, that one obtains the fruit.

Morals would be the highest branch: "By 'morals' I understand the highest and most perfect moral system, which presupposes a complete knowledge of the other sciences and is the ultimate level of wisdom." Thus, the roots (metaphysics) would be T and the highest branch (morals) would be F. By his philosophy/physics he would connect the T and the F, with two side branches of mechanics and medicine that (without pressing the point) could be seen as the N and S. He wrote on mechanics and medicine, but he never developed a moral philosophy or even suggested how he would proceed. "Provisionally" he decided to hold traditional Christian ethics (*PW*, I, 186–87), and he never went further. One commentator has observed, "Whatever the reason . . . the Cartesian ethic is missing from the system, although according to the programme laid down it should have formed its crown" (Copleston, 150).

In telling of the judgment, Descartes might allow some resolution between the T and the F. For he claimed the judgment is an act of the will, not the intellect. The will (a faculty that seeks the good) acts in response to what is in the intellect (a faculty that seeks the true). This arrangement suggests some unity between the T and F. By speaking of the judgment as an act of the will, Descartes is trying to understand human error. It is because the will becomes over-eager and affirms what is beyond what the intellect knows. For Descartes, the will is not restricted or limited in any way; he tells of not being able to conceive of it being more perfect than it is. The will is the image and likeness of God found in the human creature (*PW*, II, 39–40). Though we bear this image, we make many errors as our unlimited will acts on what it finds in our limited intellects. In explaining this, Descartes uses many phrases that associate the true and the good (T and F): when "reasons of truth and goodness point in one way" we are freer; one would not have to deliberate, if one "always saw clearly what was true and good"; yet the will "easily turns aside from what is true and good"; but since our acts depend on God, "they are wholly true and good" (*PW*, II, 40–42), for God is "supremely good and the source of truth" (*PW*, II, 15). Such passages suggest a unity of the True and the Good, a reconciliation of opposites found in many Ts and Fs, such as St. Augustine above, but not found in Ns or Ss.

Descartes's method can be seen as a way of developing our intellect so that it will be a more adequate match for our will. Thereby he hoped to bring the princess from Bohemia and others to beatitude. For fundamentally his method was aimed at delivering the soul.

As Descartes ends his First Meditation he tells of having to face "the inextricable darkness of the problems I have now raised." As he begins his Second Meditation, he tells of himself being thrown into doubts by what he has uncovered: "It feels as if I have fallen unexpectedly into a deep whirlpool which tumbles me around so that I can neither stand on the bottom nor swim up to the top" (*PW*, II, 16). But such passages seem to be a literary way of dramatizing his discovery, rather than a statement of the anguish he felt as he wrote. He seems to recall what was undoubtedly a troubled time years before only to set the scene for the great insight he possesses securely. He tells of troubling doubts many years after they had been resolved.

Thus, though Descartes presented himself as a "thinking thing," he always seems to have accepted a wide system of symbolic truth found in the Catholic faith, the poets, and his dreams. He would speak of putting on a mask to appear in public. The mask would seem to be the "thinking thing" by which he identified himself. This study would find some Jungian symbolism in Descartes, but his philosophy does not tell of the move to Integration found in many other philosophers. Perhaps that is why his philosophy has a static quality; he had a great insight that he presented many times, but it goes nowhere. It seems that the twenty-three-year-old knew anguish and struggle and came to a great insight as he sat in his overheated room. But later as a mature philosopher he was simply clarifying the great insight he had received years before.

Spinoza was a rationalist more or less contemporary with Descartes. He awakened to philosophy through reading Descartes; Descartes gave him a starting point and vocabulary. We do not know much about the life of Spinoza, but unlike Descartes he broke with his religious tradition and was left on his own to grope his way through life. From what we know of the life of Spinoza, he seems to have been a truer example of the introverted rationalist making a troubled and solitary way through life.

Notes

1. Descartes claimed his use of the word "thinking" included any conscious process ("By the word thought I mean all that we are conscious as operating within us"), that is, more than Jung would associate with the T. But in giving examples he always seemed to refer to T elements, such as in the passage just quoted where thinking was associated with the "mind, or intelligence, or intellect, or reason."

2. After coming upon his wonderful science, he had three dreams which have been widely studied. One extended study is by Marie-Louise von Franz, a Jungian who makes much of the detail that in the first dream the wind spun Descartes around "three or four" times: this is seen as Descartes wavering between the spiritual and the physical. She sees Descartes' cosmology having small spheres of the four primal elements falling into a spiral movement; she tells of the name "Descartes" originally being "de Quartis" (Jacobsohn, von Franz, Hurwitz, 92–93).

3. To illustrate this, he gives an example that seems to contain the Jungian 3:4. He considers the inference that 2 plus 2 is equal to 3 plus 1, and explains that to make the inference "not only must we intuitively perceive that 2 plus 2 make 4, and that 3 plus 1 make 4, but also that the original proposition follows from the other two" (*PW*, I, 15). In telling how we listen to music he again introduces the 3:4 symbolism: we join the third note of a melody to the first two and that gives a "triple proportion." "Thereafter, when we hear the fourth, we join them with the third so that we conceive [them] as one; thereupon, we again join

the first two with the latter two so that we conceive these four simultaneously as one" (quoted in Voss, 133). The 3:4 might also be present when Descartes tells of adopting a moral code "of just three or four maxima" (*PW*, I, 122); he tells of "three *or four* maxima" as he hesitates about the fourth and its difference from the other three. Elsewhere, he tells of three levels of wisdom and adds, "one may add a fourth category" (*PW*, I, 181).

4. Dennis Sepper has written an article on the imagination in the early works of Descartes that would support the claim that the "imagination" refers to the N. Sepper speaks of "the synthetic cognitive imagination" and calls it "the chief faculty for unifying knowledge" (in Voss, 144, 142), terms suggesting the N. He speaks of "the cognitive primacy of imagination owing to its ability to exploit the proportions in things" (Voss, 156 [proportions refer to the interrelation of elements, hence, N]). Sepper sees Descartes's *Rules for the Direction of the Mind* as really *Rules for the Direction of the Imagination;* and he judges the imagination to be "the focal point of cognition" in Descartes (Voss, 154). Descartes identifies the imagination with the *sensus communis* of medieval philosophy.

5. Descartes often presented his Three basic faculties (intellect, imagination, and sense). In one of his *Meditations,* the same Three are presented; then in the following meditation he again added memory as a Fourth (*PW*, II, 24, see 51).

6. But also consider how Augustine (F) and Descartes (T) would differ: like Descartes, Augustine saw extension as fundamental to the familiar world, but Augustine (F and extrovert) looked within to a wondrous world (the Unconscious) where he found number and timeless truths in God the teacher. Descartes as introvert readily found basic truths within himself—they were associated with his Dominant. But to get to the continuity of duration (his Recessed) he had recourse to divine intervention, to God the Preserver. He claimed that it takes the same divine power "to preserve anything at each individual moment of its duration as was required to create" it in the first place (*PW*, II, 33). For Descartes, the distinction between creation and preservation was only conceptual; God is needed to give duration. Augustine sees the wonder of God in introducing timeless Eternity (T) into creation, while Descartes finds divine intervention in giving creation the continuity of time (F).

Bibliography

Works of Descartes

PW, I and II *The Philosophical Writings of Descartes*, vol. I and vol. II, translated by John Cottingham, Robert Stoothoff, and Dugald Murdoch. Cambridge: Cambridge University Press, vol. II, 1984; vol. I, 1985.

Other Works

Cole, John R. *The Olympian Dream and Youthful Rebellion of René Descartes*. Urbana: University of Illinois Press, 1992.

Copleston, Frederick, S.J. *A History of Philosophy*, vol. IV. New York: Doubleday Image, 1963.

Frankfurt, Harry G. *Demons, Dreamers, and Madmen: The Defense of Reason in Descartes' Meditations*. New York: Bobbs-Merrill, 1970.

Jacobsohn, Helmuth, Marie-Louise von Franz, and Siegmund Hurwitz. *Timeless Documents of the Soul: Studies in Jungian Thought*. Evanston, Ill.: Northwestern University Press, 1968.

Voss, Stephen, editor. *Essays on the Philosophy and Science of René Descartes*. Oxford: Oxford University Press, 1993.

Vrooman, Jack Rochford. *René Descartes: A Biography*. New York: G. P. Putnam's Sons, 1970.

6 Spinoza: Thought and Extension United
The Dominant Quietly Allows the Repressed

Spinoza as T: Spinoza spoke of himself as "driven only by a desire for pure truth," he told of having "no other end than truth" (*CW*, 355). But this truth was wholly a priori: "What constitutes the form of the true thought must be sought in the same thought itself and must be deduced from the nature of the intellect" (*CW*, 32). He claimed, "God is Truth or that the Truth is God himself" (*CW*, 120), and the essence of the mind "consists only in thought" (*CW*, 601). But Spinoza's T identity is most evident in his general methodology: his *Ethics* is set forth "in geometrical order." As in a text of geometry, he first sets forth definitions and self-evident axioms; from these he wanted to *deduce* the rest of the book. He sought a hypothesis as starting point from which "everything which is observed in the whole of nature should be capable of being deduced"; from it all things would follow as "mathematical consequences" (*CW*, 295, 296). While he saw some people cursing or laughing at human behavior, he set out to understand it "in the geometrical style" (*CW*, 492). He would even "deduce [his politics] from the very condition of human nature" (*PT*, 288). For Spinoza's Quarternity, see figure 6.1. Spinoza's Myers-Briggs type would be INTP.

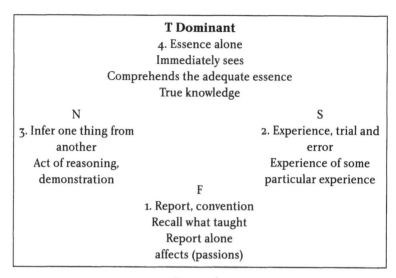

Figure 6.1

I. Spinoza Considers Thought and Extension

Benedict (Baruch, Bento) Spinoza was born on November 24, 1632, in Amsterdam, where his Jewish parents had settled after fleeing persecutions in Spain and Portugal. Benedict studied the Torah for many years before going into business with his brother. But, in 1656 his unorthodox theology brought ostracism from the Jewish community; so he left Amsterdam, retired from public life, and began a quiet life of grinding lenses, teaching, and writing. His early biographer explained, "The love of truth was so very much his ruling passion that he scarcely saw anybody" (Wolf, 44), and most of his writings were not published until after his death in 1677. As a young man he wrote and published a study of Descartes, but in introducing the work he indicated he did not always agree with Descartes. Still Descartes gave him a vocabulary and a way of doing philosophy that he used to express a vision distinctly his own.

The earliest writings of Spinoza date from 1661 and 1662 with *The Emendation of the Intellect* and *Short Treatise on God, Man, and His Well-Being*.[1] Though both of these treatises are highly abstract, they are oriented to a healing of the soul. In the first Spinoza tells of being "forced to seek a remedy" with all his strength by which he might come to "a joy entirely exempt from sadness." The remedy consisted in governing one's self entirely by the intellect. The theme of happiness-through-the-intellect-in-control runs through his writings. Thus, his major work, *The Ethics*, is said to contain only those things that would lead "to knowledge of the human mind and its highest blessedness" (*CW*, 446). As with Socrates, philosophy was seen as the search of the soul for salvation.

Both of the early works of Spinoza consider at length four kinds of perception.[2] These can be seen to correspond to the four Functions of Jung as developed in the present study: the F, S, N, and T, in that order. (See Spinoza's Quaternity above: there the F is given the lowest place "1," while the T as "4" reigns supreme.) The following text of Spinoza includes the initials of Jungian Functions in brackets:

1. There is the Perception we have from report or from some conventional sign [F].
2. There is the Perception we have from random experience. . . . and we have no other experiment that opposes it . . . [S].
3. There is the Perception that we have when the essence of a thing is inferred from another thing, but not adequately . . . [as] when we infer the cause from some effect . . . [N].
4. Finally, there is the Perception we have when a thing is perceived through its essence alone, or through knowledge of its proximate cause [T]. (*CW*, 12–13)

After telling of these Four, Spinoza illustrates them by examples that further show the similarities between Spinoza's four and Jung's. First: there are things he knows by hearsay, e.g., the date of his birth (recall the F has opinions, beliefs one cannot defend [e.g., Plato presented "opinion" as a definition of knowledge and there it was associated with F; while "authority" was of fundamental importance in St. Augustine]). Second: there are some things he knows from personal experience, e.g., oil feeds a fire and water can put it out.[3] Third: Spinoza tells of inferring one thing from another, as (he gives an example) "after we have come to know the nature of vision" we can infer that the sun is larger than it appears to us ("inferring" tells of what is Other). Fourth: when "a thing is perceived through its essence alone when, from the fact that I know something, I know what it is to know something," e.g., two plus three is five. But Spinoza is concerned that presently things known by the fourth way are very few. This his method was intended to correct; by extending this fourth knowledge he would bring peace to the soul.

To illustrate the four types of knowledge Spinoza introduces an example from mathematics, an illustration reintroduced many times in his later works. The example further associates the four perceptions of Spinoza with the Three-becoming-Four of Jung: "Suppose there are three numbers. Someone is seeking a fourth, which is to the third as the second is to the first" (*CW*, 14). Spinoza offers an example: 6 is to 8 as 9 is to x; one is seeking the fourth number. To solve the problem merchants will follow the first type of knowledge: they will simply recall what they were taught (F); Other people, the second type, will develop the rule of proportion from their experience, trial and error (S); while Mathematicians, the third type, will know by the force of the demonstration as it is found in Euclid (N). They will see it "intuitively." But, "only the fourth mode comprehends the adequate essence of the thing and is without danger of error." This is what we must chiefly use, so Spinoza would "teach the Way and Method by which we may achieve this kind of knowledge" (*CW*, 16). The *Emendation of the Intellect* would emend our minds so that this fourth and certain form of knowledge would dominate. The *Emendation* also includes geometrical examples concerning circles and squares: "Once we know the nature of the circle and also the nature of the square, we cannot then compound these two and make a square circle, or a square soul and the like" (*CW*, 29); here he tells of semicircles, triangles, and a sphere, images that Jung would also associate with the process of Integration.

The "emendation" of the intellect consists in clearly differentiating the intellect from the "imagination." For Spinoza, the confusion of these two faculties is the basis of human error (*CW*, 37). Under "imagination" Spinoza would place the first three types of perception listed above: hearsay, sense experience, and reason. That is, imagination is a generic term for faculties other than the intellect (there is some resemblance to Descartes, who saw the imagination as the N, the faculty by which sense and memory (S and F) were accessible to the intellect). For Spinoza, the intellect (the Dominant) will be mended by differentiating it from the other Three. Then the intellect will be in total control and reflecting on itself will come to a knowledge that will bring peace, for the intellect will have gained mastery and complete control. Such is the outline of what he hoped to do. But he left the work unfinished without saying why. It seems he was already working on the *Ethics*.

It was also at this time that Spinoza was writing his *Short Treatise*. There the Four kinds of perception are considered again, and again the Four are explained by the "Rule of Three": "In the rule of three you multiply the second and third numbers and divide the product by the first, you then find the fourth number." The "Rule of Three" is invoked three times in this short essay (*CW*, 97, 102, 138).[4] The four types of perception presented here further clarify the parallel with the Four types of Jung's F, S, N, and T. The first is said to work from hearsay; the second wants to test the proposition by the "experience of some particular"; the third consults true reason "which shows it could not be otherwise." "But a fourth, who has the clearest knowledge of all, has no need either of a report, or of experience, or of the art of reasoning, because through his penetration he immediately sees the proportionality in all the calculations" (*CW*, 98).

Spinoza then makes a final summary statement: "We have divided perception into four kinds: *report alone, experience, belief,* and *clear knowledge*. And since we have now seen the effects of all of these, it is evident from this that the fourth, clear knowledge, is the most perfect of all" (*CW*, 104).

The *Short Treatise* goes on to claim that our Passions arise from the first two kinds of perception, that is, from report and experience (*CW*, 138; see note on p. 97). For example, wonder is presented as a passion. We feel wonder only because, until that time, we had been holding an erroneous belief based on ignorance or prejudice; when this is rectified, we will no longer be troubled by wonder. In like manner we will free ourselves from other unsuitable passions—all passions turn out to be unsuitable except a special type of love/desire. But the process of emending the intellect must make use of both reason (the Jungian N) and intellect (T). In the process reason (N) shows itself to be the Auxiliary Function. It assists the intellect by enabling us to consider objectively the different passions; it indicates their harmful effects, but simply seeing these is not enough.

> when we use our intellect and reason properly, we can never fall into one of those [passions] we are to reject. I say our intellect, for I do not think that reason alone has the power to free us from all of these, as we shall prove later. (*CW*, 18)

In other terms, we come to happiness "both by reason [N] and by the fourth kind of knowledge" (CW, 146). This "fourth knowledge, which is the knowledge of God, is not the consequence of anything else, but immediate" (CW, 139). The reason makes us aware of the distress caused by the passions, but only the fourth knowledge can destroy the passions. Yet we do not first destroy the passions and then love God, rather our reason points out the faults of the passions, and then "only knowledge [of God] is the cause of the destruction" of the passions (CW, 146). Thus "reasoning [N] is not the principle thing in us, but only like a stairway by which we can climb to the desired place" (CW, 147). Again, reason is the process of ascent, N, but not the goal.[5] The goal is the intellect immediately united with God by knowledge and love. It is by this clear knowing of God that we are freed from the body and then we find that the passions do not have the least effect on us (CW, 133–34). This is the human well-being that is the goal of the Short Treatise. The intellect is united to God, and "God is Truth" or "Truth is God himself" (CW, 120); the intellect is in serene control; we are fully active and unaffected by the passions. We will then have been delivered, but until then everything leads to our ruin (CW, 146).

In 1670 Spinoza published anonymously a work titled A Theologico-Political Treatise. His aim was to separate philosophy from religious faith (WS, 183). So he advised that "the multitude and those of like passions with the multitude" not read the book (WS, 11). In philosophy "the doctrine taught is deduced entirely from intellectual axioms—that is, by the mere power of the understanding and logical order" (WS, 77). Philosophy is thus the T in complete control. But since this "deduction of conclusions from general truths a priori, usually requires a long chain of arguments," and most people lack the patience or skill to follow them, they need another type of guidance. This is provided by revealed religion. For Spinoza the multitudes are fickle and changing, "governed solely by emotions, not by reason" (WS, 216). So they find themselves at war with one another.

According to Spinoza, the Scriptures were given for the multitudes who are unable to follow a complicated argument. Only a few are led by reason, but ordinary folk can understand the biblical account of the Hebrews' covenant with God and so improve their behavior, but their understanding was limited for they see "as if through a cloud" (CW, 451); while the philosophers know the "eternal covenant of the knowledge of God and love is universal" (WS, 55). The philosopher sees that "the knowledge and love of God is the ultimate aim to which all our actions should be directed" (WS, 60). Divine law involves "true knowledge of God and love" (WS, 59). While the historical narratives "cannot give us the knowledge nor consequently the love of God, for love of God springs from knowledge of Him" (WS, 61). The frequency of the knowledge/love phrase (eight times in seven pages) suggest that he is telling of an important unity, a unity of the Opposites: knowledge (T) and love (F).

Throughout the work Spinoza is contrasting those "led by sound reason" and those "impelled by the passions" (WS, 201, 216). People of the first sort can be guided by philosophy and reason, while those of the second can be guided by the stories and teachings of the Scriptures. By the events and imaginative language of the Scriptures the multitudes can come to some measure of understanding. Having done so, the masses will submit to civil behavior, and this will give stability to the state. Such is the political aspect of the work. In the course of the work Spinoza shows an extensive knowledge of both the Old and the New Testaments.

The *Short Treatise on God, Man, and His Well-Being* shows the reason in firm and total control, though it does allow for a form of love. But the love (as with all affects) must first submit to the reason; then the love that the treatise sees as an ideal comes out of the intellect. The concern of the *Treatise* had been the conflict between reason and the passions, but in the abundant phrases telling of knowledge and love reconciled in God, Spinoza seems to have achieved some reconciliation of his opposites. This will emerge more clearly in his *Ethics*.

Spinoza left an unfinished work titled *A Political Treatise*. It considers different forms of government and takes a similar outlook. Since people are led "more by passion than reason, it follows, that a multitude comes together, and wishes to be guided, as it were by one mind, not at the suggestion of reason, but of some common passion" (WS, 316). To deal with the political reality, he would offer a rational consideration of different forms of government. But throughout the work, he is always affirming the reason over the unruly passions. So, in laying the foundations of a state, "it is necessary to study the human passions"; but it is not enough to develop an ideal policy; the policy must be such that whether people are "led by passion or reason" they should keep the laws firm and unbroken (WS, 328). The concern of Spinoza is that those governing the state are not "so much determined by lust as by reason" (WS, 348). Spinoza had titled his earliest writing *The Emendation of the Intellect*; the latter political treatises could be called *The Emendation of the State*. For both works involve "emendations" aimed at getting the reason in control of the passions, "as in the state of nature the man who is led by reason is most powerful and most independent, so too that commonwealth will be most powerful and most independent, which is founded and guided by reason" (WS, 303).

In the *Republic* Socrates was seen to tell of the state and soul together and one would clarify the other. That seems to be the case with Spinoza, where the state has absolute control—The Dominant reigns supreme. The subject must submit to the laws "however iniquitous the subject may think the commonwealth's decisions" (WS, 302–3). Individuals should not independently follow their reason so long as they are liable to passions (WS, 303). In the state the authorities have radical control, and this resembles the radical control that the understanding has over the soul. As in Plato, one seems to be telling of the other.

Early in this political work love was set aside as one of the "perturbations of the mind," But soon he is using phrases that reintroduce love and suggest a reconciliation of opposites: the "knowledge and the love of God," and "the true knowledge of God and the love which necessarily results" (WS, 288, 305). One could see these as telling of the rejected love returning, perhaps as cornerstone.

II. Spinoza's Ethics

Spinoza's major work, the *Ethics: Demonstrated in Geometrical Order,* was published only after his death.[6] He had worked on it for sixteen years, continually making changes and additions, but what they were and when they were made cannot be identified. In the *Ethics* Spinoza would see all people born in confusion and living in turmoil: "Like waves on the sea, driven by contrary winds, we toss about not knowing our outcome and fate" (CW, 530), for we are led by our imaginations. We would have been helplessly lost, were it not that mathematics, that which concerns only "the essences and properties of figures," has come to our rescue by showing us a different standard of truth (CW, 441). Adopting the method that first was evident in mathematics, Spinoza will demonstrate our essential human nature "more clearly than the noon light" (*CW*, 436; see also *WS*, 128). In his telling of logical necessity, mathematical clarity, and the noon light, he suggests the radical domination of the T and of Consciousness, a domination which is evident throughout the work. The work proceeds by many concise arguments and each argument is concluded with a Q.E.D.

Spinoza would like to offer a completely deductive system, so he starts with God, whose existence we can know a priori, that is, know by a form of the ontological argument (*CW*, 418). He claims we can be more certain of the existence of God than of anything else; this is his starting point. This sets him in contrast to Descartes, who had begun with the *cogito* and self-knowledge. But for Spinoza the existence of God is the only suitable starting point for philosophy (*CW*, 455). He told of knowing of God's existence as clearly as he knew the essence of a triangle. Starting from the existence of God, he would like to deduce everything else, just as from the nature of a triangle one can deduce its properties, that is, one can deduce that the sum of its angles is equal to two right angles, and so forth (*CW*, 426, 490; see Copleston, 232). In a similar way he believed the existence of the world followed necessarily from the existence of God and could be so demonstrated.

Spinoza would speak of God as having infinite attributes (*infinitis attributis*); but only two are named: thought and extension. "God is a thinking thing" and "God is an extended thing" (*CP*, 448, 449).[7] In saying that God is extended he differs from Descartes; unlike Descartes's God, Spinoza's God has a body. Thought and extension give the works of Spinoza a measure of dualism, as they did the works of Descartes. But for Spinoza the separation is not absolute, as they are reconciled in God, the real starting point of our knowledge; thus God would be the reconciliation of what Descartes saw as totally separate. The present study would associate these attributes with the T (thought) and the F (extension). In Spinoza, we know the two attributes as separate, since there is no causal flow between them: so the body cannot determine the mind to think and the mind cannot determine the body to act (*CP*, 494, 495, 450; Bennett, 48). The two act apart and in parallel, so that my decisions do not effect what my body does and my body does not effect what my mind thinks. My body follows the laws of physics and my mind follows the laws of thought. Each line of causality follows a strict determinism. The causal lines correspond with one another, but they do not interact.

Spinoza would identify God with Nature and see God as infinite Mind and infinite Extension. Some have claimed that by uniting thought and extension in God Spinoza has avoided the problem that perplexed the Cartesians (see Copleston, 229); while others have regarded the solution of Spinoza as largely verbal. In any case, for Spinoza the two attributes are united in God; and thus God can be seen as the *reconciliatio oppositorum*: for the God of Spinoza unites both thought and extension, intellect and love.

The *Ethics* would see us in bondage to our affects (Latin, *affectus*, that is, relating to the feelings or emotions); in Jungian terms, our intellect (T) is in bondage to our feelings (F). The affects (feelings) are harmful to the extent they prevent the mind from being able to think (*CW*, 601). So the *Ethics* would assist us in moderating or restraining these affects. In only "moderating" the affects, the aim of the *Ethics* would be more limited than the *Short Treatise* (above), which would put the intellect in total control. It seems Spinoza must have tried without success to achieve the total control he had wanted; so he claims that when Descartes tried to show how such control could be achieved he was simply demonstrating his cleverness (*CW*, 492, 595). He saw the ancient Stoics claiming an absolute dominion over their affects. But Spinoza, in a rare appeal to experience, objects, "Experience cries out against this" (*CW*, 595).

Some of the affects are said to be pleasant (they bring *laetitia*) and some unpleasant (they bring *tristitia*). The pleasant ones give us a sense that the power of the body is increased and the unpleasant give a sense that the power of the body is decreased. During Spinoza's early work on the *Ethics*, he had considered all affects, pleasant and unpleasant, as passions to be overcome (they are called passions, as they would act for the intellect and the intellect would be passive)—this is not the proper way. Later, he would come to allow a pleasant affect wherein the mind is active; this would lead him to rework his earlier text to introduce appropriate changes (see Bennett, 257–58). The affect that allows the mind to be active is the pleasure (*laetitia*) one has in knowing clearly. The mind is active when it has adequate ideas and passive when it has inadequate ideas. An inadequate or confused idea is called a "passion" (*CW*, 542). When the mind does not see clearly, it is no longer fully active, as it can be when the idea is adequate (that is, when the intellect has a clear and distinct idea). Whereas with an inadequate idea, the "passion" acts for the mind, so the mind is no longer the doer. When our affects act for us, we have lost control of our life and are in bondage to our affects, that is, to whatever we happen to feel, to fortune, to whatever. For ourselves to gain control and be the ones acting, we must understand, and to understand is to act (CW, 558). All such passages show the T gaining a radical control over the F.

The *Ethics* of Spinoza sets forth the difficult path by which the human intellect can achieve blessedness and the freedom to act for itself. But the final passages set forth teachings concerning immortality, knowing, and intellectual love. His teachings on these subjects late in the *Ethics* has provoked considerable opposition from even his friendly critics. For it is hard to see how the conclusions he reaches there follow according to the a priori geometrical method he had adopted at the beginning of the work.[8] Some critics have tried to excuse these final passages: Stuart Hampshire has suggested they take one "beyond the limits of literal understanding"; Frederick Pollock justifies them by saying there is "unquestionably something of an exalted and mystical temper in his expressions"; C. D. Broad considers them the "philosophic expression of certain religious and mystical experiences which Spinoza may have enjoyed" (quoted in Bennett, 373–75). Delahunty sees his claim that the mind survives bodily death raising "baffling and vexatious problems" that involve "contradictory conclusions" (Delahunty, 280, 301). But Bennett's judgment is more severe: he calls these final passages "an unmitigated and seemingly unmotivated disaster," "nonsense," "valueless," "dangerous," "rubbish"; "the burden of error and confusion has become unbearable" (Bennett, 357–75). Delahunty, in a phrase that suggests the *reconciliatio oppositorum*, sees this final book of the *Ethics* containing "two different and incompatible lines of thought which are knitted together" (Delahunty, 303).

The final passages differ from the rest of the work as they suggest several items that involve more than pure intellect. First, Spinoza claims that in death the mind is not absolutely destroyed, but something of it remains which is eternal. "We feel and know by experience that we are eternal. For the mind feels those things that it conceives in the understanding" (CW, 607–8). And note the appeal to experience—hardly part of a geometrical procedure. The result is that "our mind can be said to endure" (*CW*, 608; see 612). That is, he is claiming that beyond the essence of the mind, which is eternal and timeless, the mind itself will *endure*, a word that suggests ongoing time. It could be seen as a unity of eternity (T) and duration (F) and is said to be something that "we *feel* and *know*." It is one of the passages that his critics claim take us into the "mystical." It seems to say that the individual continues after bodily death.

A second point: In both his philosophical writings and his correspondence Spinoza had told of "the knowledge and love of God." This would be acceptable because of the intellectual understanding he had of love. But some passages in the *Ethics* that tell of the "intellectual love of God" seem to go further. He claimed, "The mind's intellectual Love of God is part of the infinite Love by which God loves himself"; from this it follows that insofar as God loves himself, he loves humans beings, so "God's love of men and the Mind's intellectual Love of God are one and the same" (*CW*, 612). Our blessedness, freedom, and salvation consist in "a constant and eternal Love of God, or in God's love for men" (*CW*, 612). This somewhat particular love seems to go against earlier passages that speak differently: "Strictly speaking God loves no one" (*CW*, 604). Now we are told that the more the mind enjoys divine Love, the more it understands. And "because the mind enjoys this divine Love or blessedness, it has the power of restraining lusts" (*CW*, 616). Here one does not enjoy blessedness because one has restrained one's lusts, but the power to restrain lusts arises from the blessedness (*CW*, 616). This love is an affect. It is the affect that Spinoza eventually came to allow and apparently went back to modify his earlier texts to do so. Originally he had claimed that the intellect should by wholly active, but this one affect is given a special status whereby the intellect can be partially passive.

The very phrase, "intellectual love of God," suggests a reconciliation of T and F, and the reconciliation itself is identified with "God's love of men" and "men's love of God." The two forms of love seem to be the same, much like the Self of Jung is either God or the image of God within the soul. But what is notable is that in this mutual love Spinoza goes into the mystical, while retaining the semblance of the geometrical method. There is no sense of mystery or awe in the wording of these passages (as is usually found when the unconscious Function is approached), but the deus ex machina quality of introducing this special love suggests more than can be concluded by the logical work of the conscious mind. The passages reach conclusions that speak of love and combine the opposing Functions in phrases that acknowledge that "we feel and know." A measure of feeling is accepted. His critics object to these final passages, but in Spinoza exceeding his method a Jungian could see him partially accepting the F he had rejected—yet it does not seem to belong.

A summary statement on Spinoza: All of his work concerns the intellect getting control over the passions (that is, "love, hate . . . and the other perturbations of the mind" [WS, 288]). Spinoza's earliest writings tell of four kinds of knowledge, and the four are readily associated with the Four Functions of Jung. Beyond the opposition of Intellect and the Affects (T & F), the *Ethics* repeats Descartes's radical separation between thinking and extension (T & F). The final passages of the *Ethics* telling of intellectual love have been called mystical, for "two different and incompatible lines of thought . . . are knitted together." That could be seen as the return of rejected love. Thus the passages criticized so heavily suggest the beginnings of a *reconciliatio oppositorum*.

Notes

1. The first is written in Latin and is unfinished. The second is available in two Dutch versions probably deriving from a Latin original; there are significant variations in these two versions. Wienpahl has suggested that the *Short Treatise* might not be directly written by Spinoza (Wienpahl, 40). But Spinoza scholars generally have accepted it as authentic.

2. In the present study, "Perception" has been associated with the N and S Functions, yet Spinoza, a T, lists four kind of perception! Consider his own distinctive use of the term. He is not speaking of perception as ordinarily understood, for he tells of "perceiving ideas or essences"—ordinarily one would say we "know" ideas. One translator has sometimes translated his *percipere* as "to conceive" (Hallett, 17). When the same Four are considered in the *Ethics* he refers to them as perception or knowledge indiscriminately (CW, 477–78); see also the Introduction to the *Short Treatise*. In the *Ethics* he explains: "I say concept rather than perception, because the word perception seems to indicate that the mind is acted upon by the object" (CW, 447). In the *Ethics* he tells of four kinds of knowledge but then runs the first two together to tell of three kinds. There he refers often to the "third kind of knowledge" (especially in Part V), but it is clear that it is what is here presented as the fourth. See

also Wienpahl, 109–10: " . . . 'four modes of perceiving,' as they are called in the *Emendation of the Intellect*, or four kinds of 'knowledge,' as they are called in the *Ethics*."

3. Note that with Spinoza (a T), hearsay (F) is lowest and sense experience is next; Plato (an N) would have S in last position and then the F: in Plato's account of the division of a line, sense experience was lowest and opinion/hearsay was second. Augustine (an F) gives a primacy to a sort of hearsay, that is, to "authority." Note the primacy of number, geometry, in Spinoza. As Augustine told of four ways of love, Spinoza told of four ways of doing arithmetic.

4. This brief work has another example of 3 becoming 4. Spinoza lists three effects of true belief and considers each; then he adds, "Having spoken up to now of everything which the third kind of effect of true belief shows us, we shall now proceed to speak of the fourth and last effect, which we did not mention on page [103]" (*CW,* 119).

5. Here Spinoza tells of an ascent. But since he proposes a radical immanence of the divine in the world, it would refer to the mental process and not an ascensional power in things.

6. From his correspondence, it seems that most of the *Ethics* was written in 1662 and 1663. By mid-1665 he seemed nearly ready to publish, but held back for political and religious reasons; he continued modifying the text until his death (*CW,* 350).

7. Wienpahl has suggested that "infinite attributes" does not mean an infinite number, but rather that each of the two attributes is infinite in itself (Weinpahl, 82; Bennett, 76-79). This is not the common opinion, and it would seem to be ruled out by *CW,* 451, which speaks of Extension, Thought, or "any other attribute."

8. Some have seen the geometrical format of the work as no more than Spinoza's way of stating his vision; many of the most important parts of the work are stated in appendices and other added passages that are apart from his stated method.

Bibliography

Works of Spinoza

CW   *The Collected Works of Spinoza,* volume I (other volumes have not yet appeared), edited and translated by Edwin Curley. Princeton: Princeton University Press, 1985.

WS   *Chief Works,* including the *Political Treatise,* the *Theologico-Political Treatise,* translated and introduced by R. H. M. Elwes, bibliographic note by Francesco Cordasco. New York: Dover Press, 1951.

Other Works

Bennett, Jonathan. *A Study of Spinoza's Ethics*. [Indianapolis]: Hackett Publishing, 1984.

Delahunty, R. J. *Spinoza*. Boston: Routledge & Kegan Paul, 1985.

Hallett, H. F. *Aeternitas*. Oxford: The Clarendon Press, 1930.

Lucas, Jean. *The Oldest Biography of Spinoza*, edited with translation and introduction by A. Wolf. Port Washington, N.Y.: Kennikat Press, 1970.

Weinpahl, Paul. *The Radical Spinoza*. New York: New York University Press, 1979.

7 Rousseau: The Heart's Uncertain Reasons
The Dominant and Suggestions of Integration

Rousseau as F: Rousseau hoped to present "the one philosophy really proper to the human heart" (*C*, 62). He invited his readers to follow him "in all the extravagances of my heart" (*C*, 65). He had achieved certitude: "I cannot go wrong about what I have felt, or about what my feelings have led me to do" (*C*, 262). To guide us we have an "inner feeling" that "makes its way through the mistakes of reason" (*RJ*, 242). A commentator tells of Rousseau's method: "Whatever 'the heart' (substituted for Descartes' 'reason') admits as clear and evident, will be true" (Crocker, 146; parenthesis in text). "In the long run, reason follows the bent of the heart" (*RW*, 386). Rousseau's autobiography has thirty-four accounts of his weeping: "weeping when I had no cause for tears, and sighing I know not why;" "I indulged my feelings, I sighed and cried like a child. How often would I stop to weep at my leisure and, sitting on a large stone would be amused to see my tears fall into the water," etc. (*C*, 49, 62). He explained his autobiography, "I should not fulfil the aim of this book if I did not . . . reveal my inner feelings" (*C*, 88). He told of "burning with love for no object" (*C*, 210, 410), and of "the succession of feelings" which marked his development (*C*, 262). His politics would center on the "citizens' hearts," for the law was to be loved (*SC*, 14). Education must be "well adapted to the human heart" (*E*, 34). For Rousseau's Quarternity, see Figure 7.1. Rousseau's Myers-Briggs type would be INFP.

T
Truth
Intelligence
Brain

General Will
A common Self

F Dominant
Feeling
Sentiment
Heart

Figure 7.1

I. A Troubled Move to Become Intelligent

Rousseau's autobiography, the *Confessions*, tells of his birth in the independent city of Geneva in 1712; soon afterwards his mother died. When he was sixteen, returning from a day in the country, he found the city gates locked, so he set out to find his fortune in the wider world. After travels in Italy and France, he settled for several years in Annecy and Chambery (Savoy, France) with a woman twelve years his senior; there he worked, read, and studied music. In 1741 he came to Paris when the French Enlightenment was well under-way and quickly became known to the major figures of the movement. They and he knew that he was different, for the leaders of the Enlightenment were mostly rationalists, while he was not. Yet they were fascinated by him.

He explained how his own mind had developed: "I felt before I thought" (*C*, 19). He believed others had the same F then T se-quence: "Our sensibility is incontestably anterior to our intelli-gence, and we had sentiments before we had ideas" (*E*, 290). In writing of education he warned that reason is the faculty "that devel-ops with the most difficulty and latest"; and even then the reason was said to be not a faculty itself but "only a composite of all the others" (*E*, 89).[1] Thus, Rousseau was a Feeler who spoke often of reason, but the reason was not even a faculty, at best it was identified with the *sensus communis*.

Though reason was not a faculty, Rousseau knew the separation between Feeling and Thinking: "I have a passionate temperament, and lively and headstrong emotions. Yet my thoughts arise slowly and con-fusedly, and are never ready until too late. It is as if my heart and my brain did not belong to the same person" (*C*, 112–13).

The double identity of heart and brain tells of his Enantiodromia. It left him shy and reserved in public, but the duality was not limited to his social self.

> But I do not suffer from this combination of quick emotion and slow thoughts only in company. I know it too when I am alone and when I am working. Ideas take shape in my head with the most incredible dif-ficulty. They go round in dull circles and ferment, agitating me and overheating me till my heart palpitates. During this stir of emotion I can see nothing clearly and cannot write a word; I have to wait. Insen-sibly all this tumult grows quiet, the chaos subsides, and everything falls into place, but slowly, and after long and confused perturbations. Have you ever been to the opera in Italy? During changes of scenery wild and prolonged disorder reigns in their great theatres. The furni-ture is higgledy-piggledy; on all sides things are being shifted and everything seems upside down; it is as if they were bent on universal destruction; but little by little everything falls into place, nothing is missing, and, to one's surprise, all the long tumult is succeeded by a delightful spectacle. That is almost exactly the process that takes place in my brain when I want to write. (*C*, 113)

He is telling of "how ideas take shape in my head," of "the process that takes place in my brain." The T appears as a disordered confu-sion, but what is most notable in the passage is that *he* does not consciously order his ideas; rather he watches as, higgledy-piggledy, ideas *order themselves* in his head. This ordering of ideas meant the Repressed T was active and the active Repressed gave him the sense of being a prophet proclaiming the truth "given" to him.

In 1749 Rousseau had a dramatic awakening that began his ca-reer as author and changed his life. His friend and a figure in the

Enlightenment, Diderot, was held in confinement in Vincennes because of his religious and political writings, so Rousseau often walked out from Paris to visit him. One day he took with him the *Mercure de France,* and as he walked he read that the Dijon Academy was sponsoring an essay contest on the question: "Has the progress of the sciences and arts done more to corrupt morals or improve them?" The effect was immediate: "The moment I read this I beheld another universe and became another man" (*C,* 327). This becoming "another" suggests the Repressed is acting in the Unconscious.

> suddenly I felt my mind dazzled by a thousand lights; crowds of lively ideas presented themselves at the same time with a strength and a confusion that threw me into an inexpressible perturbation; I feel my head seized by a dizziness similar to drunkenness. A violent palpitation oppresses me, makes me sick to the stomach. (*C&C,* 575)

Unable to breathe, he let himself drop under a tree and stayed there in great agitation so that eventually the whole front of his jacket was wet with tears though he was not aware of weeping. "Everything that I was able to retain of these crowds of great truths which illuminated me under that tree in a quarter of an hour has been weakly scattered about in my three principal writings" (*C&C,* 575. This text is from a letter written in 1762; he identified the three principal writings as his *First Discourse,* the *Second Discourse,* and *Emile*).[2] The disturbance began in his mind ("these crowds of great truths which illuminated me") and spread to his heart.

> My feelings rose with the most inconceivable rapidity to the level of my ideas. All my little passions were stifled by an enthusiasm for truth, liberty, and virtue; and the most astonishing thing is that this fermentation worked in my heart for five years. (*C,* 328)

When he arrived at Diderot's he was "in a state of agitation bordering on delirium." Diderot encouraged him to enter the contest, so he composed the essay that would launch his fame. He tells of his writing process:

> I devoted the night hours to it when I could not sleep. I meditated in bed with closed eyes, and shaped and reshaped my sentences in my head with incredible labour. Then, when I was finally content with them, I committed them to my memory to such time as I could put them on paper. (*C,* 328)

Later he would sit in bed and dictate the ideas developed the previous night. He soon produced the essay that would win the prize, an essay he would later judge "full of strength and fervor" but "completely lacking in logic and order" (*C*, 329).

In the essay he introduces himself as "an honorable man who knows nothing" but is sure of his "sentiment." Then he told of the coming of the Enlightenment wherein the light of reason dissipated darkness, but soon he is presenting the other side of any enlightenment. With examples from Greek and Roman history he tells of culture weakening human character and corrupting the soul. He sees current luxury, licentiousness, and slavery to social standards as "punishment for the arrogant attempts we have made to emerge from the happy ignorance in which eternal wisdom has placed us. The heavy veil with which she covered all her operations seemed to warn us adequately that she did not destine us for vain studies" (*FSD*, 46–47). He called for an ignorance that rejected the rational achievements of the Enlightenment, but he asked, "Are we destined then to die fixed to the edge of the pit where the truth has hidden?" "What dangers there are! What false paths when investigating the sciences! How many errors, a thousand times more dangerous than the truth is useful, must be surmounted to reach the truth?" (*FSD*, 48–49). He exclaims, "Almighty God, thou who holds all spirits in thy hands, deliver us from the enlightenment and fatal arts of our forefathers, and give back to us ignorance, innocence, and poverty, the only goods that can give us happiness and are precious in thy sight" (*FSD*, 62).

The imagery of the quotes ("heavy veil" over nature, "the pit where truth has hidden," and "What false paths . . . must be surmounted to reach the truth") suggests the T is buried in the Unconscious; and there he would have it remain. Or would he? One is surprised to find him praise three heroes of the Enlightenment, Bacon, Descartes, and Newton, as rare individuals able "to raise monuments to the glory of human intellect" (*FSD*, 63). So while calling for ignorance and an end to the Enlightenment, he allowed some Enlightenment figures had gone beyond ignorance to true greatness. In this a Jungian could see a two-step process: the rejection of the T in favor of what was "engraved in all hearts" (*FSD*, 64); but then Rousseau allows that some have achieved a higher form of T. The intellect, the cornerstone of the Enlightenment, has been rejected, yet some have restored it at a higher level.

This was his first attempt to tell of the "crowds of great truths" that revealed themselves by the roadside. His second attempt, the *Second Discourse* ("*On the Origin of Inequality,*" written in 1753) picked up many of the same themes. He called on people to know the "natural man" before society distorted him with its "mass of knowledge and errors" (*FSD*, 91). The natural man was the solitary savage living without "communication" or "commerce" with others (*FSD*, 120, 33). This savage was not guided by "arguments," rather he followed a "natural sentiment" that urged "Do what is good for you with the least possible harm to others" (*FSD*, 133). Soon societies developed and led to "sociable man, always outside himself, [who] knows how to live only in the opinion of others; and it is, so to speak, from their judgment alone that he draws the sentiment of his own existence" (*FSD*, 179). When society was proclaimed, those in the state of nature ran to embrace their chains; they soon became "an assemblage of artificial men and fictitious passions" (*FSD*, 178).

In his *First Discourse* Rousseau allowed some great individuals escaped the corruption of the Enlightenment, so in the *Second Discourse* he told of "a few great cosmopolitan souls" who follow the example of their Creator and feel benevolence for the whole human race (*FSD*, 160–61).

The *Second Discourse* again defended the solitary savage living by the natural virtues of the heart. But as Rousseau wrote the *Second Discourse* he was also writing an article on political economy that praised the "body politic"—evidently this was more than the solitary savage. He told of the state possessing a "general will" that determines what is just or unjust for all its members, and the "voice of the people is truly the voice of God" (*SC*, 8). This "general will" obviously involves far more than the free will of a savage living alone and doing as he pleases. Accordingly, Rousseau allows that his "general will" introduced an almost insuperable dilemma for human freedom (*SC*, 10); but he resolved it by claiming people are subjugated to be made free, they then obey without anyone commanding, and their wills are chained by their own consent! Such a wondrous Reconciliation of Opposites suggests the Jungian Self. This general will speaks with a "celestial voice which dictates to every citizen the precepts of public reason, teaching him to act according to the maxims of his own judgment," and the citizen must accept whatever society decrees so as "not to be in contradiction with himself" (*SC*, 11). The "celestial voice" indicates that more than consciousness is involved.

Rousseau had hoped to write an extended treatise on politics, but in 1762 he settled for a short work, *The Social Contract*, an attempt to justify civil society. Again, the state arises when free individuals gather to adopt common laws. Since people have given themselves freely to society, society is justified in making total demands on them. Though they must be totally obedient, the people are still free—such is the reconciliation of necessity with freedom! The community would become a "public person" endowed with its own "unity, its common self, its life, and its will" (*SC*, 56).

> This passage from the state of nature to the civil state produces in man a very remarkable change, replacing instinct by justice in his behavior, and conferring on his actions the moral quality that they had lacked before. It is only now, as the voice of duty succeeds to physical impulse and right to appetite, that man . . . is compelled . . . to consult his reason before he attends to his inclinations. (*SC*, 59)

By entering the social contract "a very remarkable change" takes place in that one is "to consult his reason"! In the earlier *Discourse* the works of reason were rejected so that one might return to the blissful ignorance of nature; now the natural state is left aside and reason, or a celestial voice dictating to reason, reveals the general will that all must follow. In the process, one finds "his ideas amplified, his feelings enobled, and his entire being raised so much higher." Thus, one will constantly "bless the happy moment" of transformation wherein one became no longer "a limited and stupid animal, but an intelligent being and a man" (*SC*, 59; see Jung, *PR*, 104, for the transformation into a higher being with the appearance of the Self).

Rousseau had rejected the works of the Enlightenment to discover the sentiments of the heart (F) in its natural state. But then in a blessed moment of mutual self-surrender, people rise above themselves to be endowed with a common self that speaks with the voice (authority) of God. Contradictions are resolved as the ignorant one becomes an *intelligent* being. The rejected intelligence has become the cornerstone of Rousseau's new identity. But the heart has not been neglected. This shows itself in an interesting 3:4 when Rousseau is speaking of the law: "In addition to these three categories of the law there is a fourth, which is the most important of all; it is not graven on marble or bronze, but in citizens' hearts; in it lies the true constitution of the state" (SC, 89).[3]

Though the wicked man might continue to center the world about himself and make "himself the measure of all things," the good man "measures his radius and keeps to the circumference. Then he is ordered in relation to the common center, which is God, and in relation to the concentric circles, which are the creatures" (E, 292). The ego-center has surrendered to a higher Center: God as the center of concentric circles with the ego moving around the center. This circular movement about the divine center picks up a basic Jungian image of the Self. Consider some texts of Jung: "Often one has the impression that the personal psyche is running round this central point like a shy animal, at once fascinated and frightened" (Jung, PA, 218). Dreams show the Self with people walking around it in a "circular movement" (Jung, PR, 65); for Jung the ego revolves about the Self "very much as the earth revolves round the sun—thus we come to the goal of individuation . . . . The individual ego senses itself as the object of an unknown and supraordinate subject [the Self]" (Jung, TE, 240).

II. The Philosophical Method of a Feeler

Rousseau considered the *discovery* of truth the dominant interest of his life (RSW, 59). To speak of discovery suggests that he did not already possess it; like St. Augustine, he could find Truth only after a difficult search. Descartes and Spinoza (Ts) certainly told of the importance of truth, but for them the truth was clear and securely possessed. Rousseau (as F) found the truth to be obscure: "Truth for us is covered with a veil" (quoted in Crocker, 207), and he believed he would see truth as it is only after his death (RSW, 61). Yet Rousseau would take a phrase from Juvenal as his motto: *vitam impendere vero*, to devote one's life to the truth. He told of being only too happy "to suffer for the cause of truth" (C, 535); proclaiming the truth was his "sublime vocation." But sometimes he modified this vocation: "My duty is to tell men the truth," only to add, "or what I believe to be the truth; it is for a voice more powerful than mine to make them love truth" (quoted in Cranston, 292). The passage tells of truth, a seeming truth, and a heavenly (?) voice.

Throughout his writings Rousseau regarded "opinion" as the great unseen enemy (Crocker, 59).[4] Rousseau was once an avid reader; later he believed reading had filled his mind with conflicting opinions about which he could not decide. He saw the philosophes as men proclaiming their opinions with more interest in getting attention and advancing their reputation than in the truth of what they said; Christian churchmen were seen to be doing the same. Rousseau's search for truth was a religious quest; accordingly the transcendent God of this highly sentimental man was not identified as Love, but as the supreme Intelligence. This God is obscure in the present life, but after death we will share the enlightenment "of celestial Intelligences" (*FSD*, 202)—the phrases suggest that the T is missing in the present world.

In an unfinished essay written in the 1750s Rousseau speculated on how natural man first began to philosophize; he imagined him on a lovely star-filled night when he was drawn out of himself to embrace the universe. The regular movements of stars, planets, and seasons suggested someone ordered them, but who? He was left with "a thousand confused ideas that he could not abandon or clarify. He tried vainly to penetrate the mysteries of nature." Since it was beyond his understanding, he was about to forget it all, when

> suddenly a ray of light struck his spirit and revealed to him those sublime truths that are beyond our human powers and that human reason is able to confirm but not discover. . . . The sanctuary of nature was opened to his understanding as it is to heavenly intelligences, and all the most sublime ideas which we attach to this word: *God*, presented themselves to his spirit. This grace was the reward of his sincere love for the truth. (*RW*, 83–84)

He stands upright to make the first prayer to the divine Being who arranged the whole system. This unfinished essay developed themes that will reoccur in Rousseau: the great truths (T) are beyond our human power, yet to the one who sincerely loves the unknown truth, they are revealed.

In 1761, Rousseau published a novel, *Julie, ou la nouvelle Héloïse*. Julie has a lover, yet out of a sense of duty she marries another and bears him two sons. Late in the novel she leaps heroically into the water to save one of her sons from drowning, but following the event she is about to die herself, attended by her atheist husband and her

Christian pastor. There she makes a statement of her Deist faith, "I always sought what was for the glory of God and the truth. . . . I am not so proud to think I was always right; I am perhaps wrong, but my intention was always pure." So it was with Rousseau: he was uncertain of the truth he proposed, but certain of his sincerity. Julie claims God is kind and just, and, "If God did not illumine my reason in this matter, could he hold me responsible for a gift he has not given?" Again Rousseau: truth involves a divine illumination, a gift that he cannot be blamed for lacking (LD, 15). Julie is suffering from a fatal fever, but earlier she had thought the matter through and that satisfies her now. So it will be with Rousseau. She addresses God: "O great Being! Eternal Being, supreme Intelligence, source of life, father of men and king of nature" (JNH, 704). Her atheist husband and Protestant pastor are deeply moved by her words; her pastor exclaims, "I would instruct you and you instruct me!"

Like Julie, Rousseau found himself surrounded by the atheist philosophes and the Christian clergy. By Julie's speech he tried to reconcile these opponents in a statement to which both might agree. But he, like Julie, could never be sure the Deism he believed was the truth—it might be only his opinion. But together with Julie, he was sure of his sincerity. Julie's simple sincerity sets her apart from the quarrels of philosophes and Christians.

The year after Julie appeared, Rousseau brought out Emile (on education [1762]). This is an extended account of how the child should learn directly from nature and not from the opinions of others. Emile is a hypothetical student being educated, and as he begins his teens he is hardly aware of books. From Emile's earliest days his instructor has devised occasions whereby Emile might learn directly from nature (heat and cold, the stars, etc.) and his own appetites (hunger, thirst). Emile's teacher seems to spend the whole day watching or working with the child, so that eventually he gains an authority in Emile's heart (E, 234); this further enables him to shape the boy's spirit. Emile can be read as an appalling account of social engineering[5]—for the child is spied on day and night, and one can object that he does not simply learn from nature but from artificial tricks devised to instruct him.

Since religion involves abstract terms, Rousseau did not want God or the soul mentioned to the child. At age fifteen Emile "does not know even the name of history, or what metaphysics and morals are"

(*E*, 207). He "hardly knows how to generalize ideas and how to make abstractions," for these are the source of our greatest errors (*E*, 275). Rousseau sugests that eighteen might be a suitable age to tell of God and the soul. To show how to teach religion, Rousseau interrupts the story of Emile to tell at length of himself as a troubled young man meeting a sympathetic priest, the unnamed Savoyard Vicar, who brought him peace by making a highly personal profession of Deism. Rousseau had known such a priest from Savoy, but he acknowledged that much of the vicar's profession was his own composition.

The vicar invited Rousseau to set out with him at daybreak to a hill high above the Po River; the rays of the rising sun were projecting long shadows of trees and vinyards, while the Alps stretched out in the distance. After long and silent contemplation, "the man of peace" spoke:

> My child, do not expect either learned speeches or profound reasonings from me. I am not a great philosopher, and I care little to be one. But I sometimes have good sense, and I always love the truth. I do not want to argue with you or even attempt to convince you. It is enough for me to reveal to you what I think in the simplicity of my heart. Consult yours during my speech. That is all I ask of you. If I am mistaken, it is in good faith. (*E*, 266)

As with Julie, there is a perfect setting and a loving friend speaking from the heart; the vicar will "reveal" his heart and in doing so the heart of Rousseau will respond. The vicar tells of being born in poverty and seeking the priesthood to support himself. He was soon confused as he studied the philosophers, for they seemed not to be seeking the truth at all, but only attention.

> I meditated therefore on the sad fate of mortals, floating on this sea of human opinions without rudder or compass and delivered to their stormy passions without any other guide than an inexperienced pilot who is ignorant of his route and knows neither where he is coming from nor where he is going. I said, "I love the truth, I seek it and cannot recognize it. Let it be revealed to me, and I shall remain attached to it. Why must it hide itself from the eagerness of a heart made to adore it?" (*E*, 267–68)[6]

In searching for truth we find "impenetrable mysteries surround us on all sides," and we mistakenly believe "we possess intelligence for piercing these mysteries" (*E*, 267). Many adopt an opinion at random rather than admit "that none of us can see what it [truth] is." The vicar decided to seek the truth by consulting his Inner Light, thus "yielding to sentiment more than to reason." He would accept that "to which in the sincerity of my heart I cannot refuse my consent" (*E*, 272, 270). Like Julie, he would be judged by his sincerity. This leads him to affirm the existence of a Supreme Intelligence who set up the world system and will judge our souls after death. But he warns that "reasonings" about God are always rash, and "a wise man ought to yield to them only with trembling and with certainty that he is not made to plumb their depths" (*E*, 277).

We become confused in trying to know God himself, "He escapes me, and my clouded mind no longer perceives anything" (*E*, 277). But this is only in the present life; eventually we will be delivered from the body and then we will contemplate "the Supreme Being and the eternal truths of which He is the source" (*E*, 283); the mysterious God is again associated with the T. Presently we cannot even think of God or the eternal truths.

> As my mind approaches the eternal light, its brilliance dazzles and confuses me, and I am forced to abandon all the terrestrial notions which helped me to imagine it. God is no longer corporeal and sensible. The supreme intelligence which rules the world is no longer the world itself. I lift and fatigue my mind in vain to conceive His essence. (*E*, 285)

The vicar spoke of God who "makes himself *felt* in" the universe (*E*, 293). But the above passage tells of a God "no longer corporeal," a God "no longer the world itself"—a God no longer felt? These passages could be understood in terms of a section near the end of Rousseau's *Confessions* where he told of the wonders of nature lifting the heart to God; these "upliftings of the heart" did not require "the weary effort of thought" (*C*, 593). He tells of a pious old woman who had uplifting moments in nature and prayed, "O Good mother." And Rousseau made that his prayer, "O Nature! O my mother! I am here under your sole protection" (*C*, 594). This is God as "the world itself," the God perceived when one regards the world with wonder. But in *Emile* he is telling of a supreme and *transcendent* Intelligence "no longer corporeal" and "no longer the world itself."[7]

One begins to wonder why the vicar's opinion should merit special attention. But that overlooks the setting, the sincerity of the vicar, and their honest friendship. Rousseau had come to trust the priest, and only after their friendship was established did the priest confide. ("Nothing has so much weight in the human heart as the voice of clearly recognized friendship" [E, 234].) Heart has spoken to heart. This and the lovely setting give weight to the vicar's opinion and makes him different from the philosophes and Christians speaking mindlessly in the salons of Paris where even the speakers do not believe what they say.

The vicar never tries to argue his points: "Always remember that I am not teaching my sentiment; I am revealing it" (E, 277). The vicar's heart-to-heart revelation would enable the young Rousseau to see: "It is enough for me to reveal to you what I think in the simplicity of my heart. Consult yours during my speech" (E, 266). "I wanted not to philosophize with you but to help you consult your heart" (E, 289). Here there is heart-to-heart communication, while in the salons of Paris "opinions" are not really opinions, for no one believes them; they are social ploys to get attention. For Rousseau, one should reveal the depths of one's heart, so that listeners can discover the depths of their own. This is the method of the vicar, the F. It is the method of both Augustine and Rousseau in writing their *Confessions*: the baring of the heart that allows readers to discover their own heartfelt truth. Objections might arise, but the vicar can resolve them: "This sentiment that speaks to me is stronger than the reason combatting it" (E, 280). The Rationalists spoke of innate ideas, while Rousseau would speak of innate sentiments and innate feelings (E, 290; RJ, 242). When feelings are shared, one can discover one's own. "Conscience, conscience! Divine instinct, immortal and celestial voice, certain guide of a being that is ignorant and limited." In a similar way Augustine (another F) told of a Teacher in his heart that let him know when he was hearing the truth.[8]

The vicar himself had "exhausted the vanity of human opinions," only to find the road of wisdom. He concludes his profession of faith with a disclaimer:

> The fact that I act in good faith does not mean I believe myself infallible. Those of my opinions which seem truest to me are perhaps so many lies. . . . I have done what I could to attain the truth, but its source is too elevated. If the strength for going farther is lacking to me, of what can I be guilty? It is up to the truth to come nearer. (E, 294)

Again, the real truth requires divine revelation; it must come nearer—but one cannot be blamed if it does not. When the vicar finished speaking, Rousseau adds, "He was moved, and so was I. . . . *to the extent that he spoke to me according to his conscience, mine seemed to confirm what he had told me*" (emphasis added) (*E*, 294). For Rousseau, that is philosophy! The "opinions" commonly bantered about were only social postures. But, when the vicar set postures aside and revealed his heart, the heart of Rousseau could manifest itself. Truth comes by mutual revelation. Likewise in prayer, we open our hearts to God and hope He will do the same for us; if not, we are not to blame. The vicar advised, "Seek the truth yourself. As for me, I promise you only good faith." Like Julie, the vicar has only the purity of his heart, but by speaking from the heart, others discover what their own heart is saying. Like Julie, the vicar says that God or the truth must make the next move. For a Jungian, these statements show well the method of the F; the F waits in sincerity for the T to reveal itself.

A modern critic sees the vicar's profession as "an attempt to reconstruct man's psychological unity, to harmonize reason and sentiment" (Crocker, 152). This is the reconciliation of opposites Rousseau tried to achieve, and one hesitates to say whether it occurred. Yet the vicar tells of proceeding "according to the *understanding* He [God] gives to my mind and the *sentiments* He inspires in my heart" (emphases added) (*E*, 295). The uncertainty suggests a reconciliation that is tenuous at best.

Emile was severly criticized by both Christians and atheists. So Rousseau, fearing for his life, fled Paris and went to Switzerland; but finding opposition there he took refuge in England with David Hume. He had quarrelled with friends in France and now quarrelled with friends in England. He looked for "a single human heart that opened up to his, felt his sorrows, and pitied them" (*RJ*, 225). He returned to France in 1767 with an assumed name and continued to write. From 1776 to 1778 he worked on the *Reveries of the Solitary Walker*, a collection of ten meditations made while walking in the country and published only after his death. The *Reveries* tell of his distress as friends betrayed him, but they also speak of "the holy name of truth." He explains, "In its general and abstract sense truth is the most precious of our possessions"; but again, he was not sure he possessed it (*RSW*, 66).

In *Reveries*, Rousseau tells of knowing a time of confusion many years earlier when he asked, "Shall I allow myself to be tossed eternally to and fro by the sophistries of the eloquent, when I am not even sure that the opinions they preach and press so ardently on others are really their own?" At one time, lest he be taken in by the eloquent, he considered following the common opinion, but that would leave him "searching through high seas and storms, without helm or compass, for a scarcely visible lantern which would never light my way into any port" (*RSW*, 54). So "finding on all sides impenetrable mysteries and unanswerable objections," he undertook what was "perhaps the *most ardent and sincere* investigations ever conducted by any mortal" (emphasis added). In the prime of life, he made up his mind once and for all on religious questions. He would take the opinion that seemed most clearly proved and not worry about objections he could not answer. This resulted in the Deism set forth in the vicar's profession in *Emile*. He advised us to "choose" our opinion with all the maturity of judgment of which we are capable; if we are wrong, "we cannot in justice be held responsible."[9] Now, as an old man suffering from actual and imagined persecution, these earlier conclusions "seem to have been sent down by Heaven." The "empty logic-chopping" of the salons will not make him reconsider. When he falls into doubt, "I remember the painstaking attention and sincerity of heart which led me to them, and all my confidence returns" (*RSW*, 61).

Yet sincerity did not seem to be enough; something always seemed lacking and Rousseau remained restless until his death. He had said, "Truth for us is covered with a veil." He awaited its revelation; that was all a prophet of truth could do. But he looked forward to the day he would be free of the body and then see "truth face to face" (*RSW*, 61). In the meantime, if someone on earth were to claim certitude he would only be a "charlatan." So Rousseau accepted his "sublime vocation" and proclaimed the uncertain truth. He proclaimed it by the only means he knew: with ever increasing sincerity he told the world what was in his heart. That was his mission. The *Confessions* recounts his many faults in detail, yet there he challenged his readers to say they were better than he. By "better" he did not deny they might have fewer faults, only that they were less sincere. Such is the vocation of this introverted F. When the F speaks, we can feel ourselves at the bedside of Julie, or sitting at sunrise over the Po River, or gazing at the stars with the first philosopher. At such tender moments, our hearts affirm their innate sentiments and other hearts can discover theirs.

Augustine and Rousseau are the only Fs considered in this study, and the two have much in common: they both wrote philosophic biographies that they called "Confessions," and both confessions center around a moment of conversion while weeping under a tree. But what they have in common is deeper than that. Both wrote philosophy by telling their personal story. Both developed intense friendships and wanted to speak to the heart, and both did. Both spoke of Truth as hidden behind a veil. Both told of seeking to know God and the soul, the two noncorporeal realities. Both believed that freedom can be found only by a total surrender to divine law, and both believed our yearning for happiness can be satisfied only in God, a transcendent God that both identified as Truth/Intelligence.

One does not need to be an F to appreciate the power in the writings of Rousseau. He thought readers would gain a passion and energy in their own souls from reading his sincere account (*RJ*, 218), and many of them did. A distinguished T would read *Emile* soon after it appeared and would gain this passion and energy. This was Immanuel Kant, who was to read *Emile* and find himself shaken in his T identity, for the words of the Savoyard Vicar enabled Kant to listen to his own heart as he had not done before.

Notes

1. This is developed later in the same work (*E*, 157–58) when Rousseau equates reason with the "common sense," which is said to reside in the brain and has no special organ, no faculty (Rousseau's "common sense" is the *sensus communis* of the scholastics, not "common sense" as in contemporary American usage). Here Rousseau says reason has two levels: the *"sensual or childish reason"* which forms simple ideas by joining several sensations; while *"intellectual or human reason"* joins these simple ideas together to form complex ideas. For Rousseau, reason offered only a subjective standard: "Human reason is not a common determinate standard, so that it is unjust for any man to lay down his notion of things for others" (*LD*, 14).

2. He claimed his writing did not come from "a fleeting explosion" but from "a dominant and permanent feeling which can sustain itself . . . for ten

years and produce twelve volumes always filled with one sustained zeal" (*RJ*, 217–18).

3. *The Social Contract* is the only work of Rousseau that has significant Jungian symbolism of transformation. This 3:4 occurs in a reversed form, for the separated Fourth would be Rousseau's Dominant, his F, while the Three are placed in the Unconscious. On several occasions Jung has told of this understanding of the 3:4 (see his *PA*, 108, 112). A similar reversed form of the 3:4 was found in Plato, who proposed one should study three subjects till one begins the Fourth, which he identified as philosophy/dialectic, associated with Plato's Dominant N. Likewise, Spinoza told of three indirect forms of knowledge, and one direct form, his Dominant T. It is noteworthy that the passage of Plato just cited spoke of the separated Fourth as the "coping stone." Rousseau, in the passage that speaks of the law in the hearts of the citizens, sees what is in the heart as the unshakeable *key* stone (*SC*, 90). If the Repressed is the cornerstone, could the Dominant be the keystone/coping stone? Other examples of the Dominant as the separated Fourth will be seen in the present study when Kant tells of faculties in a university and Teilhard speaks of the transformation of the Three Unconscious faculties.

4. In this study opinion has been associated with the F—and Rousseau was highly critical of opinion! But this can be easily explained: the "opinions" Rousseau criticized were not opinions at all; they were only ploys to get attention. Real opinions were few and these he would take seriously, as will be seen.

5. The same is true of the characters in *Julie*. One has the sense that Julie's husband has been manipulating Julie, her lover, and just about everyone else in the novel so that they fit into his ideal; the same social engineering is found in Rousseau's drama *Pygmalion*. Though Rousseau wrote hundreds of pages on bringing up children by direct experience, it should be noted he had no direct experience of child-rearing. Yet he had five children by his common-law wife; each time, several weeks after birth, he left the child at a foundling home—over her objections.

6. Rousseau claimed that what the vicar said was the result of his own "arduous research." Like the vicar, he would later use the image of a troubled sea voyage: taking prudence for a guide would be like "searching through high seas and storms, without helm or compass, for a scarcely visible lantern which would never light my way to port" (*RSW*, 54). His search for truth would resolve matters that baffle the human mind while "finding on all sides impenetrable mysteries and unanswerable objections" (*RSW*, 55).

7. The vicar's coming to a God "no longer corporeal" resembles the moment when St. Augustine passed beyond the corporeal to acknowledge the eternal Truth beyond his mutable mind and beyond his attempts to think of God in corporeal terms (Augustine, *Confessions*, 149, 136–37; see above). This section does not consider the time and eternity opposition in Rousseau as earlier ones did for Augustine, Descartes, and Spinoza. But Rousseau's *Confessions* tell often of his fascination with time. Note that Emile is told of the God apart from the world only when he begins to think; otherwise he would

simply idolize the world without any true idea of God. It was a similar idolatry that Augustine feared and made him hesitate so long in becoming Christian.

8. Augustine found that, when someone spoke, his inner Truth would say, "He is speaking the truth." Then he was sure (C, 260).

9. This was the plea of Julie; it is also the plea Rousseau made in his *Letter to D'Alembert* (LD, 15). In each case his defense consisted in pointing out his sincerity.

Bibliography

Works of Rousseau

C   *The Confessions*, translated by J. M. Cohen. London: Penguin Books, 1953.

C&C *The Confessions and Correspondence, Including the Letters to Malesherbes*, vol. V, *The Collected Writings of Rousseau*. Edited by Christopher Kelly, Roger D. Masters, and Peter G. Stillman; translated by Christopher Kelly. Hanover: Dartmouth College, 1995.

E   *Emile*, introduction, translation, and notes by Allan Bloom. New York: Basic Books, 1979.

FSD *The First and Second Discourses*, edited, with introduction and notes by Roger D. Masters; translated by Roger D. and Judith R. Masters. New York: St. Martin's Press, 1964.

JNH *Julie, ou la nouvelle Héloïse*. Paris: Editions Garnier Freres, 1968. My own translations.

LD   *Letter to D'Alembert*, in *The Miscellaneous Works of J. J. Rousseau*, vol. III, translator unidentified. New York: Lennox Hill, 1972.

RJ   *Rousseau: Judge of Jean-Jacques: Dialogues*, vol. I, *The Collected Writings of Rousseau*. Edited by Roger D. Masters and Christopher Kelly; translated by Judith R. Bush, Christopher Kelly, and Roger D. Masters. Hanover: Dartmouth College, 1990.

RSW *Reveries of the Solitary Walker*, translated with an introduction by Peter Walker. New York: Penguin, 1979

RW   *Rousseau: Religious Writings*, edited by Ronald Grimsley. Oxford: The Clarendon Press, 1970. The texts of Rousseau are in French with notes and comments in English. The translations here are my own.

SC *The Social Contract,* translation with introduction and notes by
Christopher Betts. New York: Oxford University Press, 1994.

Other Works

Cranston, Maurice. *Jean-Jacques: The Early Life of Jean-Jacques
Rousseau (1712–1754).* New York: W. W. Norton, 1982.

Crocker, Lester G. *Jean-Jacques Rousseau: The Prophetic Voice*
(1758–1778). New York: Macmillan, 1973.

8 Kant: Pure Reason Falters and Regains Control
The Dominant Allows Auxiliaries, Then the Repressed, and Then Reconsiders

Kant as T: Kant introduced the *Critique of Pure Reason* by saying it dealt with "nothing save reason itself and its pure thinking"; it is an "*inventory* of all our possessions through *pure* reason, systematically arranged"; it tells "what reason produces entirely out of itself" (*CPuR*, 10, 14). "A philosophy of any subject (a system of rational knowledge from concepts) requires a system of *pure rational* concepts independent of any condition of intuition (*MM*, 181; parenthesis and emphasis in text). For Kant, one knows one's self to be "intelligence"; "a rational being must regard himself as intelligence" (*FMM*, 76, 71). "Man, insofar as he is conscious of himself (object to himself) *thinks*" (*OP*, 210). Accordingly, one should do one's duty, and this "does not rest at all on feelings, impulses and inclinations" (*FMM*, 52). For "every feeling itself [is] pathological" (*CPr&O*, 183). When asked why people can accept rational arguments for virtue and still not *be* virtuous, Kant replied, because "the teachers themselves have not completely clarified their concepts" (*FMM*, 27). Jung refers to Kant as a T (Jung, *PT*, 383).[1] For Kant's Quarternity, see Figure 8.1. Kant's Myers-Briggs type would be INTP.

	T Dominant IV Modality Reason	
N III Relation Understanding	Sublime Happiness	S II Quality Sensation
	Holiness	
	F I Quantity Feelings	

Figure 8.1

I. Enantiodromia: A Thinker Discovers His Feelings

While lecturing as privat dozent at the University of Königsberg, Immanuel Kant was known for the methodical ordering of his life. But in 1762 the neighbors noticed he was missing his daily walk. The privat dozent was absorbed in reading the recently published *Emile* by Jean-Jacques Rousseau.

Kant's parents were devout Pietists who sent their son to a school which shared their values. Pietism, with its stress on the personal and inner aspects of Christianity, was not concerned with doctrines or theology. It valued the pious heart with little regard for the intelligence and its subtlety. But Kant was highly intelligent and fascinated by the ideals of the Enlightenment. He moved away from his Pietist roots and developed the metaphysical ideas of Leibniz and Wolff, writing his own rational treatises on God, freedom, and immortality. Then at age thirty-eight he came upon Rousseau and was amazed. Rousseau too was part of the Enlightenment, yet an anomaly who spoke of feelings, the heart, and the inner worth of each individual. In short, Rousseau was a voice of the Enlightenment telling of many of the Pietist values Kant had known years before. But to these Rousseau added, in the words of Kant, his "extraordinary talents and magic power of eloquence." The leading writers of the Enlightenment were fascinated by him, and, for several days after coming upon *Emile*, Immanuel Kant missed his daily walk.

Before reading *Emile* Kant had studied the British moralists. These had given him a basis for appreciating *Emile*, for they spoke of the "moral sense" or the "sense of benevolence." This they took to be a separate faculty of perception (like sight or hearing) that simply recognized the good when it saw it. They wrote without the emotional power of Rousseau. Yet their "moral sense" could more or less fit with the "heart" proposed by Rousseau. Kant awakened to the repressed F, and there appeared what one critic called a "noticeable change of tone" in his writing, and also a personal crisis that would last for years (Vleeschauwer, 42).

In 1762, the year Kant read *Emile*, he began speaking of an independent moral feeling that owed much to the British moralists and more to Rousseau. This "feeling" was apart from reason and made its own claims. In Jungian terms, Kant was a T who had discovered the Opposites: recognizing the two faculties (T and F), he claimed the distinction important and insisted the two be kept separate.

> In these times we have first begun to realize that the faculty of conceiving of truth is intellection, while that of sensing the good is feeling, and that they must not be interchanged. Just as there are unanalyzable concepts of the true, that is, what is met with in the objects of intellection considered by themselves, there is also an unanalyzable feeling for the good. (Prize Essay, in *CPr&O*, 284)

Kant praises the British moralists and tells of people having "many simple sensations of the good." He suggests an independent "moral sense" or "moral feeling" and wonders if this could be the basis of morality. Now both faculties (T and F) have been identified and "must not be interchanged." But which should dominate? The final statement of the essay leaves the issue unresolved: "It is still to be settled whether it is simply the cognitive faculty or whether it is feeling (the primary inner ground of the appetitive faculty) which decides the basic principles of practical philosophy" (*CPr&O*, 285).

The following year (1763) Kant wrote a work very different from his earlier metaphysical writings: *Observations on the Feeling of the Beautiful and Sublime*. As the title indicates, his subject is Feeling! But only the "finer feelings": "to that kind of feeling, which can take place without any thought whatever, I shall here pay no attention" (*O*, 46).

Intellectual works would be considered, if they "contain something for feeling" (*O*, 57). Now he is concerned with the unity of Thinking and Feeling. "Moral feeling" (*moralisches Gefuhl*) is his central concern; it is named eight times in this brief text, but still it is not to be trusted if it is not united with principle (*O*, 67). When feelings and principle are united, the result is sublime. In contrast, what is beautiful is evident and shallow. Day is beautiful while night is sublime. "Affability is beautiful and thoughtful silence is sublime." Feelings of the beautiful are awakened by scenes of flower-strewn meadows, while feelings of the sublime are awakened by "tall oaks and lonely shadows in a sacred grove," by "the quiet stillness of a summer evening as the shimmering light of the stars breaks through the brown shadows of the night" (*O*, 47). The feeling of the sublime often includes dread, melancholy, quiet wonder, greatness, and awe. By his images and emotions Kant's sublime suggests the Unconscious,[2] while the beautiful is simple, charming, and straightforward.

One passage of *Observations* tells of the melancholy temperament, and some commentators (aware of Kant's early problems with melancholy) have seen it as a personal reflection.[3] The melancholy individual is said to be particularly sensitive to "the higher moral feelings" and becomes melancholy "when his feelings are aroused beyond a certain degree," or when his feelings have been led astray. But the melancholy individual

> has above all a *feeling for the sublime*. . . . All emotions of the sublime have more fascination for him than the deceiving charms of the beautiful. His well-being will rather be satisfaction than pleasure. He is resolute. On that account he orders his sensations under principles. They are so much the less subject to inconstancy and change, the more universal this principle is to which they are subordinated, and the broader the high feeling is under which the lower are included. . . . Of such a nature are principles in comparison to impulses, which simply well up on isolated occasions; and thus the man of principles is in counteraction with him who is seized opportunely by a goodhearted and loving motive. . . . [The melancholy one] has a high feeling of the dignity of human nature. (*O*, 64–66)

It was Rousseau who awakened Kant to the high feeling of human dignity, and Kant, following Rousseau, began praising the lofty feelings of simple folk. Intellectual gifts are of little real benefit, for "the capacities of the soul have so great a connection that for the most part one can elucidate the talent of insight from the manifestation of feeling" (*O*, 72). In Jungian terms the soul has such an underlying unity that insights are measured by the manifestation of the repressed Function! Kant knew a manifestation of feeling when he read *Emile*, and his "talent of insight" followed. Now Kant, the great rationalist and metaphysician, is claiming it would be useless to have great intellectual gifts without "a strong feeling" for what is noble, for the elements of the soul "have so great a connection." And, furthermore, the feeling provides the motive to rightly use one's intellectual gifts (*O*, 72). At this time he is a very different philosopher from the earlier Kant and from what he would later become.

In this work *Observations on the Feeling of the Beautiful and Sublime* (1763), Kant finds it good that people generally act out of good impulses rather than on principle, for those who act on principle are frequently mistaken. Therefore, Nature endows most people with helpful impulses that resemble animal instincts urging them to act for the common good. Here Kant's F appears as urges or impulses that are *usually more helpful than reason!* Still the rationalist is present as Kant claims the feeling for humanity should unite feeling with principle.

In the *Observations*, the influence of Rousseau is evident as Kant praises the impulses of simple folk, but Rousseau is never mentioned in the text. However, in the borders of his manuscript of *Observations* Kant added many notes; ten such notes mention Rousseau. In one notation Kant speaks of a time "when I despised the masses, which know nothing. Rousseau has set me right. This blind prejudice disappears; I learn to honor men." In *Observations* this honor is evident, for he located the sublime in principles which "are not speculative rules, but the consciousness of a feeling that lives in every human breast. . . . it is the *feeling of the beauty and the dignity of human nature*" (*O*, 60; emphasis in text). It is a "universal affection" for humanity. Now Kant the Thinker is being guided by a "feeling that lives in every human breast"! Such passages recall the Pietism in which Kant was raised, but now there is talk of "principle." This unity of principle with a lofty feeling is the sublime. And the most sublime is the feeling of the dignity of humanity.

By his marginal notations on *Observations*, Kant was trying to clarify for himself how Feeling and Thinking might relate: "The simple human being very early has a *feeling* for what is right, but he gets

a *concept* of it only very late or not at all." Having accepted spontaneous feelings, he is puzzled by their inconstancy: "The universal
love of humanity has something high and noble about it, but it is
chimerical." That is, like all impulses, it comes and goes. For Kant,
things have become unsettled, and many journal notations express
only his doubts and uncertainty (Schilpp, 64). His love for humanity
is unsteady and perhaps illusory. He writes a troubled notation:

> Everything goes past like a river and the changing taste and the vari-
> ous shapes of men make the whole game uncertain and delusive.
> Where do I find fixed points in nature, which cannot be moved by
> man, and where I can indicate the markers by the shore to which he
> ought to adhere? (See Schilpp, 73)

In 1765 Kant wrote an outline for a course he intended to teach
on Moral Philosophy. There he affirmed that right and wrong can be
known directly by the human heart, but he warned lest philosophers proceed to dispense with proof. Still the outline would tell of
trusting the feelings of "the human heart."

Before reading Rousseau, Kant had read the mystical texts of
Emanuel Swedenborg (1688–1772) and at first was enthused to find
that the visions claimed by Swedenborg coincided with his own
metaphysical conclusions. But in 1765 he declared the texts of Swedenborg to be "eight volumes of sheer nonsense," the "concoctions
of a diseased brain." These denunciations are in a work that he
published anonymously, *Dreams of a Spirit Seer*. His English translator calls the work "a wanton destruction of everything he [Kant]
once held sacred," and "a caricature of all contemporary metaphysicians" (*DSS*, 14, 21; translation and introduction by John
Manolesco). In this work Kant claimed he had been taken in by
Swedenborg—and taken in by his own metaphysics! He rejected all
talk of spirits and immortal souls as pseudo-knowledge (*DSS*, 94). A
puzzled commentator asks, "Was the book [*Dreams of a Spirit Seer*]
just a by-blow of free humor, or was there concealed behind the
satyr play of the mind something resembling a tragedy of metaphysics? None of Kant's friends and critics was able to answer the
question with certainty" (Cassirer, 79). Metaphysics itself had become an insubstantial dream. Kant was deeply confused, and he
struggled to develop an entirely new philosophy—without meta-

physical dreams, that is, a philosophy that would work within the limits of what a human could know.

In this radical rejection of his own philosophy Kant was not completely at a loss. In his critique of Swedenborg he fell back to the teaching of Pietism/Rousseau: he told again of "the moral feeling." A feeling that inclines us to conform to the great Universal Will (*DSS*, 51). *Dreams of a Spirit Seer* comes to a hopeful conclusion centered on the heart, the F: "But true wisdom is the companion of simplicity, and as with the latter, the heart prescribes rules to the mind, all these huge weapons of our scholars become redundant. Its aims must not require means which cannot be at the disposal of all men. . . . Does not the heart of man contain its own moral law . . . ?" (*DSS*, 97).

The heart "prescribes rules to the mind"; the heart contains "its own moral law"! Is it any wonder that Kant published the work anonymously? For Kant the rationalist, the T and its metaphysical dreams have been set aside and the feelings of the heart are in control. Three years earlier Kant had wondered whether the knowledge faculty or the feelings determine the true principles. Now in 1765 he renounces his rational arguments: "The heart prescribes rules to the mind." Now he no longer needs rational arguments (T) for the immortality of the soul; rather he will base his "expectation of a future life upon the *feelings* of a noble soul." Now there is no need for intellectual speculation, for a "moral faith" in immortality is said to be "above the subtleties of reason and discursive arguments"!

In the Introduction to this present Jungian study of the philosophers, Enantiodromia was explained with an example. The example told of a dominant T suddenly being overcome by emotional tenderness (F) only to protest later on: "I was not myself." Kant is now being presented as a T giving way to emotion; could that be the reason *Dreams of a Spirit Seer* was published anonymously? By the anonymity Kant seemed to be saying, "In writing this I was not myself." The final line of this text appeals again to a feeling: he quotes Voltaire, "Let's seek our happiness and cultivate our garden." Happiness is a feeling, the feeling that he would later insist we should *not seek*. So concludes this puzzling work.

Late in 1765 Kant thinks back on the philosophers he has been reading and concludes: "They divide themselves into moralists of pure reason and those of the moral feeling." Such is his Enantiodromia! Again: "All systems are such as derive morality either from reason or from feeling" (Schilpp, 110–11). The T and the F are each making a claim. As the year 1765 ended, Kant again picked up the image of a sea voyage to write good news: "after many capsizings . . . I have finally reached the point where I feel secure in the method that has to be followed" (PC, 48). On the last day of the year he announced that after all his capsizing he finally has developed a suitable method. Further enlightenments continued: "The year 1769 brought great light for me." In that year he seems to have come to the insights that would result in the "critical" philosophy for which he is known. In 1770 he was promoted to professor of logic and metaphysics, and his inaugural lecture has reason back in control: "Thus moral philosophy, so far as it supplies first principles of moral judgment, is known only through the pure understanding and itself belongs to pure philosophy." "Only through the *pure understanding*" will his "pure philosophy" develop, the philosophy he wanted would be purified of any empirical data (such as movements of the heart that come and go). The moral feeling or any other feeling is empirical and thus can play no determining part in what he intends to write. "The moral judgment does not originate in the feeling, but rather the feeling in the judgment. Every feeling for morality presupposes a moral judgment in the understanding" (Schilpp, 114).

Sometime around 1770 Kant seems to have regained his equilibrium, and the Enantiodromia was over. Reason is again in control and the "sentimentalism" of Rousseau is renounced. "By that time the crisis was over. But at its height, as in the *Traume [Dreams of a Spirit Seer]*, it is acute" (Vleeschauwer, 40). Kant's new balance would take years to master and articulate. It would differ from what is found in his earlier writings, as reason would no longer act alone. It would act only in conjunction with the *understanding* and *sensibility* (that is, T will act only in conjunction with N, and S). That gives three Functions: T, N, and S. But where are the Feelings, the Fourth?

II. Kant's Architecture of Quaternity

During the turmoil of the 1760s Kant published abundantly, but the 1770s has been called his "silent decade of incubation" (Paulson, 100). Midway through this decade he complained in his journal of the person who values "his feelings, his mental agitations, images, the half-dreamed, half-thought notions that play around in his swirling mind" and lacks the "cold-bloodedness of judgment." As the decade ended, he wrote in his journal, "One should never be beside oneself [*ausser sich*], but rather in possession of one's self" (quoted in Zammito, 38, 44).

During the silent decade, Kant gained possession of himself by renouncing his feelings and working out a pure metaphysics, one that would be free of everything empirical and contingent. It was to have two parts: one theoretical and one ethical, and he hesitated about which he would write first. In 1781, twelve years after receiving his "great light," Kant brought out the theoretical part: *Critique of Pure Reason*. It is a speculative work in which motives and feelings will have no part, for "these belong to the empirical sources of knowledge" (*CPuR*, 61, 633n). Though the work is theoretical, he briefly outlines the major lines of his later writings in ethics (*CPuR*, 61, 325n, 636–44).

The first task of the *Critique of Pure Reason* is a "clearing, as it were, and leveling of what has hitherto been waste ground" (*CPuR*, 14). That is, he must reject metaphysics as it had been known. Only then can pure reason lay down its own "complete architectonic plan" and thus form an "edifice" for all speculative knowledge, a structure to contain all thinking. The unity of Kant's structure is impressive, but even a sympathetic critic would find his "monolithic schematization of concepts" somewhat excessive (Cassirer, 171). But notable for the present study is the Quaternity—a *Fourfold structure*—that constitutes what Kant called his "complete architectonic plan." He insisted it was based on logic and claimed to develop it out of the logic texts of his day.[4] He introduced it by saying, "we find that the function of thought in judgment can be brought under four heads, each of which contains three moments." But instead of listing the four in sequence one after the other in a line or one under the other, he set them in a pattern that illustrates his architectural imagery:

But the pattern also suggests the Jungian Quaternity with its two pairs of opposites set around a center; a distinctive arrangement of which Kant was fully aware. While working on the *Critique*, he wrote to a friend telling of the importance of his layout and explained he was not going to be like Aristotle, who set his predicamenta "side by side as he found them in a purely chance juxtaposition. On the contrary, I arranged them according to the way they classify themselves by their own nature" (*PC*, 73). The present author is not aware of any Kantian scholar commenting on Kant's distinctive layout.[5] This unique way of listing four elements, a way that is not "a purely chance juxtaposition," occurs *six* times in the *Critique of Pure Reason* (see Figure 8.2 for the most basic form of this listing).

	I **Quantity** Universal Particular	
II **Quality** Affirmative Negative Infinite	Singular	III **Relation** Categorical Hypothetical
	IV **Modality** Problematic Assertoric Apodeictic	Disjunctive

Figure 8.2

This is probably the most basic of the six sets of elements laid out this way. But there are numerous other sets of four in this *Critique* and many could easily appear in such a layout: There are four considerations of space (68–69); four unconditioned unities (366); four concepts of comparison (278–80); four comparisons of Leibniz (283–85); four absolutes of completeness (390); four formal conditions of a complete system (576–628); four disciplines of pure reason (576–628), four cosmological antinomies (396–421), and four main points of the system of metaphysics (662). "Four" seems to be on Kant's mind. It is often evident he is building on the original Four; but at times the connection seems tenuous, as in the following four arranged as a Quaternity:

1. I think,

2. as subject,   3. as simple subject

4. as identical subject in
every state of my thought.

Sometimes, as when he lists the four cosmological antimonies, he refers back to the original Four (Quantity, Quality, Relation, and Modality, as above) without repeating the original layout. But, even more surprising, in later writings that have less to do with logic (from whence he claims to have drawn his four), he continues to introduce the same four. For example: the categories of freedom are quantity, quality, relation, and modality (*CPr&O*, 68–69); in religion he finds there are "four tokens of the true church"—the same four (*RLR*, 92). In political matters, the laws of civil society are developed under the same four headings (*PC*, 132). In aesthetics the four moments of taste involve the same four (*CJ*, 37–77), so do the four satisfactions of the sublime (*CJ*, 85–106), and so do the four considerations of matter (*OP*, 15–22, 27–55). This is the "architectonics" or the "monolithic schematization of concepts" that runs all through Kant's mature thinking. The four elements are—with a single exception—always considered in the same order. What is this layout of elements that "classify themselves by their own nature" into a Quaternity? Kant claims it is based on the work of logicians, but it is difficult to identify these logicians. The layout of Kant's Quaternity resembles what Jung considered an Archetype of the Unconscious. But Kant suggested something similar in calling it "an edifice for which we have at least the idea in ourselves" (*CPuR*, 573). Is that not an archetype? Jung could be seen as offering an empirical basis for Kant, and Kant could be seen as giving a philosophical perspective to what Jung claimed is empirical (see Jung, *ACU*, 67). Perhaps Kant would have found in the writings of Jung what he looked for in Swedenborg: empirical evidence of his claims.

The present study has adopted an arbitrary way of listing the Functions with the T on top. To conform Kant's layout to the arrangement followed in this study, one must rotate Kant's diagrams 180 degrees to come up with the following:

IV
Modality

III   II
Relation   Quality
I
Quantity

In a Quaternity presented later in the *Critique* the same layout of four elements is involved. If one would rotate this later Quaternity one would have:

IV
Postulates of empirical
thought in general

III   II
Analogies of experience   Anticipations of perception

I
Axioms of intuition

This Kantian Quaternity will be considered at length as its four elements can readily be shown to parallel the four elements of Jung's. Here Kant maintains that we come to any experience with certain a priori principles and apart from these we can have no experience. One critic, Copleston, has compared these principles to red glasses through which one views the world. Wearing such glasses, a priori one could not say what one would see, but a priori one could say it would be red. So with these principles: they resemble four "filters" of a sort that one brings to experience. The First (I), corresponding to quantity (axioms of intuition, F), affirms "appearances are all without exception magnitudes, indeed extensive magnitudes" (*CPuR*, 198). Kant's point is that one cannot experience the unextended: e.g.: a point or a spirit. To be perceived an object must be extended in time and space (extension has been associated with the F); the perception brings the extended space together to make of it one length or one object.

The Second (II) "filter," corresponding to quality (anticipations of perception, S), affirms, "In all appearances, the real that is an object of sensation has intensive magnitude, that is, a degree" (*CPuR*, 201).

A perception involves a sensation, and a sensation is always "intensive." For example, before seeing a light I can know that the light will have *some* intensity (brightness). I cannot say how bright it will be, but I can say there will be some level of brightness; every sensation has *some* intensity. This is an a priori, a filter of sorts, that I bring to any experience.

The Third (III) filter, corresponding to relation (analogies of experience, N), is central to Kant's *Critique* and is considered at considerable length (thirty pages). This affirms, "Experience is possible only through the representation of a necessary connection of perceptions" (*CPuR*, 208). Thus, as perceptions are experienced they seem to be necessarily related to one another. This relationship would take three forms. First, I cannot think of the sensation of the present object without thinking of it as connected with the sensation I had of it a moment before. This means I must think of a permanent identity abiding "behind" the sensations (that is, a substance apart from the sensations); I have no other way of perceiving. Secondly, I must think of one event as linked to other events; I cannot think of any event as wholly new. When I claim that every event has a cause, I am simply stating what is necessary in my own thinking of an event (not a necessity in "things"). Thirdly, I must see the present abundance of sense phenomena as relating to each other. Elements are "seen" to form an interacting community.

All three of these "analogies" are saying that we can have no sense knowledge without a synthesis of our perceptions into a unity that is not sensed. Thus, the synthetic unity (in its three forms, as above) is contributed by the subject; the three forms of unity (substance, causality, community) can be affirmed a priori—before any experience. They are not found in experience; they are a prioris of the reason that are brought to experience.

The Fourth (IV) filter corresponds to modality, postulates of empirical thought in general, and it makes several claims. If I can think of something corresponding with these conditions, I judge it to be *possible*. If it also involves a sensation, I judge it to be *actual*. If the actual is determined with material conditions of experience, I judge it to be *necessary*.

Quantity I and Modality IV could be seen as contrasting with one another: Extension (time and space) is contrasted with the timeless judgments of reason, F is contrasted with T. But in relating

Kant's quaternity with Jung's, what is more striking is the close corre-spondence between Kant's *Quality II* and *Relation III* with Jung's S and N. Quality is found in sensation, for every sensation is said to have its own "intensity"—the very word suggests an "in-itself." In contrast, Re-lation always involves a reality "beyond-itself"—it points away from it-self to another; it involves a unification of diverse sense data into a unity that is not immediately sensed (e.g.: a community is not directly sensed, only individuals are). This is N; it is always looking "beyond"—beyond the multiplicity of immediate sensation—to attain a more comprehensive unity that is "behind" what is evident (e.g.: the forest is not sensed, only individual trees are; the trees are synthesized as a forest). Kant's "Relation," like Jung's N, "synthesizes" what it finds. Thus the II and III of Kant correspond well with the S and N of Jung. The same parallel between Kant's II Quality and III Relation and Jung's S and N is evident in other contexts, as when Kant uses his four elements to consider civil society. In speaking of Quality he writes, "everyone may be allowed to pursue his *own* happiness"; while Rela-tion concerns "only those *external* activities that restrict the freedom of his fellow citizens" (*PC*, 132). Thus, Quality, S, is in-itself ("his own happiness") while Relation, N, is out-of-itself ("his fellow citizens").

This is a brief account of the four elements running through the mature thought of Kant; he sees them as four a priori categories that each person adds to experience ("we can know a priori of things only what we ourselves put into them" [*CPuR*, 23]). But when Jung proposed his Quaternity, was he not making a similar claim? We "project" our inner experience onto events. Kant claims to base his Quaternity on the logic of propositions; while Jung claims to base his Quaternity on material found in alchemical texts, dreams, and so forth. The similarity of their claims and the difference of their approach suggest that one might shed light on the other.

III. The T and F Are Divinely United

Kant made only brief references to morality in the *Critique of Pure Rea-son*, but he regarded his philosophy of nature and his philosophy of morals as two parts of a single work, and the two developed together during his decade of incubation. His *Critique of Pure Reason* can even be regarded in Jungian terms as three Faculties (reason, understand-ing, and sensibility [sensation]) looking for the missing Feelings (3+1).

He never lists the faculties as three (this weakens a Jungian interpretation), though scholars do, and sometimes "reason" seems to include both reason and understanding (even in the title, *Critique of Pure Reason*).[6] So the *Critique of Pure Reason* can be seen as an account of three faculties—with Feeling absent. The three have an evident parallel with three Faculties of Jung (reason as T, understanding as N, and sensibility as S). In including N and S, Kant's first *Critique* broke with his earlier pre-critical writings where reason was acting alone. But in his first *Critique* he opposed a rational philosophy that did not include the faculties of experience (the understanding and the senses [CPuR, 23n]). Such is Kant's critical philosophy: the T can draw valid conclusions only when working with material from N and S, that is, from the necessary a prioris contained in these *faculties* of experience—but not in the *data* of experience. A Jungian would regard this addition of the N and S as the Differentiation of the Auxiliaries, what is often a first step to the Integration of the missing Fourth.

Since the three faculties can be considered a priori, they can be considered part of "pure" philosophy. But can Feeling be so considered? Or are all our feelings so contingent that we can know of them only by experience? The feelings seem to escape rational treatment (see *CPuR*, 61). So Kant would develop a philosophy of morals apart from the contingencies of feeling.

In 1785 Kant published the *Foundations of the Metaphysics of Morals* and in 1788 the *Critique of Practical Reason*. In these he affirms that the only thing good in itself is the will, and the will should be controlled by the reason. Since feelings (even feelings of benevolence) urge that I act apart from the reason, acts done with such a motive can not be moral. For example, I might help my neighbor because I enjoy the work. This deed is neither moral or immoral; I am simply enjoying myself. Good is in the will; it is not a matter of acting on a "good feeling" (e.g.: a feeling of benevolence) or producing a "good result." In rigorously denying any moral value to feelings, Kant breaks with Rousseau and all forms of eudaimonistic ethics:

> there is the alleged special sense, the moral feeling. The appeal to it is superficial, since *those who cannot think expect help from feeling*, even with respect to that which concerns universal laws; they do so even though feelings naturally differ so infinitely in degree that they are

incapable of furnishing a uniform standard of the good and bad, and also in spite of the fact that one cannot validly judge for others by means of his own feeling. (*FMM*, 61; emphasis added)

Kant is saying one cannot use one's own happiness (a feeling) as a norm to work for the happiness of humanity (as the British moralists had proposed). For how can I presume that what makes me happy will do the same for others? A priori, I cannot say what will make others happy, so this or any feeling cannot be a moral standard. Since feelings vary from person to person they cannot be the basis of a "pure" science.

Kant argues that a good will does its duty without regard to pleasure or pain. Reason indicates one's duty, and the attendant pleasure or pain has nothing to do with its morality. In fact, the moral law, "by thwarting all our inclinations, must produce a feeling which can be called pain" (*CPr&O*, 181). But morality ignores the pain. If doing something moral is pleasant, the deed is easier to do, but the pleasure (or its absence) has nothing to do with the morality of an act.

Yet there is one feeling that Kant does not dismiss: Respect for the law, the *feeling* that is central to his moral philosophy. Respect is allowed, for it is based on reason. In acting out of respect for the law, one is acting morally. Kant explains,

> though respect is a feeling, it is not one received through any [outside] influence but is self-wrought by a rational concept; thus it differs specifically from all feelings of the former kind which may be referred to inclination or fear. . . . Respect is properly the conception of a worth which thwarts my self-love. Thus it is regarded as an object neither of inclination nor of fear, though it has something analogous to both. The only object of respect is the law. . . . All respect for a person is only respect for the law (of righteousness, etc.) of which the person provides an example. (*FMM*, 17n, 18n)

Though respect for the law is a feeling, Kant approves of it, for it is wholly dependent on the duty recognized by reason. As such, it follows necessarily from the law.

In the *Critique of Practical Reason* Kant warned again of any morality based on satisfying a feeling or inclination (e.g., a desire for happiness). This would detract from the purity of duty, consequently it "always degrades mankind when they [empirical interests, inclinations, etc.] are raised to the dignity of a supreme practical principle" (*CPr&O*, 179). If a person's acts are moral, it is not because they produce a satisfying feeling, i.e., make one happy. The only incentive for a moral deed is the moral law. And, as the moral law is known a priori, so its incentive (respect for duty) must be known a priori (*CPr&O*, 181). As such, it does not depend on one's disposition, one's feelings.

The moral law causes us pain, because duty urges that we act against self-love. Pain is the negative effect of the moral law, while the positive effect is respect. Both of these can be known by pure reason apart from experience. Thus the law is

> the ground of a positive feeling which is not of empirical origin. This feeling, then, is one which can be known a priori. Respect for the moral law, therefore, is a feeling produced by an intellectual cause, and this feeling is the only one which we can know completely a priori and the necessity of which we can discern. (*CPr&O*, 181–82)

In the *Critique of Practical Reason*, Kant called all feelings pathological (*CPr&O*, 183), for feelings are selfish and seek their own satisfaction apart from the law. But there is a single feeling which is not pathological: "respect for the law," the "moral feeling." This brings no personal advantage and it satisfies no appetite; it is wholly at the disposal of reason. Since it is *necessarily* present in a rational creature, it transcends what is simply empirical. Thus, "we cannot help feeling respect"; it is "inseparably bound with the idea of the moral law in every finite rational being" (*CPr&O*, 187). That is, for an act to be moral one must obey the law from a feeling of duty and not from any appetite. Respect for duty is unique, for it follows from the law *necessarily*. As such, it can be part of "pure" philosophy The F has been rejected, but then a form of the rejected F is returned as the basis of morality—a feeling totally dependent on reason. To a very limited extent the rejected F has been restored.

Kant argues that the Gospel command, "Love God above all and thy neighbor as thyself," does not oblige us to have *feelings* of affection for our neighbor; such feelings would be "pathological," love as a personal inclination. As inclinations they cannot be commanded. But, upon hearing the command to love, we are, nevertheless, to strive to like to obey God and strive to assist our neighbor. These strivings are acts of the will. Thus the Gospel presents the moral disposition in its perfection. By speaking of love (not duty) it is telling of an "ideal of holiness unattainable by any creature" (*CPr&O*, 190). If a rational creature reached this total perfection, one would no longer have any temptation (pathological feelings that seek a personal advantage apart from the common good). We cannot reach such perfection. But if we did,. morality would be transformed into holiness and respect for the law would pass into love, a love and holiness found in God alone.

Though Kant wrote of love as an ideal, he warned against pious exhortations to love and of novels that awaken loving feelings. Since these feelings are not identical with respect for duty, they are pathological, and this becomes evident in the fanaticism they can produce. Respect for duty can never lead to fanaticism, for it is based on the law. When an exhortation to virtue is "properly commended to the human heart," it appeals only "to the subjection of the heart to duty" (*CPr&O*, 250, 252). Kant himself spoke with unaccustomed eloquence:

> Duty! Thou sublime and mighty name that dost embrace nothing charming or insinuating but requirest submission . . . [you] only holdest forth a law which of itself finds entrance into the mind and yet gains reluctant reverence (though not always obedience)—a law before which all inclinations are dumb even though they secretly work against it, what origin is there worthy of thee . . . ? (*CPr&O*, 193)

In these passages from his mature writings, Kant has radically rejected spontaneous feelings (F) and any morality based on them. But then the rejected function reappears as a feeling (F, the heart responding to duty wholly dependent on what is recognized by reason, T). Thus Kant has told of two feelings: the pathological feelings that are rejected and the feeling of respect that is retrieved with honor. Jung often told of the rejected Function being restored: "The stone that was rejected has become the cornerstone." The F was rejected; now it is retrieved. For Kant, "The former is that feeling which precedes the representation of the law; the latter, that which can only follow upon it" (*MM*, 201). For this latter feeling one has only "wonder at its inscrutable *source*" (*MM*, 201). In the extended quote above Kant had asked of this feeling, "What *origin* is worthy of thee?" The two phrases suggest a source/origin hidden in mystery— the unconscious? Should respect for the law become one's only feeling, the feeling would be transformed into love and then one would be as God, a perfect unity of T and F, of reason and feeling.

But that is not all. Somewhat surprisingly, Kant goes on to tell of a further restoration of Feeling, one to which his critics would object. The philosopher Unamuno would speak of the "restoration" as Kant's "somersault" (*TSL*, 3). Kant had already allowed that living a moral life brings a form of self-contentment. But, beyond self-contentment Kant spoke of the highest human good, the *summum bonum*. This turns out to be a union of virtue and *happiness*—happiness is a satisfaction of the feelings! Even Kant regards virtue and happiness as two "extremely heterogeneous concepts" with maxims that are "wholly heterogeneous." Then how can the two unite? They have the heterogeneousness of T and F, for virtue/morality is a purely rational ideal and happiness is a feeling. For Kant the two constitute an antinomy; yet he calls for their "synthesis" (*CPr&O*, 217). This is his somersault and what many see as a rejection of the rational purity of the ideal he had stated.[7] The difficulty is that virtue is a matter of observing the law in total disregard of one's feelings, while happiness is a satisfaction of the very feelings (inclinations) that virtue must overlook. That is why they are "extremely heterogeneous concepts." How can they be reconciled? It is difficult to explain their union; it involves a *reconciliatio oppositorum:* "the exact coincidence of happiness with morality" (*CPr&O*, 228). To claim this coincidence Kant introduced the immortality of the soul and God as the giver of appropriate rewards; so God is the "ground" of the coincidence (*CPr&O*, 228). This coincidence/synthesis is the basis for many of his writings in theology. He claims that even without this happiness God is worthy of our respect/glory, but with this synthesis God is worthy of our love (*CPr&O*, 234; RLR, 4). Such is the reconciliation. It is a rationalist losing his "rigorous purity" (Adickes) to tell of love. Thus, Kant can be seen to resemble Spinoza in moving beyond the rational purity of an ideal to tell of a personal love. Because of this reconciliation of similar heterogeneous concepts, both Kant and Spinoza were roundly criticized by their followers.

Kant's rationalist critics could see no justification for the move, but to a Jungian it is the saving move wherein one abandons the Dominant to seek Integration. It is the person coming to wholeness. For Jung this wholeness always includes the religious; that is, we seem to enter a sacred world apart from our own doing. Thus, both

Kant and Jung would speak of the move in terms of religion and holiness (Kant: "the holiness of duty" [CPr&O, 256]). Religion (holiness) comes in passing beyond the "rigorous purity" of the rational.

The Stoics called for a life of virtue and claimed virtuous living
would leave one *content*, but they never said such living would bring
happiness.[8] Their self-contentment is of the natural order; they can
respect themselves, for they have done their duty, but happiness is beyond their control. By their not claiming "happiness," Kant believed
the Stoics did not see that a rational being must have everything go
according to one's wish and will (CPr&O, 227; CPuR, 637). Our inclinations are "brought into a harmony in a wholeness which is called
happiness" (RLR, 51). A happiness that is a wholeness beyond the
present order! How better to speak of the Jungian Self?

Since virtue must overlook our desires, how can Kant allow the satisfaction of our desires? He would reply that the highest good (the
union of virtue and happiness) is possible only on the supposition of
a supreme Cause of nature who is above nature and who will bestow
an appropriate happiness on virtuous individuals in spite of the contingencies of experience. By obeying the moral law one does not automatically become happy, rather one becomes *worthy* of happiness. The
happiness itself comes from God, who acts beyond the natural system.
Such is Kant's solution. Virtue does not bring happiness; but if we are
virtuous happiness will come as a heavenly gift.[9] Likewise for Jung the
Self is not our doing; it comes as a gift. Kant explains: "morals is not
really the doctrine of how to make ourselves happy but of how we are
to be *worthy* of happiness. Only if religion is added to it can the hope
arise of someday participating in happiness in proportion as we en-
deavored not to be unworthy of it" (CPr&O, 232).

God's law requires that we should do our duty, but that is not all:
"there is added to this his glorious plan of crowning such an excellent
order with corresponding happiness" (CPr&O, 234). We can know of
this satisfaction only through a certain "pure *rational faith*"—pure as it
springs from reason, yet it is a *faith* (CPr&O, 229; see also LE, 52ff.).
Happiness does not follow *automatically* from doing one's duty (if happiness were our motive, there would be no virtue). It is only by appealing beyond the natural order to God's "glorious plan," that our
highest good (the *summum bonum*) is bestowed as a heavenly gift. Thus,
Kant introduces a sort of deus ex machina resolution. The ultimate
synthesis of virtue and happiness, T and F, is a divine gift! We live in a

world of nature, but more than nature is needed. It is a necessary idea of reason that we see ourselves living in a world of grace! (*CPuR*, 638–40).

The need to bring virtuous people to happiness is the basis for Kant's proof for the existence of God: "We must postulate a most holy and omnipotent Being which alone can unite the two elements [duty and happiness] of this highest good" (*RLR*, 4–5). But the highest human good, a synthesis of opposites (virtue and happiness), the Self, the *conjunctio oppositorum*, requires a faith that takes one beyond the system. By rational *faith* reason goes beyond itself. Thus the synthesis does not follow automatically; it is a "crowning" from elsewhere (*CPr&O*, 234). The moral man is rendered triumphant, "crowned with happiness while still here on earth" (*RLR*, 125).[10]

IV. Nature Draws Us Beyond Reason

Kant, in his mature philosophy of Nature (*Critique of Pure Reason* and *Prolegomena*), rejected the rational metaphysics that he had been doing; still his new philosophy remained highly rational. But, as seen above, in his new philosophy of Morals (*Foundations*, and *Critique of Practical Reason*) he told of "a rational *faith*" that included a synthesis of T and F. There were many Quaternities in his first *Critique*, but they did not show a balance of Thinking and Feeling, as they were entirely based on reason acting with understanding and sensation. (He had told of Quantity [associated with the F], but quantity involved space and time only as "the formal conditions of our sensibility" [*PAFM*, 31]). The balance of T and F was proclaimed in his philosophy of Morals (see above, the accounts of a "rational faith").

The final pages of the *Critique of Practical Reason* go so far as to speak of "admiration and awe"; the terms suggest one is drawn beyond the rational and into mystery:

> Two things fill the mind with ever new and increasing admiration and awe, the oftener and more steadily they are reflected on: the starry heavens above me and the moral law within me. I do not merely conjecture them and seek them as though obscured in darkness or in the transcendent region beyond my horizon: I see them before me, and I associate them directly with the consciousness of my own existence. (*CPr&O*, 258)

To one familiar with Kant, the personal quality of the passage is surprising. His consideration of the starry sky makes him aware of "an unbounded magnitude of worlds beyond worlds and systems of systems and into limitless times." But within himself the moral law shows he lives "in a world which has *true infinity.*" On the one hand, the immense extent of the universe seems to annihilate him, while, within, the moral law reveals he is free and independent of the Natural world. He calls for a study of both the world above him (Nature, unbounded, limitless) and the world within him (Morals, true infinity) in a way "suitable to the *sublimity*" of what is involved. He has reintroduced sublimity, a theme he had considered years before involving shady groves and suggesting the Unconscious. Now, to reconsider sublimity, he would write a third critique.

This was the *Critique of Judgment,* published in 1790. It would consider again beauty and the sublime. In the first *Critique,* Kant tried to show how judgments of the natural world could be understood; in the second *Critique* he tried to see how judgments of morals could be understood; in the third *Critique,* he would work with judgments of taste: the beautiful and the sublime. As indicated earlier, a Jungian would see Kant's treatment of the beautiful involving only consciousness, while the sublime suggested the unconscious. Beauty is found in objects with clearly defined boundaries, while sublime feelings are provoked by what seems formless, without bounds, the immense (e.g.: a storm-tossed ocean) (*CJ,* 82); again the sublime is connected with quantity, with the "immense," with "an unbounded *magnitude* of worlds beyond worlds" (*CPr&O,* 258; emphasis added).

For a Jungian, this third *Critique* would show two unions of opposites: beauty involving a unity of the auxiliary Functions, N and S, while the sublime involves a unity of the Dominant (T) and the Repressed (F). This can be seen in several texts wherein Kant contrasts the sublime with the beautiful. Note in the following passage that the sublime involves a unity of the J Faculties (Kant's Dominant and Repressed, the elements of his Enantiodromia), while beauty involves a unity of the P Faculties (his Auxiliaries):

> the feeling of the sublime brings with it as its characteristic feature a *movement* of the mind bound up with the judging [J] of the object, while in the case of the beautiful taste presupposes and maintains the mind in *restful* contemplation [P]. (*CJ,* 85)

Again the same contrast:

> the beautiful seems to be regarded as the presentation of an indefinite concept of understanding [N], the sublime as that of a like concept of reason [T]. Therefore the satisfaction in the one case [beauty] is bound up with the representation of *quality* [S], in the other [the sublime] with that of *quantity* [F] (*CJ*, 82).
>
> . . . just as the imagination and understanding, in judging of the beautiful, generate a subjective purposiveness of the mental powers by means of their harmony, so [with the sublime] imagination and reason do so by means of their conflict. (CJ, 97)

The mention of conflict suggests the ongoing tension of the T and F though they are united.

The first quote associates the sublime with judging (T and F are judging Faculties), and it associates beauty with contemplation (N and S are perceiving Faculties). The second quote associates *quality* (S) with the understanding (N), while it associates *quantity* (F) with the reason (T). Both beauty and the sublime effect some sort of reconciliation. Beauty is easier to achieve than is the sublime (the auxiliary Faculties are somewhat easy to reconcile); while reason (Kant's Dominant) and quantity (his Repressed) are associated "by means of their conflict." Beauty "extends our concept of nature" (*CJ*, 84), for in seeing beauty we seem to sense that Nature has a "purposiveness" (recall the N is associated with the Final Cause). In seeing beauty, Nature seems to be preadapted to ourselves (*CJ*, 82). So beauty brings a gentle sense of the furtherance of life. While the sublime produces an "emotion . . . by means of a momentary checking and a consequent more powerful outflow of the vital force" (*CJ*, 62). This feeling of emotion is bound to the sublime (*CJ*, 62). In the presence of the sublime the individual is both repelled and attracted (*CJ*, 83, 97, a repelling and attraction that recalls Otto's *Idea of the Holy* and Jung's accounts of an encounter with the unconscious Function). Thus the ongoing "conflict" that characterizes the sublime suggests the troubled union of the Dominant and the Repressed.

In speaking of the sublime, Kant introduces the sense of mystery Jung associates with the unconscious Function. It involves the "formless," with "no particular objective principles and forms" (*CJ*, 84). Also, Kant associates the sublime with Quantity: In the sublime one encounters an object that appears so great (immense) that the imagination cannot comprehend it, yet the totality of the object is present in the reason. Reason, in exceeding what can be imagined sensuously, seems to perceive itself as having a destiny beyond the sensuous world, beyond what the imagination can grasp. Nature excites us to the ideas of the sublime "in its chaos or in its wildest and most irregular disorder and desolation provided size and might are perceived" (*CJ*, 84). "Size and might" are essential; they are quantity, and "quantity" (associated with the F in Kant's Unconscious) provides the key to understanding the sublime (*CJ*, 82). [11] The sublime appears "*absolutely* great"; that is, great beyond all comparison, a quantity so great that it seems immeasurable and absolute. The reason is unable to grasp what cannot be measured. In reality there is no object beyond measure, but when one appears to be immeasurable, we feel we have a supersensitive faculty, we feel an "emotion which no mathematical estimation can bring about" (*CJ*, 92). And so "a kind of emotional satisfaction is produced" (*CJ*, 91).

Thus, the sublime is not in nature itself; it is a feeling in us, "a kind of emotional satisfaction" we experience when we face what seems to be without measure. Since it is *in us*, Kant would ask,

> Who would call sublime, e.g., shapeless mountain masses piled in wild disorder upon one another with their pyramids of ice, or the gloomy, raging sea? But the mind feels itself raised in its own judgment if, while contemplating them without any reference to their form . . . it yet finds the whole power of the imagination inadequate to its ideas. (*CJ*, 95) [12]

When our sensuous imagination is unable to grasp the extent of the "immeasurable" that we see, yet the reason has an idea of the whole, we experience a "conflict" that pains us. And this "arouses in us the feeling of our own supersensible destination" (*CJ*, 97). Then we experience pleasure in finding every standard inadequate to measure what we know. The conflict makes us feel we "possess pure self-subsistant reason" (*CJ*, 97).

But the sublime also involves a might immeasurably greater than our own. We are aware of the sublime when confronted with something fearful, yet we are not afraid. So the sublime can be provoked by "the boundless ocean in a state of tumult; the lofty waterfall of a mighty river," and so forth. Such sights attract us the more powerful and the more fearful they appear, "provided only that we are in security" (*CJ*, 100). They raise the energies of the soul above their accustomed height "and discover in us a faculty of resistance of a quite different kind, which gives us courage to measure ourselves against the apparent almightiness of nature" (*CJ*, 100–101). Then the mind feels "the proper sublimity of its destination, in comparison with nature itself" (*CJ*, 101).

But it is important to note that only those who have a developed moral feeling can experience the sublime (*CJ*, 105–6). So Kant speaks of the "moral foundation" of "our supersensible destination" (*CJ*, 134). Only the person with moral feelings can sense one's self as above nature, while the one who lives only by natural appetites knows one's self only as a natural object, a part of nature and subject to its laws. But by living according to duty one knows a higher destiny. Aware of our higher identity, we need not be afraid. We feel secure, though nature itself is fearful. These passages could be taken as accounts of Kant's own condition: his conscious mind is serene and distant from the turmoil it once had known.

Shortly before he died Kant was pressured politically because of the unorthodoxy of his religious ideas, so in 1798 he responded with *The Conflict of the Faculties*—not the faculties of the soul, but the faculties of a university. He would use Jungian symbols of 3+1 to tell of the division of the university into two ranks: "three higher faculties and *one lower* faculty." This was one way of stating the structure of German universities in his time; but in telling of three higher and one lower he claimed it corresponded to an "a priori principle"! (*CF*, 25, 31). This a priori principle seems to refer to the Jungian Archetype of 3+1: "three higher Faculties and one lower Faculty." Philosophy turns out to be the lower faculty. In speaking of Philosophy as a "lower faculty," he did not really regard it that way: he was speaking with deference. For he saw philosophy, in contrast with the other three (Theology, Law and Medicine), as concerned with truth! The others are concerned only with studying texts (*CF*, 59, 29).[13]

A Jungian reflecting on this passage would see the philosopher conforming to the T, while, without pressing the point, the law professor could be seen as N and the medical professor as S. But, in any case, Kant clearly identifies the theologian with F, for the theologian is said to work in terms of "a certain indemonstrable and inexplicable *feeling* that the Bible is divine" (*CF*, 35, emphasis in text). Since the theologian is concerned with feeling, Kant warns that he is not to meddle with using his reason, for this would result in confusion and anarchy. The theologian is simply to stick with the teaching he has received

> based on a feeling connected with it (for example, a pious feeling of supernatural influence—although, since feeling yields no positive principle, it is only subjectively valid and cannot provide the basis for a universal law). In this case the philosophy faculty must be free to examine in public and to evaluate with cold reason the source and content of this alleged basis of doctrine, unintimidated by the sacredness of the object which has supposedly been experienced and determined to bring this alleged feeling to concepts. (*CF*, 55)

Thus, in this late writing, "cold reason" is radically in control and works at bringing an "alleged feeling to concepts." Beyond that, he adds, "to claim that we *feel* as such the immediate influence of God is self-contradictory, because the idea of God lies only in reason" (*CF*, 105). The major section of this work is titled "The Philosophy Faculty versus the Theology Faculty." The philosopher with reason versus the theologian with feeling sounds like the reason-feeling Enantiodromia he had known years before, even to his warning lest the two faculties "run together" (*CF*, 37). But it would seem that the personal Enantiodromia was over long ago, and he was only insisting on a familiar theme.

Kant wrote these passages from the *Conflict of the Faculties* when he was an old man feeling his age and threatened by censors. They should be so understood. But they show the rationalist in radical control with little room for the mystery and wonder found in his writings on the sublime. This was the last work he published, but at the time of his death in 1804 there was an incomplete text left on his desk. This text suggests that he pulled back from the *summum bonum*, the synthesis of virtue and happiness (T and F) for which he once argued. He had hoped to develop these unedited pages into a fourth *Critique*, a work he had often called "his chief work" (*OP*, xvii; there are many textual problems in this incomplete work; it was published only in the twentieth century). God and matter/world are the principal themes of these pages. But though the pages tell many times of God, they do not tell of God bestowing happiness on those worthy of it. Erich Adickes, the scholar who developed the German text of *Opus Postumum*, claims this idea has "practically disappeared." Adickes sees Kant backing away from the *summum bonum* (*reconciliatio*) found in his earlier works. He sees Kant wanting to purify his text of the "heteronomy and hedonism" the *summum bonum* involved (Adickes, 832, 846; see *RLR*, lxv). Now, "the concept of God is the idea of a moral being judging and universally commanding," "a legislative force which gives these thoughts emphasis." Such phrases and an abundance of others associate God simply with Kant's Dominant T with no mention of attendant happiness, F (see *OP*, 201, 207). So Adickes argues God is no longer the Guarantor [*Burgen*] or Equalizer [*Ausgleicher*] who rewards the deserving, but only the "Ground [*Urgrund*] for the voice of the categorical imperative" (Adickes, 832–33).[14] Once Kant had claimed that only the rewarding God (the *summum bonum*) was a God worthy of love (*CPr&O*, 234); his *Opus Postumum* does not speak of our loving God. It is hard to judge an incomplete text on what is missing, but there are many places he could have introduced the union of virtue and happiness and he did not. The absence is striking.

Kant's early writings show him to be a thorough rationalist (T), but in reading Rousseau's *Emile* in 1762 he discovered his feelings (F) and this brought on years of personal turmoil (Enantiodromia) as he tried to decide whether morality was based on reason or feeling. But his insights of 1769 seem to have resolved the issue. Reason regained control as presented in an architecture of Quaternity. But in the *Critique of Practical Reason* he allowed reason to go beyond itself in a rational faith and the union of "extremely heterogeneous concepts" (T and F). But in his *Opus Postumum* he seems to have set aside the "heteronomy and hedonism" of the God who rewards and punishes. In these pages, both God and the world seem to be wholly identified with rational terms (while the God who rewards would be a God who acts in human affairs and therefore beyond rational terms).

In this final work of Kant, there is a musing at the bottom of a manuscript page that Kant left unexplained. It teases the Jungian reader: "Whether there is a threefold or a fourfold form of immateriality" (*OP*, 233). It is the ambiguity of the Three and the Four, and it seems to tell of the uncertain reconciliation that Kant himself had achieved.

Notes

1. Jung makes many passing references to Kant; only once does he treat him at any length, in *PT*, 43–45. See also Jung, *A*, 6; *TE*, 169.

2. In 1755 Kant had written a theoretical reflection on the cosmos and ended it with a passage that told of both feeling and the sublime: "the contemplation of a starry heaven on a pleasant night affords a kind of enjoyment which is felt only by noble souls. . . . [Then the soul] speaks an unnamed language and gives us implicit concepts which can be felt but not described . . . . How fortunate it is . . . a way is opened to happiness and sublimity." Again these "felt" concepts speaking "an unnamed language" suggest the F is in the unconscious.

3. Kant was generally careful not to speak of himself. He set as motto for his first *Critique*: "De nobis ipsis silemus"—We say nothing about ourself. How different this impersonal approach is from that of the Feelers: Rousseau and St. Augustine.

4. One commentator could not identify what logic text Kant was referring to; he saw Kant devising the plan himself using many texts (Vleeschauwer, 76–81). Hartnack claims that logic has developed since Kant; accordingly, "the absolute character of Kant's devision and arrangement is thereby seriously shaken." Hartnack sees Kant limiting the classes of acceptable judgments, to allow that "his system of categories works out neatly" (Hartnack, 36–37).

5. Later writings would contain less-evident Quaternities: In *Prolegomena to Any Future Metaphysics* Kant refers to the same basic elements, but arranges them differently, and in a way that is also distinct:

1	2
As to Quantity	As to Quality
3	4
As to Relation	As to Modality

Then in writing the *Critique of Practical Reason* he listed the same four underneath one another; he sets other elements in a square (*CPr&O*, 41) and the four theorems by which he begins pick up on the above four elements. In projecting his *Critique of Judgment* he explained: "there are four main parts that would follow, containing the concepts of the understanding, divided according to the four classes of categories" (*CJ*, 132). On three occasions in *The Metaphysics of Morals* he sets four elements in a block (as above) (65, 66, 200). *Four elements set in a square is clearly central to his architecture.* (One 3:4 of which I am aware is in a letter of 1793 that refers to the three questions that end the *Critique of Pure Reason* [*CPuR*, 635] and adds, "A fourth question ought to follow, finally: "What is man?" [*PC*, 205]. Here I see only a coincidental resemblance to Jung's 3:4.)

6. It was only in the course of writing the *Critique of Pure Reason* that Kant made a clear distinction between reason and understanding; the distinction is evident in a fragment dated March 1780; the understanding applies to empirical sensibility and the reason works with concepts (Vleeschauwer, 81). The overlap of the terms is considered in Copleston (26, 72) and Hartnack (98).

7. Greene's introduction to *RLR* quotes the objection of Pringle-Pattison: Kant "the preacher of duty for duty's sake, who had so rigorously purged his ethics of all considerations of happiness or natural inclination, surprises us with the baldly hedonistic lines on which he rounds off his theory" (*RLR*, lxiii). It also quotes Adickes, who sees the hedonistic introduction of happiness as a "subversive element" depriving his thought of its rigorous purity (quoted in *RLR*, lxv–lxvi).

8. Kant affirms that "intellectual feeling" is a contradiction in terms, but he accepts something similar when he allows "intellectual contentment" (*CPr&O*, 121–22). Again one could ask, is not contentment a feeling? Yes–but it is a feeling that follows on what reason has seen and is different from the spontaneous feelings.

9. In a similar way, people must work for a moral society as if everything depended on them. But the consummation of the task "can be looked for not from men but only from God Himself" (*RLR*, 92).

10. The resolution is further complicated when Kant says that without the concept of God "morality would have no incentive." He would see one must begin with morality, and "afterward it can be combined with theology, and then our morality will obtain more incentives and a morally moving power" (*LPT*, 27, 31). But does not this added incentive involve more than acting for duty's sake? The happiness that he speaks of "while still here on earth" would be completed by immortality "in a future world" (*CPuR*, 639).

11. Kant's rejection of his earlier philosophy concerned whether or not the unextended is "unthinkable" (*DSS*, 34–38). Following his "great light" of 1769, his first philosophical writing concerned the continuity of space and time.

12. Kant often makes references to mountains and raging seas, but personally he never saw either as he never left the region around Königsberg where there are neither mountains nor seas.

13. The other three are concerned with an authoritative text: one with the Bible, one with the Law, and one with books of Medical Regulations.

14. In the *Critique of Practical Reason* God was identified as "the ground of the exact coincidence of happiness with morality" (*CPr&O*, 228). This is missing, yet in the *Opus Postumum* he speaks of God eleven times in terms of the Latin triad: *Ens Summum, Summa Intelligentia, Summum Donum*. The triad suggests a reconciliation; it resembles the way Augustine would speak of the Trinity and its presence in us as our Being, Knowing and Loving (see above).

Bibliography

Works of Kant

CF *The Conflict of the Faculties*, translated and introduced by Mary J. Gregor. Lincoln and London: University of Nebraska Press, 1992.

CJ *Critique of Judgment*, translated by J. H. Bernard. New York: Hafner Press (Collier Macmillan), 1951.

CPr&O *Critique of Practical Reason and Other Writings in Moral Philosophy*, translated by Lewis White Beck. Chicago: University of Chicago Press, 1949.

CPuR *Critique of Pure Reason*, translated by Norman Kemp Smith. New York: St. Martin's Press, 1965.

DSS *Dreams of a Spirit Seer*, translated by John Manolesco. New York: Vantage Press, 1969.

FMM *Foundations of the Metaphysics of Morals*, translated by Lewis White Beck. New York: Bobbs-Merrill, 1959.

LE *Lectures on Ethics*, translated by Louis Infield, foreword by Lewis White Beck. First published in 1930. Gloucester: Peter Smith, 1978.

LPT *Lectures on Philosophical Theology*, translated by Allen W. Wood and Gertrude M. Clark. New York: Cornell University Press, 1978.

MM *The Metaphysics of Morals*, translated by Mary Gregor. Cambridge: Cambridge University Press, 1991.

O *Observations on the Feeling of the Beautiful and Sublime*, translated by John T. Goldthwait. Berkeley: University of California Press, 1981.

OP *Opus Postumum*, edited, with an introduction and notes by Eckart Forster; translated by Eckart Forster and Michael Rosen. Cambridge: Cambridge University Press, 1993.

PAFM *Prolegomena to Any Future Metaphysics*, translator not listed, edited by Lewis White Beck. New York: Bobbs-Merrill, 1950.

PC *Philosophical Correspondence*, edited and translated by Arnulf Zweig. Chicago: University of Chicago Press, 1967.

RLR *Religion within the Limits of Reason Alone*, translated with an introduction and notes by Theodore M. Greene and Hoyt H. Hudson, with a new essay by John R. Silbur. New York: Harper Torchbooks, 1960.

Other Works

Adickes, Erich. *Kant's Opus Postumum*, with notes and introduction by Adickes. Berlin: Verlag von Reuther & Reichard, 1920.

Cassirer, Ernst. *Kant's Life and Thought*, translated by James Haden. New Haven: Yale University Press, 1981.

Copleston, Frederick. *A History of Philosophy*, vol. VI, part II. New York: Doubleday, undated.

Hartnack, Justus. *Kant's Theory of Knowledge*, translated by M. Holmes Hartshorne. New York: Harcourt, Brace & World, 1967.

Paulson, Friedrich. *Immanuel Kant: His Life and Doctrine*, translated from the revised German edition by J. E. Creighton and Albert Lefevre. New York: Fredrick Ungar, 1963.

Schilpp, Paul Arthur. *Kant's Pre-Critical Ethics*, second edition. Evanston: Northwestern University Press, 1938, 1960.

Unamuno, Miguel de. *Tragic Sense of Life*, translated by J. E. Crawford Flitch. New York: Dover, 1954.

Vleeschauwer, Herman-J. de. *The Development of Kantian Thought*, translated by A. R. C. Duncan. New York: Thomas Nelson and Sons, 1962.

Zammito, John H. *The Genesis of Kant's Critique of Judgment*. Chicago: University of Chicago Press, 1992.

9 Kierkegaard: *Sacrificium Intellectus*
The Dominant Surrenders to a Troubled Conjunction

Kierkegaard as T: Kierkegaard reflected on his childhood: "Inwardly torn asunder as I was without any expectation of leading a happy earthly life . . . what wonder that in desperate despair I grasped at nought but the intellectual side in man and clung fast to it, so that the thought of my own considerable powers of mind was my only consolation, ideas my one joy, and mankind indifferent to me" (*JK*, 40). "Even as a child I was conscious of my intelligence and that such was my strength in the face of those much stronger boys" (*JK*, 243). Kierkegaard called himself "the odd thinker" and told of using his intellect to ward off attacks of moodiness (*PV*, 62; *JK*, 128). He told of writing: "I am wrapped in thought and am happy" (*D*, 52); "Above all . . . I have served Thought and Truth;" I have labored "in the service of truth" (*DS*, 58; *PV*, 7). Yet he feared that his "outstanding intellectual gifts" might tear him to pieces (*JK*, 39). For Kierkegaard's Quarternity, see Figure 9.1. Kierkegaard's Myers-Briggs type would be INTP.

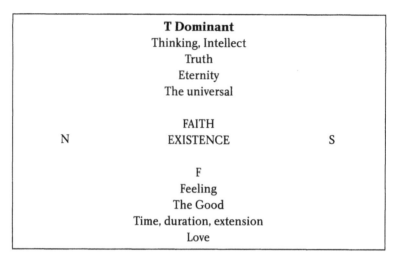

Figure 9.1

I. Personalities of a Thinker

Søren Kierkegaard was born in Copenhagen in 1813 and rarely left that city. He became a partial recluse, publishing his works under eighteen different pseudonyms, and each pseudonym can be seen as an expression or nuance of his own complicated personality. All the while he regularly published religious and edifying works under his own name, and throughout his years of writing he tells of knowing himself as religious. The pseudonyms can be seen as variations on Kierkegaard's identity as a T, for they all seem to be Thinkers: The "Young Man" is said to have been brought up "exclusively by thought" and is "essentially melancholy of thought" (*SL,* 37; *CU,* 264). In speaking at a banquet, he tells of renouncing all love, "for my thought is to me the most essential consideration," "no happiness is possible for me except my thought have free play," "my thought saves me." "Constantine Constantius" is "case-hardened understanding" (*CU,* 264). "Johannes de Silentio" boasts only of being able to think a thought whole (*FT,* 41). "A" is "a developed thinker" who keeps existence away "by the most subtle of all deceptions, by thinking, he has thought everything possible and yet he has not existed at all"; he is in "despair in thought" (*CU,* 227, 226; *EO,* II, 198–99). Several of Kierkegaard's major philosophic works are written under the pseudonym "Johannes Climacus," and in telling of the childhood of Climacus Kierkegaard tells details of his own childhood (*JC*, 103n; *JK*, 175). Climacus is undoubtedly a T: "In love he was, madly in love; but with thought, or rather with thinking" (*JC*, 103). Climacus had disciplined himself "to execute a sort of nimble dancing in the service of thought." He risks his life "to play the game of thought"; as a "privately practicing thinker" he undertakes "thought projects" (*CU*, 59). "Thinking was and remained his passion" (*JC*, 109).

In identifying with Thinking, these various personalities had difficulties with the opposite Function, Feeling: "Quidem" says, "I have lived intellectually. When in the poets I read the speeches of lovers, I smiled because I could not see how such a relationship could concern them so much." Constantine compares one in love to a marionette pulled about unwillingly, an image suggesting that the unconscious Function is thwarting the conscious intent of the Ego. Constantine reflects on the upsets of love:

> This is tragic, in a sense it is profoundly tragic, even though no one is concerned about it or is concerned about the contradiction that is so bitter to a thinker, that there is something [love] that exercises its power everywhere and yet cannot be grasped by thought, something which is capable of attacking from behind the man who is vainly trying to think it. (*SL*, 52)

The character "A" knows love, but knows it only intellectually; he is divided and has never been in love, "for then he would instantly, in a way, have been in course of consolidating himself" (*CU*, 227).

These characters tell of Kierkegaard the Thinker who as a youth "grasped at nought but the intellectual side" and then experienced his Feelings as random attacks of moodiness. Yet Kierkegaard recognized the fundamental importance of Feeling: "The immediate feeling is indeed—primary. It is the *elan vital* out of which life flows, just as it is said that the heart is the source of life" (*PH*, 113). But such spontaneous feelings produce moodiness and a disrelationship in one's inmost being (*WL*, 54). Spontaneous love was the rejected Function acting at random until it underwent the transformation of the Unconscious:

> The heat of spontaneous love is so great—no matter how great its passion is—so dangerous that this heat can easily become a fever. Spontaneity is, as it were, the fermenting element, so called because it has not yet undergone a change and therefore has not separated

from itself the poison which engenders the heat in the fermenting element. (*WL*, 49–50)

Love brought confusion into the life of the Thinker, but in the end the confusion was recognized as a "life-giving confusion." Kierkegaard told of marriage wherein love undergoes a transformation and the disrelationship is resolved; marriage is the "transfiguration of first love, not its annihilation" (*EO*, II, 32). The transfigured love is the F returning from the Unconscious. Kierkegaard would tell of "love's mysterious ground," but more often he will speak of it with the water images associated with the Unconscious.

> As the quiet lake is fed deep down by the flow of hidden springs, which no eye sees, so a human being's love is grounded, still more deeply, in God's love. If there were no spring at the bottom, if God were not love, then there would be neither a little lake nor a man's love. As the still waters begin obscurely in the deep spring, so a man's love mysteriously begins in God's love. As the quiet lake invites you to look at it but the mirror of darkness prevents you from seeing through it, so love's mysterious ground in God's love prevents you from seeing its source. When you think you are seeing it, then it is a reflection which deceives you, as if it were the bottom, this which only conceals the deeper bottom. . . . As the still waters, however quietly they lie, are really running water, for is not the wellspring at the bottom: so love flows, however still it is in its hiddenness. (*WL*, 27)

> There is a place in a human being's most inward depths; from this place proceeds the life of love, for "from the heart proceeds life." But this place you cannot see, no matter how far you thrust in; the source withdraws itself into remoteness and hiding; even if you have thrust in as far as possible, the source is always a bit farther in, like the source of a spring which just when you are nearest to it is farther away. (*WL*, 26)

Many additional texts make passing reference to the F in images of water: "Feeling is like the river Niger in Africa, its source is not known" (*CU*, 212); "Spiritual love contains the spring which flows into eternal life" (*WL*, 288); that "God is love" is an "inexhaustible fountain of joy that always renews itself" (*DS*, 134).

There was a turning point in the life of Kierkegaard that greatly affected all his writing: He became passionately in love with Regina Olson ("Thou queen of my heart ["Regina"]. . . . Everywhere, in every girl's face, I see features reminding me of your beauty," etc.). In September of 1840 at the age of twenty-seven, he proposed and two days later she, aged sixteen, accepted with the approval of her family. Only then did he have misgivings: "I saw I had made a mistake." In October of the following year, he broke the engagement. Her father protested to him, telling of her anguish, "She was in deep despair." He reflects, "I was quite shaken, but I held on to my own view." As she and he were about to part she said, "'Promise me that you will think of me.' I did. She said, 'Kiss me.' I did—but without passion. Merciful God! . . . I spent the nights weeping on my bed" (DS, 40–41). Years later he would call it "an example of what it is to die" (FS, 98). The turmoil of the event launched him as a writer; many of his texts make allusions to the event and many others were written and published for Regina to read.

To recover from the break, he went to Berlin for several months and spent most of his time there writing. Upon his return he set about publishing a work that tells of a young man who had fallen in love, but soon after the engagement found he was capable of containing all of his love in his mind without further need of his beloved: "Before he begins he has taken such a terrible stride that he has leapt over the whole of life. Though the girl die tomorrow it will produce no essential change . . . at the very first instant he has become an old man with respect to the whole relationship" (R, 38-39).

So the young man breaks his engagement and, freed of the girl, he leaps ecstatically into his T:

> I belong to the idea. . . . When the idea calls I forsake everything, or rather I have nothing to forsake. . . . Long life to the high flight of thought, to moral danger in the service of the idea! Hail to the danger of battle! Hail to the solemn exultation of victory! Hail to the dance in the vortex of the infinite! Hail to the breaking wave which covers me in the abyss! Hail to the breaking wave which hurls me to the stars! (R, 126–27)

The exultation of this "high flight of thought" has a sense of unreality; it is the triumph of one who has severed himself from his Unconscious. He lives purely in idea, in thought, and in renouncing love he has no unexpected moods to plague him—or does he?

This flight of ecstasy would scarcely describe the life of Søren Kierkegaard. On the same day he published *Repetition* he also published *Fear and Trembling*. Here his broken engagement is considered in its religious significance. *Fear and Trembling* tells of two

Knights, and each Knight finds he has no more need of the beloved for the growth of his love. The first Knight makes the very difficult act of renouncing her; in this he resembles Kierkegaard and the young man in *Repetition*. He is called the Knight of Infinite Resignation. The second Knight, the Knight of Faith, also makes the difficult act of renunciation, but the second Knight follows this with the act of faith. The second Knight says: "I believe nevertheless that I shall get her, in virtue, that is, of the absurd, in virtue of the fact that with God all things are possible" (*FT*, 57).

This Knight has renounced his beloved, and then by virtue of his faith receives her back. There is a double process: rejection followed by reception as a gift. In Jungian terms, the stone must be rejected before it can be received back as cornerstone.[1] *Fear and Trembling* considers at length the story of Abraham and Isaac. Abraham is asked by God to sacrifice his beloved son Isaac; in preparing to do so he makes the act of Infinite Resignation, for it is in total opposition to his feelings. But Abraham is also a Knight of Faith, for after having renounced Isaac (renounced his F) he can lovingly receive Isaac back. "It is great to give up one's wish, but it is greater to hold it fast after having given it up" (*FT*, 33). Isaac is received back as a gift from God, and Abraham can so receive him because he had faith.[2] Abraham's resignation allows him to live the purity of an ideal (T), but Faith goes beyond the ideal and he receives Isaac back.

The Knight of Faith makes a double movement: first, he must renounce his beloved, and then on a higher level receive the beloved back. Renouncing his beloved required a human courage of which both Knights felt capable, but to receive the beloved back was beyond what reason can conceive. But, nonetheless, the Knight of Faith received her back. The renunciation can be seen as a renunciation of F to live as T, and it is followed by a reception of F on a transcendent level. Such a sequence characterizes the ascent of the T. And Kierkegaard insists on how radical the first break must be: "Only at the moment when his act is in absolute contradiction to his feeling is his act a sacrifice" (*FT*, 84). The beloved first must be renounced totally and only then recovered; one must know the pain of rejecting the immediacy of love only to discover "the rebirth of love" (*ED*, 192). When the rejected love is reborn it serves as cornerstone; it appears in its archetypal character as coming from a land of mystery: "when love awakens it is older than everything, for when it is, it is as if it had been there a long time, it presupposes itself far back into the distant past until all search for its origin ends in the inexplicable" (*ED*, 182). This reborn love is also said to have a "miraculous beginning."

Kierkegaard told of his youth when he grasped at nought but his intellectual side, but later he repeatedly criticized this one-sided intellectualism. He writes of the radical Thinker:

> an abstract thinker is a duplex being: a fantastic creature who moves in the pure being of abstract thought, and on the other hand, a somewhat pitiful professorial figure which the former deposits, about as one sets down a walking stick. When one reads the story of such a thinker's life (for his writings are perhaps excellent), one trembles to think of what it means to be a man. (*CU*, 268)

Such a thinker proclaims, "Thought and being are one." He can say this because he himself is only a thought—otherwise he has disappeared. Kierkegaard reflects: "A thinker erects an immense building, a system"; this philosophical system involves the entirety of being and all of world history, but "if we contemplate his personal life . . . we discover that he himself personally does not live in this immense high-vaulted palace, but in a barn alongside of it" (*FT*, 177). Thought has taken everything from the thinker and given him nothing in return (*EO*, II, 207). Kierkegaard describes the encounter with such a thinker:

> If you meet someone who suffers from such a derangement of feeling, the derangement consisting in his not having any, you listen to what he says in a cold and awful dread, scarcely knowing whether it is a human being who speaks, or a cunningly contrived walking stick in which a talking machine has been concealed (*CU*, 175)

Jung, in telling of the confinement one knows when living purely by the Dominant Function, used the image of Laocoön, the man coiled about by a serpent, constricted and limited. Kierkegaard uses the same image to tell of Johannes Climacus: "Thought twined itself painfully about him (like the serpent, like Laocoön)" (*JC*, 130). The Laocoön image is implied again when Kierkegaard tells of another who "has not the passion to tear himself from the coils . . . of reflection" (*PA*, 34); he tells of another who "had run riot in overmuch deliberation and had become the prisoner of his many thoughts so that he could not act" (*ED*, 150). In his *Journals*, Kierkegaard wrote:

"It is reason that has conquered: reason that has tyrannised enthusiasm and the like, making it ridiculous" (*JK*, 173). Kierkegaard believed that Thought so dominated the present age that should one consider suicide, he would do so with such care that he "literally chokes with thought"; it would not be suicide at all, for "it is really thought that takes his life" (*PA*, 33).

To avoid the constriction of thought, Kierkegaard required that a man unify thought, imagination, and feeling. Thought and feeling are easily identified with the corresponding terms of Jung. The addition of imagination as third could recall Jung's suggestion that the Imagination is the play-Faculty forming the Symbol (Self) in which opposites are united.[3] Kierkegaard claims that it is "a miserable mode of existence for a thinker who is also an existential individual to lose imagination and feeling, which is quite as bad as losing his reason" (*CU*, 311). For Kierkegaard: "The task is not to exalt one at the expense of the other, but to give them an equal status, to unify them in simultaneity" (*CU*, 311). The same three are involved elsewhere when Kierkegaard speaks of uniting the Good and True (a union frequently postulated by Kierkegaard [see *WL*, 53; *PV*, 88; *PH*, 136]). But he also tells of relating "the Good and the True *through Imagination*" (*FT*, 208).

Fear and Trembling had called for a double movement: first one renounces feelings to live in the idea (T), then one renounces the idea to make the absurd movement of faith. The intellect cannot even think the second movement, yet it becomes the thinker's passion: it is "the supreme passion of the Reason to seek a collision, though this collision must in one way or another prove its undoing. The supreme paradox of all thought is the attempt to discover something that thought cannot think" (*PF*, 46). In his *Journal* Kierkegaard writes that life is not a "long continuous growth in understanding," rather one must "experience the maturity of discovering that there comes a critical moment where everything is reversed, after which the point becomes to understand more and more that there is something which cannot be understood" (*JK*, 172). The "moment where everything is reversed" is the moment wherein the Thinker turns back to the rejected F.

The same idea is present when Kierkegaard says "it is necessary to work *through*" reflection and cleverness:

The stages of all actions which are performed with enthusiasm are as follows: first of all comes immediate enthusiasm, then follows the stage of cleverness [T] which, because immediate enthusiasm does not calculate, assumes with a calculating cleverness the appearance of being the higher; and finally comes the highest and most intensive enthusiasm which follows the stage of cleverness, and is therefore able to see the shrewdest plan of action but disdain it, and thereby receive the intensity of an eternal enthusiasm. (PA, 84)

In other words, "immediate goodness" (F) must be set aside by the understanding (T), but eventually one also "acts against understanding" and receives goodness back. But, Kierkegaard explains, when one acts against understanding, "it requires a religious *impetus* to set goodness afloat again" (PA, 85). Immediate Goodness is rejected, but religion takes one beyond rejection to the final stage wherein the rejected Goodness is restored.

The only way the one-sided domination of Thought can be ended is by its encounter with the unthinkable. Thought confronts a Paradox and knows it must relinquish its domineering role, for the Paradox cannot be thought. It offends the Reason, yet Reason finds that it "cannot free itself from the cross to which it is nailed" (PF, 62). So Kierkegaard urged the Reason to yield to the Paradox. Then the Paradox bestows itself and there is "a synthesis in some third entity" (PF, 67). The third entity is the "happy passion" of faith:

It comes to pass when the Reason and the Paradox encounter one another happily in the Moment, when the Reason sets itself aside and the Paradox bestows itself. The third entity in which this union is realized (for it is not realized in the Reason, since it is set aside: nor in the Paradox, which bestows itself—hence it is realized *in* something) is that happy passion to which we will now assign a name, though it is not the name that so much matters. We shall call this passion: *Faith*. (PF, 73)

Faith is the happy passion that unites the opposites. When Faith first appears it is a nameless presence, but Jung would see that the reconciling Self generally appears as unknown (as did the "Stranger" in Plato). Just as Faith enabled the Knight of Faith to receive back his beloved, so Faith resolves the Paradox that defies mediation. "Faith is a miracle, and yet no man is excluded from it; for that in which all human life is unified is a passion, and faith is a passion" (FT, 77). By Faith a "private personality" is established within, and this is identified as a sort of "Holy of Holies." To tell of this mysterious personal depth Kierkegaard uses an image that suggests both Quaternity and the opposites in balance: "just as the entrance to a house is barred by the crossed bayonets of the guards, the approach to a man's personality is barred by the dialectical cross of qualitative opposites in an ideal equilibrium" (PA, 70). Faith is the new reality that establishes the opposites in "an ideal equilibrium."

The rational person knows "universals"; thinking is in terms of these abstract essences. The universal concept "man" ("the human") serves as the norm that one must follow to live an ethical life. There is no paradox involved in understanding the universal; "the ethical is always quite consistently very easy to understand" (CU, 350). Each must do one's duty as a human being; that duty is easy to understand, though often difficult to live. Should one renounce the universal human norm and act according to one's feelings, one would have given in to temptation (FT, 80). So in claiming an absolute duty towards God one is involved in Paradox; this requires that one renounce the universal human duty (T), much as Abraham did. The paradox of faith is the claim that the universal (the ethical norm known by Thought) is not the highest: there is something higher that the Reason is unable to think. Beneath thought is the tendency to act because of feeling and mood (temptation), while above thought is the passion of faith. Both are apart from the universal human duty.

The Knight of Resignation "has the universal as his home, his friendly abiding place" (FT, 86); it is "glorious to belong to the universal" and demonstrate to everyone the intelligibility of one's deeds. But the Knight of Faith must renounce the universal and walk a solitary path beyond what can be thought; one is intelligible only to God. The Knight of Resignation has not gone this far; he lives purely by abstract norms, that is, the T is dominant; this is identified as the religion of one's childhood (CU, 532). It involves no faith and is not Christianity; for this Knight, God is identified with the universal and so becomes impotent, "an invisible vanishing point, a powerless thought" (FT, 78). One cannot relate to such a God. In order to relate to God one must know God as a reality beyond the universal. Some do not do so and put God aside as they mature, but this is only "a childish and superstitious overvaluation of thought" (FT, 59). To avoid this, one must put thought aside and make an act of faith. To put thought aside is the suffering of the Christian: it involves "giving up reason and becoming crucified to a paradox" (*DS*, 149).

II. Time, Eternity and Existence

The Knight of Faith was seen to make two movements: First, feelings were renounced to live in Thought, then Thought was renounced to achieve a higher synthesis of Thought and Feeling that Kierkegaard called Faith. The same sequence of rejection and acceptance in a higher synthesis is presented in other terms: first, time is renounced for eternity, then eternity is renounced for a union of time and eternity, time is the cornerstone returned. The Knight must renounce the *temporal* to gain an eternal consciousness (the act of Infinite Resignation). By this first step the Knight of Resignation can still affirm that God is love through all eternity, but in the temporal world he and God have nothing to say to one another. How could they? The whole of the temporal has been renounced; the Knight of Infinite Resignation has no reason to pray about any temporal affair, as he is indifferent to the things of time.

But the Knight of Faith makes a second movement: faith. By faith he regains the temporal that he has given up. The temporal has been identified with F and the eternal with T; so in terms of time and eternity the double movement tells again of the F renounced for T, and then the T is renounced for a higher form of F (F united with T). "It is great to grasp the eternal, but it is greater to hold fast to the temporal after having given it up" (*FT*, 33). In the double movement time is renounced and then regained; the regained temporal is united with eternity in a transcendent third, Existence.

> A purely human courage is required to renounce the whole of the temporal to gain the eternal; but this I gain, and to all eternity I cannot renounce it—that is a self-contradiction. But a paradoxical and humble courage is required to grasp the whole of the temporal by virtue of the absurd, and this is the courage of faith. (*FT*, 59)

The opposition of time (F) and eternity (T) is a frequent theme in Kierkegaard: a devotional work explains, "The temporal order is in conflict with the Eternal" (*PH*, 136). The conflict is Kierkegaard's Enantiodromia. He found his choice of the intellectual side had separated him from "the historical continuity of domestic family life," that is, from the temporal (*DS*, 31). As a pure intellect he could live *sub specie aeternitatis*. But to marry he must regain the temporal; it is through a woman that man can be "again reconciled with time" (*EO*, II, 312). Note the *again*—it is only after having given up the temporal that one can marry! In breaking with Regina he had renounced the temporal, but can he marry? Can he become the Knight of Faith and receive her back by the absurd?

Kierkegaard tells of Johannes Climacus (the pseudonym used in telling of his own childhood) having a "love of grammar and of the divine status of rule," but while drawn to divine rules (T) he became fascinated with something different: extension (F).

> When it was explained to Johannes Climacus that, for example, the accusative implies extension in time and space . . . then new vistas opened out to his mind. The preposition disappeared, and expansion in time and space became like a huge empty picture before his gaze, fleeting as clouds. His imagination was set in motion, but in a different way than hitherto. . . . he took in nothing except the enormous extension. (*JC*, 106)

Extension (F) involves "new vistas"; it suggests a distant region "fleeting as clouds"—the Unconscious.

Kierkegaard tells of the need to reject time and the temporal order in many different contexts and different phrases: Time has a seductive power and time is the heaviest burden laid on man (*WL*, 135–36); The temporal is sin and signifies sin (*CD*, 82–83); it is "the primeval forest of evasion" (*PH*, 186); Time is "the most dangerous enemy," the "cunning power which invents everything," the "alert enemy which never slumbers" (*EO*, II, 141; *FT*, 33). Eternity and Time are in opposition, yet they strive for a reconciliation, that is, "the Eternal and the temporal seek to make themselves intelligible to each other" (*PH*, 43). This would be the process of Integration.

The first expression of a person's relation to the absolute is the renunciation of what binds one to the temporal. Plants and animals can say, "All has its time, there is a time to be born and a time to die; there is a time to jest lightheartedly in the spring breeze." But humans differ from other forms of life, for they are not entirely extended in time: they contain eternity. So time can be the human downfall: "Duration, duration of time is indeed the demand which brings the majority into bankruptcy" (*PH*, 34; *WL*, 286).

Time is continually interfering with our relationship with God and the contemplation of timeless Truth:

> Time, that was ignored by contemplation, begins to assert its validity. . . . the double-minded person lets time cut him off from contemplation. Is this not double-mindedness: to be in time without any contemplation, without any distinct thoughts, or to put it more exactly, to be within time deceived over and over again about having or having had an experience of contemplation! (*PH*, 115)

> But one ingredient in the lowliness of a human being is that he is temporal, and cannot endure to lead uninterruptedly the life of the eternal in time. And if his life is in time, then it is *eo ipso* piecemeal; and if it is piecemeal, it is sprinkled with diversions and distractions; and in the diversion the human being is absent from his God-relationship, or present in it, yet not as in the strong moment. (*CU*, 439)

In Kierkegaard the temporal is associated with the Feelings and the love that must be rejected: for "erotic love, the most beautiful but nevertheless frail invention of temporality, belongs to time" (*WL*, 289). Such love is a disappearance in time (*EO*, I, 194). The one who lives by the erotic lives only for the passing moment. Each moment has its intensity, but, like the love affairs of Don Juan, the erotic moments repeat endlessly without continuity or meaning. To escape the momentary and meaningless life, one must reflect. That is, one steps back from the moment and lives an eternal consciousness. Such a one might eventually become a speculative philosopher, but he too has a meaningless life; he does not live, he only thinks.

An abstract eternity is "the medium of all thought" (*CU*, 268); it is the realm of everlasting truth. There the thinker would live as a contemplative *sub specie aeternitatis*. In his earlier years Kierkegaard had great interest in speculative philosophy, especially the thought of Spinoza and Hegel; he kept repeating to himself that he should "ally himself to Eternal Philosophy" (*JC*, 131). "It is not only at certain moments that I view everything *aeterno modo*, as Spinoza says, but I live constantly *aeterno modo*" (*EO*, I, 37–38; for Kierkegaard on Spinoza, see *PF*, 51–52). He lives apart from life, "hovering above himself" in pure thought. But this is hard to maintain, so many a thinker from time to time swoops down into the world of time to lose himself briefly in the moment; he lives for these forays when he forgets himself, forgets his eternal identity and lives only for a momentary love affair. But such moments cannot last and one returns to eternal solitude. In living *aeterno modo,* one is isolated from the continuity of real love and is bewildered by time. But all the while he suspects that if he ever did love (as opposed to having erotic affairs), he might become reconciled to time (*EO,* II, 140–45). Love by its nature must be in time, it must be historical, it must have continuity (*EO,* II, 140–47). This is the love found in marriage. The life of Don Juan had no continuity; "Everything for him is a matter of the moment only," and "in the same moment everything is over and everything repeats itself endlessly," so "his life is the sum of repellent moments which have no coherence" (*EO,* I, 93, 95).

Don Juan (the Don Juan of Mozart) illustrates what Kierkegaard calls Immediacy. His love affairs are highly damaging to others, but he proceeds with a childlike innocence; he lives completely "in the moment" without thinking of past or future: "To see her and to love her is the same thing." He does not reflect, so he endlessly repeats the same act of seduction. But if a person follows each momentary passion, one finds life is made of "nothing but instants" (*PH,* 51) without continuity.

Most people do not stay long in this immediacy, for they reflect. This reflective stage takes many forms: it gives rise to the abstract thinker, the speculative philosopher, Johannes the Seducer, the Romantic poets such as Lord Byron—and the mystic. They reflect on life from the distance of eternity (T), and the poets among them weep because the world is transitory (F). Though the poets live in eternity, they cannot really make the break with time. So they become double-minded and weep over the things of time, for such things cannot bring the eternal satisfaction for which the poets long. The Romantic poets wrote of their sorrows and disappointments with the temporal, but they would not break with it. For they observe, "What if some temporal help should suddenly appear, then I would be trapped, I, who by commitment to the Eternal had died to the temporal?" (*PH,* 167). They know that time will never satisfy them, yet, unwilling to break with it they become victims of melancholy.

Kierkegaard (writing as "Judge William" to his friend "A") calls on the aesthete to break with the temporal (F). That is, the Judge advises, "Despair," despair of finding satisfaction in the things of time. Kierkegaard sees the mystic as one who has actually made the break: "The temporal vanishes before his eyes" (*EO,* II, 235). The instant of renunciation fills the mystic with indescribable bliss, but it does not last, for soon "the temporal advances its claim." Then time appears as the enemy of the mystic, for the mystic knows anguished stretches of time between brief moments of eternal delight. He recalls the moment of eternal bliss and is unwilling to live in the world of time; though time rightly received would be "the greatest of all the gifts of grace" (*EO*, II, 254). It can be received back as a divine gift, much as Isaac was received back by Abraham! But instead of receiving time back, the mystic lives *aeterno modo*, purely as a T. He has made the break with time, and unlike the poet he does not descend to it again. But he is stranded in his T and will not make the next move that would receive time back as a gift of grace. Christian marriage would be such a move; the eternal vows of marriage would reconcile the Thinker with time.

The aesthete fears marriage (Byron: "Love is heaven; marriage is hell"), for marriage seems to eliminate the spontaneous movements of temporal love (F) that so appealed to the Romantic poets (*EO*, II, 32). But in *Either/Or* Kierkegaard claims that when the temporal is renounced in the vows of marriage, it returns, that is, the F is restored. A 170-page section of *Either/Or* is titled "Equilibrium of the Aesthetical and Ethical in the Composition of the Personality." That is, the personality is the equilibrium of spontaneous love (F) and eternal duty (T). The very title of this extended section tells of the Opposites joined "in the Composition of the Personality," a balance of opposites as recommended by both Kierkegaard and Jung. To achieve this balance, one must first renounce the temporal stirring of love by a promise of enduring fidelity, only to have spontaneous love returned "transfigured" in the marriage (*EO*, II, 34). A man must first live *aeterno modo* in timeless fidelity; only after this might he regain the temporal through a woman, for woman possesses a "secret rapport with time" (*EO*, II, 312).[4] Married love unites the temporal and the Eternal to give a continuity to what would otherwise be the repellent moments of passion. Only married love can be historical, that is, continuous (*EO*, II, 96).

Kierkegaard made the first part of the double movement in rejecting Regina; by doing so he rejected both love and time to live in the philosophical *aeternitas*. He had hopes of making the second part of the double movement, of reaccepting a woman's love and thereby regaining the temporal; one would be "again reconciled with time"

(*EO*, II, 312). For woman resolves "the problem which has cost many a philosopher his reason, the problem of time" (*EO*, II, 313). Kierkegaard's critique of the philosophical *aeternitas* constitutes the second part of the movement by which he hoped to move beyond his reason, "to grasp the whole of the temporal by virtue of the absurd," "to hold fast to the temporal after having given it up" (*FT*, 59, 33).

Having praised the Eternal, Kierkegaard proceeds to show that it is an error and an illusion for temporal man to live as though he were purely eternal—the failing of both the mystic and the speculative philosophers. Kierkegaard criticizes them for they try to live beyond time. They do not realize that the human is a synthesis:

> Since man is a synthesis of the temporal and the eternal, the happiness that the speculative philosopher may enjoy will be an illusion, in that he desires in time to be merely eternal. Herein lies the error of the speculative philosopher. Higher than this speculative happiness, therefore, is the infinite passionate interest in a personal eternal happiness. (*CU*, 54)

The speculative philosopher identifies being with thought and thereby loses his own reality: "being" is an eternal reality apart from time, and into this abstraction the philosopher himself vanishes. He has become a "chimera of abstraction," yet, in fact, "the knower is an existential individual for whom the truth cannot be such an identity as long as he lives in time" (*CU*, 176). Though one might try to live in the eternal world of pure thought, time intervenes to make this impossible; for "time cannot find a place within pure thought" (*CU*, 278). The individual is thus torn between time and eternity, and this draws forth a passion, the passion called existence, *the union of time and eternity.*

Kierkegaard compares the existing individual to the driver of a team of horses; one of the horses is Pegasus and the other is a worn-out jade, one is T and the other is F. "And it is just this that it means to exist, if one is to become conscious of it. Eternity is the winged horse, infinitely fast, and time is a worn-out jade, the individual is the driver" (*CU*, 276). However the duality of eternity and time leaves the individual "double-minded." One type of double-minded person "forgets the Eternal and on that account misuses time, the other misuses eternity" (*PH*, 103). The first is the one who simply lives for the moment; the second is the one that lives *aeterno modo,* as if there were no time. The driver of the team of horses must deal with the Enantiodromia!

Socrates claimed that he knew nothing, and thereby he advanced as far as one could go on one's own. By claiming ignorance he rejected the possibiility of recollecting himself into eternity. He renounced a home in thought and became an existing individual. But Christianity would go further: it accuses the individual of sin, and this leaves one incapable of reflecting one's self into eternity (*CU*, 186). Socrates at least had the possibility of escaping from time into the eternal; but, for Kierkegaard, the Christian, burdened with sin, does not have even the possibility of escape and is forced to exist. The Christian must go further than ignorance and believe what is absurd; this further separates the Christian from the eternity of thought and forces a more passionate existence. The absurdity that the Christian believes is that the eternal Truth has come into being in time (*CU*, 188). The temporal must first be rejected for the eternal, then time is accepted in the absurd, the union of the eternal God with time. This is the double movement of faith; "It is great to grasp the eternal, but it is greater to hold fast to the temporal after having given it up" (*FT*, 33). The temporal is the stone rejected; it has become the eternal God in time, the cornerstone of Christian faith.

Kierkegaard spoke abundantly of the aesthetic. The aesthete (from the Greek, *aesthesis*, perception) is the one who simply observes; perhaps he contemplates the whole of being. And, with special reference to the philosophy of Hegel, he might contemplate the entirety of world history, he might know perfectly the whole of objective truth. But still the one contemplating might be a "no-one"—the abstract thinker has become an airy ghost. Such a thinker might claim "immortality," having identified immortality with eternity, but whether the thinker or any other individual is immortal the thinker does not even stop to inquire.[5] To pass beyond being only the impersonal observer (the aesthete), one must make a free decision. This is what those lost in the contemplation of being (or contemplation of process) cannot do. For they have disappeared as subjects; they are wholly lost in the truth they contemplate. But for Kierkegaard this is all wrong; truth is subjectivity, a matter of inwardness. To gain inwardness, one must break with objective being and make an irrevocable decision; only by making a free and irrevocable choice can one become a subject. By the decision one comes into being as a someone. Kierkegaard advises, "Choose yourself," and "Give birth to yourself" (*EO*, II, 210, 171, 181). Without such a choice one is an airy no-one; by the choice and only by the choice "the personality is consolidated."

The philosopher can avoid all choice and even demonstrate that choice is impossible; there is only the necessity of the historical process. The philosopher can even speak of God, but "God" is like the rest of his thought, only an abstraction. It takes a free and irrevocable decision for both God and the self to become existential, that is, real, and then one can live a real life. After the choice, one has become a someone and only a real someone can relate to a real God. Thus freedom of choice is said to be the true Aladdin's lamp: "When a man rubs it with ethical passion, God comes into being for him" (*CU*, 124). By the decision one has achieved a self, what the pure contemplative lacks. This newborn self can relate to God, something that the no-ones (the mystics, contemplatives, aesthetes, etc.) cannot do. The eternal decision (e.g., marriage) brings together Time and Eternity and one can have a history before God. This allows religion, what Kierkegaard called Religion A; it involves a relation to God that is possible only for the existing individual. It is the first form of religion.

Socrates could know Religion A. But with Christianity something further is required: Religion B. Here

> The eternal happiness of the individual is decided in time through the relationship to something historical, which is furthermore of such a character as to include in its composition that which by virtue of its essence cannot become historical, and must therefore become such by virtue of an absurdity. (*CU*, 345)

Not only, as in Religion A, must one leave objective contemplation to make an inward decision, now one is also obliged to accept the claim that the eternal God ("that which by virtue of its essence cannot become historical") has become historical. This is the Incarnation, the Paradox that the Christian is obliged to believe. "Existence is paradoxically accentuated for the reason that the eternal itself came into the world at a moment of time" (*CU*, 505). This goes beyond the ignorance of Socrates; as such it gives rise to the "crucifixion of the understanding" (*CU*, 496, 500, 501).[6] So at the crucifixion of Christ "the view of the moment and the view of Eternity . . .

have never stood in such opposition" (*PH*, 138). The Enantiodromia is at its height! The ethical person with Religion A had to hold faithful to a decision he or she had made; this gave one a certain existential reality. But with Religion B one must hold fast to an objective absurdity that defies the intellect. This deepens one's existential pathos. Such a one cannot play intellectual games and show one's self to be a theological genius, for the absurdity of the claim can not be rendered intelligible by the greatest genius. With the Paradox, divine Authority has become the decisive quality, and the mind finds Authority comes to it from "elsewhere," from beyond itself (*PA*, 96). Authority is supreme and it defies the understanding (T). (Recall authority has been associated with the F, as in St. Augustine.)

Religion A and Religion B could be contrasted: by Religion A one affirms eternity in time by a vow (e.g., marriage); in Religion B (Christian faith) one affirms the absurd: that the eternal God has entered time. The first gives rise to the existing individual; the second requires one "to exist constantly on the extremest verge of existence by virtue of the absurd" (*CU*, 505). Living on the "extremest verge of existence" involves an intensity of existential passion; for one lives the faith that holds to the objective union of eternity (T) and time (F). Thus, the Reconciliation of the Opposites for Kierkegaard is a troubled Reconciliation achieved only by the absurd. His *Journal* states vividly his situation: "We shudder to read about the sufferings a beast undergoes when it is used for vivisection; yet this gives only a glimmering of the pain involved in being a Christian: to be kept alive in a state of death" (quoted from Kierkegaard's *Journal* in Thompson, 212).

In coming to this position Kierkegaard has told abundantly of "fear and trembling," "the concept of dread," "despair" and other anguished states. But he was not the only philosopher to speak in such terms. Many spoke this way as they passed beyond the Dominant and tried to achieve a synthesis of the opposites. For example, in Plato's *Sophist*, the Stranger, in attempting to reconcile the opposites, speaks of it as a "perilous enterprise," for he must make the paradoxical claim, "Being in a sense is not." He adds: "I tremble at the thought of what I have said, and expect that you will deem me mad, when you hear of my sudden changes and shiftings" (II, 249). Teilhard told of his reconciliation of opposites and said one "will not be able to shake off a feeling of terror. . . . He will be frightened by the novelty, the boldness and at the same time the paradoxical potentialities of attitudes that he finds himself, intellectually and emotionally, obliged to adopt" (*HM*, 46–47). In each case, as in Kierkegaard, the fear and trembling concern the paradoxical unity of opposites. Jung often spoke in similar terms of the fearful process of Integration:

> because individuation is an heroic and often tragic task, the most difficult of all, it involves suffering, a passion of the ego: the ordinary empirical man we once were is burdened with the fate of losing himself in a greater dimension and being robbed of his fancied freedom of will. He suffers, so to speak, from the violence done to him by the self. The analogous passion of Christ signifies God's suffering on account of the injustice of the world and the darkness of man. (*PR*, 157)

The suffering and violence of which Jung speaks here often are part of the philosopher's story, and this has been indicated. But no other philosopher testified to the anguish as eloquently as Kierkegaard: "Faith is against understanding; faith is on the other side of death" (*SU*, 101). He judged his major philosophic work (*Concluding Unscientific Postscript*) to be an account of "all the inner sufferings involved in becoming a Christian, the fact of giving up reason and becoming crucified to a paradox" (*DS*, 149). Jung would understand what he was saying.

Spinoza, Kant, and Kierkegaard were all Ts and all saw God in terms of rational *duty*. But some texts of Kierkegaard bear a likeness to an additional theme in Kant that is worth noting. Kierkegaard claimed that "To will the Good for the sake of reward is double-mindedness" (*PH*, 72). Therefore, for both Kant and Kierkegaard, one must will the Good without any consideration of reward. Yet for both of them the reward *is given* to one who does one's duty, but it comes extrinsic to the duty. This was the substance of Kant's argument for the existence of God. So it is with Kierkegaard: "That the Good has its own reward is indeed forever certain. It is not even more certain that God exists, for that is one and the same thing" (*PH*, 72). For both Kant and Kierkegaard the proof for the existence of God is centered on the need of having virtue rewarded, yet for both the reward cannot be the reason for the act or it would not be virtue.

Each of the three Thinkers recently considered (Spinoza, Kant, and Kierkegaard) proposed a highly rational system; then each seems to have stepped beyond the rational system to affirm a more personal God than pure reason allows, a God that also involved the F. As indicated in the study of Spinoza presented above, Spinoza was roundly criticized for going beyond the logic of his system to suggest a personal immortality (his critics cried, "nonsense," "valueless," "rubbish"). Yet Spinoza himself did not seem to acknowledge the move. Kant, though, was well aware of what he was doing when he went beyond his system to see God as uniting two "extremely heterogeneous concepts" (virtue and happiness), that is, the good man was rewarded with happiness (F) apart from the system (T). But going further Kierkegaard seemed to revel in speaking of a God he knew in radical opposition to the rational. He attained only a troubled Reconciliation. Jung would generally see the Auxiliaries (with Kierkegaard the N and S) as helps in assisting the Reconciliation (see the passages quoted in Myers and Myers, 18). But Kierkegaard does not seem to deal with the Auxiliaries; perhaps that is why his Reconciliation is so troubled. This would be in line with the suggestions of Myers and Myers indicated above.

Kierkegaard can well be compared with other Thinkers. But a very different comparison can be made if Kierkegaard as a T is set in contrast with St. Augustine as an F. They had many similarities: Each was a highly religious author and each had a period of dissipation followed by a conversion; each told much of sin, of divine Omnipotence, and so forth. Both are on the J Axis, so (together with Descartes, Spinoza, Kant, etc.) they each spoke of God as a union of the Good and the True (F and T) (Kierkegaard, WL, 53; FT, 208; PV, 88; PH, 136; the F and T, Good and True, association in Descartes, Spinoza, and Kant are indicated above). But beyond this, Kierkegaard was a T and Augustine was an F, and this would mean the authors were significantly different. The present Jungian reflection could bring out their difference by contrasting the two authors in terms of three points.

1. Kierkegaard as T was at home with Truth (his Dominant) and was told of his underwater search for Love, while Augustine as F was at home with Love and told of his underwater search for Truth.

2. Kierkegaard was at home with Reason and encountered Authority, while Augustine was at home with Authority and encountered Reason.

3. Kierkegaard was at home in Eternity and could accept the Temporal only by divine grace, while Augustine was at home in the Temporal and could accept the Eternal only by divine grace.

These points could be developed. As to the first: Kierkegaard told of his youth when he grasped at naught but the intellectual side and suppressed his emotions; he found the logic of grammar to be his favorite subject (JC, 106; EO, II, 274). To the contrary, the young Augustine developed his feelings and suppressed his analytic/rational side; he disliked analysis and grammar (C, 30). Before his conversion, Kierkegaard lived by his abstract reason; before his conversion, Augustine lived by his feelings.

Both St. Augustine and Kierkegaard could be seen as searching for their opposite Function. St. Augustine's opposite Function was Thinking, so he was searching for Truth; Kierkegaard's opposite Function was Feeling, so he was searching for Love. But the very character of their searches shows their individual types: Kierkegaard was analytic in his search for Love, while Augustine was emotional in his search for Truth. Kierkegaard found Love elusive, so he compared Love to Proteus (EO, II, 151); Augustine found Truth elusive, so he compared Truth to Proteus ("Proteus portrays and personates the truth which no one can lay hold of" [HL, 182]; Proteus is "discloser of universal truth" [HL, 319]). Proteus was the underwater God who changed his shape; Jung associates Proteus with the repressed Function (A, 216–17); so it was love for one and truth for the other.

Both Augustine and Kierkegaard used the sea as a symbol, but they used it in opposite ways (for Jung the sea was the primary symbol for the Unconscious). Augustine told of going on an elusive, under-the-sea quest for Truth, while Kierkegaard told of an elusive, under-the-sea quest for Love (WL, 19). Ultimately St. Augustine found human truth based on divine Truth; in contrast, Kierkegaard found human love based on divine Love. Consider a passage wherein Augustine told of human *truth* participating in divine Truth: "If you and I both see that which you say is true, and both see that which I say is true, where do we see this? Not I in you, nor you in me; but both of us in the Unchangeable truth itself, which is above our minds" (*C*, 12, 35). Compare this with a passage wherein Kierkegaard told of human *love* participating in divine Love: "O God of Love, source of all love in heaven and earth, you who spared nothing but gave all in love, You who are love, so that one who loves is what he is only by being in you!" (*WL*, 19).

Both Augustine and Kierkegaard made a double movement: they rejected their opposite and then received back what was rejected. As a youth St. Augustine rejected the analytic pursuit of grammar and arithmetic only to receive them back as transformed on a higher level: he came to speak of them in wondrous terms: "the almost heavenly power and nature of grammar," and he called "sempiternal number" the "discloser of universal truth" (*HL*, 322, 318, 319). St. Augustine saw Truth as a gift of God given to the human mind: truths are manifested "by God revealing them to one's inner self." In contrast, Kierkegaard began his double movement by a rejection of love, but later it was the gift given him by God: "It is God, the creator, who must implant love in each person, he who himself is love" (*WL*, 205). Kierkegaard could speak of a "crucifixion of the understanding" in coming to faith, and one could imagine Augustine telling of the crucifixion of the heart as he came to the faith.

A second point of contrast: both Augustine and Kierkegaard told of the difference between Reason (T) and Authority (F). But they came to the issues from opposite sides: Augustine often argued that authority was the necessary starting place from which one could proceed to reason ("There is no sounder principle in the Catholic Church than that authority would precede reason" [*WL*, 39]). While Kierkegaard saw reason as the necessary starting place from which one could proceed to the Authority that is beyond reason (faith is beyond philosophy, so it "cannot be taught, but only believed," etc. [*PA*, 99]). St. Augustine could be seen as saying *Fides quaerens intellectum.* One could see Kierkegaard telling of *Intellectus quaerens fidem.*

A third item of contrast between the two authors is found in their concern with time and Eternity. For years Augustine could not accept any nonextended reality; all reality was within time. A major event in his conversion was when divine grace showed him that "above my changing mind was the unchangeable and true *eternity* of truth" (*C*, 154). Kierkegaard readily acknowledged eternal truth, he lived *aeterno modo* and spoke of the mind as an eternal consciousness; but divine help was needed for him to accept the temporal

(*FT,* 59). For Augustine faith came when he accepted the Eternal, for Kierkegaard faith came when he accepted the Temporal. Eternal Truth was the goal for which Augustine strove in his emotional acceptance of the faith, so Eternal Truth came as a gift. Temporal Love was the goal for which Kierkegaard strove in his analytic acceptance of the faith, so Temporal Love came as a gift. Kierkegaard spoke of holding "fast to the temporal after having given it up." One could speak of Augustine as holding fast to the Eternal after having given it up.

The above set of contrasts brings out ways that a Dominant F and a Dominant T might be compared; each has as a Repressed Function what the other has as a Dominant. So their philosophies begin at opposite points, and each one labors to acquire what the other had to start with. But they are both Judgers on the J Axis and this gives them many issues in common, as was just shown. Their writings have a very different character than that of the Perceiving philosophers on the P Axis. On the P Axis the Enantiodromia concerns issues of S and N: Trees or Forests, units or systems, tangibility or vision, atoms or relations, present or future. This difference was considered earlier with accounts of Plato, Locke, and Sartre; now those on the P Axis will be considered further with studies of Whitehead, Hume, and Teilhard de Chardin.

Notes

1. At the time as he was writing *Fear and Trembling* Kierkegaard noted in his *Journals:* "If I had faith I would have remained with Regina."
2. In telling the story, Kierkegaard says Abraham and Isaac "rode in silence for *three* days. On the *fourth* day Abraham said never a word, but he lifted his eyes and saw Mt. Moriah afar off" (*FT,* 27). The Scripture has it, "On the *third* day Abraham lifted up his eyes and saw the place afar off" (Gen. 22:4). Kierkegaard has changed the day of seeing and the sacrifice from day Three to day Four.
3. Jung develops this in an essay on Schiller, the German poet: "Schiller calls the symbol-creating function a third instinct, the *play* instinct; it bears no resemblance to the two opposing functions, but stands between them and does justice to both their natures." "The third element, in which the opposites merge, is *fantasy activity,* which is creative and receptive at once" (*PT,* 106–7). Later Jung speaks of "the creative *fantasy*" able to produce a content "that can unite the opposites" (*PT,* 115). These suggestions concerning "fantasy activity" as a reconciling third might apply to Kierkegaard's reconciliation of Thought and Feeling in the imagination.

4. One could interpret such passages to say that the feminine (what Jung called the Anima) is associated with the opposite Function, time, the F. Perhaps a similar association is found in Kierkegaard's claim that woman "is much closer to God than man is" (*EO*, II, 54). Kierkegaard claims that marriage belongs essentially to Christianity (*EO*, II, 29). He sees the Romantic poets weeping over the beauty of love as pagan, for they cannot take the first step and break with the temporal.

5. Perhaps the idea might go back to Kierkegaard's reading of Spinoza. It could be recalled that in the Fifth Book of his *Ethics* Spinoza went beyond the immortality of pure thought to suggest the immortality of the individual. Kierkegaard points out the same difference. See *CU*, 54 where he tells of "a personal eternal happiness" that is beyond "speculative happiness."

6. Many have compared Kierkegaard and Tertullian, an early Christian writer who is famous for his line: *Credo quia absurdum est.* Kierkegaard quotes the phrase (*PF*, 65–67). Jung considers the same phrase: "I believe because it is absurd," and quotes further from Tertullian: "The Son of God died, which is immediately credible because it is absurd." Jung tells of Tertullian rejecting all gnostic claims (much as Kierkegaard rejected the claims of the speculative philosophers). Jung adds, "The self-mutilation performed by Tertullian in the *sacrificium intellectus* led him to an unqualified recognition of the irrational inner-reality, the true rock of his faith" (*PT*, 13). It is easy to see a similar *sacrificium* in Kierkegaard. Jung identifies Tertullian as "the Creator of the Latin Church that lasted for more than a thousand years" (*PT*, 12). This is hardly the case: he was never called a saint, was rejected as a heretic, and was dismissed by the scholastics.

Bibliography

Works of Kierkegaard

CD *The Concept of Dread*, translated by Walter Lowrie. Princeton: Princeton University Press, 1957.

CU *Concluding Unscientific Postscript*, translated by David F. Swenson and Walter Lowrie. Princeton: Princeton University Press, 1968.

DS *The Diary of Søren Kierkegaard*, translator unidentified, edited by Peter Rohde. New York: Philosophical Library, 1960.

ED *Edifying Discourses: A Selection*, edited with an introduction by Paul L. Holmer, translated by David F. and Lillian Marvin Swenson. New York: Harper Torchbooks, 1958.

EO *Either/Or*, two volumes, translated by David and Lillian Swenson, revised by H. Johnson. New York: Doubleday-Anchor, 1959.

FT *Fear and Trembling* (1–132) and *The Sickness unto Death* (133–262), translated, with an introduction and notes, by Walter Lowrie. Princeton: Princeton University Press, 1968.

JC *Johannes Climacus, or De Omnibus Dubitandum Est*, translated, with an assessment, by T. H. Croxall. Stanford: Stanford University Press, 1958.

JK *The Journals of Kierkegaard*, translated and edited by Alexander Dru. New York: Harper Torchbooks, 1959.

PA *The Present Age* and *Of the Difference between a Genius and an Apostle*, translated by Alexander Dru, introduction by Walter Kaufmann. New York: Harper Torchbooks, 1962.

PF *Philosophical Fragments*, originally translated and introduced by David Swenson, new introduction and commentary by Neils Thulstrup, translation revised and commentary translated by Howard V. Hong. Princeton: Princeton University Press, 1962.

PH *Purity of Heart*, translated and introduced by Douglas V. Steere. New York: Harper Torchbooks, 1956.

PV *The Point of View for My Work as an Author: A Report to History, and Related Writings*, translated with introduction and notes by Walter Lowrie; newly edited with a preface by Benjamin Nelson. New York: Harper Torchbooks, 1962.

R *Repetition*, translated with introduction and notes by Walter Lowrie. New York: Harper Torchbooks, 1964.

SE *For Self-Examination* and *Judge for Yourselves!* translated, with an introduction and notes, by Walter Lowrie. Princeton: Princeton University Press, 1968.

SL *Stages on Life's Way*, translated by Walter Lowrie. Princeton: Princeton University Press, 1945.

WL *Works of Love: Some Christian Reflections in the Form of Discourses*, translated by Howard and Edna Hong, preface by R. Gregor Smith. New York: Harper Torchbooks, 1964.

Other Works

Thompson, Josiah. *The Lonely Labyrinth: Kierkegaard's Pseudonymous Works*. Carbondale: Southern Illinois University Press, 1967.

Works by Plato, Teilhard, and Augustine cited in this chapter use the same abbreviations as found in the chapters dedicated to them.

Part III
Three with a Perceiving Faculty as Dominant

10 Whitehead: Process Leads to Peace
Weaving Together the Dominant and the Repressed

Whitehead as N: Whitehead introduces his major book: Here "'relatedness' is dominant over 'quality' [N is dominant over S]" (*PR*, ix). "Actuality is through and through togetherness" (*SM*, 157). "There is no entity which enjoys an isolated self-sufficiency of existence" (*ES*, 102). "The world is a community of organisms" (*S*, 79). "Connectedness is of the essence of all things. . . . No fact is merely itself" (*MT*, 13). "All general truths condition each other" (*PR*, 15). "Every proposition proposing a fact must, in its complete analysis, propose the general character of the universe required for that fact. There are no self-sustained facts floating in nonentity" (*PR*, 17). He claimed that his basic ideas "presuppose each other so that in isolation they are meaningless" (*PR*, 5). "One all-pervasive fact, inherent in the very character of what is real, is the transition of things, the passage of one to another. This passage is not a mere linear procession of discrete entities. However we fix a determinate entity [for consideration] . . . there is always a wider determination into which our first choice fades by transition beyond itself. The general aspect of nature is that of evolutionary expansiveness" (*SM*, 88–89). In telling of opposing philosophers he stated his own Enantiodromia: "One side makes process ultimate; the other side makes fact ultimate" (*PR*, 11). For Whitehead's Quaternity, see Figure 10.1. Whitehead's Myers-Briggs type would be INTJ.

		T	
	3.	Conceptual feeling	
N Dominant	4.	True	S
1. Final cause, lure			Efficient cause
2. Theory, abstractions		COMPLETE FACT	Facts, details
3. Comparative feeling			Dative ingression PR, 241
4. Beauty		PEACE	Details of character (art) AI, 283
5. Primordial nature		CONSEQUENT NATURE OF GOD	Creativity
of God		WISDOM	Instinct
6. Intelligence			
		F	
	3.	Conformal physical feeling	
	4.	Good, (adventure)	

Figure 10.1

I. An Intuitive Situates Himself among Philosophers

Alfred North Whitehead (1861–1947) was a mathematician who became a philosopher only late in life. He had read widely in the history of philosophy, so in stating his own position he often did so by situating himself in that history. He saw his philosophy as a contemporary form of Platonism (*PR*, 63), but he also told how his philosophy differed from that of others. Here the differences could be seen in terms of the Jungian Four: First, he would claim to be a perceiver (a P, not a J) and then situate himself as an N (not an S). In differentiating himself from the Ts he tells of an understanding of mental processes found in Descartes, Kant, and their rationalist followers; these philosophers would give primacy to cogitation or thinking and, therefore, consider perception as a derived form of thinking. In contrast he endorses an understanding typified by Locke, who regarded perception as the fundamental experience—thinking is only a derived form of perception.

Whitehead writes, "The metaphysical doctrine here expounded finds the foundations of the world in the aesthetic experience, rather than—as with Kant—in the cognitive and conceptive experience." He objects that Descartes reflected apart from experience so that he could reach the actual world only by an appeal to the power and goodness of God (PR, 77, 78). Many of the followers of Descartes had less faith in God than he and found themselves with a theory of "representative perception"; they knew only "representations" and could not get to the actual world at all, so they became Idealists. In contrast, Whitehead argued that philosophy must begin with perception: he states succinctly his opposition to Descartes and others on the J Axis: "The principle that I am adopting is that consciousness presupposes experience, and not experience consciousness" (PR, 83). He would start with experience, with the "aesthetic order," not the order of mind or consciousness.

The aesthetic (from Greek, aesthesis = "perception") order is the order of perception, but the English word "aesthetic" also implies the Beautiful.[1] Whitehead would see Descartes burdening philosophy with the "unfortunate notion" that the method of philosophy is to indicate premises that are clear and certain and deduce the rest of philosophy from these (PR, 11). For Whitehead, philosophy was led astray because of "the unfortunate notion that its method is dogmatically to indicate premises which are severally clear, distinct, and certain; and to erect upon those premises a deductive system of thought" (PR, 11–12; see Leclerc, Whitehead's Metaphysics, 41, MT, 143). This "unfortunate notion" is the ideal of the T, and is rejected by Whitehead.

Having identified with the P Axis, Whitehead goes on to further situate himself. Locke was a Perceiver, but when Locke went on to identify perception with the data of sense, Whitehead could not agree. For him the data of sensation are not the fundamental elements in experience, for there is a perception presupposed by sense experience (PR, 12, 268; AI, 180; see SM, 137–39). At times he would call this nonsensate perception "intuition" or an aesthetic awareness. He found many things that he liked in Locke, but these were the passages wherein Locke developed ideas that Whitehead, Hume, and many others found inconsistent with Locke's "purely sensationalist philosophy" (PR, 89).

As an N, Whitehead would proceed from the general to the particular. This can be seen in a passage wherein Whitehead speaks of mathematics, a study that overlooks particulars:

> In other words, we are more clear as to the interrelations of the numbers than as to their separate individual characters. We use the interrelations as a step towards the determinations of the things related. This is an instance of the general truth, that our progress in the clarity of knowledge is primarily from the composition to its ingredients. (*ES*, 213)

This claim can be evaluated only by setting it in contrast to the approach he found in Locke and the Sensate philosophers. For example, Bacon claimed he wanted to begin with the experiential facts; he wanted to start with the data gained from experiment and from there induce the general laws of nature. But Whitehead objects: "Experiment is nothing else than a mode of cooking the facts for the sake of exemplifying the law" (*AI*, 94). He imagines Bacon claiming: "We ought to describe detailed matters of fact, and elicit the laws with a generality strictly limited to the systematization of these described details" (*PR*, 21). But Whitehead replies, "Unfortunately for this objection, there are no brute, self-contained matters of fact, capable of being understood apart from interpretation as an element in a system."

He was thinking of both Bacon and Hume when he told of those for whom all perception is rooted in our bodily sense-organs and all percepta are base *sensa* in the immediate present (*AI*, 179–80). He tells of powerful schools of thought which have rejected this claim, so he wonders why the sensates have not heeded these objections. He allows that one might decide to restrict the word "perception" to impressions arising from the stimulation of sense organs. Thus, sense-perception "essentially exhibits percepta as *here, now, immediate,* and *discrete*" (*A*, 182; emphasis in text)—all these terms tell of the Jungian Sensate. He would see David Hume guilty of a similar fault in claiming, "Every impression of sensation is a distinct existence." Whitehead allows this claim of "barren sensa" might satisfy our common sense (Locke, the philosopher of common sense). But it ignores the fact that all individual sense-perceptions are fused with a vast background and foreground of "non-sensuous perception" which take us beyond the here and now and the discrete; without this wider perception the individual sense perception of Hume or others could never occur. In experiencing the *sensa* there are also "*other* influences," "*other* values," "*other* purposes" (*AI*, 183; emphasis in text). This "otherness" apart from the barren *sensa* again shows Whitehead to be an N; N—the Faculty of Otherness.

This could be put as: Every tree must be *other* than itself in order to be part of the wider forest. At one point, Whitehead even uses the tree/forest image: an isolated tree would find it difficult to survive, so "in nature the normal way in which trees flourish is by their association in a forest" (*SM*, 184). That is, individual trees are not simply themselves.

And it is the wider "forest" we know first. We begin with the inter-relationships and proceed to the relata. It is a "general truth that our progress in the clarity of knowledge is primarily from the composition to its ingredients" (*ES*, 213). From the forest to the trees—it is the reverse order of Locke, Bacon, and Hume. Instead of starting with facts, Whitehead can approach a fact only as an element in a system. Philosophy concerns itself with generalities so that by providing the generic notions it might "make it easier to conceive the infinite variety of specific instances which rest unrealized in the womb of nature" (*PR*, 26). "Specific instances" (S) rest unrealized in the womb—of the Unconscious.

Whitehead objects to Aristotle and his individual substances. He says that Aristotle went on to develop a logic which leaves each thing

> as complete in itself, without any reference to any other substantial thing. Such an account of the ultimate atoms, or of the ultimate monads, or of the ultimate subjects enjoying experience, renders an interconnected world of real individuals unintelligible. The universe is shivered into a multitude of disconnected substantial things. (*AI*, 137)

In a similar way the physics of Newton is seen to contain the idea of separate units; it is "based upon the independent individuality of each bit of matter. Each stone is conceived as fully describable apart from any reference to any other portion of matter" (*AI*, 160). For Newton, relations were simply extrinsic to the reality of things. Descartes likewise told of independent substances and thus made a virtue out of "incoherence" (*PR*, 10). For Whitehead, the worlds of Aristotle, Newton, and Descartes have been left behind by Relativity. Now we must think of a world of "intrinsic relations," that is, a world where each thing is what it is by its relationships. He termed his own philosophy one of "organism," to indicate all its elements were inter-related, as is the whole of nature.

Whitehead would speak of nature being made of "prehensions," or as "a process of prehensive unification" (*SM*, 68). He gives an extended statement of his philosophy that will be quoted here although much of it cannot be understood without considerable explanation. But the passage is presented because it has many phrases that show the mind of the intuitive:

> nature is conceived as a complex of prehensive unifications. Space and time exhibit the general scheme of interlocked relations of these prehensions. You cannot tear any of them out of its context. Yet each one of them within its context has all the reality that attaches to the whole complex. Conversely, the totality has the same reality as each prehension; for each prehension unifies the modalities to be ascribed, from its standpoint, to every part of the whole. A prehension is a process of unifying. Accordingly, nature is a process of expansive development, necessarily transitional from prehension to prehension. (*SM*, 70)

As Whitehead rejected individual units in his cosmology, so he rejected individual units in his economics: the notion of an individual with private property is only a legal fiction. As an individual could not fit into Whitehead's economics, so an individual thing with private properties (qualities) could not fit into his cosmology. "The self-sufficing independent man, with his peculiar property which concerns no one else, is a concept without any validity for modern civilization" (*AI*, 34). (Recall that the individual and his private property were the basis of both the politics and economics of Locke.) Even the individualism of separate nations is rejected (*AI*, 66). "The whole concept of absolute individuals with absolute rights . . . has broken down" (*AI*, 71). In language there are no independent sentences, no "adequate separate premises from which argument can proceed" (*ES*, 95). A word or a sentence can have meaning only in a context (*ES*, 96). An idea can have "its being [only] as one of a system of ideas." And even a single system of ideas is inadequate; different systems must elucidate one another (*AI*, 32). Every entity exists only insofar as it is interwoven with all other entities. This is the law of being that Whitehead saw in the universe, in economics, in politics, in language, and even in theology—for God himself is no exception (*ES*, 83). In each case Whitehead is making the same objection: there are no separate and independent units. "There is no entity which enjoys an isolated self-sufficiency of existence." Whitehead uses a term that suggests the Unconscious when he claims that the notion of "independent existence" has "*haunted* philosophic literature throughout the centuries" (*ES*, 83).

II. The Development of an Intuitive

Looking at the life of Whitehead as a whole, one finds a marked development in his thought. One commentator speaks of it as a radical reversal of emphasis; another refers to his change as a somersault (W. Wightman, in Leclerc, *Revelance of Whitehead* (*RW*), 340), a change that occurred mostly during three years (1922-25) when he did little writing. His distinctive philosophy developed after this time and is the material treated in this study. Yet to understand the man one must consider how he had been known: as a mathematician.

Whitehead was born in England in February 1861, and his ability in mathematics was evident when he went to Cambridge in 1880; five years later he was a Fellow there. In 1895 he began a long and happy marriage; he and his wife had three children. Thus, he is the only family man considered in this study![2] Whitehead's earliest publications were in mathematics; his first book, *A Treatise on Universal Algebra*, appeared in 1898. A Whitehead scholar writes of it, "His constant theme was the broad power a mathematical system has by virtue of its abstract generality" (Lowe, 192), suggesting the domination of the N at this time. This was soon followed by two books in geometry. He regarded his most original contribution to mathematics a paper written in 1905; there he "views the material world as a set of relations and of the entities forming the fields of these relations" (Lowe, 297). With Bertrand Russell he co-authored *Principia Mathematica*, a study in mathematics and logic. During this time discoveries in physics were shaking the accepted cosmology of Newton, so Whitehead set out to develop a philosophy of nature suitable for the new situation. He began to see "events" as the basic units of the cosmos, and events were "processes of unifying." He soon saw that he would have to undertake a complete metaphysical study, but by this time he was in his sixties. In 1924 he was invited to teach at Harvard University. He quickly accepted and while teaching there, and while giving the Gifford lectures in Scotland, he wrote the philosophical works for which he is known—in his sixties and early seventies.

The strictly intuitive approach of his early years can be seen in his interest in mathematics: he would speak of mathematics as an investigation of patterns of connectedness in abstraction from the particular relata (*AI*, 157; see *SM*, chapter 2). His move to physics can be seen as a turning away from the unlimited abstraction of mathematics towards the concrete and empirical, the S. By his philosophy of science he told of seeking "what we are aware of in perception." So he introduced his *Principle of Relativity* (1922): "Our ultimate aim must be to describe the sensible in terms of the sensible" (Leclerc, *RW*, 337). The sensible—that is what he had ignored as a mathematician. But he came to see the limits of the mathematics and logic he himself had developed; they were a dead end (Wightman, in Leclerc, *RW*, 339): "Logic is the chosen resort of clearheaded people, severally convinced of the complete adequacy of their doctrines. It is such a pity that they cannot agree with each other" (*ES*, 211; *MT*, 2). This was said by the co-author of one of the great books on logic—who could not agree with his co-author, Bertrand Russell (who had a Dominant T). As mathematician and logician he had sought out the more general: "The essence of mathematics is perpetually to be discarding more special ideas in favor of more general ideas, and special methods in favor of general methods" (*Anth*, 109);—the claim states well the mind of an N. For in mathematics "we have always got rid of the particular instance" (*SM*, 26)—the S. But a Jungian would object that the time would come when the particular would have to return. Whitehead would even state the matter in psychological terms: "In the dim recesses behind consciousness there is the sense of realities behind abstractions"; these realities were the concrete objects that the mathematician had been ignoring. So the very process of abstraction points back to its origin, "a return to the concrete" (*MT*, 170).

Perhaps a psychological meaning can be seen in Whitehead's critique of people locked in a shell of abstractions: "They hold you to their abstractions by the sheer grip of personality" (*SM*, 58). The final phrase suggests the constricting Persona developed by an N; such a one dwells in a world of abstractions unable to acknowledge concrete experience (the S). He termed such disinterested intellectualism a "psychological error." He criticized people who have no sympathy for the dim perspective: such people use only their reason, "healthy, manly, upstanding reason; but, of one-eyed reason, deficient in its vision of depth" (*SM*, 59). "One-eyed reason" describes the conscious function acting alone. It is "manly, " but something is lacking: the depth of the feminine Unconscious. One-eyed reason maintains "a celibacy of the intellect which is divorced from the concrete contemplation of the complete facts" (*SM*, 176).[3] Facts (and action) have been relegated to the feminine Unconscious. Yet there they can be obscurely perceived: "Amid the infinitude of the connected universe, we can discern vaguely finite units of fact" (*MT*, 120) "Vaguely finite units of fact"! Other passages mentioning facts likewise use the imagery of the Unconscious: he speaks of a "bare welter of facts" and sees facts forming "an unrealized swamp, pestilential with mystery and magic" (*AI*, 145, 146).

When Whitehead became a philosopher he looked back on his work in mathematics and logic: "Too large a generalization leads to mere barrenness. It is the large generalisation, limited by a happy particularity, which is the fruitful conception" (*SM*, 35). The S (the happy *particularity*) has appeared. He would parallel his own development with a change he saw in eighteenth-century thought: "As mathematics withdrew increasingly into the upper regions of ever greater extremes of abstract thought, it returned back to earth with a corresponding growth of importance for the analysis of concrete fact" (*SM*, 36–37). The passage concerning eighteenth-century thought also tells of Whitehead's own move away from the N and his return "back to earth," to the S.

What is involved is an ascent into the N and then a return to the S. He would state the sequence involved: "The true method of discovery is like the flight of an aeroplane. It starts from the ground of particular observation; it makes a flight in the thin air of imaginative generalization; and it again lands for renewed observation rendered acute by rational interpretation" (*PR*, 7). This is a clear example of the stone (particular observation) being rejected only to return as cornerstone. It recalls Kierkegaard's accepting the temporal after having given it up. Or in terms of another Intuitive, Sartre: "The total concrete was what we [students] wanted to leave behind us; the absolute concrete was what we wanted to achieve." One is leaving the concrete only later to discover the real concrete, so

231

Whitehead is leaving particular observation only later to discover what is truly concrete. This "reversal" is his "somersault."

It is in this context that one can understand what Whitehead saw as the goal of his metaphysics: "The final problem is to conceive a complete [παντελής] fact" (AI, 162).[4] Most people would understand a "fact" to be an isolated unit that is simply identified with the S. But in saying "a complete fact" Whitehead is seeking more than the "barren sensa" he had rejected. It is the sensa *in context*, the individual tree seen and known as part of the forest. What he had rejected were the self-contained individual units, the separate substances of Aristotle or the atoms of Lucretius and Hume. Then later these individual units are restored as cornerstone; as Whitehead writes, "The ultimate metaphysical truth is atomism. The creatures are atomic" (PR, 53). These "atoms" are the complete facts and the concrete elements that were missing. Ivor Leclerc identified Whitehead's "complete fact" with what Aristotle was seeking when he sought to understand being as substance: it is "a distinct ontological unit which is able to subsist in itself and can be defined by itself" (WM, 19). Yet these atomic units are not simply what Whitehead had rejected; they have a nonatomic character: "Atomism does not exclude complexity and universal relativity. Each atom is a system of all things" (PR, 53). In terming each *atom* (S) a *system* (N) he is telling of a reconciliation of opposites; the rejected stone (the atoms) is now the cornerstone. Whitehead identified his cosmology as one of internal (S) relations (N). The opposites are united, so in *Adventures in Ideas*, a work written late in life (1932), he affirmed, "Throughout the universe there reigns the union of opposites" (AI, 193).

The reconciliation of Intuition and Sensation could be seen in Whitehead's accounts of the history of philosophy. The worlds of Plato (N) and Bacon (S) are seen in conflict: Plato presented an ideal of final harmony, while Bacon told of the strife of single events; the "strife" of the singular again suggests the Unconscious. The two of them together formed the elements of Whitehead's Enantiodromia, and he called for a reconciliation:

> Strife is at least as real a fact in the world as Harmony. If you side with Francis Bacon and concentrate on the efficient causes, you can interpret large features of the growth of structure in terms of "strife." If, with Plato, you fix your attention on the end, rationally worthy, you

can interpret large features in terms of "harmony." But until some outline of understanding has been reached which elucidates the inter-
fusion of strife and harmony, the intellectual driving force of successive generations will sway uneasily between the two. (*AI*, 39)

The resolution of the Enantiodromia is expressed in many
phrases: a fundamental task of metaphysics is "to exhibit final and
efficient causes in relation to each other" (*PR*, 129). Society is seen
as alternating between an emphasis on the relativity (N) and the individuality (S) of humans (*AI*, 50). And the history of science was like a
pendulum swinging between reason and stubborn fact (*SM*, 16). Science itself alternates between continuity and atomicity (*AI*, 187–88;
SM, 94). The creative process involves a similar back and forth:

> it swings from the publicity of many things to the individual privacy;
> and it swings back from the private individual to the publicity of the
> objectified individual. The former swing is the final cause, which is
> the ideal; and the latter swing is dominated by the efficient cause
> which is actual. (*PR*, 229)

The Enantiodromia is being resolved as opposites are woven together. "As the relations modify the natures of the relata, so the relata
modify the nature of the relation" (*AI*, 161). The "crux" of philosophy is
said to be in maintaining the balance between the relativity (N) and
the individuality (S) of existence (*ES*, 111). Science and philosophy are
"both concerned with the understanding of individual facts as illus-
trations of general principles" (*AI*, 144). But "the emphasis of science
is upon observation of particular occurrences. . . . The emphasis of
philosophy is upon generalizations" (*AI*, 147). Religion seems to be the
same: "Religion starts from the generalization of final truths first perceived as exemplified in particular instances" (*RM*, 120).

In a late essay (1941) summarizing his thought, Whitehead told of
two worlds: the World of Value and the World of Fact (*ES*, 77). The
World of Value is said to contain purpose, intention, the union of
many; its essential character is termed the coordination of all possibilities. The World of Fact is the world of finite multiplicity and finite actuality; it is the world of action. Each of the worlds is said to
be futile except in its function of embracing the other. "Value refers
to Fact, and Fact refers to Value" (*ES*, 80). Mere fact or mere possibility are termed only abstractions of thought:

> In the universe the status of the World of Fact is that of an abstraction requiring, for the completion of its concrete reality, Value and Purpose. Also in the Universe the status of the World of Value is that of an abstraction, requiring for the completion of its concrete reality, the factuality of Finite Activity. (*ES*, 92)

> But the World of Value emphasizes the essential unity of the many; whereas the World of Fact emphasizes the essential multiplicity in the realization of this unity. Thus the Universe, which embraces both Worlds, exhibits the one as many, and the many as one. (*ES*, 89)

All such passages show a common theme running through the later texts of Whitehead: with a variety of terms and contexts he is working together elements of his N and his S.

The Unconscious is often seen as unruly and its primary symbol is water; Jung warns that the Unconscious can burst into Consciousness and overwhelm it as waters in a flood. Whitehead speaks of forming a unity through a "coincidence of forces derived from both sides of the world. . . . Mere physical nature lets loose a flood, but it requires intelligence to provide a system of irrigation" (*AI*, 25). By the *system* of irrigation the abstract harmony of Consciousness is irrigated by what could have been a devastating flood from "physical nature"—the Unconscious (see Jung, *PT*, 261–65 where the danger of "inundation" by the Unconscious gives way to ordered streams and a new fruitfulness).

Whitehead wrote many accounts of the history of ideas, especially of that history over the past five centuries. These tell both of the development of science and Whitehead's own development. He explains, "The great periods of history act as an enlightenment. They reveal ourselves to ourselves" (*AI*, 168). So he prefaces his *Adventures of Ideas* by telling of two meanings in the title: one concerns the slow drift of humanity towards civilization; "the other meaning is the author's adventure in framing a speculative scheme of ideas which will be explanatory of the historical adventure" (*AI*, 7). The same double meaning (both social history and personal history) can be found in the opening essay of *Science and the Modern World*. First he tells of the predominance of Reason and final causality that characterized the Middle Ages (this reflects his own early interest in mathematics and logic). Then there was the emphasis on efficient causality and the facts that characterized the Renaissance (his turn to physics and philosophy). But contemporary science has established a balance between theory and fact. He is telling of the history of ideas in terms of his own personal history.

In a wider historical context Whitehead tells the same story: the Greeks developed a speculative thought that was "lucid and logical," but in their disregard for detail they lacked "the complete scientific mentality" (*SM*, 14). Their minds did not include the "muddled suspense" (a phrase suggestive of the Unconscious) of empirical research. He saw the Greeks concentrating on finality and the ultimate end of things. Their thought gave rise to medieval theology and the "rationalistic orgy of the Middle Ages" when rationality permeated all society (*SM*, 19, 23). But with Galileo and other experimeters there was a stirring of empirical interest apart from claims of finality. Both Galileo and Luther are seen as appealing to efficient causality and experiment: "This appeal to the origins of Christianity and Francis Bacon's appeal to efficient causes as against final causes were two sides of the same movement of thought." There suddenly developed a great interest in and awareness of "irreducible and stubborn fact." This involved a "return to contemplation of brute fact and was based on a recoil from the inflexible rationality of mediaeval thought." A *"return* to contemplation of brute fact"—having made its flight, the aeroplane (see above) has returned to the ground, to see it for the first time. Whitehead traces the opposing influences that have shaped the modern world to conclude that contemporary science has reached a balance with an interest in both theory and fact:

> This new tinge to modern minds is a vehement and passionate interest in the relation of general principles to irreducible and stubborn facts. All the world over and at all times there have been practical men, absorbed in "irreducible and stubborn facts": all the world over and at all times there have been men of philosophical temperament who have been absorbed in the weaving of general principles. It is this union of passionate interest in the detailed facts with equal devotion to abstract generalization which forms the novelty in our present society. Previously it had appeared sporadically and as if by chance. This balance of mind has now become part of the tradition which infests cultivated thought. (*SM*, 10–11)

Both elements are involved when Whitehead tells of science needing two kinds of faith: First, a faith in reason, a trust that the ultimate natures lie together in a harmony; but the growth of science
involves a deeper faith, a faith that concerns the nature of things
found in immediate and present existence (*SM*, 23–24). It is first a
faith in the N, and then a deeper faith in the S; and the achievement
of the modern world is that the two have reached an ongoing balance. To consider the reverse (how reality would appear to an S):
One could imagine Locke or Hume readily accepting "immediate
and present existence" but requiring a "*deeper* faith" to affirm that
"ultimate natures lie together in harmony."

This essay of Whitehead's on the development of science is an
analogue for his own development; this can be seen as he concludes
the essay:

> There is no parting from your own shadow. To experience this faith is
> to know that in being ourselves we are more than ourselves: to know
> that our experience, dim and fragmentary as it is, yet sounds the ut-
> most depths of reality: to know that detached details merely in order
> to be themselves demand that they should find themselves in a system
> of things. (*SM*, 25)

Thus the essay ends with a psychological touch: we cannot part
from our own shadow; in being ourselves we are more than ourselves. As detached details are integrated into a system, we find the
Self: that which is "ourselves" and "more than ourselves." As involving more than ourselves Jung would see this conclusion as religious;
it reconciles the opposites.

Whitehead sees religion involving a similar reconciliation: "Religion starts from the generalization of *final truths* first perceived as
exemplified in *particular instances*" (*RM*, 120). Or, "Religious truth
must be developed from knowledge acquired when our ordinary
senses and *intellectual operations* are at their highest pitch of discipline" (*RM*, 120).

III. Metaphysics and Theology

Whitehead set out to provide a metaphysics of process that would
avoid the difficulties modern physics was having with the cosmology
of Newton and the primacy it gave to things located in space. In con-

trast, Whitehead granted primacy to process and found it to be of two types: concrescence and transition (*PR,* 320; *AI,* 237)—the terms roughly approximate growth and perishing. Concrescence (he explains that the term is derivative from the Latin verb meaning "growing together") is the unification of a plurality into an actual entity; transition is the passing of the actual entity into the succeeding concrescence. Thus the two processes alternate.

In concrescence the universe of many things acquires an individual unity; each item of the many becomes subordinate to the constitution of the novel one (*PR,* 321). Into this process God has entered, for God is seen as supplying a telos, a lure, a final cause, the as yet unrealized unity towards which the many develop. The final cause had to be present at the outset.

The concrescence is the growth of the many towards this final cause, and in Whitehead's telling of this movement there is a striking 3:4. First, he tells of *Three* forms of "feeling" and then of *Four* ways that "eternal objects" ("universals") enter the process.[5] That is, the Three was extended to include a Fourth. In the following text the F, T, and N (the three Conscious Functions of an Intuitive) are all identified as "feeling"; but it is important to note that what Whitehead meant by feeling is not the same as the Feeling of Jung. Whitehead associates feeling with a form of intuition or a type of prehension.[6] The three "feelings" are presented as successive phases that conform well to the F, the T, and the N. They could be seen as the steps by which the "dative ingression" (the Fourth) rises to full Consciousness (N). "There are three successive phases of feelings, namely a phase of conformal feelings, one of 'conceptual' feelings and one of 'comparative' feelings, including 'propositional' feelings in this last species." Then he goes on to tell of the Four while picking up again the Three feelings: "there are four modes of functioning whereby an eternal object has ingression into the constitution of an actual entity: (i) as dative ingression, (ii) in conformal physical feeling, (iii) in conceptual feeling, (iv) in comparative feeling" (*PR,* 249).

The Three "feelings" and the Fourth constitute the four "modes"; they are an evident 3:4. And the correspondence is more evident when the Four modes are identified in ways that correspond with the Four of Jung. The first mode (*dative ingression*—not a feeling at all) tells of the many past actualities which enter into a new concrescence;

these act as efficient causes and to some extent are outside of the concrescence (they are the separated Fourth, the S); they are the total of past fact from which the concrescence proceeds.

The second mode (*conformal physical feeling*) is called "emotional—blind emotion—received as felt elsewhere"; it is "sympathy, that is, feeling the feeling in another and feeling conformally with another" (*PR*, 246); it is the F of Jung. The primitive feelings are emotional feelings which conform to the data.

The third mode (*conceptual feeling*): the physical feeling in conforming to the data receives from them a form. This form can be viewed as an abstract idea or one of a subsequent feeling. This is the conceptual feeling; it is derived from the physical. "The physical feeling is feeling a real fact; the conceptual feeling is valuing an abstract possibility" (*PR*, 421); the conceptual feeling is T.

The fourth mode (*comparative feeling*): this is said to include an infinite variety of more complex types of feelings. Only one of these many types of feeling is explained here to show its association with the N, "propositional feeling." The primary function of a proposition is that it act as a "lure for feeling." The basic "lure" in a concrescence is supplied by God, the unifying principle of growth and the final cause of the concrescence. However the lure for feeling that is found in the proposition is one that was derived from the data. As a lure it acts as a final cause guiding the further concrescence of feelings (*PR*, 281). This new lure should accord with and add to the basic lure of the entire concrescence. To illustrate by an example: at bedtime a man consciously reviews the day's events and projects them against a welter of possibilities. He is unconsciously deciding feelings so as to maximize his primary feeling; he is considering propositions or proposals as capable of emphasizing or actualizing his own reality (*PR*, 285). Thus, the proposition plays a role in "generating purpose" and also inductive thought; it is the N (purpose and induction are associated with N). So (i) is presented as efficient cause and (iv) as final cause; they are again the elements of Whitehead's Enantiodromia, with F and T (the Auxiliaries) acting as mediators.[7] (See fig. 10.1)

Consider again the man contemplating possibilities in reviewing the day: The possibilities that had a reference to the actual world were seen as lures arising from the data. If the lure from the data, called the objective lure, can harmonize with the subjective lure (in this example, the person considering), the objective lure can be admitted and by this process growth and development take place. The subject thus becomes actualized by admitting elements from the actual world into his own possibility, while the elements from the actual world are thus entering into unity and purpose. This is an example of the World of Value and the World of Fact each attaining to concrete reality only in their union. The *subjective* lure provides the concrescence with its basic unity, while the lure proceeding from the data gives the richness and ultimately the satisfaction of completion to the subject.

When by concrescence the goal is attained, the result is the concrete or an "actual entity"; it is then a fact, an atom, a part of the brute past that can serve as a datum for succeeding concrescences. As datum or data it acts as efficient cause for the new concrescence, and the process continues. This gives a sort of pulsation within the universe: the final cause, having been realized, becomes the efficient cause for the future in which it serves as data giving rise to a new concrescence. Thus Whitehead speaks of a vector moving from efficient to final cause and back again to efficient cause. "Concrescence moves towards its final cause, which is its subjective aim; transition is the vehicle of the efficient cause, which is the immortal past" (*PR,* 320, 229).

Looked at in one way, there is a simple pulsation between efficient and final causes. But regarded in another way, each new actuality is of a higher order; for each old set of efficient causes arises from a more complex set of syntheses. The process of the world is then an ascending process of synthesis of syntheses, or as Whitehead wrote: "The Universe achieves its values by reason of its coordination into societies of societies, and into societies of societies of societies" (*AI,* 207). The phrase states well the ascending process of the Intuitive: forests of forests are developing.

In addition to the temporal world, Whitehead recognizes what he terms the temporal world's three formative elements: the Creativity of the universe, the Primordial nature of God and the Consequent nature of God. Any understanding of Whitehead's metaphysics must center around these three. In this study they will be shown to conform to the Unconscious (creativity), to the Conscious (Primordial nature of God), and the Self (Consequent nature of God).

Whitehead speaks of the protean character of Creativity and sees it as difficult to describe.[8] It is activity and freedom and he proposes it to replace the traditional notion of primary substance; it is the ultimate (*RM*, 90; see *PR*, 11, 32).

> Creativity is another rendering of the Aristotelian "matter" and of the modern "neutral stuff." But it is divested of the notion of passive receptivity, either of "form," or of external relations. Creativity is without character of its own in exactly the same sense in which Aristotelian matter is without a character of its own. (*PR*, 46)

Whitehead will often spell creativity with a capital C; he would speak of this "Immanent Creativity" replacing the "transcendent Creator" of the Christian tradition; it thus gives an air of paradox or pantheism (*AI*, 237). In his descriptions of the formlessness, protean character, paradox, and energy of Creativity, he is associating it with the Unconscious. Though it has no character of its own, it is said to be characterized by the dead data of the past (*PR*, 249). The Creativity in actualizing the dead data (the efficient cause of Concresence) resembles the Unconscious energy actualizing the repressed S.

In contrast to the Creativity is the Primordial nature of God; it is beyond the temporal order. It is the conceptual side of God's nature (*PR*, 46). It is not the totality of abstract forms each in isolation; rather, it is the abstract forms as unified in an ordered system; it is the general system of mutual relationships among the forms (see *SM*, 145; *RM*, 154, 156). It is the N. Whitehead sees it as the ultimate basic adjustment among the forms upon which all created order depends; it is the conceptual adjustment of all appetites. The Primordial nature is present in the world as an urge to the future, an ordered goal for all appetites, a lure for the ordered progress of the universe; it exerts final causality on the world. It is the ground of all order and supplies each being with its subjective aim (*PR*, 164, 248, 287; *SM*, 159). Whitehead says he almost called the Primordial nature of God "Intuition" but backed away as this connoted something physical; he almost called it "Vision" but this did not allow that the Primordial nature included a yearning after concrete particular facts (*PR*, 50, 529). In any case, it is God in abstraction and is easily seen to conform with Jung's Intuitive Function and with what Jung means by Consciousness.

This Primordial nature in its lack of particulars cannot be called actual. It is a purely conceptual harmony, but it leads the world onward by its "vision of truth, beauty and goodness" (*PR*, 526). These three conform to the three conscious functions (T, N, and F).[9] They are not actual, as the Function of actuality is missing: the S. The Three parts of the primordial Vision—without the Fourth—shows its incompletion; it contains a "vision of truth, beauty and goodness" (T, N, F). But it is only a vision. The Fourth is the particulars (S) for which it yearns.

But in addition to being promordial, God is also Consequent; He is the Beginning *and the End* (PR, 523, 530). The creative advance of the world is said to react on God giving an eventual completion to God's nature by adding a fullness of the physical. God receives completion in the individual and the passing satisfactions of each finite fact (PR, 527). This is the Consequent nature of God; it is God as actual; it is the God of the religions providing refreshment and companionship. The Consequent nature of God is God as really actual. Completing the deficiency of His conceptual nature, God introduces the particulars of the universe into the primordial concepts; "The primordial nature is conceptual, the consequent nature is weaving of God's physical feelings upon His primordial concepts" (PR, 524).

In the same process in which God assumes the physical, the world undergoes an opposite transformation: the world of disordered particulars acquires order, meaning, and purpose. As to God, he is primordially one, but

> in the process he acquires a consequent multiplicity, which the primordial character absorbs into its own unity. The World is primordially many, namely, the many actual occasions with their physical finitude; in the process it acquires a consequent unity. (PR, 529)

To attain its final state the disordered multitude of the world passes through societies and societies of societies as it ascends to what is ultimately the Apotheosis of the World (PR, 529). As the world's particulars are woven into God, God is woven into the world; and the world has its life only because of the incarnation of God into it (RM, 149). In the ongoing process the opposites are joined together to form the Consequent nature of God. So God is the beginning and also the end.

Like the Self in Jung, the Consequent nature of God can be described only by antitheses in apparent contradiction. Whitehead enumerated many of these: the many become one in complete unity and yet they retain their own individuality with no loss in their identity and completeness; unity is reconciled with individual self-realization;

diversities are together but they no longer oppose (*PR*, 528, 531, 532). Thus the universe is to be conceived as attaining the active self-expression of its own variety of opposites: of its own freedom and necessity, of its own multiplicity and its unity, of its imperfection and its perfection. All the "opposites" that are found in the nature of things are incorrigibly there (*PR*, 531).

In *Adventures of Ideas* the ultimate phase is presented more personally than in the metaphysics of *Process and Reality*. *Adventures of Ideas* has been called his most personal text. Here the wondrous unity is called Peace, and the phrases by which Whitehead tells of Peace recall what Jung said of the Self. This Peace involves a momentous coordination of values (*AI*, 283). "Peace" is introduced after Whitehead has told of the Four qualities that together constitute civilization (Beauty, Truth, Adventure, and Art), and, of the Four, Beauty was given primacy. Whitehead goes on to explain,

> We are in a way seeking for the notion of a Harmony of Harmonies, which shall bind together the other four qualities, so as to exclude from our notion of civilization the restless egotism with which they have often in fact been pursued. "Impersonality" is too dead a notion, and "Tenderness" too narrow. I choose the term "Peace" for that Harmony of Harmonies which calms destructive turbulence and completes civilization (*AI*, 283).[10]

Notice that "Peace" (like the Self in Jung) puts an end to "restless egotism, " for Something greater than the Ego is said to be within: Peace. It is not a deadening of the mind, but "a positive feeling which crowns the 'life and motion' of the soul" (*AI*, 283; recall the "Self" as crown in Kant). With Peace everything changes: "Its first effect is the removal of the stress of acquisitive feeling arising from the soul's preoccupation with itself. Thus Peace carries with it a surpassing of personality"; it is "the sublimation of the egoistic aim by its inclusion of the transcendent whole" (*AI*, 283, 293). Whitehead illustrates by telling of Regulus, a legendary Roman who was tortured to death for the Roman Republic. Whitehead believed Regulus was mistaken in his estimate of the Republic; but, "the point is that with that belief, he achieved magnificence by the sacrifice of himself" (*AI*, 288). This sacrifice of personal identity by Regulus is Whitehead's model of what occurs as the ego surrenders to a final Peace; in terms of Jung, it is the ego surrendering to the Self.

For Jung, ego concerns diminish when the Self appears. So Whitehead has it: "Interest has been transferred to coordinations wider than personality." Jung claims we cannot bring about the Self on our own (*PT*, 261). Whitehead has it that Peace is "largely beyond the control of purpose. It comes as a gift" (*AI*, 284). Jung would situate the Self between Consciousness and the Unconscious. Whitehead has it that Peace "is habitually lurking on the edge of consciousness" (*AI*, 283). Jung has it that the Self brings about an end to a period of turmoil. Whitehead saw Peace bringing a "subsidence of turbulence." Jung would tell of the Self allowing the energy of the Unconscious to give us new life. So the Peace of Whitehead "preserves the springs of energy, and at the same time masters them" (*AI*, 284). Amidst the tribulations and tragedies of the world, "Peace is then the Intuition of permanence" (*AI*, 285). It is "the harmony of the soul's activities with the ideal aims that lie beyond any personal satisfaction" (*AI*, 286).

The Peace that coordinates the personality, mastering the springs of energy and widening human consciousness, is also the Peace that harmonizes civilization. It is presented indiscriminately as a psychic reality within and a social reality without. In many similar instances the activities of Whitehead's inner faculties have corresponded to the processes that Whitehead observed in the universe (much as Socrates set up a correspondence between the soul within and the state without). The correspondence is most obvious in Whitehead's religious thought, where the acts of his faculties parallel the divine activity.

The three formative elements of the world (the Creativity, the Primordial and the Consequent nature of God) are seen to parallel the human psyche presented by Whitehead when he presents his "threefold division of human nature": instinct, intelligence, and Wisdom (*AI*, 24). Like the Creativity, instinct proceeds out of the settled fact of the past. Like the Primordial nature of God, human intelligence coordinates notions into a logically coherent system. And, just as the Consequent nature of God determines the mode of coalescence between the Creativity and the Primordial nature, so Wisdom is said to determine the mode of coalescence between instinct and intelligence and thus to produce a decided outcome (*AI*, 24). That is, the divine processes resemble those of Whitehead's own psyche.

The parallel is further evident if Whitehead's own psychological advance is compared to the advance that occurs in God as his Primordial nature acquires the completion of his Consequent nature. The initial stage in both God and Whitehead consisted in an abstract harmony-intuition devoid of the particular but yearning after concrete fact. This stage was followed by the gradual incorporation of the particular fact into the harmony. The disordered world of particular fact being woven into the Primordial harmony recalls the disordered Unconscious (characterized by particular data, facts) being brought into ordered Consciousness. Both Whitehead and God are involved in the same process, and both of them resemble the act of knowledge that begins with the generalization and seeks to conceive the facts; it begins with the relationship and then seeks the relata. Whitehead, Whitehead's God, and the generalizations in his mind could say together: "The final problem is to conceive a complete [παντελής] fact." Whitehead and his God are taking part in the same ultimate quest: the conception of the complete fact, for as yet the facts, the specific instances, "rest unrealized in the womb of nature."

Whitehead was a Perceiver and thus had a very different spirit from the Judging philosophers considered in the previous six chapters. He identified himself with Plato, whom he quoted abundantly; he was particularly drawn to Plato's *Sophist* (see the many references in *Adventures of Ideas*), a work that told of the theorist coming to accept the world of Sense—like Whitehead himself—and a work that was central to the presentation of Plato in the present study. In contrast to Plato and Whitehead, the philosophers of the J Axis told abundantly of forms in time and space. But in opposition to them Whitehead proposed a philosophy that he called Organism; it was a cosmology that saw all things interrelated with no absolute time and space. The "organic," a sort of "world-soul," could also describe the cosmology of other Intuitives: Teilhard and the final philosophy of Plato, as presented above.

David Hume will be the next philosopher considered. Though both Whitehead and Hume were on the P Axis their philosophies have very different spirits. Whitehead often criticized Hume (see abundant passages in *PR*, also *S*, 30–37). Both started with perception, but they approached it in different ways. Hume started with the world of sense and tried to come to the world of Theory, but he had great difficulties in getting beyond sensation and the concrete particular. Like Whitehead, Hume was on the P Axis, but he came at the problem of knowledge in an opposite way: he tried to construct a philosophy out of the data of sensation. In his attempts he knew the fear and trembling of one seeking Integration. The difficulties of the process are presented in his *Treatise of Human Nature*.

Notes

1. The central importance of Beauty runs through the texts of Whitehead: "The teleology of the universe is directed to the production of Beauty. Thus any system of things which in any wide sense is beautiful is to that extent justified in its existence" (*AI*, 264). Social evils are seen as lacking in beauty (*SM*, 182). Physical pain, mental pain, sorrow, and horror are termed "aesthetic destruction" (*AI*, 256). A judge on the Supreme Court gives his decision "on the basis of the aesthetic satisfaction" in blending the American Constitution with the activities of modern America (*ES*, 130). In physics he would tell of the beauty of equations (*SM*, 61–62). Truth is said to derive its power "from its services in the promotion of Beauty. Apart from Beauty, truth is neither good or bad" (*AI*, 266). So that, "beauty is left as the one aim which by its very nature is self-justifying" (*AI*, 265).

2. Rousseau had a long-time common-law marriage, and finally a recognized marriage. All the others were bachelors.

3. A similar image is involved when he writes, "Celibacy does not suit a university. It must mate itself with action" (*ES*, 219).

4. In *Religion in the Making*, God is identified as "the one systematic, complete fact" (*RM*, 148). The process theology of Whitehead has much in common with the process theology of Teilhard. Both were Intuitives trying to make their thought down-to-earth and concrete. Teilhard has a line that resembles this key line in Whitehead: he told of "the empty fragility of even the noblest theorizings as compared with the definitive plenitude of the smallest *fact* grasped in its total, concrete reality" (*HM*, 72; emphasis in text). Again, he was seeking the *fact* in context.

5. The eternal objects are more or less equivalent to the "forms" of Plato, but they include forms like "green" and "stone, " to which Plato might have hesitated to assign a form.

6. Here and elsewhere Whitehead makes much of "feeling, " but he uses the term in a different sense than the Feeling of Jung. For Whitehead it is a form of perception: he speaks of "'feeling' the many data": "Here 'feeling' is the term used for the basic generic operation of passing from the objectivity of the data to the subjectivity of the actual entity in question" (*PR*, 65). He associates it with Bergson's "intuition" and Descartes's *sentire*. He would also identify it with his own word, "prehension" (*MT*, 32). Wightman would see

him using the word "feeling" to avoid Hume's "impression" and its mechanical association (*RW*, in Leclerc, 344).

7. Many additional Quaternities can be identified in Whitehead: consider the following: "In conclusion there are four main types of entities in the universe, of which two are primary types and two are hybrid types. The primary types are actual entities and pure potentials (eternal objects); the hybrid types are feelings and propositions (theories)" (*PR*, 247). Here the primary would be S and T; the secondary would be F and N.

Consider another: "We can classify the topics of physical science under four headings: (l) The true and real things which endure, (2) The true and real things which occur, (3) The abstract things which recur, (4) the Laws of Nature" (*AI*, 46). He gives an example of each: l, a rock, human individuality; 2, any happening; 3, the shape of a rock; 4, the geometrical relations of things. The Four have some parallel with Plato's division of the line into two higher and two lower. The example shows the four more or less conform with Jung's: the conformity with F is not evident, while those of S, T, and N are.

A 3:4 is present when Whitehead tells of Gravitation in Aristotle: there are Three classes of moving objects and a separated Fourth, the Earth itself: "In this classification of the complements of physical nature yet a fourth component remains over, in its character unique and thus the only member of its class. This component is the Earth, the centre of the Universe, by reference to which all these other types of being are defined" (*AI*, 145). Though the first three cannot reasonably be identified with any specific Functions, the earth as separated Fourth is clearly the S, the cornerstone by which the others are defined.

The Four seem involved when he writes, "Civilization is constituted out of four elements. (l) Patterns of Behavior, (2) Patterns of Emotion, (3) Patterns of Belief, and (4) Technologies." He then proceeds to separate one of the Four, the one most likely associated with the S: "We can at once dismiss Technologies as beyond our topic, though all four constitutive elements interact upon each other" (*AI*, 175). He considers only the interacting Three.

The Four are again suggested: "There are four main types of objects, namely, 'eternal objects,' 'propositions,' 'objectified' actual entities and nexus" (*PR*, 82). This could possibly be T, F, S, and N; but the four terms are not sufficiently explained to justify the identification with particular Functions.

8. *RM*, 90. Whitehead will speak of Creativity as Proteus; recall above that Augustine (an F) spoke of Truth as Proteus, while Kierkegaard (a T) spoke of Love as Proteus. Like Whitehead, they each identify the missing Function with Proteus; it is the formless one in the Unconscious.

Lewis Ford argues that Whitehead only began speaking of God after giving the lectures presented in *Science and the Modern World*; the chapter on God was not a lecture but was added to the printed work. Russell insists Whitehead was unquestionably agnostic during the years he knew him well (1898–1912); he suggests that the death of Whitehead's son Eric in World War I turned him away from a mechanistic universe (Ford, 4, 6, 102). One can see the beginnings of his theology of creativity, Primordial and Consequent natures in *RM*, 85–90.

9. These same Three ideals are identified by Whitehead in other contexts: in writing of the "intellectual understanding" of a society, he tells of the members sharing "judgements of 'true or false,' and of 'beautiful or ugly,' and of 'good or bad.'" (*AI*, 17). These three (the True, the Beautiful, and the Good) would shape the social lures in the same way as the identical transcendentals in God's Primordial nature would shape the cosmic lures. The same three are found when he tells of the need to weave ideas into structures "with the attributes either of truth, or of beauty, or of moral elevation"; the problem was "whether the sentence when framed was true or false, beautiful or ugly, moral or shocking" (*ES*, 214). In each case it is the three Conscious Functions listed in the same order.

10. The Ultimate Peace that binds together Four qualities could recall Plato's presentation of Being—which also united Four qualities: Other and Same, Motion and Rest. It also recalls Teilhard's Omega which bound together Four attributes: Actuality, Autonomy, Irreversibility, and Transcendence. For each of the authors the Quaternity of elements is the final ideal that reconciles opposites. As Whitehead approaches his account of Peace, he wrote a passage that tells of 3 and 4: "for example, triplicity or the abstract relationship of sets of numbers, such as the squareness of the number four" (*AI*, 253).

Bibliography

Works of Whitehead

AI   *Adventures of Ideas.* New York: New American Library, 1955.
Anth *Alfred North Whitehead; an Anthology.* New York: Macmillan, 1953.
ES   *Essays in Science and Philosophy.* New York: The Philosophical Library, 1947.
MT   *Modes of Thought.* New York: Capricorn Books, 1955.
PR   *Process and Reality.* New York: The Humanities Press, 1957.
RM   *Religion in the Making.* New York: Meridian Books, 1954.
S   *Symbolism.* New York: Macmillan, first edition, 1927.
SM   *Science and the Modern World.* New York: New American Library, 1948.

Other Works

Lowe, Victor. *Alfred North Whitehead: the Man and His Work*, vol. I. Baltimore: Johns Hopkins University Press, 1985.

Ford, Lewis S. *The Emergence of Whitehead's Metaphysics, 1925–1929*. Albany: State University of New York Press, 1984.

Leclerc, Ivor, ed. *The Relevance of Whitehead*, a collection of articles. New York: Macmillan, 1961.

Leclerc, Ivor. *Whitehead's Metaphysics*. New York: Macmillan, 1958.

11 Hume: A Philosopher Turns to History
The Dominant Cedes to Nature

Hume as an S: Aside from mathematics and logic, "reasoning is nothing but a species of sensation" derived entirely from a "present impression" (*T*, 103). "The most lively thought is still inferior to the dullest sensation" (*EW*, 53). A commentator on Hume writes, "Virtue for Hume takes its origin in quotidian reality, in sensation, in the world of things. Sentient taste leads to moral taste" (Siebert, 168). Another commentator sees Hume "wedded to a particular metaphysic—a belief in ultimate simple entities" (Passmore, 110). Hume himself wrote that "everything in nature is individual, " and "objects have no discoverable connection together" (*T*, 19, 103). The unconnected "individuals" include our perceptions and ourselves: "All our perceptions are different from each other, and from every thing else in the universe, they are also distinct and separable, and may be considered as separately existant" (*T*, 233). "All events seem entirely loose and separate. One event follows another, but we never can observe any tye between them" (*EW*, 98). We ourselves are no more than a "succession of perceptions which constitutes our self or person," and even this could be reduced to the "perceptions which are immediately present to our consciousness" (*T*, 265). For Hume's Quarternity, see figure 11.1. (Hume's Myers-Briggs type would be ISTJ.)

```
                              T
                           Reason
                        Understanding
         N                                      S Dominant
      Foundation                            Present impressions
   Principles, spring                         Empirical facts
                              F                  Practical
                          Sentiment           Pleasure, pain
                            Belief
```

Figure 11.1

I. Radical Skepticism and Practical Living

David Hume was born in Edinburgh, Scotland, in 1711. He studied the English, French, and Latin classics and spoke of literature as the ruling passion of his life. He began writing philosophy at the age of sixteen. Finding himself entirely unsuited for business, he went to France in 1734 to seriously pursue his writing. Having finished his *Treatise of Human Nature*, he returned to Scotland in 1737 and sought a publisher for the work. He regarded it as "very sceptical" for it would show the "narrow limits of human understanding"; in terms of this study, human understanding would be limited to the dominant Function, S. But though his philosophy greatly restricted what the mind can know, nature gave him a way out: Philosophy would make us all skeptics, "were not nature too strong for it" (*EW*, 539). Here "nature" is simply accepted as apart from philosophy.

Hume wanted to study human knowing as he judged it to be "the capital and center" of all other sciences. He was taken by the empirical method of "my Lord Bacon" and the achievement of Newton, "the greatest and rarest genius that ever arose for the instruction of the species." What Newton did for the physical world, Hume hoped to do for the moral world, that is, for the human world (Passmore, 8, 43; Noxon, 75–80).[1] He introduced his *Treatise* by saying he would "render all our principles as universal as possible, by tracing up our experiments to the utmost" (*T*, xvii). When he had finished the work he knew the limits he would put on human knowledge, so in writing the Introduction he advised his readers to take pleasure in their lack of success. Pleasure would be a significant element in his philosophy, while principles are more or less lacking. Hume worked on the

Treatise with such intensity that he entered "a highly wrought-up state of mind" that amounted to a nervous breakdown. He wrote to a friend saying that his study of philosophy had shown him only endless disputes, so he had to look about for a new way of establishing truth.

> After much study and reflection of this, at last, when I was about 18 years of Age, there seemed to be opened up to me a new scene of thought, which transported me beyond measure and made me, with an ardor natural to young men, throw up every other pleasure or business to apply entirely to it. (Siebert, 172)[2]

But this enthusiasm was not to last: "all my ardor seemed in a moment to be extinguished, and I could no longer raise my mind to that pitch, which formerly gave me such excessive pleasure. . . . In this condition I remained for nine months." He compared his case to that of the mystics who tell of their elevation of spirit and also tell of their torments as all spirit deserts them. To explain both the mystics and himself he suggested that ardor and enthusiasm had decomposed his nerves and brain. His accounts of enthusiasm and anguish while writing the *Treatise* show his personal involvement with philosophy at this time, an involvement he often concealed. The present study will claim that his later writings were written with an easy objectivity and show little of the same intensity or involvement.

But apart from such statements in his letters, Hume's anguish was evident in the *Treatise* itself. Towards the midpoint of the text, he paused to survey the "voyage" he had made so far and the "immense depths of philosophy" still lying before him. He tells of "having struck on many shoals, and having narrowly escaped ship-wreck," yet he will continue setting out on the "boundless ocean" in a leaky, weather-beaten vessel (*T*, 263). Contemplating "the wretched condition, weakness and disorder of the faculties" with which he must work, he tells of being reduced "almost to despair." Philosophy has left him in "forlorn solitude" as "some strange uncouth monster" repellent to others. "Everyone keeps at a distance and dreads that storm which beats upon me from every side" (*T*, 264).

Believing his *Treatise* has broken with established opinion, Hume wonders about his criterion of truth. He identifies this as a propensity "to consider objects *strongly* in that view under which they appear to me" (*T*, 265); he will consider what appears, the phenomena. But this leads to distressful conclusions: We can comprehend objects only "in that succession of perceptions which constitutes our self or person, " or perhaps only "those perceptions which are immediately present to our consciousness" (*T*, 265).

While telling of a strong attraction to present perceptions, Hume also tells of the mind not being content until it comes to the "original and ultimate principle." But this is hard to find:

> This [ultimate principle] is our aim in all our studies and reflections: And how must we be disappointed, when we learn that this connection, tie or energy lies merely in ourselves and is nothing but that determination of mind which is acquired by custom and causes us to make the transition from an object to its usual attendant and from the impression of one to the lively impression of the other? (*T*, 266)

Thus, "events are entirely loose and separate," and the only thing that unites them is our mind; if our mind often sees one event after the other, our mind ties them together and talks of cause and effect. But, reflecting on the situation, the mind gains no satisfaction, for the mind can find no ultimate and operating principle in things, but only its own tendency to associate certain perceptions. Such reflections leave his brain so "heated" that he begins to reject all belief; unable to find any principle (N), he fancies himself "environed with the deepest darkness and utterly deprived of the use of every member and faculty" (*T*, 269).

In these dramatic and personal passages Hume presents a philosophy centered on the immediate data of sense phenomena (S), while at the same time he tells of the mind wanting to discover some fundamental and ultimate principle (N) of explanation. Seeking a principle drew him out on a stormy sea, and after a long search left him "environed with the deepest darkness" and deprived of all possibility of success. The principle could not be found. There are only particulars.

Hume had proposed a philosophy based on individual perceptions: these included sensations (colors, sounds, fears, etc.) and reflections (ideas of colors, ideas of sounds, ideas of fears, etc.).[3] But it took him nowhere: "All our distinct perceptions are distinct existences." Then how might things interrelate? For "the mind never perceives any real connection among distinct existences" (*T*, 636). Though perceiving no connection, we continue to claim that things are connected. Why? For example, why do we claim the fundamental interrelation of cause and effect to be real when we never see it?

Every "present impression" is a unit in itself, and it is *we* who associate impressions together.

Hume goes on to say we associate impressions according to three different ways: (1) two impressions resemble each other; (2) two are perceived as contiguous; (3) one is seen as cause of the other. He presses the meaning of causality and concludes that one event is considered to be the cause of the other only because we have seen one appearance regularly follow the appearance of the other. Thus, we make the association of the two and speak of the first event as a cause and the second as an effect. The connecting link is not in the phenomena; it comes from ourselves, from our customary way of expecting one event will follow after the other.

Thus, perceptions are associated in three ways (by resemblance, contiguity, cause and effect), and any association of perceptions comes from us; we are "the cement of the universe." The unifying principle is "the principle of the association of ideas" (*EW*, 547). The unity is only of ideas and not part of the objective world ("this connection, tie, or energy lies merely in ourselves, and is nothing but that determination of the mind, which is acquired by custom" [*T*, 266]). This conclusion leaves him "environed with the deepest darkness" and without a "faculty" (N) to rescue himself. It is the world Sartre presented in *Nausea*, where reality is simply heaps of separate things and all relations are only in the mind. In each case it is the radical separation of the S and N.[4]

Philosophy has left him in dire straits, but Nature rescues him and dispels his melancholy. How? He leaves his room, dines with friends, plays backgammon—and the chimeras vanish. "Philosophy would render us entirely *Pyrrhonian*, were not nature too strong for it" (*EW*, 543). Nature has delivered him. "When we leave our closet and engage in the common affairs of life, its [philosophy's] conclusions seem to vanish like the phantoms of the night on the appearing of the morning" (*T*, 455). Later he returns to his room and looks at his speculative writings, and hardly has the heart to take them up again. Eventually he gets back to work and the *Treatise* continues for hundreds of additional pages. The only unifying principle he has found is that two perceptions habitually next to one another in time or space are associated. This "relationship" is entirely extrinsic to the individual units; the unity that comes from being situated next

to another or immediately after another is about as minimal a relation as one could imagine. Thus, Hume offers a philosophy of separate trees and no forest. In a similar way many other elements in his
thought are composed of distinct units: "Time, as it exists, must be
composed of indivisible moments" (*T*, 31). That is, time is not a con-
tinuum, it is composed of small indivisible atoms: "Every moment
must be distinct." Space is the same: he tells of looking at the top of a
table, "My senses convey to me only the impressions of coloured
points, dispos'd in a certain manner" (*T*, 34). For Hume the "points"
are not like the dimensionless points in geometry; rather they are like
the pixels of color on a TV screen, which are small areas. Because of
their smallness and proximity, they are united by the eye of the beholder to appear as a table top. But reality consists in separate points.

This is the basic difficulty of the Sensate and it is evident again
in a much later work, *Dialogues Concerning Natural Religion*, written
in 1751 or 1752. One character in these *Dialogues* (whom most commentators see as Hume) wonders about "the coherence of the parts
of a stone, or even that composition of parts which render it extended"; the coherence is termed "inexplicable" (*EW*, 307); and another character in the dialogue agrees, "The cohesion of the parts
of matter is still incomprehensible" (*EW*, 311). "Coherence," "composition," and "cohesion" make no sense to Hume because the N, the
faculty of unification, is lacking. This lack recalls a very similar difficulty in Locke (presented earlier in this study). They both were Sensates and saw reality constituted by separate units.

Such is Hume the philosophic skeptic, but beyond this there is
Hume the man of action. He finds that "nature by an absolute and
uncontroulable necessity has determin'd us to judge" (*T*, 183). Spontaneously we make judgments that ignore our philosophic doubts.
To refute skepticism Hume appeals to a psychological fact (Passmore, 149). Nature takes over and we live like everyone else. Perhaps
that is appropriate for the Sensate; skepticism is just not practical,
and they are practical. Though "Nature" played a large part in the
thought of the time, Hume never tried to philosophize about this
source of deliverance; he accepted nature much as Descartes accepted the Catholic Church—a reality apart from his philosophy
that brought him deliverance.

The problem of the *Treatise* is the problem of the Sensate: to find
the unifying principle, that which will make a unity of the individu-

als, a forest of the trees. Hume first encounters the problem when he tries to understand how the mind forms general ideas (universals) out of particular impressions. He suggests they are "collected by a kind of magical faculty in the soul, which, tho' it be always most perfect in the greatest geniuses . . . is however inexplicable by the utmost efforts of human understanding" (T, 24). Note his claim: the unifying is done by some "magical faculty" beyond the "utmost efforts of human understanding"; in Jungian terms the "magical faculty" is the N buried beyond the efforts of Consciousness. The "magical" faculty is particularly active in the great geniuses (this allows for the work of Newton). Copleston sees Hume uniting individuals by a "mysterious" process (C, 78). For Hume, the mystery and the magic are associated with whatever unites the many, that is, the N.

Hume finally found a publisher for his Treatise but was disappointed when it fell "dead-born from the press" (EW, 3). So, in 1748, he brought out a radical revision of the first part of his Treatise in an essay eventually called An Enquiry Concerning Human Understanding. He begins by telling of two ways to philosophize about human nature. The first is not quite serious and would see humans made for actions to express one's tastes and sentiments. Such a philosopher would write in an easy manner, using poetry and eloquence to engage the affections of the reader, "alluring us into the paths of virtue," and moving us to action. The other type of philosopher would see the human as a reasonable rather than an active being. This second type would seek "those principles which regulate our understanding, excite our sentiments, and make us approve or blame" certain types of behavior. The second type would hope to "discover some hidden truths." But this type of philosopher cannot enter into practical affairs, for his abstruse conclusions vanish in the light of ordinary life. Hume sees nature giving him advice:

> Abstruse thought and profound researches I prohibit, and will severely punish, by the pensive melancholy which they introduce, by the endless uncertainly in which they involve you, and by the cold reception which your pretended discoveries shall meet with, when communicated. Be a philosopher; but amidst all your philosophy, be still a man. (EW, 47)

Hume would still defend his philosophy. He compared it to the artist who must begin by studying anatomy, yet anatomy enters only indirectly into his finished work. It shows him the limits within which he can work. Hume believed many metaphysicians were making claims that extended beyond what we can know. When telling of these metaphysicians Hume's imagery suggested the Unconscious: "Chased from the open country, these robbers fly into the forest, and lie in wait to break in upon every unguarded avenue of the mind, and overwhelm it with religious fears and prejudices" (EW, 48). To deal with them it is necessary to carry "the war into the most secret recesses of the enemy"—which recesses would also be in the mind. Meanwhile he knew that young and adventurous philosophers would seek to go beyond the limits: "each adventurous genius will leap at the arduous prize . . . while he hopes that the glory of achieving so hard an adventure is reserved for him alone."[5] The only way to stop this nonsense is to show clearly the limits of what we can know. Thereby we can "undermine the foundations of an abstruse philosophy, which seems to have hitherto served only as a shelter to superstition, and a cover to absurdity and error" (EW, 52). His exploration of our "mental geography" would show us radically unfit for such subjects. This is where serious philosophy has its value. By showing the limits of our knowledge, it will free us from extravagant metaphysical claims. Stating these limits is the purpose of true metaphysics, the second type of philosophy, the philosophy that is serious.

In doing this latter philosophy Hume tells of wanting to "discover, at least in some degree, the secret springs and principles, by which the human mind is actuated in its operations" (EW, 51). The "secret springs and principles" suggests the Unconscious where (for a Dominant S) the principles, N, might be found.

But the Enquiry does not take long to conclude, "These ultimate springs and principles are totally shut up from human curiosity and enquiry" (EW, 66).[6] We may consider ourselves lucky if "we can trace up the particular phenomena to, or near to, these general principles" (EW, 66), but we cannot reach them. The "general principles" (N) are beyond us. Should we try to grasp the principles, we find "we are got into fairy land, long ere we have reached the last steps of our theory" (EW, 97). This "fairy land" of "theory," or "forest" and "secret recesses of the enemy" suggest the Unconscious; they can be understood by setting these phrases in contrast to passages in Whitehead. As an N, Whitehead had no trouble with theory; his land of mystery was the facts: he spoke of "the facts of physical nature" as "an uninterrupted swamp, pestilential with mystery and magic" (*AI*, 146). For Hume, the "fairy land" and "magic" concern principles and theory, while for Whitehead the "mystery and magic" concerns the physical facts. Hume was S and Whitehead was N; what was self-evident to one was magic and mystery to the other.

Hume picks up an image from Locke to claim that our line is too short to fathom such immense abysses. So, Philosophy would do well to leave "a scene so full of obscurities and perplexities, return, with suitable modesty, to her true and proper province, the examination of common life . . . without launching into so boundless an ocean of doubt, uncertainty, and contradiction" (*EW*, 120)!

The obscurity causes the mind to lose confidence "of the ground on which she treads." Hume sums up his situation: the rational mind "sees a full light, which illuminates certain places; but that light borders upon the most profound darkness" (*EW*, 161). In Jungian terms, there is only the full light of Consciousness that borders on the profound darkness of the Unconscious. There is no middle ground, no semi-lit area of symbolic knowledge.

Hume believed his skeptical conclusions would not make a great difference to society. For the refutation of skepticism is found in ordinary life where the skeptical conclusions "vanish like smoke, " "like the phantoms of the night, " and leave the skeptic in the same human situation as anybody else. Then he too must go about his business guided by habit and custom. So Hume's chief objection to radical skepticism is that one cannot live by it. So what difference does it make? And, for a practical man, it does not benefit society.

However, a mitigated form of skepticism can be of value: many people are taken by some unproven principle and lose perspective on those taken by a different principle; this gives rise to religious wars. So, if all people would develop a mitigated skepticism, they might become tolerant of one another and exercise restraint. They can avoid lofty enquiries and leave the "more sublime topics" to poets and orators. Hume states this in a phrase that could contain a Three-with-missing-Fourth: he speaks of a "mankind, who must act and reason and believe [S, T, and F—?], though they are not able, by their most diligent enquiry, to satisfy themselves concerning the foundation of these operations" (*EW*, 163). The "foundation" (N) of the three Conscious functions is not to be found, but the other three constitute what we need for ordinary life.

This first *Enquiry* began by telling of two different kinds of philosophy: the first would lure us "into the paths of virtue" using poetry and eloquence; the second would seek for ultimate springs and principles and show only the limits of what we can know. As the work ends, Hume seems to have decided to leave aside his skeptical reflections and return to the first kind of philosophy.[7] He seems to have decided there was nothing to be gained in writing skeptical and unpopular accounts; rather, he resolves to write edifying accounts for the benefit of humanity. When he introduced his *Treatise*, he again told of two types of philosophy: one proceeds by reason and the other by eloquence. Philosophy was seen as a type of warfare, and, in the *Treatise*, Hume added with bewilderment, "The victory is not gained by the men at arms who manage the pike and sword, but by the trumpeters, drummers and musicians of the army." When his *Treatise* fell "dead-born" from the press, he decided to join the drummers and musicians. The change would bring him success.

II. Hume the Moralist

In his earlier *Treatise* Hume considered morals at length and reached conclusions resembling what he later presented in his *Enquiry Concerning the Principles of Morals*, published in 1751. He regarded this *Enquiry* as "incomparably the best" of his writings, though history has not. By his title he tells of seeking a principle, or the foundation of a principle, that will be based on the experimental method. The data for his study would be human judgments; he would propose different behaviors and see if diverse peoples would consider them virtue or vice. Thus, by "following the empirical method, " he will be dealing with a "question of fact" and not an abstract theory (*EW*, 184). He warns against "sublime theorists" who devise policies that lead to harmful results (*EW*, 195). To oppose this he presents abundant historical examples from which he concludes that *utility* is "the SOLE source of the moral approbation paid to fidelity, justice, veracity, integrity, and those other estimable and useful qualities and principles." In announcing his conclusion, he compares his methodology to Newton's (*EW*, 206, 226). He sees further evidence for the primacy of utility by an aesthetic theory that proposes what is useful to self and society brings pleasure to the beholder, while what is pernicious brings pain. And pleasure and pain are the ultimate ends that cannot be questioned (EW, 271).

His moral principle centers virtue around behavior that pleases the individual and ameliorates society, a basis for morality that is so evident he wonders why others have not presented it before. But this is the utilitarianism of the S: virtue is what works. As a utilitarian he warns against someone "who delivers a theory, however true, which he must confess, leads to a practice dangerous and pernicious." Virtue is not in a theoretical truth, so, "Why dig up the pestilence from the pit in which it is buried?" If it turns out that there are pernicious truths, they will only surrender anyway to "errors that are salutary and advantageous" (EW, 260). Again, beneficient nature is stronger than the conclusions of philosophy.

When Hume began his Enquiry Concerning the Principles of Morals, he said that people committed to irrational principles do not yield to argument. Therefore, one must speak to their affections. He seems to have decided to write in emotional language with a conscious effort to be eloquent. That leaves the spirit of Hume's earlier skeptical philosophy radically different than the sentimentalism of his text on morals. He himself was not an emotional man. One of his commentators claims, "There is something in the spirit of Humean philosophy fundamentally opposed to sentimental values."[8] Yet sentimental values form a constant overlay to Hume's study of morals. He makes abundant use of historical and literary stories that show a nobility of character for us to emulate. He defines virtues in highly sentimental terms: he sees "confident courage" as it "engages the affections, and diffuses, by sympathy, a like sublimity of sentiment over every spectator." He tells of benevolence, "the very softness and tenderness of the sentiment, its engaging endearments, its fond expressions ... enters into a warm attachment of love and friendship. . . . The tear naturally starts in our eye on the apprehension of a warm sentiment of this nature" (EW, 242, 244). Such teary-eyed passages abound and seem to be part of a conscious effort to move us and persuade. For the work began with the claim that an argument "which speaks not to the affections" will never lead others to change their minds (EW, 180). So he speaks instead to our affections. Yet he seems not to experience these sentiments himself, rather he uses them to lead the sentiments of his reader to virtue.

Hume saw that morality involved both reason and emotion, and he was insistent that they remain separate: "This partition between the faculties of understanding and sentiment, in all moral decisions, seems clear" (*EW*, 265; see *T*, 457, 458). This separation of understanding and sentiment makes his texts read like well-stated rational arguments that were afterwards gussied up with sentimental touches. The understanding and the sentiment could be seen as the *T* and the *F*. That is, he is Differentiating the Auxiliaries; and in the process he is conscious of the difference between an argument and the sentimental additions.

Hume believed that many ancient accounts of heroes do not move us as they are written. But "an eloquent recital of the case" will immediately catch up our hearts (*EW*, 225). He decided to write eloquent recitals to catch the heart. In 1752 Hume began writing a history of England that would eventually become six large volumes, a work that dominated his attention for a decade. He had already developed utility as the basic principle of morality; now he would use stories from English history to instruct and edify by adding an emotional overlay. For example, he considers King Charles I, one for whom no man could resist shedding "a generous tear"; he was "a kind husband, an indulgent father, a gentle master, a steadfast friend." He was "sustained by his magnanimous courage, the majesty of a monarch, " and talking with his son filled his "eyes with tears of joy and admiration." These emotional touches go beyond Hume's historical sources. At the execution of Charles he tells how some "fell into convulsions, or sunk into such a melancholy as attended them to their grave." Again, he is adding to his source. A scholar of Hume explains, "Hume clearly shapes historical fact for sentimental purposes and in so doing becomes emotionally caught up in the hero of his own creation."[9]

While writing his *History of England* Hume was obsessed with religion and its detrimental influence on civilization (Siebert, 63). Crazed spiritual claims were seen as threats to the "calm sunshine of the mind." Yet Hume believed the religious urge was fundamental to human nature, so he did not believe it could be eliminated or argued away. For the root of religion strikes "deeper into the mind, and springs from the essential and universal properties of human nature," yet the first religious principles are secondary (*PWR*, 134). There will always be religion as long as people suffer pain and fear death. It is no wonder that those in "absolute ignorance of causes, and being at the same time so anxious concerning their future fortunes . . . should immediately acknowledge a dependence on invisible powers, possest of sentiment and intelligence." Hume saw religion having great power, generally a pernicious power throwing people into a frenzy.

Hume had a general anti-Catholic orientation and often spoke of Catholicism as "the superstition." But Siebert claims that a close reading of Hume's *History* reveals that, as the text advanced, extreme Protestants replaced Catholics as chief mischief-makers (Siebert, 90). Hume even approved of the religion of the late Middle Ages, as it was largely a matter of formal practices that were carelessly performed. But then the zeal of the Reformers caused the Catholics to respond with a comparable zeal. It was the zeal itself that distressed him, because this was the great source of human misery.

At one time Hume had ridiculed church liturgies, but later he gave them a qualified endorsement ("pictures, postures, vestments, buildings, and all the fine arts") as a means of insulating people from unchecked zeal. These symbols released the pent-up energies of religion. In his political writing, he wanted the civil magistrates to be supreme, but he also called for an established church. It was not that he believed in any church, but he felt an established church would innoculate the citizens against the religious disease (Siebert, 115). He saw the Church of England as he knew it in his own time as a good example of what he would recommend: its clergy were learned and worldly, and they retained just enough ritual and liturgy to speak to the religious urges, but by their moderation they prevented people from being overwhelmed with fear and enthusiasm. (He had friends among churchmen.)

In such texts, *utility* is the norm for all virtue; the S is supreme. In contrast to this the religious fanatics are caught up in their *theories* or *principles* ("pompous theological theories," "habitual reverence for the principles of religion" [EW, 382, 306]), and theories and principles are associated with the N. For Hume, these ultimate principles would always remain in total darkness: "We are placed in this world as in a great theater, where the true springs and causes are entirely concealed from us" (PWR, 140). But since most people would always have a need to deal with religious questions, Hume called for a state church that would use appropriate symbols. His

study of history was calculated to show the chaos that religious enthusiasm had produced. He wanted the symbols of religion to remain to reduce the enthusiasm of the masses. He could be seen,
then, as an S with a T as Auxiliary. His *Enquiry Concerning the Principles of Morals* and his *History* showed Sensation as Dominant; but
Sensation (the experimental method) worked well with Thinking
and Feeling (understanding and sentiment) to present a unified
message. Still, for Hume, the Fourth was missing. This is most evident as he comes to the end of his *History* and speaks in high praise
of Newton: he was "cautious in admitting no principle but such as
were founded on experiment." His account of Newton ends with a
statement of reserve:

> While Newton seemed to draw off the veil from some of the mysteries
> of nature, he showed at the same time the imperfections of the me-
> chanical philosophy; and thereby restored her ultimate secrets to that
> obscurity in which they ever did and ever will remain. (*HE*, vol. 5, 433)

The mention of "veil, " "mysteries of nature, " "obscurity, " etc. suggest the Unconscious. But Newton only "seemed to draw off the
veil" from such mysteries. The ultimate secrets remain in "that obscurity in which they ever did and ever will remain." There is again
the radical division between light and dark Hume had presented
years before.

Hume often spoke of beauty, but the beauty was not that of the N.
The beautiful was simply the practical. Machinery was beautiful, if it
worked. Prosperity and vineyards laden with fruit were beautiful.
Barren landscapes and storm clouds had an opposite effect (*EW*,
234). His aesthetics centered around the practical, and, just as philosophic truth could be set aside if it did not work, so, religion, morality, art, and government were good only if they ameliorated society.

The texts of Hume show him to be a man with little or no personal sense of religion, but there is good reason to believe that he
remained a theist or Deist.[10] In his *Dialogues Concerning Natural Religion*, he seems to allow some minimal knowledge of God (at least for
a God that might be known as Mind or Thought). But this would be
the abstract God associated with his conscious Function or auxiliary Function; it involved no mystery. Hume had drawn a clear line
between what can be known and what cannot, and he saw no possibility of passing beyond this into the night where nothing was visi-

ble. Should a religious fanatic (or even the physics of Newton) seem to advance further, Hume was firm in claiming they were mistaken.

A commentator saw the hallmark of Hume's style in "a certain detachment, a striving for control . . . overall, an air of Olympian superiority. The importance of detachment and self-possession is in fact what Humean philosophy teaches—certainly as a goal for the elite" (Siebert, 171). Siebert speaks of Hume being "meticulously controlled," "he speaks from a comfortable distance," "he has detached himself from metaphysical anguish," etc. (Siebert, 173, 174, 177). All such characteristics are indications that he had decided not to probe into the Unconscious. As Descartes accepted the values of the Catholic Church without question and this gave him a balance not found in his philosophy, so David Hume accepted the values of the Enlightenment and a balance that Hume the philosopher could not justify. They both had more Integration in their lives than was in their philosophy.

The texts of Hume do not say much to a Jungian, but even that could be significant. He had no interest in a personal religion. A personal religion involves confronting the mystery associated with the Unconscious and trying to come to some terms with it (perhaps finding the Fourth and the Union of Opposites). Perhaps he had some such confrontation as a young man with personal dilemmas, but apart from this he has left no evidence of a personal religious interest. Yet he retained an interest in the religion of others and an interest in Natural Theology, both of which concern only the Conscious reflective mind. Since Hume maintained an Olympian standpoint of detachment and control, his texts would involve no Enantiodromias, Integrations, Quaternities, or an appearance of the Self. He became a bon vivant who found it more useful to keep to "the calm sunshine of the mind" with no desire to intrude into regions totally dark. Should other people be troubled by religious urges, he recommended liturgical practices to help abate their enthusiasm.

Notes

1. Noxon presents well an extensive account of the influence of Newton on Hume, an influence that was strong in his early days: "After his early,

reclusive, system-building day, history, politics, and religion gained priority . . . natural philosophy shifted quickly to the periphery"—so did the influence of Newton (Noxon, 75). Hume had practically no involvement in experimental science. When Locke was considered in the present study, his interest in experimental science was seen as integral to his S identity; Hume was an S without such an interest. But Locke was an Extrovert, and Hume an Introvert. The Introvert is interested in observing his own psyche; so it was with Hume.

2. What the new scene was, he does not say, nor is it evident. Norman Kemp Smith thought it was that science rests on feeling; Passmore thought it associationism. In terms of it appearing this early in his reflections, I suggest it concerned using immediate perception as the basis of all knowledge (Smith, 20; Passmore, 131).

3. The ideas follow after the sensations so that we have no idea without first having a sensation. But the sensations are vivid and lively, while ideas are considered nothing but weaker forms of sensation. Recall how Whitehead saw Descartes beginning with a judgment and then having difficulty in getting to perception; but Whitehead praised Hume for beginning with perception. Like Whitehead, Hume would begin with perception, but his perception was different from Whitehead's.

4. The common reading of Hume would see no real causal necessity in things, but Galen Strawson argues that Hume is only saying we can know nothing of the true nature of causal power. He sees Hume claiming only that there is no logical contradiction in saying something might arise without a cause (Strawson, 101). I acknowledge his claim but am not totally convinced.

5. Jung has written abundant studies of works of literature that tell of a hero setting out to enter the dark forest, and so on. He sees the hero as one setting out to find the lost maiden (the Anima) in the Unconscious. She is often associated with the Repressed and can lead to the rise of the Self, the Transcendent Function. Here Hume would warn aspiring heroes that there is no "arduous prize"; the so-called prizes are only varieties of superstition.

6. Hume regularly speaks of us not attaining the "springs and principles." It is not always clear if Hume uses the word "spring" to refer to the spring in a machine or to a spring of water. In either case it could have Jungian overtones. Hume's *Dialogue Concerning Natural Religion* tells of four ways misery enters human affairs. The Fourth *might* be understood as N. "The *fourth* circumstance, whence arises the misery and ill in the universe, is the inaccurate workmanship of all the springs and principles of the great machine of nature" (*EW*, 372). That is, he allows that rain is beneficial, but in excess it causes flooding! The flooding shows that the ultimate springs and principles are not quite right. This same work identifies God as the "being who knows the secret springs of the universe" (*EW*, 370).

7. The same two types of philosophy were presented at the beginning of his *Treatise*; for there he complained that the prize went to the eloquent as opposed to those who use their reason. In the *Enquiry*, he seemed to recognize the value of each. After writing the *Enquiry*, he seems to have decided to

write an eloquent philosophy rather than the rational and skeptical philosophy that no one wanted to read.

8. See Siebert, p. 28. Consider the following lines from the *Treatise* that show little tender sentiment: "Nothing has a greater tendency to give us an esteem for any person than his power and riches; or a contempt than his poverty and meanness" (*T*, 357). This is far from the emotional appeals that run through Hume's later writings. These emotional appeals are part of Hume's conscious effort to win over opponents to a philosophy that he does not argue. He presents the common judgments of people as empirical facts, for he believed such philosophy might do some good.

9. Siebert, 56. Much of the material presented here is taken from Siebert's insightful study.

10. His *Dialogue Concerning Natural Religion* was published only after his death. He had written it some time before, but did not seek publication. The *Dialogue* has three persons presenting accounts of the natural knowledge of God. It is difficult to say which, if any, of the characters he favored. Perhaps he was only trying to think through the matter for himself. In any case, the dialogue concerns the conscious ability to know and does not touch on the symbolic knowing found in "religion." Siebert quotes a text of Hume's *Treatise* where poets are said to be guided "by a certain taste or common instinct, which in most kinds of reasoning goes farther than any of that art and philosophy with which we have been yet acquainted" (*T*, 494). Siebert sees this as the only text wherein Hume "almost ventured into the . . . region of the numinous and mystical" (Siebert, 168).

Bibliography

Works of Hume

EW   *Essential Works of David Hume*, edited and with an introduction by Ralph Cohen. New York: Bantam, 1965. To assist those using other editions in locating a passage, the pages of the individual works are: *An Enquiry Concerning Human Understanding*, pp. 44–167; *An Enquiry Concerning the Principles of Morals*, pp. 180–292; *Dialogues Concerning Natural Religion*, pp. 303–90; *Essays*, pp. 411–531; *An Abstract of a Book Lately Published*, pp. 534–47.

HE   *A History of England*, vol. V. Philadelphia: Porter & Coates, no date, but about 1900.

PWR *Principle Writings on Religion*, edited and with introduction by J. C. A. Gaskin. New York: Oxford University Press, 1993.

T   *Treatise of Human Nature*. Buffalo: Prometheus Books, 1992.

Other Works

Copleston, Frederick, S. J. *A History of Philosophy,* vol. V, part II, *The British Philosophers.* New York: Doubleday-Image, 1964.

Noxon, James. *Hume's Philosophical Development: A Study of his Methods.* Oxford: The Clarendon Press, 1973.

Passmore, John. *Hume's Intentions* (revised edition). London: Gerald Duckworth, 1968; first published in 1952, Cambridge University Press.

Siebert, Donald T. *The Moral Animus of David Hume.* Newark: University of Delaware Press, 1990.

Strawson, Galen. *The Secret Connexion.* Oxford: The Clarendon Press, 1989.

12 Teilhard: Quaternity in Omega
The Process of Transformation

Teilhard as an N: Teilhard called for a "scientific re-casting of knowing: intuition replacing deduction" (J, 2/July/52); he wanted a metaphysics based on "intuitive induction" (J, 23/July/52) and regarded his major work, *The Phenomenon of Man*, as the expression of an intuition (*PM*, 300). He spoke endlessly of "vision" and the "eyes": the Foreword to *The Phenomenon of Man* is titled "Vision" and claims "the whole of life lies in that verb, " and "vision is really fuller being." One seven-page essay has it that "the universe has appeared to human eyes," "takes shape before our eyes," is "distinguishable to our eyes," to "researchers' eyes," "beneath our eyes," all "within the vision of natural science" (*VP,* 238ff). In contrast to Hume and the Sensates, Teilhard knows no separate units: "There is no fact that exists in isolation" (*PM*, 30), and he would "not admit that things can exist in isolation" (*WW*, 167). He states well the mind of an N: "Every increase of internal vision is essentially the germ of a further vision which includes all the others and carries still farther on" (*PM*, 231). Teilhard would call himself "a pilgrim of the future" and explained: "The world holds no interest for me unless I look forward, but when my eyes are on the future it is full of excitement" (*LT*, 140).[1] For Teilhard's Quarternity, see figure 12.1. Teilhard's Myers-Briggs type would be INTJ.

			T			
			3.	Mind		
			4.	Thoughts		
	N Dominant				S	
1.	*La Vision*	SUPREME CENTER			*La Sensation*	WT
2.	The eye, seeing, visible	CHRIST, WORLD SOUL			The hand, sensing, tangible	
3.	Eyes				(intangible)	WT, 108
4.	—	DIVINE MILIEU			Sensations	DM, 129
5.	The Without				The Within	
6.	Transcending (transience)	OMEGA			Immanence	
7.	*en dehors d'elle*				*en soi, centre*	
8.	Science	F			Humanity	PM, 248 & ff
9.	Evolution	3.	Heart		Involution	PM, 301 & ff.
		4.	Sentiments			

Figure 12.1

I. An Account of Integration

Pierre Teilhard de Chardin was a thirty-three-year-old Jesuit priest studying geology at the University of Paris in December of 1914 when he was drafted into the French army. While serving as a stretcher bearer in World War I, he was involved in several major battles. During these years, Teilhard underwent a profound personal transformation and wrote an ongoing account of the changes that illustrate vividly what Jung called Integration; these accounts bring out well the religious dimension of the process. The accounts are found in his *Journal* and a series of articles circulated among friends. He was almost thirty-five in April 1916 when he finished the first article, "Cosmic Life." The essay tells of the Cosmos itself awakening, and the awakening is divided into subsections titled: *La Vision* and *La Sensation*, evident references to the N (*Vision*) and the S (*Sensation*), the elements of his Enantiodromia.

The importance of *La Sensation* (and related words, *sens, sentir*) for Teilhard is often lost in English translation, as *Sensation* is sometimes translated as sensation (sense, to sense) and sometimes as feeling (feel, to feel). Because of the two translations the frequency and importance of the term is lost in English. The present study will introduce Teilhard's French, *sensation, sens, sentir*, both to make evident the frequency of the terms and affirm their relation to Jung's Sensation.

Jung wrote of the Functions as faculties of the psyche, and faculties of the psyche were central to Teilhard's first essay. He would contrast *La Vision* and *La Sensation*, and the two faculties are implied in many phrases. For example: Teilhard says he writes "only for those who can *see* and *feel* [*sentir*]"; his essay will help people "*see* and make them *feel* [*sentir*]" (*WT*, 15). The elements continue to recur in the same order: one uses one's "*eyes* and *hands*" and eventually discovers "the *visible* and *tangible* universe" (*WT*, 38, 60).

In the section titled *La Vision*, Teilhard appeals to the contemporary scientific picture wherein all things are *seen* to have "a reciprocal influence on one another." All things share a common origin and a common growth; all things are *seen* as elements of the total development of the cosmos. (As "total development," vision is aware of the forest and not the trees.)

Having briefly stated the scientific view, Teilhard adds it is not enough to "*observe* [*regarder*] from the *outside* the cosmic currents taking shape . . . we must be able to feel [*sentir*] them" (*WT*, 25). Then he moves to the *inside* and the section titled *La Sensation;* but here he no longer considers the objective world of science. His imagery tells of a personal descent into the unconscious:

> And I allowed my consciousness to sweep back to the farthest limit of my body, to ascertain whether I might not extend outside myself. I stepped down into the most hidden depths of my being, lamp in hand and ears alert, to discover whether, in the deepest recesses of the blackness within me, I might not see the glint of the waters of the current that flows on, whether I might not hear the murmur of their mysterious waters that rise from the uttermost depths and will burst forth, no man knows where. With terror and intoxicating emotion, I realized that my own poor trifling existence was one with the immensity of all that is and all that is still in process of becoming. I can feel [*sens*] it: matter, which I thought was most my own, eludes and escapes me. (*WT*, 25)

He soon concludes *La Sensation* with the claim that his life is not his own, for his inmost soul is one with the life of the universe. The personal freedom of which he had been conscious seems to be only a minute point surrounded by a mass of unconscious forces that escape his control.

> If, as I said before, we step down into ourselves, we shall be horrified to find there, *beneath the man of surface relationships and reflection,* an unknown—someone as yet hardly emerged from unconsciousness,

still, for lack of the appropriate stimulus, no more than half-awake: one whose features, seen in half-shadow, seem to be merging into the countenance of the world. (*WT*, 27; translation amended)

He comes to realize that it is not so much himself acting as the world acting through him. It is not so much his own awakening as the Cosmos itself awakening within him. The exploration of *La Sensation* fills him "with religious horror," a phrase that further suggests the unconscious. Though he is awed by this new and startling awareness, he decides to plunge into the unknown and see where it will take him.

In these passages the evident scientific world of *Vision* is set in contrast with the hidden and mysterious world of *Sensation;* the different tones of the sections illustrate the difference between the Conscious and the Unconscious mind. In Jungian terms the repressed Function is being sought in the dark waters of the Unconscious. Jung often would see a feminine presence in a man's Unconscious. So with Teilhard, his experience of *la Sensation* has brought him to "the rich, the mother, the divine"; he has encountered the "fertile generatrix, the Terra Mater."

As the essay continues, Teilhard allows himself to sink into the allurement of "divine matter" unable to imagine that what he was seeking "could fail to coincide with the enchantment of the *senses*." But as he drifted to ever more diffuse stages "of primordial consciousness, he finds the light of life was dimmed." While seeking a "bliss-giving repose" in the "little-known depths, " he experienced "a diminution of personality." In Jungian terms, the diminution of ego-identity attends the descent into the unconscious.

But Teilhard's descent to the lower regions suddenly is halted by what he called "faith in life." Now he feels called to make a radical about-turn, a "reversal." He stops his descent into primordial matter, turns about, and aligns himself with the rising movement of evolution. He announces, "We must travel with our backs turned to matter and not try to return to it and be absorbed into it." He has become aware that he was drifting towards "Nirvana." "Now, like a diver who regains control and masters his inertia, I must make a vigorous effort, reverse my course and ascend again to the higher levels" (*WT*, 32). He believes that in making the descent he had been following a "temptress." By his reversal he turned from her and thereby could "win back ground from the unconscious" (*WT*, 40; "unconscious" is Teilhard's term).

Teilhard can be seen as an Intuitive surprised by a disturbing encounter with Sensation. He tells of making the descent because we have "an *immanent* need to put our *hands*" on what is "absolute." Eventually his hand will discover the *"tangible"* universe and also "the Hand of God," "a contact with the hand of God, " God's "creative Hands" (*WT*, 60, 65). (Teilhard's writings include at least a hundred such references to the hand(s) of God; he would also speak of the Eyes of God, but unlike these references, the divine Hands are encountered in a context of mystery [for other mysterious meetings with the Divine Hands, see *WT*, 146; *DM*, 76–79; *HM*, 122]).

Judging by this account of "reversal" one would think that Teilhard has rejected matter, but that is not the case. Rather Teilhard would claim that one first must make a descent into matter (the unconscious), and then reverse direction and ascend. It is only in making the descent that one can gain the support one needs to rise to God. Thus, this essay tells first of our Communion with the Earth (the descent into the unconscious), and then of a rising to Communion with God. So the point of the essay is to tell of a "Communion with God through the Earth." To achieve this Communion, one must first descend into the earth (matter, the unconscious) and then rise to divine union.[2] God is identified as the heavenly Word, Light and consciousness, but the way to attain communion with God is indirect: it begins with a descent to earthly silence, darkness, and unconsciousness. And Teilhard would claim that it is only by first making the descent that one can obtain the energy needed to rise to heaven.

The descent and rising is presented at length in this first essay, but the account of the final Communion with God is only briefly stated. That is, he identifies the Supreme Center as Christ and adds "all things were moving towards the Child born of Woman, " but he says little more (*WT*, 59). It is as though this new Center (Christ, the Self, etc.) had recently appeared; he was fascinated by it, but he did not have much to say about it. In the essays that followed he would speak of it in increasing abundance.

In 1898, many years before his wartime service when Teilhard first considered entering the Jesuits, he wrote to his parents that he felt called "to leave the world," a phrase suggesting a Platonic rising up to the light. His entrance into the Jesuits could be seen as a rejection of his S to follow his N to God. Years later, during the war, he sees he cannot go directly to God; he must first descend to earth. Entering the Jesuits was the way he "rejected the tangible" (*HM*, 71), for matter had its evident limitations. Matter is confining, one keeps coming up against opaque walls, and one is "never finding in *sense* experience (always superficial) the clue to anything" (*WT*, 101; translation amended; parenthesis in the text).[3] So Teilhard decided to "leave the world." But World War I involved a forcible encounter with the tangible he had rejected. To tell of retrieving the missing Function Jung would often quote the Scriptures: "The stone the builders rejected has become the cornerstone." For Teilhard (N), the rejected stone was the tangible, the S (much as the T philosophers considered above were seen to reject the F).

Writing in March of the following year, 1917, Teilhard tells of "the saint . . . losing one's materiality" and he seems to be telling of himself. Such a one can see all things in God; for all things are seen as Christ. Such an object

> as the eyes can see, the heart feel, and the mind apprehend—exhausts the truth and beauties of heaven and earth, the faculties of the soul converge; there they meet one another, are fused together in the flame of a unique act where perception is blended with love. The formal effect of the act of purity is to unite the inner powers of the soul in the act of a single passion of extraordinary richness and intensity. (*WT*, 108; translation amended)

It can be noted that "the faculties of the soul converge" into a single act, but "the faculties" include only the *eyes*, the *heart* and the *mind* (N, F, and T); the Sense faculty has been left out of the process. That is because the saint has become immaterial, much as Teilhard had done in entering the Jesuits. So the saint is said to find Christ "intangible." Sensation is missing. To include Sensation with the other Three, the conscious mind and its Faculty (vision, N) must renounce control. The phrases by which Teilhard tells of the process sound like the phrases of Jung: Teilhard claims the pain that "decomposes is essential . . . if [one] is to live and become spirit" (*WT*, 112). One's original identity "will be broken down before the true simplicity that he awaits and has been promised is realized." Thus, to achieve the ultimate unity one first "must suffer a sort of decomposition." The individual must "suffer an eclipse which will seem to annihilate it." For Teilhard this means his Dominant N, the ability *to see*, must diminish so that he might better be able *to sense*. He states it directly himself: "the mystical effort to *see* must give way to the effort to *feel* [*sentir*] and to surrender" (*WT*, 125). This is the switching of Faculties! The dominant N must renounce control to allow development of the rejected S. The process involves distress, disintegration, loss, and sorrow. But only by the N renouncing its dominance can one find the S. Teilhard tells of the finding: the "Godhead gradually assumes, in our sentient faculty [*notre faculté de sentir*], the higher Reality it possesses in the nature of things" (*WT*, 127). God, or rather, the Godhead, appears in the *sense* faculty! The stone that was rejected has been found, and containing the Godhead it will become the cornerstone. Yet to locate the sense faculty at all required a movement away from the Dominant (the eyes, or even the three faculties: eyes, heart, and mind [N, F, and T as above]); only then does one discover the Godhead appearing *in Sensation*. The S faculty, that which was dismissed as "always superficial" and unable to offer a clue to anything, is now *notre faculté de sentir* containing the Godhead! The cornerstone has been located.

Teilhard claims the process is hard to put into words, even for those who have been "initiated," a term suggesting a religious rite. He has again told of his descent to Sensation using the language of religious mystery; his language further suggests to Jungians the disintegration of the ego as one descends into the unconscious.

Each succeeding essay of Teilhard tells of his struggle to understand the transformation he was undergoing. In the summer of 1917 he tried writing a somewhat systematic piece, "The Mystical Milieu," that tells of passing out of himself and into Christ. He begins "at one point, in a person: my own person." But his person must be renounced should he want to travel to another Point/Person, Jesus. He feels drawn out of himself by an intense sensation ("a limpid sound rises midst silence, a trail of pure color drifts through the glass"). These vivid sense impressions tend to "break up our autonomy"; he claims they "took possession of me and bore me away."[4] The appeal is said to originate in "the hallowed function of *sense perception*," in fact, there is a "vocation contained in all *sense perception*" (*WT*, 118).

The essay speaks of our being drawn out of ourselves "into an ever richer and more spiritual rhythm that was imperceptible and endlessly becoming the measure of all growth and all beauty." Now we begin to see God present everywhere in the *tangible* universe: "Under this single *tangible* stuff, Lord, you make yourself manifest to us and fill us with rapture" (*WT*, 122). This involves an expansive movement that he called the "second phase of our perceptions"; it is the descent. Now the entire world is seen in a different way. "At first we might have mistaken it for a mere projection of our emotions." But it is more than that, for we have been drawn out of ourselves to be united with all things. This is the loss of ego identity as one enters into the great All—into the unconscious.

Teilhard tells of dissolving into the universe, only to find once again the dissolution "seemed to be reversed" (In Jungian terms the descent into the unconscious is reversed), much like the reversal presented in "Cosmic Life" above. With the reversal the decentering seems to end, and the universe begins recentering itself, but not on him. It is being centered on Another, on Christ: "I recognized that it was all coming to centre *on a single point*, on a Person: your Person: Jesus! . . . Every presence makes me feel [*sentir*] that you are near me; every touch is the touch of your *hand*" (*WT*, 146).

In this essay ("The Mystical Milieu"), Teilhard started with his ego identity, "at one point, in a person: my own person." But then in passing out of himself his ego seemed to dissolve into all things. The dissolution was "reversed" and all things gathered around another point, "your Person, Jesus," and the Jesus he senses/touches is located at the Center of a set of concentric circles (*WT*, 148; recall the image as in Rousseau, above). This essay in Jungian terms tells of a movement from the ego (a point) to the Self or Transcendent Function (also a Point); in calling it a Point he is saying it is reaching a personal focus. Recall that when the "divine" had first shown itself, it was more or less unfocused (an "unknown," the "Godhead"—somewhat impersonal terms; the Self had not yet developed to become Personal or hyper-Personal as it is now).

"The Mystical Milieu" (written sixteen months after the first essay) began like the first with a strong sense of the divine presence in the rejected S Function. But it includes an advance over the earlier essay in that there is now a detailed account of the final Christ, the mysterious and very personal Focus that resembles what Jung associates with the Christ of the mystics and called the Transcen-

dent Function or the Self. Jung saw this mysterious Other as ourselves and more than ourselves, and Teilhard insists on the same
point. For Teilhard this Other is found "immediately behind us, as
though it were an extension of ourselves" (*WT,* 182); "a Divinity is
being born among us" (*WT,* 184). We experience within ourselves, *ad
intra,* a "Reality more absolute and more precious than ourselves . . .
a cosmic extension of our personality"; we find we can "worship in
ourselves something that is 'us.' God with us!" (*WT,* 187). It is ourselves, yet more than ourselves.

In his accounts of descent, the Christian or personal character
of what he was finding was not evident. For then the impersonal
"Divine" was spread over everything the sense faculty could touch;
it was the impersonal Godhead. Now it is an inner and Personal
Presence, and it will be seen to reconcile the opposites.

In the month after writing "The Mystical Milieu," Teilhard wrote
"Nostalgia for the Front." The essay tells of nostalgic feelings for the
battlefield, and to explain this feeling to himself he tells of resorting
to "almost mystical considerations." At the Front he felt "freed and
relieved from even my own self" (loss of ego). But this is "no more
than the negative part" of a process of "initiation"—a religious involvement—wherein all his vital powers were directed "upon a *tangible* object" (*HM,* 174); there he was "baptized . . . into a higher Life."
Again, he is telling of a loss of self that leads to finding a higher Self.
Again, when this higher Self first appears, there is ambiguity about
its personal character. He speaks of it as "another *Thing,*" a "Presence" (impersonal), but also as "a Soul greater than my own," a "new
and super-human Soul," "a *personality* of another order" (personal
terms) (*HM,* 175–76). Having known this higher Self on the battlefield, he decides he must proceed with his life "not in a spirit of
selfishness as before, but religiously" (*HM,* 179).[5]

In January 1918 he would write "The Soul of the World, " an essay
that tells abundantly of this higher Soul (Self).[6] He struggles to
name the wonder that seems to be both his own Center and the
Center of the cosmos:

> There can be no doubt that we are conscious of carrying within us
> something greater and more indispensable than ourselves: something
> that existed before we did and could have continued to exist without
> us: something in which we live, and that we cannot exhaust: something
> that serves us but of which we are not masters: something that will

gather us up when, through death, we slip away from ourselves and our whole being seems to be evaporating. (*WT,* 181)

His individual soul is "dominated and filled to overflowing by a Power beside which it is as nothing, and with which, nevertheless, it is but one." And "confronted by this masterful guest . . . the soul would be overcome by a profound and sacred feeling of awe" (*WT,* 181). Such passages show that in the course of two years the mysterious Identity within him—briefly indicated in "Cosmic Life"—has become an evident reality of which he could and did write at length.

In the following years Teilhard spoke abundantly about this Other within and found his own Christian commitment strengthened as the Other became increasingly personal. Before the war he had known only the descent and the impersonal All that he had found difficult to reconcile with his Christian faith, for Christianity insists on the personal nature of God, not on an impersonal Godhead. Teilhard would soon call this personal Center "Omega" or "the Omega Point." Omega is the final letter of the Greek alphabet, and Teilhard picked the term to indicate the fullness of Christ at the end of time (Christ identified himself as "the Alpha and the Omega, the first and the last, the beginning and the end" [Rev. 22:13; see Rev. 1:8, 17; 21:6]). By adding the word "Point," Teilhard was saying the final end of the universe is centered and personal.

Teilhard often contrasted this *personal* Center with the "Eastern way" which generally spoke of deliverance into an impersonal unity, into what Teilhard had called the Godhead. So Teilhard spoke of the Eastern mystic seeking Nirvana, a state that could be seen to end with the descent into the unconscious, that is, there would be no reversal. The Eastern mystic would descend to where all ego or personal identity is lost; there would be no reversal and no appearance of a divine Someone. This denial of *all* personhood is called "anatta" and is a basic teaching of Buddhism. Neither Teilhard nor Jung was sympathetic to the claim that one could be free from all individuality, a claim more or less integral to Buddhist texts.[7] At the same time, Teilhard expressed considerable appreciation for the Buddhists' sense of the All and the divine matter to which one would descend. Teilhard found this descent (which he regarded as the first and almost essential part of a process) lacking in much Christianity.

II. The Divine Milieu

When Teilhard's military service ended, he returned to continue studies in geology. While in those studies he gave a lecture ("Science and Christ") telling again of the descent, reversal, and rise that ran through his wartime essays. But here he is telling of his scientific work. The essay is subtitled, "Analysis and Synthesis." By analysis one proceeds "in a manner of speaking downwards, " but in the work of synthesis, "starting from the lowest term at which it arrives, let us try moving upwards." (Analysis is discovering the individual trees, while synthesis is reconstituting the forest.) Here Teilhard would see the scientific work of *synthesizing* one's research as ultimately bringing one to the unique center of things, which is God our Lord (*SC*, 21–22)

When Teilhard finished his doctorate, he went to China where he did extensive fieldwork in geology and became involved with the fossils and tools of early humans (Peking Man). In China in 1926–27, he wrote a devotional work, *The Divine Milieu*, that tells of the mind (conscious mind) working "within an incredibly small radius of light." But beyond this limited light he was aware of a "vast, rich, troubled and complex" darkness, a darkness "heavy with promises and threats." He sets out to explore this mysterious region:

> I went down into my inmost self, to the deep abyss whence I feel dimly that my power of action emanates. But as I moved further and further away from the conventional certainties by which social life is superficially illuminated, I became aware that I was losing contact with myself. At each step of the descent a new person was disclosed within me of whose name I was no longer sure, and who no longer obeyed me. And when I had to stop my exploration because the path faded from beneath my steps, I found a bottomless abyss at my feet, and out of it came—arising I know not from where—the current I dare to call *my* life. (*DM*, 76–77)

The passage recalls the descent recounted in his first essay, and again he realizes a depth completely beyond the familiar. He is troubled by his findings and backs away from the inner current to return to the daylight, hoping to live again on the surface. But now, even the surface is seen to contain the mystery he wanted to avoid. That is, he found before his gaze "the web of chance," that which seems to rule all events; chance seems to have brought him into being, and only chance sustains him; he feels helpless and knows the distress of a particle adrift in the universe. But at this moment he encounters "the two marvellous hands" of Christ: one hand is acting within him and the other is guiding the external universe. Again, as in his first essay, Teilhard has told of a descent into mystery that ends by his finding salvation in the divine *Hands*.

In *The Divine Milieu* (as ten years earlier), the transformation began with an appeal found in Sensation, and then the three *less* conscious Faculties become involved:

> It began with a particular and unique resonance. . . . All the elements of psychological life were in turn affected; *sensations, feelings, thoughts [sensations, sentiments, pensées]*. Day by day they became more fragrant, more coloured, more intense by means of an indefinable thing—the same thing. Then the vague note, and fragrance, and light began to define themselves. . . . I had in fact acquired a new sense [*sens*], the *sense of a new quality* or *of a new dimension*. Deeper still: a transformation had taken place for me *in the very perception of being*. Thenceforward being had become, in some way, tangible and savorous to me. (*DM*, 129)

In telling of things becoming "more fragrant, more coloured, " becoming "tangible and savorous," he is telling of a new quality in Sensation. But soon all three of the less conscious Faculties are affected: "sensations, feelings, thoughts"—S, F, T. By the change he finds himself dwelling in the Divine Milieu; this is identified as God revealing himself "as the ultimate point, " as a "personal unity, " and "the common centre of all consummation." Now he has discovered a Center "incomparably near and *tangible;*" it is the Center where all the elements of the universe "*touch each other* by that which is most inward and ultimate." The Milieu "assembles and harmonises within itself qualities which appear to us to be contradictory." The Milieu includes the S ("tangible") and has harmonized apparent contradictions—the reconciliation of opposites that Jung considered the primary characteristic of the Self.

The first essay of Teilhard, "Cosmic Life" (above), has only a brief and indirect statement concerning the Self. But in the essays that followed, Teilhard tells increasingly of finding the Self as an abiding presence filling him with awe; he would speak of it abundantly and with ease. His Integration continued after the war, so his accounts continued to be filled with a sense of wonder (see *DM*, 113–21).

III. The Macrocosm Becomes Centered on Omega

In reading of Teilhard's transformation, one becomes aware of how closely his accounts parallel the Integration process of Jung, a more detailed and closer parallel than with any of the other authors considered here. But so far this study has presented Teilhard's personal transformation with only minimal recognition of his wider philosophy. Now a similar process will be shown in his cosmology. Teilhard saw the transformation as both personal and cosmic, so he spoke of the individual as a Microcosm undergoing the same transformation as the Macrocosm (see *AM,* 241); that is, the micro and macro are in the same process. In his wartime writings, Teilhard was already aware of the "cosmic" importance of his transformation and from the beginning he had related it to the evolution of life. The Christ (the Transcendent Function) that he knew "within" was also seen as the goal of evolution, the Soul of the World that was coming into being. His scientific and philosophic thought developed in a long series of essays after the war; eventually he brought his ideas together in his major work, *The Phenomenon of Man,* a work that contains much science, much philosophy, much religious awareness—and much that suggests a Jungian Integration.

In 1918 Teilhard wrote that all particles in the universe—what he often called monads—could be considered as units *en soi.* Beyond this he based his cosmology on the fact that elements are constituted more by their *"en dehors d'elle, plutôt que par leur centre,"* that is, by their "beyond self, rather than by their center," their in self (*J,* 185). The "beyond self" is evidently the N, while the "in self" is the S. The "beyond self" and the "in self" can be seen in parallel with Plato's "Other" and "Same," with Sartre's (and Hegel's) "for-itself" and "in-itself." Teilhard would sometimes call the "beyond self" "transience." As a good Intuitive he would not allow that things could exist in isolation: "Since every being can subsist and hold together only through confluence with others, transience, far from being inexplicable, is the very condition for the monad's existence" (*WT,* 167). Note: "transience," extending beyond oneself, is part of the very being of things; that is, things are "incompletely individualized." Thus, each individual is said to have a double identity, being "at the same time itself [S] and something else [N]" (*WT,* 167). Later he will claim that every being is "constructed like an ellipse on two conjugate foci" (*PM*, 61; see also *J*, 267, 304; *AM*, 241), and the foci are identified as the beyond self and the in self. His terminology would vary in many ways: he once called the "beyond self" a "collective centration" (forest rather than trees) and the "in self" an "individual super-centration" (tree rather than forest) (*T*, 183n). But here and elsewhere the two are the N and the S, here presented as two foci within each being; they are like the two centers around which one can draw an ellipse. They are also *La Vision* and *La Sensation*, the two points within each being that must come together so that the ellipses they presently form might become Circles. The two foci are implicit when Teilhard speaks of the human as "the two-fold center of the world" (*PM*, 31), and when the human is identified as the one "*on* whom [N] and *in* whom [S] the universe enfolds itself" (*PM*, 92).

Teilhard's cosmology is most developed in his central work, *The Phenomenon of Man*, written in 1938–40 and revised in 1948. The Foreword is titled "Seeing": "We might say that the whole of life lies in that verb" (*PM*, 31). The Foreword tells of the vision of the world that has developed in contemporary science. But to share this *vision* one must develop "a whole series of '*senses*'" (a sense of the immensity of the universe, a sense of the organic, etc.). "Without these [sense] *qualities* to illuminate our *vision*, man will remain . . . an erratic object in a disjointed world." Thus in his Foreword, Teilhard is again appealing to a combination of Vision and Sensation (N and S) as he did years before in "Cosmic Life." He is saying that the two poles need each other and unless we develop a "sense" of immensity, a sense of the organic, our vision cannot increase.

The first chapter of *The Phenomenon of Man* considers the elementary particles of matter. Our gaze undergoes a "disintegration as it goes downward" into ever-simpler particles; finally, when analysis can proceed no farther, he claims we are obliged to turn our perspective "upside down" (*PM*, 43). The disintegration is the descent; the turning of perspective upside down is the reversal; then the rise of which he will speak is the ever-increasing synthesis of living organisms. The account of this increasing synthesis constitutes the body of the book. To consider the rise of life, Teilhard speaks of the Without and the Within, and the same two elements (N and S) *en dehors d'elle* and *en soi* are involved. The Without refers to the objective world that science can study (*La Vision* of his first essay), and the Within refers to what each individual knows "within," one's *quant a soi* ("reserve," *PM,* 54); it is *La Sensation.* The Without refers to what is *seen;* the Within to what is *sensed* personally. To illustrate the difference: by observing a dog's behavior, one learns of the dog's "Without"—what appears to an observer. The Within refers to the dog's own awareness—what cannot be seen by an observer. One can only guess what the dog is "thinking."

Teilhard claims that all units of matter, subatomic particles, etc., have both a Without and a Within (a trace of consciousness): "There is some sort of psyche in every corpuscle" (*PM,* 301). (This understanding is often called pan-psychism. Though claims of pan-psychism are highly controversial, still a number of scientists and philosophers have accepted it, e.g, J. B. S. Haldane, and A. N. Whitehead.) In any case, for Teilhard the Within is an element's *en soi,* its *quant a soi,* its inscape, its "immanence," its S.

Teilhard believed the thoroughgoing materialist recognized only the Without, the external world, while others allowed only the psyche (this opposition resembles the conflict of Giants and the Gods in Plato's *Sophist*). In coming to speak of the Within, Teilhard set the materialists in opposition to the idealist philosophers; the materialists recognized only the Without (transience) and the Idealists recognized only the Within (immanence).

> On the one hand the materialists insist on talking about objects as though they only consisted of *external* actions in *transient* relationships. On the other hand the upholders of a spiritual interpretation are obstinately determined not to go outside a kind of solitary introspection in which things are only looked upon as being *shut in upon themselves* in their "*immanent*" workings. (*PM,* 53; emphasis added)

The conflicting philosophies are the elements of Teilhard's Enantiodromia, the N and the S, the Other and Same of Plato, the for-itself and the in-itself of Sartre, and the value and fact of Whitehead. Since a scientist deals only with the Without (vision), when writing as a scientist Teilhard will write in direct and objective language (his scientific writings in geology have been collected in ten volumes). But in his philosophic or religious works he introduces the Within (S) and this involves a sense of mystery (the unconscious) not appropriate for scientific writing: thus, when *The Phenomenon of Man* speaks of the Within, it is "half-seen in this one flash of light"; it appears as if "it were seen through a rent"; it is "a spectrum of shifting shades whose lower terms are lost in the night" (*PM*, 56, 60). It is again the S retaining its mystery.

The Phenomenon of Man begins by telling of the original minerals present billions of years ago (elementary monads with their two foci); these gradually would be transformed as the earth gave rise to living organisms. Each particle (atom, electron, etc.) of the minerals has an original *immanence*, a Within, by which it is locked into itself. That is, each has a trace of psyche, but should the particles remain minerals their situation "has closed them prematurely in upon themselves." To develop "they have to get out of themselves," that is, they have to become other (N). The minerals are the rejected S function, closed on themselves. What is needed is *transience*, the N by which they might proceed out of themselves. They must become other than themselves or there will be no evolution, no buildup in structures.

To understand the meaning of this other-than-themselves consider the carbon, oxygen, and additional atoms of which a dog is made. The atoms are still themselves, but they are also other than themselves, for they comprise the dog. In being the dog, they "escape" being simply carbon atoms; they pass out of themselves to attain a common canine identity, a living organism that is formed by their union. They still retain an individual immanence (Within), but by their *transience* they have passed out of simply being themselves to become the dog. The dog is a unit with its own Within (consciousness), a Within much greater than the minute consciousness of its atoms. There is then a sequence: immanence (the Within of each atom), then the transience of the atoms going out of themselves to attain a common life, and then the new and more intense immanence, the consciousness (the soul) of the dog. The atoms have left aside the separate immanence they once had, only to find a common inmanence returning as cornerstone.

This same sequence, S to N to S (rejecting immanence for transience and later taking up immanence again to make it of central importance), could be seen to resemble Kierkegaard's F to T to F (rejecting the temporal only to take it up again, and so forth with other philosophers). The result of the sequence is evident when Teilhard speaks of the entire planet attaining a "common Immanence," a "tenuous Immanence." The phrases tell of a planetary immanence that is now appearing and is presently tenuous. This immanence is the final S making its appearance. This ultimate immanence is the "Soul of the World." The term picks up again a classical theme (the term was common among the Stoics), but what is original in Teilhard is that this Soul is in process of coming to be, coming increasingly to animate the world. To understand the word "Soul" here, consider the carbon and oxygen atoms in a dog: each atom has its own immanence/Within/S and together these elements give rise to the immanence/Within of the dog; the consciousness (soul) of the dog is a common immanence for all the atoms of which the dog is composed. Teilhard believed the planet was in a similar process of developing its own immanence. This "common Immanence" (world Soul) is beginning to make a tenuous appearance. Today the world is gaining a Unity. "*The sum* of the universe's *transience* will continue to increase until the time when it attains the value of an *immanence* that will embrace all things in a sort of common soul" (*WT*, 167–68, emphasis in text).

The full process could be stated: an original immanence (S, particles unrelated) must give way to increasing transience (N, evolution, things proceeding out of themselves to become related); they finally gain a universal immanence that seems to be a cornerstone for the new balance. This immanence is the Great Within, the Soul of the World, Omega. In it the opposites are united: "In it everything climbs as to a focus of *immanence*. But everything also descends from it as from a peak of *transcendence*" (*HE*, 70). Teilhard sees this developing process underlying the evolution of Life and this is presented in detail in *The Phenomenon of Man;* the process tells of a divided universe coming to attain its single Soul.

In considering evolution, Teilhard stresses the "passing out of self" that is essential for each atom to enter the wider process (as in telling of his own transformation he had to lose his own individuality):

> By the phenomenon of association, the living particle is wrenched from itself. Caught up in an aggregate greater than itself, it becomes to some extent its slave. It no longer belongs to itself. . . . From being a centre it is changed into being an intermediary, a link—no longer *existing*, but *transmitting*. (*PM*, 111)

The result is

> The least molecule is, in nature and in position, a function of the whole sidereal process, and the least of the protozoa is structurally so knit into the web of life that its existence cannot be hypothetically

annihilated without *ipso facto* undoing the whole network of the biosphere. (*PM*, 218)

The protozoan is integral to the web of life much as the individual tree is integral to the forest! These passages show the radical dominance of the N; elements are hardly more than parts of a wider whole, or parts of a universe in passage.

Every living element is said to pass out of itself in *three* ways (by associating with others, by extending in time, by transmitting what it is), but with the appearance of the first human being Teilhard tells of the Three ways becoming Four: "these are the *three* headings under which life rises up by virtue of its elementary mechanisms. There is also a *fourth* heading which embraces them all—that of *global unity*" (P, 111–12; the emphasis of "three" and "fourth" has been added). The Three are all forms of transience, while the missing Fourth is an immanence; it is identified as "the illuminating involution of the being upon itself" (*PM*, 258). And the "*in*volution" again suggests the S.

The Phenomenon of Man told of a world wherein, until the appearance of the first human, the elements (with their three "transient" properties of associating, extending, and transmitting, each term suggesting "otherness") seem to lack one fundamental property of being, immanence: things were not quite themselves, not entirely units in themselves (each element was "positively woven from all the others" [*PM*, 44]). It is true that Teilhard had spoken of the units of matter as "radically particulate" (S), but they were also "essentially related" (N), that is, essentially "other" (*PM*, 40). As such, they were not fully units to begin with, for they were other than themselves. Thus, he would speak of "material corpuscles [S] . . . as transient [N] reservoirs" (*PM*, 42). This would mean that any single particle (any atom, molecule, or other unit) cannot *be* apart from its relationship to the rest. In Teilhard's terms, things are so connected that "it is impossible to cut into this network, to isolate a portion without it becoming frayed and unravelled at all its edges" (*PM*, 44). For Teilhard, no unit can exist simply in itself (trees exist only as part of a forest); this is true of any unit: an electron, a cell, a human. The very being of each unit makes it part of a wider system.

When telling of the Three before they became Four, Teilhard spoke of things "no longer *existing*, but *transmitting*" (*PM*, 111); as transmitting, they were fundamentally Other than selves. But when he came to tell of the appearance of the first human, he introduced the Fourth. Then Life attained "its paroxysm of feeling [*son parox-ysme senti*]." This paroxysm *senti* is the first human, the first reflective immanence. In saying *senti*, the added Fourth is readily associated with the missing "unit in-itself, " the Sense Function. In the course of evolution a new and more intense immanence has appeared, the human being. The human appears with a vastly increased immanence, *en soi*.

Now something new has arrived, for the animals were hardly doing more than "transmitting"; they were hardly more than N. But with the coming of the human, something new has appeared: each human has a value *in one's self* (S). Earlier, transience (N) had dominated the process; but, in the reflective consciousness of the human individual, each unit is a center *in one's self*. Transmitting has given way to a new immanence. Accordingly, to explain human reflection, Teilhard introduces an image of the N and the S functioning together: "the *eyes* . . . were able to converge and fix on what the *hands* held . . . the external counterpart of reflexion." Thus, the reflective individual is said to constitute a "knot, " a unity in itself, "a knot whose strands have been for all time converging from the four corners of space" (*PM*, 170)—a striking image of the Jungian Self.[8]

Just as Teilhard gave a careful account of what Jung called Integration, so his texts would include an abundance of Threes that become Fours. Many of these Threes or Fours cannot be clearly associated with particular Functions so they are not integral to Teilhard's thought and are not discussed in this study; but the abundance of the Three-Four image in Teilhard is worth noting. A selection of them are gathered in a footnote.[9]

Teilhard would see reflection introducing a crisis in evolution, for in coming to reflection one begins to see the world centered about one's self—after all, one is the knot that has emerged from the four corners of space! One begins to think of one's self as the goal of evolution and center of the cosmos. But there are many humans who are similar "knots." The individual is only one of many cosmic centers; many "knots" have discovered themselves to be "in-selves." Each could simply turn in on itself in isolation, producing a dust of human particles with each particle imprisoned in a private perspective (its individual Within). There would be many trees, but no forest. To avoid this Teilhard recommends that we give ourselves to one another in love. Again it is a matter of passing out (N) of ourselves so that we might become more deeply our selves (S): in love "the more 'other' they become in conjunction, the more they find themselves as 'self'" (PM, 262). Love is thus a paradoxical unity of opposites. The course of evolution has brought about increasing stages of immanence: the molecule was more deeply immanent than the atom, the cell was more deeply immanent than the molecule, so with the animal, so with the human. Teilhard believed that humans must continue the process by coming together to form the society of the future, a society that could be seen as a common human organism.

Science will play an important part in the unification, for science draws individuals out of their private world to share a common vision. Just as particles of the original dust were drawn out of their selves to share a common evolution, so human individuals are drawn out of their isolation to develop a common scientific world view. This is the fundamental importance of science for Teilhard; it establishes a common outlook for humanity. Science can draw nations out of their limited and chauvinist outlooks. The common outlook of science (N—recall how science was associated with *la Vision* in Teilhard's first essay) that is now developing will lead humanity to recognize it has a common soul (S). Thus, for Teilhard, it is science (the study of the Without) that gives rise to humanity (the Within, the S, the immanence of the planet).

The conjunction of the N and the S is again evident as *The Phenomenon of Man* speaks of *science* as the "twin sister" of *humanity* (PM, 248). These two were "born together" in the last century, and the two assumed a religious value (the religion of science, the religion of humanity) as the century continued. The twin sisters are correlates of N (vision, science) and S (sensation, humanity, sense of man). For science is presented as a "supreme act of collective *vision*," while humanity (S) is presented again in the imagery of the unconscious: it first appeared as "a vague entity, *felt* [*senti*] rather than thought out . . . an obscure feeling [*sensation*]" (PM, 245). The two (science highly conscious and humanity less so) constitute the two foci presently developing within the earth.

In past ages, humanity, the less conscious focus, was not recognized. And even two centuries ago, Teilhard claims, it would have taken "divination" "to *feel* [*sentir*] the beating heart of that sort of embryo." But the "magic" of humanity has continued to shape the politics of the world; humanity appears as "the still unnamed

Thing." Again we find the correlate (humanity) of the repressed S Function is associated with an embryo. It gradually appears in our depths as a mystery difficult to name.[10]

In telling of the "Sense of Man" or humanity, Teilhard was not telling of an "objective" reality seen before our eyes, but of a deeper identity that we *sense* within; and together we sense that we (humanity) are the wave of the future. He would see the motto of the French revolution, "Liberty, Fraternity, Equality," speaking obscurely to the common humanity that all of us share. "Even today the magical words are much more *felt (senti)* than understood" (*FM*, 251; emphasis in text). Again, the appeal arises from the "magical words" that we sense (unconscious), rather than from the clear words of science that we understand (conscious). But Teilhard will often pair the two: "Science and Humanity, " "science and society, " "technology and higher co-consciousness," etc. (*AE*, 379; 304); it is the "coming of science" that is "welding people and individuals one to another" (*TF*, 20).

When Teilhard wrote the first of his wartime essays and told of a presence arising in his own depths, he spoke of it as a somewhat impersonal Presence not fully Personal. So, in *The Phenomenon of Man*, the conclusion of evolution is first identified as a "still unnamed Thing." But the Thing gradually clarifies itself as personal or, rather, as Hyper-Personal. It is a planetary "Unanimity" (Latin: *una anima*), a world Soul, humanity with a single Within. It is more than the human Collectivity; it is the Collectivity united as a single Someone. In later texts he would speak of three stages of reflection. There is first the individual human (R1); then there is the human collectivity (R2), the society forming today wherein many individuals share a common vision. But he would go on to tell of R3, humanity united as a single Someone, humanity (R2) centered around Christ the divine Person.[11]

In *The Phenomenon of Man*, this single Soul is termed the Omega Point, the point suggesting a personal Center. It is the Center of human centers: "a distinct Centre radiating at the core of a system of centres" (*PM*, 262). The "system of centres" refers to the human multitude made up of many souls (R2); this multitude will eventually "reflect upon itself at a single point" (R3—*PM*, 187). This point is Omega, the goal of evolution, and the goal has four attributes, with the Fourth attribute set apart from the first three: "Autonomy, actuality, irreversibility, and finally transcendence are the four attributes of Omega" (*PM*, 271). Teilhard told often of the Omega Point and on two other occasions he listed it as having *four* properties. There would be slight differences in how he would name the four, [12] but in each case the Fourth transcends the process and is distinguished from the other Three. The Jungian symbolism is evident.

"Transcendence" can sound very similar to "transience," but the meanings are very different. "Transcendence" means that Omega must *transcend* the evolutionary process; thus Omega could be said to be three parts evolutionary process (transience) and one part transcendent God, 3-becomes-4. Omega obviously resembles what Jung called the Self. It unites Four qualities, it is the "higher Pole of evolution," and the place where the "radii meet" (*PM*, 259). The evolutionary process itself involves much transience; but the term of the process is the transcendent God. God is entering the process of evolution; by doing so the transcendent God gives the transient process what the process does not have, Stability. The appearance of the Fourth is again "religious."

In 1948, eight years after finishing *The Phenomenon of Man* and before it was published, Teilhard added a "Postscript" titled "The Essence of *The Phenomenon of Man*." It is excessively abstract, but "The Essence" can be understood as a bare-bones statement of the relationship of the N and the S, the Without and the Within presented earlier. The postscript tells of the planet's "organic *involution*" involving an "increase in interiorisation, that is to say in the psyche or consciousness" (*PM*, 301). "Involution" (folding inward) is a somewhat original word that Teilhard devised and set in contrast to Evolution (folding outward). Thus, one term tells of the S and the other of the N. In the beginning there was a "pre-cosmic phase of involution" (see *CE*, 192, 50). "Pre"-cosmic, because when there was only involution (S) there was no common world, no cosmos, only a dust of separate particles; each unit was radically turned in on itself. For there to be a cosmos, the dust particles had to turn out of themselves and relate; communality, N, was needed. This turning out of self made the dust a "cosmos" (made the separate trees a forest). This Teilhard would call the "cosmic, historical phase of evolution"; the elements share in a common process. Evolution and Involution are the N and the S, Vision and Sensation, the two foci of the ellipse presented earlier.

But Teilhard warns that all particles might not reach the final goal; for the particles could rebel and abandon the process. That is, they could involute in isolation. Thus, there is a conflict wherein each element is drawn "to evolution (life) and to involution (entropy)" (HE, 23; parentheses in text). The "involution (entropy)" would mean that the particles sink back into their isolation. Evolution (Latin root means an unfolding, an opening *out*; it is the N) is opposed to entropy (Greek root means a turning *in*; it is the S). Since evolution draws the elements together in a common process it opposes their turning in on themselves. This contrast between *Evolution* and *Entropy* runs through the texts of Teilhard (See *FM*, 50, 81, 91, 188; *HE*, 22, 98; *CE*, 109; *TF*, 114, etc.) The frequency with which he mentions the two and their opposition can be seen as a statement of his Enantiodromia. Teilhard favors Evolution and thus supports the N (out of self) over the S (in self)—till finally a higher form of the S is divinely given. This constitutes "the wholesale *introversion* upon itself of the noosphere" (*PM*, 287).

To partake in Evolution the dust particles must renounce their centers and proceed out of themselves, but then the rejected S Function must be restored; this means that Evolution itself will reach a final "Involution" in which the planet will turn in on itself to form a single psyche or World Soul (much as the carbon and oxygen atoms in the dog had to come out of themselves [N] to become part of the dog, but the dog has a common "soul," "within" [S], that is deeper than that of the atoms). Thus the postscript would tell of a final Omega, "a supreme pole of *interiorization*," a "transcendent focus" that is "born of involution" (*PM*, 309, 307). It is the universe involuting on itself. The elemental involutions of the cosmic dust had to be set aside so that a cosmos could come into being and evolve. But eventually the cosmos itself will attain its final involution. The involution that was rejected will return as cornerstone.

The original *Phenomenon of Man*, as finished in 1940, told of immanence being rejected for transience, a transience that leads to the final immanence. The 1948 "Summing Up or Postscript" omitted much of the scientific material of his original account and changed the vocabulary, but a Jungian could see it as the same story: involution was rejected for evolution, an evolution that leads to the final Involution. In both the text and the "Summing Up" the Jungian message stands out: the S is rejected for the N, and the N leads to a return of the S as cornerstone.

Jung said the Intuitive has a special relation with the unconscious, and this would seem to be verified by the Intuitives considered in the present study. The four Intuitive philosophers considered here offer clearer accounts of Integration than the other philosophers considered (with the possible exception of St. Augustine). But no account of Integration is as complete as the one found in the writings of Teilhard. These told of his seeking the S by making a descent to the unconscious. This required that his original identity "be broken down"; he had to suffer "a sort of decomposition" *(WT,* 125). "The mystical effort *to see* [N] must give way to the effort *to feel* [*sentir,* S] and to surrender" *(WT,* 125). This could recall similar claims by Jung and even passages from other Intuitives: Whitehead spoke of a final "Peace" that involves "the sublimation of the egoistic aim"; to explain the "surrender" Whitehead told of a noble Roman achieving greatness "by the sacrifice of himself" *(AI,* 293, 288). That is, to find the Repressed, the ego identity must be sacrificed. Sartre told of Antoine in Bouville: "Bouville: The vegetation has only surrounded three sides of it. On the fourth side there is a great hole of black water that moves by itself." "I am quietly slipping into the water's depths" *(N,* 156, 8). In the process he has discovered his rejected S, but only by surrendering his ego: "A pale reflection of myself wavers in my consciousness. . . . and suddenly the 'I' pales, pales, and fades out" *(N,* 170). Again, a loss of ego. This could also be seen in Plato: In his earlier dialogues Plato wrote of the death of Socrates. But years later he reintroduced the theme of Socrates going to his death at the end of the *Theaetetus.* If one recalls that Plato did not have the psychological vocabulary to tell of the loss of ego and disintegration of the Dominant, this reintroduction of the passing of Socrates (associated above with Plato's N) going to his death could be a way of telling of such a loss. Recall it is directly after this that the Stranger appears and accepts Sensation as Socrates could not. Only after the second account of the passing of Socrates is Plato able to accept the Giants (S) and proceed to Integration. Thus, all four Intuitives treated here could be seen as sacrificing the ego before either the Repressed or the Self (Transcendent Function) could appear.

But there is another common element in three of these Intuitives: after telling of the sacrifice of ego, Plato, Whitehead, and Teilhard tell of finding what are striking examples of the Jungian

Self. The three of these tell in their own vocabulary of passing beyond the ego to find a "Self" that consists in *a Quaternity of elements in balance*. In Plato it is found in his new understanding of Being, a reality that reconciled the Four opposing elements: Same and Other, Motion and Rest. In Whitehead it is found in his accounts of Peace, the "Harmony of harmonies" that reconciled Four qualities: Beauty, Truth, Adventure, and Art. While in Teilhard it is found in the Omega Point, the "Center of centers" that reconciled Four attributes: "Autonomy, actuality, irreversibility, and finally transcendence" (*PM*, 32). All three of these authors went through a time of conflict that was resolved only when they came upon a Quaternity of elements that united oppositions and gave them rest.

Sartre did not tell of such a final Quaternity, but one could argue he was moving in that direction by his continued striving to work the In-itself and the For-itself together; perhaps his atheism held back his complete Integration. Still in his final interviews Sartre seems to have suggested a somewhat messianic understanding of the future that involved a heavenly intervention that would even restore the dead to life. One could argue that the outside intervention (a characteristic of the Self—Whitehead: Peace "comes as a gift" [*AI*, 284]) alluded to in these controversial interviews suggest the possibility of help from a Divinity of sorts.[13] In any case an intervention apart from the system was involved, what Jung would refer to as "grace."

But the striking fact for the present study is that all of the Intuitives considered here told of what could be seen as a surrender/sacrifice of the ego/Dominant. And three of these Intuitives, Plato, Whitehead, and Teilhard, went on to tell of a wondrous reconciliation of Opposites in a Quaternity of Four elements in balance. That is the basic Jungian paradigm of Integration, and it is particularly evident in the Intuitive personality (Jung suggested the Intuitive has better access to the unconscious).

But beyond the Intuitives, the present study has shown how this paradigm, with its Quaternities and Three-Fours, can be found in philosophers of all four Dominants. By using the Jungian paradigm one can gain a fresh and unified perspective on the works of the great philosophers. Perhaps a terminology for dealing with the differences among philosophers could be developed out of this study. But this terminology would have to allow for the fact that some philosophers simply have presented a philosophy of the Dominant (Descartes), while others did not start writing philosophy until Integration began (Teilhard), while still others first developed a philosophy of the Dominant and then developed a second philosophy telling of Integration (Plato).

It is far from clear why some people leave the beaten path of common opinion to engage in a personal struggle with what Jung called the Collective Unconscious. But many people have done so and among these are the creative philosophers. The present study has considered many such struggles and seen their writings as personal statements.

Today the history of philosophy shows radical differences among philosophers of the greatest distinction. The present work uses the Types of Jung to understand the different starting points of the philosophers, then uses Jung's paradigms of Enantiodromia, and Integration to tell of their development. Jung's accounts of the Types, Enantiodromia, and Integration readily suggest philosophic implications, but I am not aware of other sustained attempts to relate them to figures in the history of philosophy. This I have tried to do. But I claim to show something else: the great texts in philosophy telling of Being, humanity, the cosmos, and so forth, also show what Socrates knew at the beginning of Western philosophy: philosophy involves the quest of the soul for salvation.

Notes

1. Teilhard was aware of Jung: in 1934 he read one of his articles ("Does the World Stand on the Verge of a Spiritual Rebirth?") and recommended it to a friend: "The ideas substantially are curiously akin to mine" (*LTS*, 15). A friend tells of Teilhard having in the 1950s a "wide knowledge and appreciation of Jung's theories" (Cuenot, 312). The present author has worked for years with the texts of Teilhard and even read many of his *carnets des lectures;* he sees little basis for this claim. The unpublished journals of Teilhard have five references to Jung from May 19, 1946 to January 14, 1955. The final reference is the most substantial and it reflects on an article on Jung that appeared in *Time.* But the limited extent of Teilhard's familiarity is best seen in the way he spells Jung as "Young" or "Yung." A friend of Jung's (Miguel Serrano) tells of visiting Jung shortly before his death and coming into his room: "On the small table beside the chair where Jung was sitting was a book called *The Phenomenon of Man* by Teilhard de Chardin. I asked Jung whether he had read it. 'It is a great book,' he said" (Serrano, 100–101).

2. This descent and rising is not unknown in the Christian tradition.

St. Paul tells of Christ having "descended into the lower parts of the earth. He who descended is he who also ascended far above all the heavens" (Eph. 4:11). The descent and rising is present when Paul claims that we have been buried with Christ and will rise with him. St. Augustine uses the same descent and rising up. In his *Confessions* he picks up on Christ's descent and rising; then he asks the proud: "But how can you raise yourselves when you are already high in the air . . . ? Come down, so that you may go up and go up toward God" (*CE*, 82). This descent and rising became a regular theme in Teilhard: he tells of a cycle that brings one "down to the bowels of matter in its full multiplicity, thence to climb back to the center of spiritual unification" (*SC*, 36); it is found again when he tells of a first phase wherein he felt "the need to descend, step by step, to ever more elementary beliefs," and "in a second phase, I try to re-ascend the natural series" (*CE*, 99). Jung would see the descent and rising referring to the descent from the ego and the rising to the Self; Jung would see the same process in terms that speak of dissolution and reconstitution. Teilhard would use a similar terminology.

3. To be a mystic Teilhard had rejected the tangible; Teilhard was an N rejecting his Repressed. Kierkegaard told of the mystic rejecting time; Kierkegaard as T was rejecting a different Repressed.

4. Jung writes: "Sensation creates ties to the object, it even pulls the subject into the object; hence the "danger" for the naive type consists in his vanishing into it altogether" (*PT*, 133). So Teilhard tells of being pulled into the object, into the sensation.

5. Here the texts of Teilhard speak of the change in terms of being "not selfish" but religious. Teilhard will speak often of this other Identity within him and always speak of it in religious terms. See my presentation in *Teilhard de Chardin*, 142.

6. Recall that Plato had come to a form of the world soul as a reconciliation of his N and S (see above)—so with Teilhard. Jung tells of Egyptians symbolizing the world soul by a cross inside a circle.

7. See my treatment of this in *Teilhard de Chardin*, 144–58.

8. Teilhard uses similar phrases on other occasions: he tells of humans coming together "from the four corners of space" (*AE*, 350), "universalization causes the four currents to converge" (*AE*, 95), and so forth. He had seen the human symbolized in a special way as the union of eye and hand; the same union is implied when he speaks of the final Omega: "Omega . . . . only forms for our *eyes* and offers itself for our *touch*" (*HE*, 149). Quaternity and the union of N and S is again implied when he explains "at a universal crossroads, everything can be *seen*, can be *felt (senti)*" (*AE*, 87). All such phrases suggest the union of *Vision* and *Sensation* considered in his first essay.

9. Consider a dozen texts wherein Teilhard tells of Threes-becoming-Fours: he speaks of "Three successive pairs of alternatives offering four possibilities," so that there are "Four separate roads [that] lie open to us, one back and three f orward." "The four roads are not a fiction" (*FM*, 49). "The three characteristics which make the human individual a truly unique object in the

eyes of Science . . . to these must be added a fourth" (*FM*, 90; note, the fourth is apart from Science, from the faculty of consciousness). He tells of "three aspects of one and the same fundamental process; they are aspects of a fourth mystery. . . . To distinguish this mystery from the other three we must. . . ." (*CE*, 133; note the missing element is "mystery"). There are "the following three (or even four) successive theorems" (*FM*, 223; parenthesis in the text). "Three currents today, or to speak more precisely four, are sweeping us. . . . Behold the fourth spirit [Christianity]" (*SC*, 128). He claimed his spiritual autobiography "has to be woven from four (and not only three) threads" (*HM*, 77; *LTF*, 212; parenthesis in the text). There are four parts to *The Phenomenon of Man*: "The fourth is my pet" (*LTF*, 137). His unpublished journal tells of "three discoveries" and then he lists four (J, 4/Nov./50); it tells of "the Christic" involving three reflections plus an emergence (J, 11/July/52). His retreat notes ask, "Is there not a sort of fourth mystery in Christianity—distinct from" Creation, Incarnation and Redemption? The fourth (Pleromatization) "is a synthesis and crowning of the three" (Retreat Notes, 1945). "For various reasons, all three of these solutions are to be feared. . . . There is, without possible doubt, a fourth way out of the problem" (*DM*, 52–53). Additional Three-Fours in Teilhard will be presented as this study continues.

10. In my earlier writings on Teilhard I have shown in detail how the "twin sisters," science and humanity, include what had been twin aspects of the Cosmic awakening, *La Vision* and *La Sensation* (see King, *Teilhard's Mysticism of Knowing*, 92–101; *Teilhard de Chardin*, 119–20). The association of Humanity with the S is further evident in the many times that Teilhard will use the terms Humanity and Sense of Man as equivalent.

11. The abbreviations R1, R2, and R3 are found only once in Teilhard's published works but occur many times in his unpublished journals. Still the three-phase sequence is evident in many places in his published writings. For an extended treatment of the three reflections, see my *Teilhard de Chardin*, pp. 130–43.

12. On one occasion he identifies the four as: centered, individual, actual, and transcendent (*AE*, 112). On another occasion he tells of them as three: reality, totalising power, and irreversibility; having done so, he asks if they form "three sufficient attributes." They do not, so he suggests as fourth a "necessary being" who is "already existing" (*AM*, 271–72).

13. Many interesting comparisons can be made in terms of the present study. One such comparison would indicate that Sartre and Teilhard made much of "knowing" (consciousness) and the known, but they identified them differently. Sartre, mindful of the intentionality of consciousness, identified it with the N; while Teilhard, mindful of the interiority and privacy of consciousness, identified it with the S. Thus, Sartre identified the subject with N and the object with S, while Teilhard did the reverse. Yet both of them tried to work the N and S together.

Bibliography

Works of Teilhard

AE   *Activation of Energy*, translated by René Hague. New York: Harcourt Brace Jovanovich, 1963.

AM   *The Appearance of Man*, translated by J. M. Cohen. New York: Harper & Row: 1965.

CE   *Christianity and Evolution*, translated by René Hague. New York: Harcourt Brace Jovanovich, Harvest Books, 1971.

DM   *The Divine Milieu*, translator unidentified. New York: Harper & Row, Harper Torchbooks, 1960.

FM   *The Future of Man*, translated by Norman Denny. New York: Harper Colophon, 1969.

HE   *Human Energy*, translated by J. M. Cohen. New York: Harcourt Brace Jovanovich, Harvest Books, 1969.

HM   *The Heart of Matter*, translated by René Hague. New York: Harcourt Brace Jovanovich, 1978.

J   *Journal*, volume I, (August 26, 1915—January 4, 1919), edited by Nicole and Karl Schmitz-Moormann. Paris: Fayard, 1975. *J* followed by a date refers to the unpublished notebooks from the final years of Teilhard's life. They are at the Jesuit House at Chantilly, France.

LTS *The Letters of Teilhard de Chardin and Lucile Swan*, edited and annotated by Thomas M. King, S.J., and Mary Wood Gilbert. Washington: Georgetown University Press, 1993.

LT   *Letters from a Traveler*, translator not identified. New York: Harper & Row, 1965.

PM   *The Phenomenon of Man*, translated by Bernard Wall. New York: Harper Colophon, 1975.

SC   *Science and Christ*, translated by René Hague. New York: Harper & Row, 1968.

TF   *Towards the Future*, translated by René Hague. New York: Harcourt Brace Jovanovich, A Helen & Kurt Wolff Book, 1975.

VP   *The Vision of the Past*, translated by J. M. Cohen. New York: Harper & Row, 1966.

WT   *Writings in Time of War*, translated by René Hague. New York: Harper & Row, 1968.

Other Works

Cuénot, Claude. *Teilhard de Chardin: A Biographical Study,* translated by Vincent Colimore. London: Burns & Oates, 1965.

King, Thomas M. *Teilhard de Chardin.* Collegeville, Minn.: Glazier/ Liturgical Press, 1988.

King, Thomas M. *Teilhard's Mysticism of Knowing.* New York: Seabury, 1981.

Serrano, Miguel. *C. G. Jung and Hermann Hesse: A Record of Two Friendships.* New York: Schocken, 1968.

EPILOGUE
A Final Reflection

I hope to have shown that many philosophical differences can be considered in terms of Jung's psychological types; but having done so I find it difficult to state my own philosophy. I know I have a dominant T (only a T would have written this study) and I am wary of claiming the truth of a philosophy that simply reflects my Dominant. Yet I believe that everyone must have a philosophy, explicitly or implicitly, and some sort of stance on religion. I have read much philosophy mindful of Jungian types and remain more philosopher than psychologist; that is, I am unwilling to allow psychological types and processes of Integration to answer what remain real philosophic and religious questions.

I

Others writers have suggested that psychology or personal taste is at the basis of philosophical differences. Most notably, William James: "The history of philosophy is to a great extent that of a certain clash of human temperaments." Accordingly, he would "explain a good many of the divergences of philosophers by it [temperament]." Though he would apply his categories of temperament (tough-minded and tender-minded) to evaluate philosophers, he did not think his study would change the situation; for "temperaments with their cravings and refusals do determine men in their philosophies and always will" (James, 11, 24).[1] Rudolf Carnap noted the importance of psychological types in philosophy when he wrote an early presentation of linguistic philosophy. He suggested that Jung's distinction between Extrovert and Introvert might explain the difference between Realists and Idealists (Carnap, 30). The difference between Extrovert and Introvert would be a good place to begin a personal and philosophic reflection: In the Introduction I told of setting aside the present work for many years. It was largely because I felt Jung had left me enclosed within my mind—and I wanted out. So I set the project aside and came to a more Extroverted understanding of both Jung and myself; it developed out of my awareness of two ideas from medieval philosophy: the Four Transcendental Properties of Being and the Intentionality of Consciousness.

The Transcendental Properties are four qualities possessed by every being: every being is One, True, Good, and Beautiful, properties that readily coincide with Sensation, Thinking, Feeling, and Intuition. These four Properties were seen to differ from other properties in that they did not depend on the existence of their opposites: e.g., the existence of "one" does not require the existence of "many, " but this cannot be reversed (for there to be many there *first* must be one).[2] As Four properties possessed by any and every *being*, the Quaternity would be taken out of the psyche and put into the object known: every *being* is one, true, good, and beautiful.

But placing the Four in the object known does not explain how different people have different philosophic perspectives (different Dominants). These differences seem better explained by different Functions in the psyche rather than by differences in the object. So much is evident, but this could mean no more than one person has a greater sensitivity to a particular transcendental Property (the True, the Good) much as one person might have better hearing and another better sight, while what is heard or seen is objective. An N would be more aware of interrelationships and Beauty, while an S would be more sensitive to detail and the concrete singular. But still each is aware of something "given" in the world. As aware of a property in the world, one is again a Realist.

But beyond speaking of the transcendentals, medieval philosophers also spoke of intentionality, an important element in contemporary phenomenology. The intentionality of consciousness would claim that consciousness is fundamentally an orientation to the object known. Both the transcendental properties and intentionality bring one out of the psyche.

Jung spoke abundantly of psychological Functions or Faculties, and this suggests a strongly Introverted orientation. But occasionally Jung spoke as if the Types are based upon properties of the external world—properties of Being:

> Only one part of the world, therefore, can be grasped by thinking, another part only by feeling, a third only through sensation, and so on. That is probably why there are different psychic functions; for, biologically, the psychic system can be understood only as a system of adaptation, just as eyes exist presumably because there is light. (*PT*, 99)

This passage seems to make the Functions secondary to a Property in the objective world, as eyes are secondary to the light. In speaking of "a system of *adaptation*," Jung suggests that the Functions developed as adaptations to *properties of Being*. The intentionality of consciousness also gets one out of the psyche and into the world. Thus, in terms of the present study, a Thinker would be dealing with the Truth of Being and a Feeler with its Goodness. Each would be dealing with an objective reality, and each would have a blind spot corresponding to the Repressed. Thus, their philosophies could not be reduced to their psychology and they would each have a real and differing insight into being.

I find this somewhat Extroverted reading of the philosophers more congenial than one that would stay within archetypes of the psyche. But at the same time I do not believe its superiority can be proven, just as the history of philosophy has shown (to me) that Idealists and Realists cannot refute each other. But the Idealists and many passages of Jung leave me too much within my mind, so I am freed by accepting the intentionality of consciousness. Have I taken this stand only because I am not a *radical* Introvert? Radical Idealism and radical Realism are not to my "liking"; but, beyond that, either of these radical positions seems to ignore some of the material about which one should philosophize.

I am a *moderate* Introvert, but still an Introvert, so I maintain that, beyond the intentionality of consciousness, there is also the *non*intentionality of consciousness and thus some value in speaking of psychic faculties. That is, every observation also tells of the mind of the observer. What would this mean in the present context?

Consider some of the philosophers presented. In the *Republic* Socrates/Plato sets out to tell of justice *in the soul*. But finding the soul difficult to "see," Socrates spoke explicitly of the state, as there justice and injustice are more evident (*I*, 631). Today the *Republic* is generally considered a political text, though Socrates' partners in dialogue knew he really was telling of the soul—or was he? In reading the *Republic* one realizes that one was the analogue of the other. Perhaps this is frequently the case, that is, whenever we speak philosophically, we also tell of ourselves—and vice versa. This double quality (speaking of both object and soul) is evident in many other philosophers. A commentator on St. Augustine would see his *Confessions* telling of a personal conversion while his *City of God* told the same story, this time as the conversion of culture.[3] Whitehead did the same: he told of the awakening to physical science that occurred from the Middle Ages to the present, but he was also telling of his own movement from abstract mathematics (N) to a physics and philosophy that involved his S as well as his N; he acknowledged that both the objective and subjective elements were involved: "The great periods of history. . . . reveal ourselves to ourselves" (*AI*, 168). Could not Socrates have made a similar claim, "Political structures reveal ourselves to ourselves"?

A similar double account of object and soul is evident in Teilhard's first essay telling of a Cosmic Awakening: he was telling of human consciousness "awaking" in the course of evolution and also telling of his own soul awaking to its cosmic dimension. By telling of both together, Teilhard was integrating his soul into the Soul of the Cosmos. So he spoke of his soul as a microcosm within the cosmic macrocosm. His accounts of the two in a common evolution have enabled me to situate myself in the scheme of things. Teilhard was a research scientist who worked for years in the classification of fossil bones, yet he asked if zoologists really discovered evolution in the world, "or quite simply and unconsciously have they recognized and expressed themselves in it?" (*VP*, 69). If that could be true of the scientific studies of Teilhard, could it not be true in the social studies of Augustine or the political studies of Socrates? Was not each expressing himself and situating himself into an ideal state as a microcosm within a macrocosm, while Augustine and Whitehead were situating themselves into social and cultural changes of their times? I find this double reading of philosophical texts more "satisfying" than the radical dualism (subject and object) implicit in much philosophy, a dualism that leaves the conscious ego facing an objective world that is alien to the observer. I would argue that this alienation between subject and object tells of the individual before Integration.

Many philosophers in the course of their writing came to see the "subject" of consciousness as "wider" or "deeper" than the ego. Teilhard would see the *subject* of consciousness as including the World: "We are the world come to consciousness," "We have found the world in our souls." This Subject more ultimate than the ego is what Jung has called the Self; the Self of Teilhard included Humanity ("We" in the above passages), Matter, and God. Accordingly, Teilhard would speak of finding what is "myself and more than myself . . . God with us"; Whitehead put it: "In being ourselves we are more than ourselves." (I have written at length of this higher "Self" in Teilhard: *Teilhard's Mysticism of Knowing*, 101–8; *Teilhard de Chardin*, 65–102; in *Zygon*, March, 1995, vol. 30: 1). All such phrases suggest that the radical opposition between subject and object is not the final truth.

I would find Jung's Integrated individual (four Functions in balance) in a better position than the non-Integrated individual working only with the Ego-and-Dominant. But I am not willing to make the claim that a Dominant T is superior to a Dominant F, and so forth.[4]

At one time philosophy was seen as a healing of the soul, and I would like to see that understanding restored. Philosophy has developed out of the advice given to Socrates, "Know thyself." This is what many of the great philosophers were trying to do, so their philosophic texts tell of their troubled souls as well as their thoughts on being. That could mean that our souls are not alien to the universe. Teilhard has claimed, "It is through that which is most deeply personal in us that we make contact with the universal" (*CE*, 98). This claim is radically opposed to a dualism, often assumed, that would set the knowing subject as wholly other than the world. But Teilhard's claim also brings to mind the phrase telling of Hindu enlightment, "Atman is Brahman"; that is, the ultimate subject coincides with the ultimate object, a claim that can be realized only at the end of a difficult process (Integration?). To come to this awareness there must be a double exploration, a probing of both the personal soul and the objective universe—a double exploration found in the great philosophers—but finally the two explorations are found to be one. By exploring their own souls they learned of objective Being, and by exploring Being they learned of their own souls. So philosophers came to speak, often with amazement, of discovering what is both Another and one's self, the Jungian Self.

But in seeing philosophy as a deliverance of the soul, I see a distinction made by Jung of some significance. Jung told of both a Personal Unconscious and the Collective Unconscious, a difference not invoked earlier in the present work. The Personal Unconscious would contain the repressed images which have originated in one's personal past, while the Collective Unconscious, often said to be "beneath" the Personal Unconscious, would deal with the "cosmic" themes philosophers are wont to consider (God and the universe, life and death, good and evil, etc.). Jung claimed most dreams deal with matter from the Personal Unconscious and many people need only a healing of their personal life. "In practice it quite often happens that the whole treatment takes place on the personal plane, without the patient having any inner experiences that are definite enough to necessitate his coming to terms with the collective beliefs" (PR, 308). But none of the individuals considered in the present text would be of this type, for if they did not have to deal with the "big" issues, "collective beliefs," they would not be considered philosophers. They each had to deal with what Jung calls the Archetypes of the Collective Unconscious, and these introduce philosophical and religious issues. In general Jung believed that the elements of the Personal Unconscious should be dealt with first, if that is possible. Coming to terms with the Personal Unconscious was called the apprentice-piece, while coming to terms with the Collective Unconscious is the masterpiece. The masterpiece would contain the great cosmic images that run through the history of philosophy. The present work has considered many such masterpieces.

When St. Augustine spoke of the City of God, it was both a change in culture and a conversion of his psyche. Perhaps a healing at this deeper level can come about only through a personal struggle with the cosmic questions, a struggle that one does not undertake on one's own and for which one cannot predict the outcome. But this struggle runs through the writers considered in the present text.[5] And, starting with Plato's Stranger telling of a "perilous enterprise" and apparent madness, I have often cited the anguished passages of the great philosophers as these tell in a unique way of the work of the philosopher struggling to state what has taken one beyond the clarity of the conscious mind.

II

Psychologists often speak of "projection," and the present Jungian reflection will encourage some to dismiss philosophy as nothing more than that. Thus, Plato was simply projecting his psyche onto politics; Augustine and Whitehead were simply projecting their psyches onto cultural history. But this claim arises from an unexamined conviction that the dualism of subject and object is the great and final truth to which all must conform. But, for one who accepts the value of Integration as presented by Jung, the final truth must take one beyond the radical opposition of a knowing subject facing the object known.

To pass beyond the subject-object dichotomy it seems one must first work within it. So just as one might argue that it is all projection, one could also argue the reverse: one is able to understand a political or social situation only because of one's personal situation, much as an alcoholic can quickly recognize another alcoholic, it takes a thief to catch a thief, and so forth. When the behavior of an alcoholic gives me an understanding of my own behavior, I might speak of "introjection." Likewise, in terms of Plato: by hearing Socrates tell of corruption ruining the state, his listeners could recognize the corruption ruining their souls. In each case one's own life gives one a special insight into the state, or history, or evolution, etc. I would suggest that generally there is both projection and introjection; or, speaking more truly, I claim that in fact each of us is integrated into a wider context wherein the subject-object dichotomy is not the final word.

I would see the ego/subject in opposition to the world/object as the position of one with a strong Dominant. The descent to the Unconscious and the appearance of the Self ends the radical opposition between ego and world; and that is why it is so frightening, for the ego boundary disappears. For the Self is myself and more than that; it is within me and yet is more than I; it is my integration into the scheme of things, something that the ego before Integration can never know. It would seem the ego is always a unit facing a world (as Descartes and others would have it), facing it with Intellect or Heart, with Intuition or Sense. But in each case there is a subject and object dualism, while Jung would speak of the Self as a unity of subject and object. As Unity of the Opposites it would be I and more than I; it would also be the world (the object) as subject. Whitehead: "In being ourselves we are more than ourselves" (*SM*, 25). Such a claim can be made only by one who knows a Self that is more than the ego.

In identifying only with the ego I know the world before me as objective and somewhat alien, and other people are wholly other. The most common way of reducing the alienation is for an individual to "identify" with another human being. This usually happens within one's family—and, if it does not, one might seek a therapist. Then one might "project" a parental role onto the therapist, and also "introject" the therapist into one's inner life. Thereby the therapist becomes a supportive element in the patient's soul, and this works towards a personal healing. One is no longer alone and facing an alien world, for one has known the healing of human rapport. It is as if another is within me and *facing the same world I have to face;* the other "understands."[6] So in telling of his work Jung would speak of an "attentive entering into the personality of the patient" (*MDR*, 128). After one has been attentively entered, one's ego is no longer simply "facing" the rest of the universe; there is at least one other facing the same world and with whom one can identify. This is human rapport: the dualism of ego vs. the universe has ended; *every-thing other than the ego is no longer alien.*

The doctor has entered "into the personality of the patient." Perhaps the patient talks within to this other, and the other (the doctor) does not threaten but understands. But still there is an "intentionality," for the other within refers to someone who is without; if one would quarrel with the other without (perhaps one's therapist), the inner dialogue is stymied. I present this reflection on personal healing only to argue that intentionality continues to be present in all consciousness. The other (the therapist or friend) is both within and without. The "personal unconscious" is being healed in having another who is within/without; healing means one is no longer a lonely ego facing the world.

So much for the Personal Unconscious. But what of the "Collective Unconscious" and what of the Self?

Here the problem of projection occurs in a special way, for one could claim that God is simply a projection of the psyche. But perhaps both projection and introjection are involved. Jung puts it well when considering "the archetypes of Deity": he says that these archetypes "not only give one the feeling of pointing to the *Ens realissimum* but make one convinced that they actually express it and establish it as a fact" (*PR*, 363). He explains, "The image and the statement are psychic processes which are different from their transcendental object; they do not posit it, they merely point to it" (*PR*, 363). And again, "pointing" suggests the intentionality of consciousness. Within we have the Image of God, but like all images it points to what it images; that is, like all consciousness it too is intentional.

Jung is here relating the Image of God to the "Self," as he often did. But that is not the whole story of Jung's references to God. Beyond his association of God with the Self, he sometimes associated God with two other elements of the psyche: sometimes with the Conscious mind, and sometimes with the (Collective) Unconscious.[7] And Jung could justify these *three* ways of associating elements of the psyche with God by appealing to religious texts—or to philosophic texts. To avoid generalities one might consider a specific author to which one might appeal: Whitehead. In considering Whitehead (above) many parallels were drawn between Whitehead's theology and his psyche: his "cosmic" triad (Creativity, Primordial nature of God, and Consequent nature of God) was compared with his psychic triad: Instinct, Intelligence and Wisdom. One could ask if his theology was only his psychology writ large. (Was Whitehead formed in the image of God or was his God formed in the image of Whitehead?) Perhaps God and the mind are so deeply related that to know one necessitates knowing the other (and blindness to one leaves one blind to the other). Whitehead spoke of God as "the mirror which discloses to every creature its own greatness" (*RM*, 155). Which is the image and which is the mirror? Must the answer be one-sided? Augustine and Rousseau insisted they wanted to know only God and the soul; for them it was a single quest.

Whitehead had proposed "a reciprocal law of being." According to this reciprocity, a being "is only itself as drawing together into its own limitation the larger whole in which it finds itself. Conversely it is only itself by lending its aspects to this same environment in which it finds itself" (*SM*, 89). For Whitehead this environment included God, so he could become himself only by drawing God into himself and in the process lend an aspect of himself to God (to form the consequent nature of God). Would it be adequate to call this introjection and projection? Ultimately, I would not see it that way, for both terms suggest a disruption of a true order. It could be an awakening: Atman is Brahman. It was only by coming to this understanding that Whitehead could again consider himself a theist. But in asking what part of the psyche imaged God and in responding with the texts of Whitehead, I am suggesting that *three* aspects of Whitehead imaged God (Instinct, Intelligence, and Wisdom). In the treatment of Whitehead included here I identified these three with, respectively, his (Collective) Unconscious, his Consciousness, and his Self. Having suggested that all three image God, I will go further and suggest there are significant parallels between the triad of Whitehead, Jung, and others and the Christian Trinity.[8]

That is, I would claim that the Persons of the Trinity, Father, Son and Spirit, and their interrelations have significant parallels with the Unconscious, Consciousness, and Self of Jung. I would also see the Trinity reflected in Whitehead's Creativity, Primordial and Consequent Natures of God. The Father, the Godhead, would parallel the mysterious Unconscious, but before all ages He has given birth to the Son, known as the Logos, a term that suggests Consciousness. Christ (the divine Son) is thus the knowability of God, and for some time Christ as a knowable and human ideal was enough for his disciples and many Christians. But the time came for the Paschal mystery, a mystery that included his painful death (sometimes the Christian tradition spoke of the death in psychological terms as a *sacrificium intellectus*, or *incendium mentis*).

There was even a suggestion of Enantiodromia (conflict of the Opposites) as Christ prayed, "My Father, if it be possible, let this cup pass from me." But he surrendered to the Father's will: "Not as I will, but as thou wilt." Christ the Logos must die (consciousness must surrender to the great mystery that presses upon it; in Jungian terms, "the *deus absconditus* shall rise to the surface and press the god of our ideals [here Christ] to the wall" [Jung, *PR*, 96]). Christian theology has not done well in explaining why Christ had to die; perhaps it is because any rational explanation would involve only the conscious mind, and it is precisely this that must surrender (*sacrificium intellectus*). The Conscious mind, the ego, must die (and be buried); only then can the mysterious Spirit appear. Jesus, in saying farewell to his disciples, told them, "It is to your advantage that I go away, for if I do not go away the Counselor [Spirit] will not come to you" (John 16:7). The same phrase could be said by the Conscious mind as it makes its surrender (could Socrates have said, "It is to your advantage that I go away," as he departed in the *Theaetetus?*) and allows the Self to appear, that is, to be born within. So in the Gospels the coming of the Spirit is associated with a birth, a second birth (John 3:4–6; 16:21). Jung spoke abundantly of the "birth" of the Self.[9]

Thus, I propose a way of associating the Trinity with the Jungian structure; it would see the Father, Son, and Spirit in analogy with the Unconscious, Consciousness, and the Self. It would also tell well of the subtle interrelations by which Christians have spoken of the Persons of the Trinity: The Son proceeds from the Father, while the Spirit proceeds from both Father and Son (the Western understanding of the Trinity).[10] In Jungian terms the Self proceeds from both the Unconscious and the Conscious mind. The West developed a natural theology (as the Christian East did not); this suggests that our conscious mind on its own can argue to some understanding of God, a God that can be seen to resemble the Conscious mind rendered absolute. This can be seen in writings of those proposing a natural theology from Plato to Whitehead (his Primordial Nature of God). But, following St. Paul, we also can know supernatural religion (the great Mystery), but only by a death with Christ (*crucifixio intellectus?*) and being buried with him—and what follows is beyond natural theology.[11] It is the Spirit as gift.

In the present context the Paschal mystery (the death and resurrection of Jesus) would be the story of our own deliverance, a deliverance that proceeds only by what St. Paul presented as the foolishness of the cross (1 Cor. 1:16). It is called a foolishness because it goes beyond Consciousness. It would parallel the foolishness that Spinoza was accused of in some of the phrases that told of

God as Intellectual Love and of humans with personal immortality. His critics were quick to point out that he went beyond his rational and geometric method; likewise, Kant was criticized for introducing God to reconcile Knowledge and Feeling, after he had carefully kept them apart. In each case one goes beyond the God that is simply the God of one's conscious mind. Perhaps Spinoza and Kant could be seen as passing beyond their methods to offer a personal testimony that was beyond the natural theologies they had intended to write.

St. Augustine wrote of an extended psychological analogue of the Trinity. I cannot see the present sequence (Son from Father and Spirit from Father and Son) in what he has written, yet his account of the Trinity does tell of God as being, loving, and knowing; this triad would suggest the elements of his Enantiodromia (F and T united in Being), elements he found united in Being or in what Jung would call the Self (Kant's *Opus Postumum* often spoke of a similar Triad: *Ens Summum, Summa Intelligentia, Summum Bonum*). Such is an outline of how the basic Jungian structure might coordinate with Christian theology. That is, the Unconscious and its associated Function would suggest the Father; Consciousness and its associated Function would suggest the Son (the Logos); and the Transcendent Function would suggest the Spirit within, a Spirit that proceeds from both the Father and the Son, a Spirit that is said to be one with our own spirit ("He who is united to the Lord becomes *one spirit* with him" [1 Cor. 6:17]). The Spirit is God within us, the Image of God.

III

In writing the opening section I identified myself as a T, and so I am. But as I complete the work I recognize how largely my conclusions could suggest that I have been working as an F. After Rousseau listened to the Savoyard Vicar, he said, "To the extent that he spoke to me according to his conscience, mine seemed to confirm what he had told me" (*E*, 294). And that expresses well how I have listened to the philosophers considered here. At times many of them took on a special tone as if they were speaking straight from their conscience, and when they seemed to do so my own conscience was confirming what they said. I have considered a broad spread of philosophers, but I have probably given a prominence to "religious" philosophers:

Plato, Augustine, Kierkegaard, Whitehead, Teilhard, and even Sartre (for Sartre as religious see my *Sartre and the Sacred*). By including Sartre I am saying that "religion" concerns those who have to deal with the Collective Unconscious. The prominence of religious philosophers says something about the authors that appeal to me, but it also introduces Jung's understanding of the value of religion: "When a problem is grasped as a religious one, it means, psychologically, it is seen as something very important, of particular value, something that concerns the whole man, and hence also the unconscious (the realm of the gods, the other world)" (*PT*, 192).

Jung tells of working with hundreds of patients, and concerning those older than thirty-five he writes,

> there has not been one whose problem in the last resort was not that of finding a religious outlook on life. It is safe to say that every one of them fell ill because he had lost what the living religions of every age have given to their followers, and none of them has been really healed who did not regain his religious outlook. (*PR*, 334)

In the present study I have treated some impressive philosophers who have *not* really gone beyond the conscious Function (or Functions) as philosophers. This was most notable with Descartes and Hume, both of whom probed into mystery—and then backed away. I clearly favor those who seek Integration of the missing Function after a difficult struggle. Thus I would see religion involving a descent into the land of mystery. One who stays with a single conscious Function might well believe in God, but the writings of such a one would not have a religious or "numinous" tone. The difference could well be seen in the famous line of Pascal: "Not the God of the philosophers, but the God of Abraham, Isaac and Jacob." Pascal's "God of the philosophers" is the God of Consciousness, while the God of Abraham takes one into the turmoil beyond, a God with whom the "religious philosophers" had to deal (some philosophers can be faithful believers but not be religious philosophers). It is the development of one's own religious philosophy that the present study considers important.[12] Like Jung, I favor those who, as philosophers, have struggled to find a "religious outlook."

I have found a passage of Henri Bergson that speaks of the great philosophers having much in common—it too would favor the "religious" philosophers:

> The divergencies between the schools [of philosophy]—that is, broadly speaking, between the groups of disciples formed round a few great masters—are certainly striking. But would we find them as marked between the masters themselves? Something here dominates the diversity of systems, something, we repeat, which is simple and definite like a sounding, about which one feels that it has touched at greater or less depth the bottom of the same ocean, though each time it brings up to the surface very different materials. It is on the materials that the disciples usually work; in this lies the function of analysis. And the master, in so far as he formulates, develops, and translates into abstract ideas what he brings, is already in a way his own disciple. (*IM*, 60)

I suggest that Descartes and Hume spent their later years as their own disciples, clarifying and presenting anew what they had found. The image of sounding the ocean bottom suggests a probing of the Unconscious, and in presenting this passage I am again indicating a preference for the philosophers who have descended into mystery. The passage suggests that the great philosophers have probed a common ocean and told of it in words that find a universal echo.

The probe itself makes a philosopher religious; without it one might well believe in God—there seems to be a minimal theology in Hume (he is often considered a Deist), but he was not religious. Kierkegaard spoke of those for whom "God becomes an invisible vanishing point, a powerless thought" (*FT*, 78). Kierkegaard was a T, and this phrase tells of those who align God with the dominant Function and go no further. Such a God is the Function writ large ("a powerless thought"); it is not a God with whom one might have dealings, and it would not involve one in the great mystery of Being. In a similar way, Whitehead said the Primordial nature of God was not the God of religions; this study would claim the Primordial nature is simply the God reflecting his Dominant. Jung spoke of the "descent to the *deus absconditus*, who possesses qualities very different from those of the God who shines by day" (*PT*, 253). This descent could be identified with the descent of Jesus to the underworld, to his Father. The descent is the willingness to come to know the dark divinity, the Unknown God that dwells apart from Consciousness, and this descent makes one religious. It is a search for the God ignored by the rationalists, whether they be atheists or theologians.

I value in a special way the philosophers who descended to the

deus absconditus, the mysterious divinity of which their consciousness could not conceive. My three favorite books tell of such a descent: the *Confessions* of St. Augustine, the *Either/Or* of Kierkegaard,
and the *Writings in Time of War* of Teilhard. The three texts were written by a dominant F, a dominant T, and a dominant N, and they are
all radically different. But each of them tells of a descent to the *deus
absconditus* and a struggle to put what they found into new words.

Hume was not a religious man, nor was he sympathetic to religion. But he called for a state church and religious symbols, for he
believed these could neutralize the religious drive so it would no
longer be fanatical and destructive. As both a priest and a philosopher and one deeply affected by Jung, I have worked for decades
with religious symbols. These symbols and a study of comparative
religions have left me less fanatical, but they have not made me less
religious. I could point out that Ludwig Wittgenstein had a philosophy that was apart from religion, yet in telling of his favorite authors
he—somewhat like myself—turned to Augustine and Kierkegaard
and spoke much of religion. He was a student of language, but he
was drawn to the *mysterium tremendens et fascinans* that was beyond
language. Many of his disciples analyze and discuss his texts, but
they are bewildered by the mystery of his personal interests. In contrast to them, it is the man struggling to articulate his soundings of
the depths who moves me. Walt Whitman said of one of his books:
"Who touches this book touches a man"; William James quoted him
and added, "The books of all the great philosophers are like so many
men" (James, 24).

I have never had much interest in the philosophy that does not
include the soul of the philosopher, nor do I care for what is sup-
posed to be talk only of the soul (self-help books?). I am drawn to
Socrates, Augustine, Teilhard, Kierkegaard, Jung, and the others as
they tell of both the soul and objective being. In working with their
texts, I have identified with them, and because of them know I am
not standing alone. Together we have been taken into a great mystery, a religious Mystery that is us and more than Us. Their struggles
to articulate the Mystery have illumined my own.

Notes

1. Others have made similar suggestions. David Hume: "Tis not solely in

poetry and music we must follow our taste and sentiment, but likewise in philosophy. When I am convinced on any principle it is only an idea which strikes more strongly upon me" (*T*, 103). Unamuno sees philosophy more like poetry than science, for significant philosophic systems are expressions of "the integral spiritual yearning of their author" (Unamuno, 2).

2. "One" as a transcendental predicate was defined by the scholastics as *unitum in se et divisum ab omni alio;* it is what Locke meant in defining substance as "an entire thing by itself having all qualities in itself and independent of other things" (*E*, II, 260). It is what Teilhard and Whitehead would deny.

Jung seemed not to recognize the nonreciprocal nature of the transcendentals; he regularly insisted that any quality could be itself only in terms of its opposite; this was often said of the Good: to have the Good there must be Evil (see *PR*, 168, 197). The medieval philosophers saw the Four Transcendentals as exceptions to this requirement. Their point is most easily shown in regard to the "one." A unit could exist by itself and no multiplicity; the single (one) would make sense. But there could not be two or more items without there first being a one. Thus, one and many are not reciprocal terms. Likewise, in terms of the "true." Something can be "true" without the need of any falsity; but there must be truth for falsity to exist. Spinoza put it: "Truth becomes clear through Truth, i.e., through itself, as Falsity is also clear through Truth. But Falsity is never manifested or indicated through itself" (*CW*, 120). Likewise, the Scholastic philosophers argued that for something to be "good" no evil is necessary. Evil is a corruption, a secondary quality: corruption can occur only when a Good exists to be corrupted. This noncomplementarity is unique to the Four Transcendental Properties; other properties depend on their opposites: for example, big and little, hot and cold are reciprocal, while the Transcendental Four are not.

3. "Plato was right when he said that man was the State writ small, and Augustine has the advantage of realizing this dictum in a more vivid and historical way. What he gives us in the *Confessions* is primarily the history of his soul, but the macrocosm which this history reflects is the history of the Roman Empire. In the *City of God* we see the outer drama in which the inner drama was involved. St. Augustine's conversion was the conversion of a culture" (Marthinus Versfeld, *A Guide to the City of God*, New York: Sheed & Ward, 1958).

4. Jung gave small indications of his preference in claiming that the Intuitive has the best ability to contact the Unconscious [see *PR*, 165 where Intuition is called "perception via the unconscious"]). This would give the Intuitive some advantage in seeking integration; it might explain why the four Intuitives considered here (Plato, Teilhard, Whitehead, Sartre) did well in locating and integrating their Repressed, while the Sensates considered here (Locke and Hume) had only a moderate contact with the Unconscious. I would not press the point.

5. I would see both Descartes and Hume not continuing the philosophic

struggle and thus not reaching Integration *as philosophers*. Descartes found the teachings of the Church as a suitable context of meaning; Hume found "nature" and the ideals of the Enlightenment serve as a context for him. That is, both accepted a value context apart from their philosophic struggles.

6. So Jung would have it that the doctor is effective only when he himself is affected; the healing process centers around the patient making a human contact (*MDR*, 133). Rollo May has suggested a similar understanding: he writes that a surge of "a genuine human feeling of sympathy, simple as it may be, is a critical point in psychotherapy" (May, 302). He regarded this rapport as central to the healing. By human sympathy the patient is no longer facing the world alone. May suggests a patient is not helped according to a psychological theory, but is helped by the human concern that the doctor and patient come to feel for each other (May, 298). A striking claim! Is that what has been lacking? A healing of the soul could mean the escape from isolation. C. S. Lewis has claimed the reason that one writes is *not to be alone*. Could that explain much philosophical writing—and reading?

7. "We cannot tell whether God and the unconscious are two different entities" (*PR*, 468). Consider the following text that tells of godliness in (or as) Consciousness and the *deus absconditus* in (or as) the Unconscious: "in the same measure that the conscious attitude may pride itself on a certain godliness by reason of its lofty and absolute standpoint, an unconscious attitude develops with a godlikeness oriented downwards to an archaic god whose nature is sensual and brutal. The enantiodromia of Heraclites ensures that the time will come when the *deus absconditus* shall rise to the surface and press the God of our ideals to the wall" (*PT*, 96) The God of our ideals is the god of Consciousness; while the hidden god is in the Unconscious.

8. Jung has seen the Quaternity as the great truth, claiming it is found in the soul's image of God, while Christians speak of the Trinity. Jung, being aware of the Catholic teaching of Mary's Assumption, suggested that the imagery of Three becoming Four tells of Mary completing the Quaternity as the earthly Fourth—the separated Feminine drawn from the Unconscious (see *PA*, 22; *PR*, 63, 170–71). With reason, Jung has seen Mary symbolized this way in some religious art and devotional texts, but to speak of Mary as part of the Trinity is clearly unorthodox, as Jung knew well. Yet there are orthodox phrases that relate her closely to the Trinity, e.g., "Mary Immaculata of the Trinity," etc. The heavenly Trinity with the addition of an element from earth to give it balance is well illustrated in a text of Teilhard. To emphasize its importance Teilhard set several phrases in block letters: he speaks of the ideal Christian achieving a vital balance in his soul "BY ALLOWING ALL THE LIFE-SAP OF THE WORLD to pass into HIS EFFORT TOWARDS THE DIVINE TRINITY" (*WT*, 88).

9. This theme is developed at length by Kierkegaard: "The life-giving Spirit. . . .[comes] only when thou are deceased." He was not referring to physical death, but to what could be called the death of the ego; Kierkegaard develops the point: "And when thou didst die, or didst die to thyself, to the world, thou didst die at the same time to all immediacy in thyself, and also to

thine understanding. That is to say, when it is dark as in the dark night—it is in fact death that we are describing—then comes the life-giving Spirit" (*FSE*, 100–101). In the Christian mystical tradition, such is the "dark night of the soul," a night that must precede the mystical union wherein one becomes a single Spirit with the living God.

10. A significant element in the split between the Eastern and Western Churches concerned the term "*filioque,*" a term accepted in the West and not accepted by the Orthodox Churches of the East. The term tells of the Spirit proceeding from both the Father and the Son (*filioque*); it was added to the Nicene Creed by the Western Church. The Eastern Church generally spoke of the Spirit proceeding from the Father *through* the Son. The difference is subtle and the controversy included much of the politics of the time. The *filioque* would seem a closer parallel with Jung: the Self must have some of the qualities of the Conscious Function in addition to those of the Unconscious one; only thus is it a Union of Opposites; this union is suggested by the Spirit proceeding from the Father *and* the Son (Jung writes, "The tendencies of the conscious and the unconscious are the two factors that *together* make up the transcendent function" [*SDP,* 73]). The Eastern Church would have a greater tradition of surrender to the Father (Consciousness surrenders to the Unconscious) as evidenced in the mysticism of unknowing that dominated Eastern Christian thought; while the West would have a greater role for the Logos, as is evidenced in the rational theology developed in the West. Perhaps both traditions tell us something. For an account of the controversy, see Jaroslav Pelikan, *The Spirit of Eastern Christendom,* pp. 183–98. See also my *Enchantments,* p. 209.

11. A similar sequence can be found in Sartre (as presented above). He seemed to speak of a three-phase sequence: the In-itself was first, and out of this proceeded the For-itself (Consciousness), then out of the two proceeded the ideal but impossible (contradictory) Third, the In-itself-for-itself (*BN,* 693). At times he would identify each of these with God; the atheism of *Being and Nothingness* was an insistent denial of the Third; I have argued that in his later works he urges that history will eventually bring about the existence of the Third and that he denies the radical separation of First and Second he once had presented. But the sequence of elements picks up the Trinitarian sequence (Father, Son, and Spirit) as well as the sequence of Unconscious, Consciousness, and Self. See King, "On the Atheism of Jean-Paul Sartre," in S. A. Matczac, *God and Modern Philosophy,* pp. 851–64.

12. According to this understanding of "religion," Sartre, a militant atheist, would be religious. This might sound like a frivolous way of speaking, but the texts of Sartre are filled with religious themes ("Everything within me calls out for God, and this I can never forget"). On the other hand, Descartes, who, after his troubled youth, seems to have been a serene believer, would not qualify as religious. Whatever one thinks of Descartes's proofs for God's existence, accepting them or not does not have much "religious" value. God clearly existed for the conscious mind of Descartes. But for Jung and others

religion involves a passage beyond consciousness into a land of mystery; such a "descent" could be spoken of as an "initiation," the term used by Teilhard, or a "burial with Christ," the term used by St. Paul. The evidently religious philosophers treated in this book have gone through such an initiation and come to a resolution that (in the terms of Jung) included their Unconscious.

Bibliography

Bergson, Henri. *An Introduction to Metaphysics,* translated by T. E. Hulme, introduction by Thomas Goudge. New York: Macmillan, 1955.

Carnap, Rudolph. *Philosophy and Logical Syntax.* London: Kegan Paul, Trench, Trubner & Co., 1935.

James, William. *Pragmatism: The Works of William James.* Cambridge: Harvard University Press, 1975.

Jung, C. G. *Memories, Dreams, Reflections.* Edited by Aneila Jaffe. Translated by R. and C. Winston. New York: Pantheon, 1963.

King, Thomas M. "The Atheism of Jean-Paul Sartre." An essay in Metczak, *God and Modern Philosophy.* New York: Learned Books, 1976.

King, Thomas M. *Enchantments: Religion and the Power of the Word.* Kansas City: Sheed & Ward, 1989.

King, Thomas M. *Sartre and the Sacred.* Chicago: University of Chicago Press, 1974.

May, Rollo. *Love and Will.* New York: Laurel Dell Publishing, 1974.

Pelikan, Jaroslav. *The Spirit of Eastern Christendom (600–1700).* Chicago: University of Chicago Press, 1974.

Unamuno, Miguel de. *The Tragic Sense of Life.* New York: Dover, 1954.

Index